DON TROIANI'S

CAMPAIGN TO SARATOGA—1777

The Turning Point of the Revolutionary War in Paintings, Artifacts, and Historical Narrative

Eric Schnitzer and Don Troiani

STACKPOLE
BOOKS

Guilford, Connecticut

Published by Stackpole Books

An imprint of The Rowman & Littlefield Publishing Group, Inc.

4501 Forbes Boulevard, Suite 200

Lanham, MD 20706

www.rowman.com

Distributed by NATIONAL BOOK NETWORK

For free information about the artwork and limited edition prints of Don Troiani, contact:

W. Britain

10420 Geiser Road

Holland OH 43528

(419) 865-5077

www.wbritain.com

For information on licensing images in this book, visit Bridgeman Images, www.bridgemanimages.com

British Library Cataloguing in Publication Information Available

Library of Congress Cataloging-in-Publication Data

Names: Schnitzer, Eric, author. | Troiani, Don, author.

Title: Don Troiani's campaign to Saratoga—1777 : the turning point of the Revolutionary War in paintings, artifacts, and historical narrative / Eric Schnitzer and Don Troiani.

Description: Guilford, Connecticut : Stackpole Books, [2019] | Includes bibliographical references.

Identifiers: LCCN 2019007984 (print) | LCCN 2019008426 (ebook) | ISBN 9780811768535 (e-book) | ISBN 9780811738521 (hbk. : alk. paper) | ISBN 9780811768535 (ebook)

Subjects: LCSH: Burgoyne's Invasion, 1777. | Saratoga Campaign, N.Y., 1777. | Saratoga Campaign, N.Y., 1777—Pictorial works. | Burgoyne's Invasion, 1777—Pictorial works.

Classification: LCC E233 (ebook) | LCC E233 .S36 2019 (print) | DDC 973.3/33—dc23

LC record available at https://lccn.loc.gov/2019007984

Printed in the United States of America

Contents

Acknowledgments

Special thanks to James L. Kochan, who generously shared his research and knowledge of Revolutionary War military material culture, which helped inform many uniform details.

His Majesty's "Savage" Allies: British Policy and the Northern Indians During the Revolutionary War: The Carleton Years, 1774–1778, by Stevens, Paul Lawrence, PhD, State University of New York (SUNY) at Buffalo, 1984, provided many details related to the participation of American Indian and First Nations people in the Northern Campaign of 1777.

Many thanks to those who helped make this book possible: Gavin Ashworth, Greg Austin, Michael Barbieri, Thomas M. Barker, PhD, Bill Bartley, Sara Elizabeth Blakeslee, Daniel Blanchette Sr., Joel Bohy, Todd Braisted, Christopher Bryant, Rene Chartrand, Henry Cooke, Douglas Copeley, Christopher Fox, Jamie Franklin, David Geiger, Erik Goldstein, Tom Grinslade, Don Hagist, Corinna Lady Hamilton of Dalzell, DL, John A. Houlding, PhD, Les Jensen, Chris Jones, Jennifer Locke Jones, Paul Jones, Matthew Keagle, Dr. Rex Kessler, Angelika R. Kuettner, Bob Lavoy, Stuart Lilie, Lt. Colonel Donald M. Londahl-Smidt, Mike McAfee, Bob McDonald, Philip Mead, Grant Miller, Joe Moran, James F. Morrison, Colonel J. Craig Nannos, Dean Nelson, Tom Nesbitt, Ward Oles, Shaun Pekar, Miranda Peters, Kristy Putorti, Claus Reuter, Steve Rogers, Jenna Schnitzer, Robert A. Selig, PhD, Margaret Staudter, Gary Storm, Anthony Wayne Tommell, Richard Ulbrich (deceased), Chris Valosin, Gavin Watt, and Dave Zabelski (deceased).

Many thanks to the institutions that helped make this book possible: Bennington Museum, Bonhams Auction House, Brown University Library, Colonial Williamsburg Foundation, Concord Museum, Connecticut Museum of History, Cowan's Auctions, David Library of the American Revolution, Fort Ticonderoga Museum, Harvard University Houghton Library, Hessisches Staatsarchiv Marburg, Library of Congress, Longfellow's Wayside Inn, Massachusetts Historical Society, Massachusetts State Archives, Metropolitan Museum of Art, Morphy Auctions, Museum of the American Revolution, Museumslandschaft Hessen Kassel, National Trust, New Hampshire Historical Society, New-York Historical Society, New York Public Library, New York State Archives, New York State Office of Parks, Recreation and Historic Preservation, Pocumtuck Valley Memorial Association, Royal Collection Trust, Rutherford B. Hayes Presidential Library & Museums, Saratoga National Historical Park, Skinner Auctioneers and Appraisers, Smithsonian Institution, University of Michigan William L. Clements Library, West Point Museum, and Yale University Art Gallery.

Foreword

By Matthew Keagle

EVERY FEW GENERATIONS A BOOK APPEARS THAT SPEAKS PROFOUNDLY TO the past and the future. I believe this is one of those volumes. Its subject is the legendary northern campaign of 1777, arguably the first assertion of the viability of the United States during the Revolutionary War. While the campaign has been a subject of intense interest for over two centuries Don Troiani and Eric Schnitzer have approached it with a precision, humility, and mastery that are rare. By engaging the myths, legends, and drama of the campaign they have ably reconstructed the past and established a standard for future students of this campaign.

From the Colonial Wars through the Civil War, Don Troiani's paintings are the standard by which modern historical artists are judged. With unrivaled technical skill, working in a medium familiar to the age of the Revolution, Troiani brings a profound historical sensibility and attention to detail to his works. Viewers can be confident that every brushstroke has been the subject of intense consideration by the artist who seeks to document even the smallest of details. What is more, Troiani works closely with the best scholars in the field and responds to changing research and new perspectives, rather than simply perpetuating outdated interpretations.

This volume's author, Eric Schnitzer, follows in the same spirit of critical analysis. Eric is well-known as the park ranger/historian of the Saratoga National Historical Park and is *the* authority on the campaign of 1777. While focused on that campaign, from the Continental and British-allied perspectives, his extensive research has made him one of the foremost resources on the broader institutions these forces represented. Schnitzer scrutinizes and interprets even small details, those that contribute to a nuanced understanding of historical events and actors with sympathy, understanding, and accuracy.

It is fitting, then, that these two have paired to deliver a volume that functions equally as history and art. The campaign of 1777 in the north is not unfamiliar territory. As one of the most discrete military campaigns of the Revolution, one with a discernable beginning and end, with profound consequences, it has long attracted the attention of artists, scholars, and the general public. Too often, however, such attention has repeated fallacies and outright fictions that have been passed down for generations as truths. Schnitzer's deeply researched text, incorporating sources from all the combatants, provides a powerful and corrective account of the campaign in rich and exacting detail. No doubt this content will be, for the foreseeable future, the most thorough and transparent exploration of the campaign.

Complementing Schnitzer's rigorous and approachable content, Troiani has with his brush so ably reconstructed these moments and individuals. His scenes and figures allow one's imagination to activate the text. For centuries illustration has provided the spark for the imagination, particularly for historical events prior to the age of photography. Like the work of Meissonier, de Neuville, and Detaille, Troiani's paintings ignite the mind and reward lingering views that uncover minute details and actions. But illustration, which has populated volumes on the Revolutionary War for centuries, like prose, has often repeated tired historical chestnuts. The best historical art, on the other hand, draws its inspiration from the historical sources, allowing the actors of the past to speak through images as well as text.

Augmenting all of this is the collaborators' decision to enhance this volume with photographs of the original artifacts from this groundbreaking campaign. Drawn from collections on both sides of the Atlantic, these serve for Troiani's art, like Schnitzer's footnotes, as the material documentation for the historical scenes. The combination of interpretation through art and text and documentation through footnotes and artifacts solidifies this volume's place in the historiography of the campaign that defines the Revolutionary War. It is unlikely that such a capable combination of historical sources and skilled interpretations will be matched for some time to come. Of course, that is probably the goal. Perhaps a dog-eared, worn, and well-loved edition of Schnitzer's and Troiani's book will sit on the shelf of the next century's historian or artist, having provided the inspiration and the path for ongoing research on this critical campaign of the American Revolution.

Matthew Keagle
Curator
Fort Ticonderoga

Introduction

D on Troiani's Campaign to Saratoga—1777 is hardly the first book written about the Northern Campaign of 1777, which culminated in the surrender of the British Army from Canada commanded by Lieutenant-General John Burgoyne at Saratoga on October 17, 1777. The first published book solely dedicated to its history, titled *An Original, Compiled and Corrected Account of Burgoyne's Campaign, and the Memorable Battles of Bemis's Heights*, was published in 1844, and many have since followed. Saratoga's legacy is unprecedented in the annals of American War for Independence history. The Battles of Saratoga, and Burgoyne's surrender in particular, are acknowledged as the "Turning Point" upon which success in the war's outcome depended.

While many battle sites have since claimed the title for their own, the term "Turning Point" was literally coined for Saratoga, forming the title of Hoffman Nickerson's 1928 tome *The Turning Point of the American Revolution: or, Burgoyne in America*. Burgoyne's surrender marked the first time in world history that the British Army ever surrendered, and that such an army surrendered to the new army of a new nation instead of, say, France's ancien régime, is surprising to this very day. John Trumbull's monumental painting, *Surrender of General Burgoyne*, hangs in the rotunda of the United States Capitol. Burgoyne's surrender is depicted on US postage stamps and currency. Sites associated with the military events of the campaign are preserved and protected by over a dozen national parks, New York and Vermont state historic sites, and private sites. No wonder the *New York Times Magazine*'s "The Best" millennium issue rated the Battle of Saratoga as the most important "battle" fought throughout the world in the last 1,000 years![1] It therefore stands to reason that the Saratoga story deserves significant study, but not in the form of yet another rehash of the same oft-told tale. It is with that in mind that this book was created.

Historical revisionism is a necessity. The practice is best used to reconsider historical orthodoxy after the discovery of new sources or by the reassessment of existing ones. Sometimes, historical narratives are based upon surprisingly scant evidence, or even evidence that is later proven fraudulent. But history is more than just source material—it's also created by the interpretations of historians and enthusiasts, particularly teachers and authors. Sometimes, mistakes are made. If left untreated, successive generations are doomed to repeat flawed interpretations or factual inaccuracies which, over time, grow into new, increasingly faulty orthodoxy. This pitfall is typically seen when secondary sources build on each other, since, like the proverbial telephone game, the process does not apply new research. Other times, a more accurate narrative of past events is developed simply when different people with fresh perspectives and knowledge are engaged; new discoveries are often made that way.

I have regularly applied the practice of historical revisionism throughout this narrative, based upon the largest scope of applied primary sources, historiographical cognizance, and applied knowledge related to the nontraditional but highly relevant topics of material culture and military forces personnel study. It's surprising how these considerations produce a story somewhat different from the traditional narrative. Sometimes, these conclusions are contrary to oft-repeated, long-standing tenets which, when broken down, had no basis in the first place.

Students and scholars of the American War for Independence will notice that while I place significant focus on the strategic aspects of the campaign, I give little attention to the biographies of its participants. Instead, I provide a vibrantly new type of military history that spotlights logistical, tactical, foodway, and military personnel study. Too often, these aspects are relegated to stereotypes that are commonly inaccurate. Further, although only very rarely given consideration in traditional histories, material culture is given some focus in this book. Artifacts matter. Not only do original objects provide tangible connections to the past in a manner that manuscripts are sometimes unable to do, but military material culture had direct relevance to the way war was waged and battles fought. Sometimes, this impact was so important that battles were won, or lost, because of material culture. Understanding the material culture often helps explain how and why things happened that are otherwise unexplainable. Military historians who research and write about battle while ignoring military material culture do so at their peril.

Like other events in history, the Northern Campaign of 1777 is associated with an overabundance of pervasive myths and legends. I did not go out of my way to seek and destroy all known fiction associated with the campaign, but I have done my share of eradication. Nineteenth-century Romanticism took its toll on early histories of the campaign, far beyond what any of us have imagined. Most writers of that era—some of whom were themselves battle participants, such as Ebenezer Wakefield and Samuel Woodruff—used hyperbole and invented dialogue in order to inspire the readers of their time.[2] Unfortunately, their contrived accounts (and others like theirs) have been readily taken as factual by authors and historians for generations.

Although important to historiography, these stories, purpose-built for the enjoyment of nineteenth- and twentieth-century readers, have no place here. You will not find outrageous anecdotes about a supposed "mentally retarded" Hanjost Schuyler duping "simpleton" Indians, impossible dialogue concerning shooting General Fraser, or nonsense about a "Witch of the Wilderness" in this book. I liberally quote from primary sources throughout, since it's often more interesting to read original passages than a historian's rewording of them. While some of these accounts will be recognized by those familiar with the Northern Campaign, many others have never been used before in any study of it. American veteran pension record depositions from the nineteenth century populate the narrative, and this traditionally unused source material has been carefully curated for inclusion based upon interest and, of course, veracity. Original writing is contained within quotation marks, and no attempt has been made to alter spelling or punctuation. Bracketed text is used sparingly, but is inserted within quoted material in order to provide clarifications to original accounts when needed. Endnotes are annotated, and often provide further insight into details too technical to address in the main text. This includes military rank and unit identifications for most people introduced in the book.

In most instances throughout the book, I use historical names and terms for units, places, and objects of material culture. Sometimes, the result is something different from the norm—I use "Bemus Heights" instead of the modern "Bemis Heights," for example. I prefer to use the term "Revolutionary" instead of "patriot," since British royalists and Americans fighting for the United States alike considered themselves "patriots" and called themselves such. Similarly, I use the term "royalist" instead of "loyalist." Although "loyalist" is now commonly used to identify Americans who fought for the crown in the Northern Campaign of 1777, "royalist" was more typically used by the British and royalist Americans themselves (and, if they were being nice, by their Revolutionary opponents). Readers will notice that, barring what is found in contemporary quotes, I avoid using the pejoratives "rebel" and "Tory." Revolutionaries were universally identified as "rebels" by their enemies, but by 1777, Revolutionary Americans were fighting for the survival of a new nation, the United States of America. With the war's termination in 1783 and the existence of the United States officially recognized by Britain, the country's 1776 founding was validated. Similarly, "Tory" was the standard moniker given to royalists, but it was meant as a derogatory play upon the Tory political persuasion and did not gauge one's loyalty to Great Britain. Most royalist Americans were not Tories, and even many British officers were not either.

In many cases, I use non-English words, which are often found in italics (excepting proper nouns) and are followed by English definitions in parentheses. German words used are of the spellings commonly found in the eighteenth century. In most cases, the names of First Nations and American Indian nations are given in the manner that the English or French recorded them in the eighteenth century.

The maxim "There are three kinds of lies: lies, damned lies, and statistics" seems to have been tailor-made for military historians. As frustrating as it is for researchers, comparisons of contemporary records consisting of casualty numbers are commonly contradictory. Not only that, most references to enemy numbers, be they the size of an army or the number of casualties, were usually outrageously inflated. With few exceptions, numbers related to unit sizes or battle casualties found in this book are rounded and are not meant to be exact. For example, if I identify a regiment as consisting of 380 officers and soldiers, it is meant to be an accurate estimate, not necessarily an absolutely precise number. Generally, most numbers in the thousands are rounded to the nearest hundred, and numbers in the hundreds are rounded to the nearest ten.

Scholars and students alike of the American War for Independence will happily note that the old, tired, standby illustrations typically used to illustrate events of the campaign will not be found here. Inaccurate nineteenth-century pictures from Currier and Ives or *Harper's New Monthly Magazine*, or artwork produced in commemoration of the war's sesquicentennial or in the mid-twentieth century, have long outlived their usefulness. While every historian would admit that a historical narrative should be as truthful as possible, that same, noble standard is rarely applied to artwork. Depictions of, say, a dozen weapon-wielding Indians dancing around Jane McCrea, who is mysteriously tied to a tree, or battle scenes showing soldiers dressed in uniforms fifty years out of date are the visual equivalents of lying to readers. Visuals teach us just as much as words do. Sometimes even more. But by eschewing old, traditional historical artwork, how does one illustrate a book?

Don Troiani needs no introduction. His battle scenes and single-figure illustrations are second to none in the genre of contemporary military artwork. He is famous for having that rare combination of artistic talent and an eye for accuracy. Not only does he take scrupulous care to accurately portray natural and cultural landscapes, but he paints with precision on points of detail as minute as coat button spacing, musket pattern type, and even cocked hat braid width. The models he uses are dressed in accurate, hand-sewn uniforms and accoutrements made by some of the greatest tradespeople in the field and are reflective of the most up-to-date research. They are posed with original firearms, swords, and polearms in order to create the most perfect proportions. Unlike what is seen in most other historical narratives, Don's paintings are not relegated to mere dressing for the narrative, but form an integral complement to it. Paintings are meant to be read like a story, not only through their captions but by everything depicted, including the settings and material culture. Viewers learn from these illustrations, so when the wrong illustrations are used, the wrong stories are told. Readers should feel confident that Don's artwork, most of which has never been published before, provides the same level of accuracy that is provided in the text.

Ultimately, our intention is to present a new, definitive military history of the Northern Campaign of 1777, including both the latest historical research and interpretations. Rarely seen artifacts form a key part of the book. Don Troiani's brilliantly illuminating paintings form the new standard for accurate visual representations. We hope you enjoy!

Eric Schnitzer
White Creek, New York

Private, Colonel John Philip de Haas's 1st Pennsylvania Battalion, 1776

Raised in Philadelphia during the fall and winter of 1775–76, de Haas's battalion was sent north to reinforce American troops invading Canada. Withdrawn with the rest of the army that summer, de Haas's battalion formed part of Ticonderoga's defenses in the fall. Having "suffered from . . . excessive fatigue," de Haas's men were "almost naked," particularly for want of shirts; had "bad" accoutrements; and wanted bayonets. In lieu of breeches and stockings, this soldier wears "overalls," a military garment that the British generically referred to as "trousers."

De Hass to unknown, n.d., in *Pennsylvania Archives*, vol. 10, 53.

Inevitability

*I am anxious to have you here as soon as possible, as maintaining our
naval Superiority is of the last Importance.*
— Major General Horatio Gates, July 13, 1776[1]

In October 1776 it was up to Benedict Arnold to protect the northern reaches of the United States from British invasion. Considering the number of military successes American Revolutionaries had enjoyed in the north the previous year, this was a dramatic turnabout. In 1775 a string of springtime initiatives resulted in the capture of British forts at Ticonderoga and Crown Point, as well as gaining control of all of Lake Champlain. In the fall St. Johns (Saint-Jean), Montréal, and Three Rivers (Trois-Rivières) all fell to the American invasion of Canada. At Québec City, winter weather, a strong British-Canadien garrison, and the city's defenses defeated the attacking Congressional forces in the December 31, 1775, Battle of Québec. Their all-conquering wave of the province thwarted, the Americans mounted a siege of the fortified city over the winter. If left unsupported, the British garrison would not be able to survive indefinitely.

Spring brought new hope for the besiegers. With the weather improving and Revolutionary reinforcements on the way, the fall of Québec City seemed likely. The British, however, unprepared for overwhelming American aggressiveness in Massachusetts and Canada in 1775, prepared to strike back in 1776. Reinforced and reorganized, the main British Army under the command of General William Howe returned to the American colonies after having evacuated Boston in March 1776.[2] During the summer, his troops attacked American forces on Long Island, Manhattan, and in the Hudson Highlands. His professional troops, retrained after having learned costly tactical lessons in the Lexington and Concord expedition and the Battle of Bunker Hill in 1775, were now more than a match for their American counterparts. Howe easily trounced the Americans at every turn, easily outmaneuvering and defeating General George Washington's poorly trained troops.[3] Bad weather, privation, and desertion further beset Washington's men, but Howe could neither trap nor obliterate them. Still, after retreating across New Jersey and into Pennsylvania in late fall, Washington's army was on the brink of collapse. With most enlistments set to expire by year's end, the army's dissolution appeared certain.

**1st Pennsylvania Battalion Button
ca. 1775**
Don Troiani collection
First Pennsylvania Battalion enlisted men's buttons not only had their unit designation displayed on the face, but also included CONTINENTAL ARMY around the perimeter, a feature unique to this particular regiment. This cast-pewter button was recovered from the Champlain Valley.

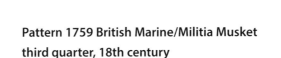

Pattern 1759 British Marine/Militia Musket
third quarter, 18th century
Don Troiani collection
Over the winter of 1775–76, Québec City's defenders consisted of British Army and American royalist troops, British and Canadien militia, artificers, and naval personnel drawn from a variety of nearby Royal Navy and merchant vessels tasked with "doing duty as Soldier[s]." Included were nearly thirty-five men from the Corps of Marines contingent assigned to His Majesty's (H.M.) Ship *Lizard*. Regulated by the admiralty instead of the army, the redcoated Corps of Marines typically carried "Marine" muskets, pattern guns that differed only slightly from the Short Land muskets carried by soldiers in many marching regiments of foot.

H.M. Ship *Lizard* journal, December 1, 1775, in *Naval Documents*, vol. 2, 1214.

Canteen
1776
Colonel J. Craig Nannos collection
This staved wooden canteen was carried by a soldier in the 1st Pennsylvania Battalion. Wooden canteens were typically suspended over the shoulder with cord, leather, or webbing belts.

The American Northern Army's situation was hardly better. Having enjoyed dominion over most of the province of Québec since fall 1775, the British and Canadien defenders of the province's namesake city held firm, and the American invasion force devolved into a retreat to northern New York. Plagued by smallpox, thrashed in the Battles of the Cedars and Three Rivers, and dogged by a massively reinforced British military, the ruined Northern Army, ousted from Canada in summer 1776, returned to the centerpiece of military operations in the north, Fort Ticonderoga. Despite the insurmountable setbacks, the Northern Army still maintained complete control of Lake Champlain, thereby preventing the British from immediately following up on their victories in Canada. But that was only a matter of time.

General Guy Carleton was the architect of Québec City's successful defense and the counterattack against the American invaders.[4] But reclaiming the province for the crown was only the start. The forts at Ticonderoga and Crown Point had been in American hands since May 1775 and would undoubtedly be used as a staging area for future operations against Québec. Not only was it strategically necessary to reclaim the forts, but it was Carleton's particular responsibility to do so. The principal challenge facing him was in how to accomplish it.

While the answer was simple—regain dominance of Lake Champlain—the solution was not. When the Americans evacuated Canada, they took away or destroyed every boat within reach, thereby forcing Carleton to take the time to scratch-build a fleet in order to transport his troops up Lake Champlain (south).

Private, Canadien Company de Boucherville

In 1776 Governor Carleton mobilized three provisional *compagnies canadiennes* (Canadien companies) formed from the ranks of the Canadien militia. Uniformed in round hats, green jackets with red facings, and buff smallclothes, the *compagnies* were issued old French muskets and bayonets captured in the previous war. Reraised in spring 1777 to serve with Burgoyne and St. Leger, the *compagnies* wore round hats and dark brown jackets and vests "nearly the colour of the bark of trees" and trimmed in colored laces that distinguished the companies.

Money, *A Letter to the Right Honorable William Windham*, 12.

Cartridge Pouch Device, 29th Regiment of Foot

ca. 1770s

Private collection

This ornament, which originally adorned the flap of a British soldier's cartridge pouch, was recovered from an American campsite. It may have been taken during operations in Canada in 1776 or in northern New York after 1777.

Waist Belt Clasp, 29th Regiment of Foot

ca. 1770s

Private collection

Typical British soldier waist belt clasps of this form included two studs on the reverse, which protruded through holes in the leather belt. The heads were peened down over a double-holed washer, thus securing the clasp in place. A hook slipped through a hole in the belt, thereby securing it around the soldier's waist or over the shoulder. The process of attaching the studs and hook typically resulted in a three-point blemish on the clasp's face.

What's worse for Carleton, because American forces dominated the lake with armed vessels, he would also have to ensure that the fleet he built was large and well-armed. Such an endeavor would take substantial manpower, materials, and, most importantly, time. With work begun in early July on the construction of a number of small vessels at St. Johns, a town located on the Richelieu River with direct access to Lake Champlain, the British had something more ambitious in mind. In order to construct "a sufficient Naval Force . . . with all speed" to control the lake, Royal Navy command ordered the overland transportation of larger vessels up the Richelieu River (south) from Chambly to St. Johns, a distance of about twelve miles.[5]

While Royal Navy personnel received instructions to disassemble some of their larger vessels for overland transport, almost 110 miles up the lake (south), American commanders of the Continental Army's Northern Department were meeting in a council of war at Crown Point in order to determine their next steps. Present was the commander in chief of the department, Major General Philip Schuyler; his second in command, Major General Horatio Gates; and brigadier generals, including Benedict Arnold. With the Canada campaign having come to a disastrous close, now under consideration was what to do about Carleton's inevitable ascent on Lake Champlain. The council determined that Crown Point should be evacuated and that it would be "prudent to retire Immediately to the Strong Ground [Rattlesnake Hill], on the East Side of the Lake opposite to Ticonderoga" with the army's healthy troops, where it appeared "Clearly to the Council, that the Post opposite to Ticonderoga, will the most Effectually secure the Country." Further resolved was that "the most Effectual Measures be taken to secure our Superiority on Lake Champlain, by a Naval Armament of Gundolas, Row Gallies, Armed Batteaus."[6]

Schuyler returned to his home headquarters near Albany, leaving Gates to command the northern defenses from Ticonderoga. Arnold, appointed "commander-in-chief of the Fleet on Lake Champlain," immediately set out to oversee and coordinate the construction of new vessels at Skenesborough (present-day Whitehall, New York). Within days after the council's meeting, American Northern Army commanders received their first intelligence as to what the British were up to, confirming their worst fears. Although the information was secondhand, it was reported that "seamen were daily employed in cutting wood . . . that they were building 3 sloops and 2 schooners at St. Johns, which they expected would be soon finished and that they intended immediately to proceed to Crown Point."[7]

Private, Colonel William Maxwell's 2nd New Jersey Regiment, 1776

Raised in the fall of 1775, the 2nd New Jersey Regiment was transferred to Québec in order to bolster invading American forces besieging the province's namesake city. Evacuated with the rest of the army there in May, Maxwell's regiment fought in the disastrous June 8 Battle of Trois-Rivières (Three Rivers). Withdrawn to Ticonderoga, the battalion formed part of the peninsula's defense during Carlton's October incursion. Expiring enlistments prompted Gates to release the 2nd New Jersey Regiment, along with other expiring regiments, on November 15.

Pattern 1738 Wall Gun
1744

Don Troiani collection

Wall or rampart guns, such as this British model, were used to defend fortifications and were commonly mounted aboard ships such as the ones operating on Lake Champlain. With a .98-caliber fifty-four-inch barrel, the piece fired a ball measuring nearly one inch in diameter. Mounted on an iron swivel, the ensemble weighs over thirty-five pounds!

Lacking any similar intelligence, the British were completely unaware of American shipbuilding endeavors.

While Arnold's oversight of the Lake Champlain fleet being constructed at Skenesborough was well managed, a series of personal and professional crises threatened to disrupt the work. His authority was challenged by an underling captain, Jacobus Wynkoop, which was summarily quashed with Gates's unyielding support.[8] Not everything went Arnold's way, however. He accused another officer, Colonel Moses Hazen, of neglect of duty, which triggered a court-martial, in which Hazen was exonerated with honor.[9] Arnold's longtime dispute with Lieutenant Colonel John Brown was on the rise, with each accusing the other of slander, criminality, and treachery.[10] Arnold was reaching his breaking point. Despite the imminent threat of British invasion, he unguardedly informed Gates that he had "some thoughts of going to Congress, & beging leave to resign" from the army, hoping that the threat would inspire the governing body to "make me a Major General—(Entre Nous)."[11]

The most important development that took place over the summer was the nature of the war itself. With passage of the July 2 congressional resolution for independency and the July 4 ratification of "The unanimous Declaration of the thirteen United States of America," the "United Colonies" became the "United States." Now, officers and soldiers in the newly named "Army of the United States" were building defenses at Ticonderoga and Rattlesnake Hill, and the vessels at Skenesborough, to fight for the very existence of a newly declared nation. The forthcoming 1776 fall campaign season was going to be a vital time for the nascent United States.

In advance of the American fleet's completion, Gates provided Arnold with instructions regarding what he was to do, and not do, with it. Among Gates's instructions was his direction to deploy the fleet far "down Lake Champlain to the narrow Pass," near the island-riddled bottom waters that the British would have to take during their impending advance south. Gates also made sure to relay to Arnold the importance of his charge:

A Survey of Lake Champlain, including Lake George, Crown Point and St John; a Particular Plan of Lake George

published by Robert Sayer and John Bennett, August 5, 1776, after William Furness Brassier, 1762; Captain Jackson, 1756

The Library of Congress, gm72002093
This map shows most of the Lake George and Lake Champlain watersheds and includes many important natural and man-made features such as St. Johns (at top), "Isle de Valcour," and Fort Ticonderoga. Note the depiction of the 45th parallel, which then (and now) defined the boundary between New York and the province of Québec. This delineation also marked the important territorial divides between the British domains commanded by Howe and Carleton, respectively. Various icons representing both Arnold's and Carleton's vessels are depicted on Lake Champlain, and the dashed line follows Arnold's southerly avenue of retreat. This map was published in December 1776 as part of a set of six for *The American Military Pocket Atlas*, a volume that was primarily intended "for the use of the Military Gentlemen."

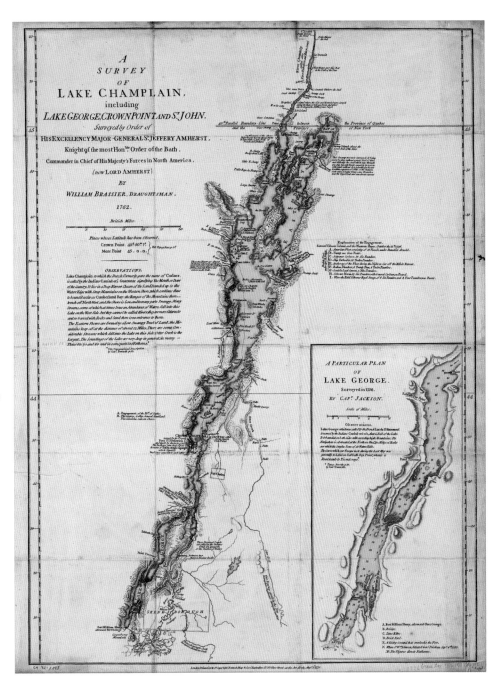

Artillery Worm

ca. 1770s

National Museum of American History;
photograph by Don Troiani

Artillery worms cleaned out a
cannon's fouled bore contents
between shots. This particular piece
was recovered from the wreckage of
the three-gun gondola *Philadelphia*,
which was sunk during the Battle
of Valcour Island. The worm's long
wooden half is no longer extant.

Preventing the Enemys invasion of our Country, is the ultimate
End of the important Command, with which you are now intrusted.
It is a defensive War we are carrying on; therefore, no wanton risque,
or unnecessary Display of the Power of the Fleet, is at any Time, to
influence your Conduct.[12]

Thus instructed, Arnold proceeded down the lake (north) and eventually
settled in with fifteen vessels at Valcour Island, snugly nestled in an "excellent
harbour" between the island and the New York shore. Over sixty miles north
of Ticonderoga, the spot was nowhere near where Gates ordered the fleet to
deploy, but Arnold believed it to be the superior position. His reasoning, as he
informed his superior, was that only a "few vessells" could attack him at once in
the Valcour Island location, and those that did would "be exposed to the fire of
the whole fleet."[13] What's more, Arnold's
flotilla was positioned in such a way so as to
be obscured from view by the southbound
Royal Navy, making the forthcoming battle
a surprise attack. There the Americans
waited.

Just as Arnold planned, most of the
British fleet of over thirty vessels missed
the American flotilla and "passed [Val-
cour Island] . . . before they knew it and
were obliged to tack in order to get into
the Bay."[14] Late-morning fire from some
of Arnold's advance vessels provided the
opening shots for the Battle of Valcour
Island, after which one of them accidentally
ran aground on the island while trying to
pull back to the main body in the harbor.
The remaining "small flee[t] of 14 Sail cum
to anker In a Line when a most obstinat

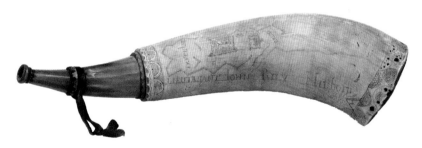

John Riley's Powder Horn

1776

Fort Ticonderoga Museum collection, PH-032; photograph by Margaret Staudter

This horn was owned by John Riley, a second lieutenant in Colonel Charles
Burrell's Connecticut State Battalion sent "to Reinforce the Northern Army"
in 1776. The horn depicts the defensive networks at Ticonderoga and Mount
Independence, the bridge between them, and much of Lake Champlain,
places reflective of Riley's service.

NARA, Revolutionary War Pension Files, John Riley (S.14,304).

Uzel Hurd's Powder Horn
1776

Cowan's Auctions, Historic Firearms and Militaria, October 25, 2012

Engraved at Mount Independence and dated November 15, 1776, this horn was owned by Uzel Hurd, a private soldier in Colonel Isaac Wyman's battalion of New Hampshire militia. Hurd "marched to Ticonderoga & Mount Independence, & joined the continental troops there under the command of General Gates" in summer 1776, where he remained until the battalion was disbanded in December.

NARA, Revolutionary War Pension Files, Uzzel Hurd (S.13,484).

Private, 18th Continental Regiment Commanded by Colonel Edmund Phinney

Reflective of the system used by British Army regiments, New England's Continental battalions reorganized for the "new army" of 1776 used a consecutive numbering system. From September through November 1776, the 18th Continental Regiment garrisoned Mount Independence, where the men improved the works, transported provisions up from Lake George, and populated the Mount's defenses during Carleton's foray up Lake Champlain. Disbanded that December, most reenlisted personnel were reorganized into Colonel Brewer's (12th) Massachusetts Regiment.

25th Continental Regiment Enlisted Button
ca. 1776

Don Troiani collection

The 1776 reorganization of the Continental Army resulted in New England's regiments receiving successive numerical designations, and their regimental buttons bore their new numbers. This pewter button was recovered in the Lake Champlain Valley. Disbanded at the end of 1776, this regiment's reenlistees were consolidated with those of the 24th Continental Regiment to form the core of Colonel John Greaton's (3rd) Massachusetts Regiment, which served in the Northern Campaign of 1777.

Ingagement then Insud," during which the Americans "fought most Breaivley and maid a most vigurus Stand Aganst a much Supero foe."[15] Because most of the larger British vessels were too far away to engage effectively, their "Gun Boats bore the blunt" of the Americans' fire for "the Greatest part of that day," until His Majesty's (H.M.) Schooner *Carleton* went in to assist. But the singular British schooner became a focal point of American cannonading and was "very Soon in Such a Shattered Condition as to be towed out of the Bay by the boats of the fleet for fear of her being taken."[16] Landed British forces fired on the Americans "from the main Land & the Island wich killed our men . . . till whe Brogt our our [*sic*] Brod Sides to Bar" on them and "gave them Such Doses of greap Shot wich cassed them to Retreet in the whouds." Some of the British vessels even came "up so Nigh that theay fireed Plattoons on us from thear Ships our Decks War Staind with Blud."[17]

After more than six hours fighting, the British broke off their attack and arrayed the fleet in a line south of Valcour Island with the intention of preventing the Americans from escaping overnight. But the deployment was poorly managed by the Royal Navy commander, Captain Thomas Pringle, and a gap of over one mile was left between the westernmost British vessel and the New York shoreline.[18] Blockaded, bested in battle, and having little remaining ammunition, Arnold "thoght Proper to Retreet that Night" in order to save as much of his shattered flotilla as possible. In a feat reflective of Washington's secret overnight evacuation of Long Island one and a half months earlier, Arnold's remaining vessels escaped through the blockade's substantial gap.

Pringle pursued Arnold up the lake (south) the following morning in a chase that extended into October 13. During the race south, the British found many of Arnold's severely battle-battered vessels run aground, most of them set on fire by the Americans who abandoned them. The British captured some boats, one of which surrendered with a crew of over one hundred aboard. Arnold and most of his officers and soldiers escaped, but only four of the fifteen vessels that made up the fleet made it back to Ticonderoga.[19] Carleton's advance party arrived at Crown Point on October 14, where, over the following days, the remainder of the British fleet joined them.

With 11 vessels destroyed or captured, about 80 men killed or wounded, and another 120 troops captured by the British, Arnold's Valcour Island gamble was an unmitigated disaster. British losses amounted to a few small gunboats and about forty men killed or wounded. Arnold's ambitious surprise attack hadn't delayed Carleton in the slightest and, with the fleet swept aside, the British regained instantaneous control over most of the lake, a benefit they would enjoy for the remainder of the war.

Carleton proceeded unfettered toward Ticonderoga, but that too was all for naught. Awaiting the oncoming British was not only the expanded defenses at Ticonderoga, but also the substantial new works across the lake

Sergeant, 24th Continental Regiment Commanded by Colonel John Greaton

This regiment was sent to Canada in spring 1776 to reinforce the American invasion, during which time the men fell so "ill with the small pox" that the remainder were inoculated. Stationed at Mount Independence and Ticonderoga during Carleton's October incursion, the regiment was afterward sent to bolster Washington's forces in New Jersey. Disbanded in January 1777, most reenlisted personnel were reorganized into Colonel Greaton's (3rd) Massachusetts Regiment. This sergeant is armed with a halberd, the traditional polearm of those bearing that rank.

Gordon to Washington, June 19–20, 1776, in *The Papers of George Washington*, vol. 5, 39.

on Rattlesnake Hill—renamed Mount Independence by the Americans. The latter fort was a completely unforeseen development; what's more, a "report said the Enemy had from 12 to 16 Thousand Men" on hand, along with a substantial array of artillery.[20] While the estimate was somewhat inflated—Gates had nearly 40 battalions composed of over 9,000 officers and soldiers present and fit for duty—the Northern Army was more than a match for the few thousand troops Carleton brought with him.[21] After Carleton personally reconnoitered the American positions and confirmed the situation for himself, he made the practical decision to return to Canada.

The British withdrawal came at a critical time. With confirmation of Carleton's departure in early November, Gates began to dismantle his garrisons. In truth, a full third of his corps were militia or levies, and their service enlistments were soon set to expire. Some of the Continental regiments reached their sunset dates—or even surpassed them—and their personnel were released to go home. Washington's pressing call for reinforcements could now be answered, and over half of the remaining Continental Army regiments were marched south to bolster Washington's beaten, bedraggled forces. Some regiments were dispatched to New York's Hudson Highlands and Morristown, New Jersey, while four regiments, commanded by Brigadier General Arthur St. Clair, joined Washington in December.[22] Thus reinforced, Washington had the strength needed to cross the Delaware River and attack the German winter-quarters garrison at Trenton, New Jersey, on December 26, a fight in which St. Clair's troops played a central part. This masterful victory was followed up by yet another in the January 3 Battle of Princeton, New Jersey.

The connection between Carleton's withdrawal and Washington's capacity to strike at Trenton was not lost on Lord George Germain, King George III's secretary of state for the colonies.[23] In a biting admonishment of the Canadian governor, Germain wrote:

> I have had the mortification to learn, that, upon your repassing Lake Champlain, a very considerable number of the Insurgents, finding their Presence no longer necessary near Ticonderoga, immediately marched from thence, and joined the Rebel Forces in the Provinces of New York & Jersey.—That unexpected Reinforcement was more particularly unfortunate for us, as it enabled the Rebels to break in, with some degree of Success, upon parts of the Winter Quarters that were taken up by the Army under the Command of Sir Wm Howe.[24]

John Barker's Powder Horn
1776
courtesy of Morphy Auctions
When this horn was "MAde AT MOUNT IN DEPENdANC" in the latter half of November 1776, the majority of the fort's garrison had been withdrawn due to expired terms of service or in order to bolster Washington's forces to the south. The horn is decorated with ships, flags, a view of the city of New York, and a pentagonal, bastioned fort.

Although grossly underplaying Washington's Trenton and Princeton victories—the British had yet to realize their ramifications—Germain's point was accurate. Carlton cogently defended his actions, explaining to the secretary:

> A little reflection on the nature of this climate, will, I hope, convince your Lordship. Troops cannot encamp in that advanced season, without perishing from the cold alone. . . . In spight of every obstruction a greater marine was built and equipt [at St. Johns]; a greater marine force was defeated than had ever appeared on that Lake before; two Brigades were taken across, and remained at Crown Point till the 2ᵈ of November, for the sole purpose of drawing off the attention of the Rebels from Mr. Howe, and to facilitate his victories the remainder of the campaign. Nature had then put an end to ours. His winter-quarters, I confess, I never thought of covering. . . . I never could imagine, while an army to the southward found it necessary to finish their campaign, and go into winter-quarters, Your Lordship could possibly expect Troops so far North should continue their operations, least Mr. Howe should be disturbed during the winter; if that great army, near the sea coast, had their quarters insulted, what could Your Lordship expect would be the fate of a small corps, detached into the heart of the rebel country in that season.[25]

Thus, Carleton's return to Canada in the fall of 1776 was as inevitable as his naval supremacy of Lake Champlain, with or without Arnold's heroic but fruitless fight at Valcour Island. With Britain's dominance of the lake and with Forts Ticonderoga and Independence in American hands, it was also inevitable that the British would return in 1777 to finish the job.

Stratagem

It was a plan of junction of co-operation, not a junction of the bodies of the armies.

—Henry Dundas, M.P., March 19, 1778[1]

His Majesty's Frigate *Apollo* entered Québec Harbor on May 6, 1777. Aboard the vessel was Lieutenant-General John Burgoyne, second in command of the Canada Army in 1776, having wintered in England and now returned with new orders for General Carleton.[2] While Burgoyne's return was fully anticipated, not expected was the nature of a March 26 letter in which Carleton was directed to hand off most of the Canada Army to his subordinate general as part of a bold plan to conquer Lakes Champlain and George, the Mohawk and upper Hudson River Valleys, and the city of Albany.

The primary architect of this plan was Burgoyne himself. While in England over the winter of 1776–77, he updated officials about the events in Canada and northern New York and submitted Carleton's "Memoranda . . . relative to the next Campaign communicated to Lt. Genl. Burgoyne to be laid before Government." The plan offered a conservative approach, in which Lake Champlain would be reconquered, and if possible, the Mohawk and Connecticut River Valleys might be quelled. But Burgoyne subverted this by submitting a plan of his own, "Thoughts for Conducting the War from the Side of Canada." It was an ambitious series of proposals, in which Burgoyne not only suggested that the Army from Canada could reconquer valleys, but that it could go much further and form a juncture with the main army, commanded by General Sir William Howe.

The official who held the power to secure approval of such an endeavor, as well as the appointment of its commander, was Lord George Germain. One of his responsibilities was in the coordination of the various military strategies proposed between the two supreme leaders in North America—Sir William Howe and Sir Guy Carleton, both of whom were newly knighted for their 1776 military successes. While it was incumbent upon Howe to lead military campaigns against the rebellion within the thirteen colonies, Carleton, as governor of the province of Québec, was expected to focus upon the protection of his domain. Germain himself informed the governor that "the security and good government of Canada

The Honble Sr Wm Howe
by Charles Corbutt (Richard Purcell),
1777

Anne S. K. Brown Military Collection, Brown
University, bdr:227278

As "General and Commander in Chief of all His Majesty's Forces, within the Colonies, laying on the Atlantic Ocean, from Nova Scotia to West Florida inclusive," Howe was entrusted with eliminating Revolutionary military resistance in the American colonies. This famous print was published in England to fulfill commercial demand for portraits of the war's famous personages. It is a fantasy piece, and does not reflect Howe's physical appearance or correct military uniform. Unfortunately, no authentic portrait of Howe is confirmed to exist.

The HON.^BLE S.^R W.^M HOWE.
Knight of the Bath, & Commander in Chief of his Majestys Forces in America
LONDON: Publish'd as the Act directs, 10.th Novr 1777, by JOHN MORRIS, Rathbone Place.

George III

by Benjamin West, R.A., 1779

Royal Collection Trust/© Her Majesty Queen Elizabeth II 2019

King of Great Britain, Ireland, and, as claimed by the English crown since 1340, France, George III was the first Hanoverian monarch who spoke English as his first language. Ultimate responsibility for approving major military operations in America, such as Howe's and Burgoyne's, rested on his shoulders. Here, George III wears the embroidered frock of the captain-general of the forces, the British Army's highest-ranking officer.

absolutely require your presence there," which, while the outcome was tenuous for a time, ended with the successful ousting of the Revolutionary invaders in 1776.[3] The Canada Army, however, was obviously poised for further offensive action, and all that was needed was a strategic plan and a general to execute it.

Burgoyne's "Thoughts for Conducting the War" was in fact a presentation of three proposals. Retaking Lake Champlain and Ticonderoga was paramount in all options, after which the Army from Canada would be poised to either take Lake George and Albany or join the British Army in Rhode Island via a campaign through New England's Connecticut River Valley. In either case, a secondary offensive by way of Lake Ontario and the Mohawk River Valley was proposed, which would serve "as a diversion to facilitate every proposed operation." If, after Ticonderoga's fall, both the Albany and Rhode Island routes were deemed too dangerous, then "the alternative remains of embarking the army at Quebec, in order to effect a junction with General Howe by sea," or strike at other Revolutionary strongholds along the coast. But Burgoyne pointed out clearly that the proposed Albany route was "formed upon the supposition that it be the sole purpose of the Canada army to effect a junction with General Howe; or, after co-operating so far as to get possession of Albany and open the communication to New-York, to remain upon the Hudson's-River, and thereby enable that general to act with his whole force to the southward."[4]

Nowhere in the plan was there a mandate for Howe to ascend the Hudson River and link with the Army from Canada at Albany, or anywhere else for that matter. After due consideration, George III approved of Burgoyne's plan; unsurprisingly, Burgoyne was chosen as the expedition's commander, and was instructed to "force his way to Albany" after securing Lakes Champlain and George.[5] From Albany, Burgoyne would await further operational instructions via a juncture of communication with his new commander in chief, Howe. As planned, the Army from Canada's success had little to do with Howe's operations, apart from the fact that Burgoyne would be under the expectation of taking direction from Howe.

As for Howe, he too had developed a series of proposals for the 1777 campaign year, each one modified from the previous based upon changing strategic situations. As early as December 20, 1776, Howe wrote a letter notifying Germain that his primary target for the 1777 campaign season would be an overland operation against the Revolutionary capital of Philadelphia, Pennsylvania. When he wrote this proposal, Howe had good reason to think that British victory in the war was certain. Washington soon changed his mind when, in one of the war's most exceptional military moves, he attacked Trenton and defeated its garrison of 1,000 Hessians. Washington not only brilliantly outmaneuvered British troops sent to force a counterattack, but was also victorious in the subsequent Battle of Assunpink Creek (January 2) and the seminal Battle of Princeton (January 3). Afterward, Washington skillfully withdrew to the hills around Morristown, New Jersey, where his army settled into winter quarters. In less than two weeks, he turned what appeared to be the inevitable ruin of the newly declared United States of America into a fighting chance for survival. It was based upon these realities that Germain wrote to Howe on March 3, informing him that the king approved his plan for an overland operation against Philadelphia.

The Right Honourable Lord George Germaine
by James McArdell after Joshua Reynolds, 1777
The New York Public Library Digital Collections, 419929

Named George Sackville at birth, Sackville rose to the rank of lieutenant-general during the Seven Years' War. A 1760 general court-martial triggered by accusations that he disobeyed orders given by a superior officer during the Battle of Minden found him guilty and "unfit to serve his Majesty [George II] in any military capacity whatever." With George III's accession to the throne, Sackville—whose surname was changed to Germaine in 1770—accepted the appointment of third secretary of state (for the colonies) in 1775. This print was copied from Reynolds's portrait of Sackville painted in 1759, the very year of the Battle of Minden.

The Proceedings of a General Court-Martial . . . upon the Trial of Lord George Sackville, 249.

General George Washington

by Charles Willson Peale, ca. 1780

The Metropolitan Museum of Art, 97.33

Howe's original plan to obliterate Revolutionary forces was drastically altered after Washington's victories at Trenton and Princeton, New Jersey. This portrait of Washington is one of many copies made by Peale after his sensational original painted in 1779. Unlike the original painting and other copies of it, which commemorated both victories, this version was made to commemorate the victory at Trenton in particular. Note Washington's blue moiré silk ribband, which was used during the forepart of the war to denote his position of commander in chief of the Continental Army, as well as two Hessen-Cassel colours captured at Trenton.

With Burgoyne commanding the Albany-bound Army from Canada, Lieutenant-Colonel Barry St. Leger was appointed to take charge of the diversionary force tasked with moving from Lake Ontario up to Oneida Lake via the Oswego River and then down into the Mohawk River Valley. St. Leger, who commanded the expedition at Burgoyne's request, planned to enter Albany after quelling Revolutionary resistance along his campaign route. Although the force St. Leger commanded was small, Burgoyne deemed it adequate for the task, since "it is not to be imagined that any detachment of such force as that of [General Philip] Schuyler can be supplied by the enemy for the Mohawk."[6]

Notable is the fact that George III approved Howe's plan weeks before Burgoyne's was likewise confirmed, and Burgoyne was made aware of Howe's overland operation against Philadelphia before he left England to take command of the Army from Canada. Howe was dutifully informed that Burgoyne would advance from Canada to Albany, after which he was expected to send Burgoyne further instruction. There was, apparently, little concern over the efficacy of these divergent campaigns. Rather, the government saw them as complementary, and if the commanders involved fulfilled their orders as instructed, all was expected to go as planned.

Invasion

The Passage of the Army over the Lake was one of the finest Sights in the World.

—Captain Sir Francis Clerke, Bt., July 5, 1777[1]

The Army from Canada assembling in mid-June was more impressive in size than in quality. Most of the army's regiments had been part of the Canada relief task force sent from Europe the previous year. The most recent general reviews for Burgoyne's British regiments, performed in 1774 or 1775, had lauded the 9th, 20th, 21st (Royal North British Fusiliers), and 24th Regiments of Foot as being "Excellent," "very Serviceable," or "fit for immediate Service," but such was not the case with others.[2] The 53rd was given an embarrassing audit, which stated that it "may with care and pains be made much better," but was nonetheless cleared for deployment.[3] The 62nd could not even meet a passing grade, having been "very much drafted, [and] are . . . but very indifferent," although by the termination of the

Captain Sir Francis Carr Clerke, 7th Baronet
by Jeremiah Meyer, R.A., ca. 1777
courtesy of Bonhams
A lieutenant in the 3rd Regiment of Foot Guards and captain in the army, Sir Francis served as Burgoyne's junior aide-de-camp in 1776–77. A primary reason for his appointment to the position was his trilingual skills: The twenty-eight-year-old could read and write in English, French, and German, the latter ability being particularly rare among British officers. In this portrait, Sir Francis wears the embroidered frock of a general officer's aide-de-camp.

Private, Battalion Company, 62nd Regiment of Foot

Crown warrant called for corps with buff-colored facings to wear buff-colored pouch and waist belts in lieu of white ones, a regulation consistently flouted by this regiment. As with other British regiments in Canada, their worn woolen breeches were replaced by linen ones cut from "old Tents" made by the regiment's women followers in spring 1777. Originally left to garrison Mount Independence in July, the 62nd Regiment's soldiers had ample time there to kill timber rattlesnakes *(Crotalus horridus)* and "cover their bayonet Scabbards with the Skins."

Green to Bainton, January 26, 1781, National Army Museum, 7201/36/1.

Cap Device, 62nd Regiment of Foot
1777
Saratoga National Historical Park, SARA 2623
Lacking expected shipments of new uniforms, British regiments in the Canada Army trimmed coats and hats in spring 1777. In some battalions their horsehair-crested caps were adorned with small, locally manufactured, pattern pewter ornaments; the 62nd Regiment adopted this "starburst" design for theirs.

1776 campaign, it was singled out as being "one of the finest English regiments" in the Canada Army.[4]

Notably, only one of Burgoyne's British regiments, the 47th, had endured major combat within the past few years, specifically in the 1775 Lexington-Concord expedition and the Battle of Bunker Hill. Otherwise, comparatively few British personnel in the Army from Canada had seen recent, if any, combat. Since most of the army's officers and soldiers were only children during the previous war (1754–63), a majority of the army's redcoats were, in fact, green.

His most capable, experienced British soldiers were his grenadiers and light infantrymen. Grenadiers were, on average, the taller soldiers of a British regiment who were army service veterans, if not veterans of battle. Likewise, British light infantrymen were soldiers who had a few years' service under their belts, and the younger, smaller men were usually chosen for the duty. Following British Army standard operating procedure, British regiments of the Canada Army transferred their grenadier and light infantry companies to form one battalion each of grenadiers and light infantry. This provided army leadership with increased tactical flexibility, allowing British commanders to deploy these elite troops en masse as cohesive bodies, rather than allowing each regiment to use them piecemeal.[5]

While no redcoats were armed with rifles, a provisional company of British Rangers was formed under the command of Captain Alexander Fraser. This unit, composed of soldiers drawn from the Army from Canada's battalion companies, was formed of men "of good character, sober, active,

British Commissioned Officer's Spontoon Head
second half, 18th century
Don Troiani collection
Despite being the regulation polearm for commissioned officers of non-fusilier British infantry and marine battalion, or "hat," companies, spontoons were laid aside at the beginning of the war in favor of fusees and bayonets. This spontoon head, marked to an officer in the 20th Regiment of Foot, is missing its crossbar.

31st Regiment of Foot Rank-and-File Button

ca. 1770s

Don Troiani collection

This cast-pewter button includes the "cable" border motif around its perimeter, a common decorative feature seen on British button faces of the 1770s.

robust, healthy" and provided with "a very good Firelock and to be in every Respect proper to Form a Body of Marksmen."[6] In order to maximize the tactical potency of the army's most elite British troops—the 24th Regiment of Foot, the British Grenadier and Light Infantry Battalions, Captain Walker's Company of Royal Artillery, and Captain Fraser's Company of Marksmen—all were brigaded under the command of Brigadier-General Simon Fraser and given the name the Advanced Corps.[7]

All told, Burgoyne's British Division of infantry numbered about 3,750 officers and soldiers.

Most of the British regiments remaining behind for Canada's protection were the worst of the lot. The 31st was deemed "not equally in order with the other regiments for services of activity,"[8] while the 34th suffered from substandard leadership, it having been recently admonished for being "fit for Service" but only if "the Officers took as much Pains as the men" in attention to their duty.[9] Most regiments going upon Burgoyne's expedition had to leave a cadre of troops behind in order to assist with the province's defenses. Carleton complained that those left behind were "the sick, infirm, and such as the Regiments usually disburthen themselves of on like occasions."[10]

While Burgoyne's redcoat infantry were not Britain's best, their average was brought lower still by the necessity of hiring Germans in Hanover in order to fill regimental establishments. With the war being relatively unpopular, a British Army all but reliant on gaining recruits by voluntary enlistment in Great Britain and Ireland wasn't capable of generating the required numbers. The Germans recruited to serve in the British ranks were a mixed lot, some having had prior military experience, others having none. Even though they were willing to serve King George III—he was their *Kurfürst* (elector), after all—they were thrust into a new, foreign world.[11]

Unsurprisingly, the British officer corps was in general united in their disdain for the German recruits. Burgoyne was incensed with the policy, and claimed that the Canada Army

> comprised a good deal of useless stuff, viz, men recruited in Germany for the British Regiments, and sent over last year, not one tenth of whom in the opinion of the Officers of those Regiments will be fit for the Ranks, from Infirmities, malingering Habits, Dejection, or Profligacy of Disposition; many of the Irish recruits and drafts [men taken from other British regiments not being deployed to North America] are equally bad.[12]

Corporal, German Recruit for the British Army

King George III's Electorate of Hanover provided 2,000 German recruits to fill Britain's redcoat ranks. While most British regiments in Canada received a few dozen German recruits in 1776, some got over a hundred. Each recruit was issued a stand of arms, frock, cocked hat, white woolen smallclothes, and other necessaries. Upon joining their parent regiments, these recruits were given regimental accoutrements, but most serving in Burgoyne's army never received their regimental clothing. The single ring of tape around each cuff signified the rank of corporal.

Waist Belt Clasp, 33rd Regiment of Foot
ca. 1770s

Don Troiani collection

Recruits intended for the 33rd Regiment of Foot were kept as a cohesive body during the Northern Campaign of 1777—an atypical decision, since standard procedure was to draft wayward bodies of men into other battalions. However, the 33rd was exceptional in the British Army. Not only did many of the recruits protest the idea of being assimilated into other units, but the regiment's colonel, Charles, Earl Cornwallis, incurred "greater expense . . . in fitting them out than other Colonels might chuse to reimburse." This regimental buckle, which constituted part of that "greater expense," was recovered near Saratoga.

Carleton to Barrington, ca. November 29, 1776, TNA, WO 1/11.

Burgoyne's Royal Regiment of Artillery—four companies' worth, numbering about 260 officers and soldiers drawn from the regiment's 1st and 3rd Battalions—constituted his best-trained British Army troops. The massive artillery train consisted of nearly 80 cannons, a dozen howitzers, and over 40 mortars—130 pieces in all. Most of the pieces were cast in the 1750s and '60s during the Seven Years' War (French and Indian War), although some of the guns—the fifteen light three-pounder "grasshopper" cannons—were of a new pattern cast in 1776 for the express purpose of being used in North America.[13] Demands for additional personnel to operate the army's artillery pieces warranted the incorporation of seventy men drafted from the Royal Irish Regiment of Artillery—the artillery regiment of the Kingdom of Ireland.[14] Also attached to Burgoyne's British artillery was a group of about 150 British infantry recruits destined for regiments in Howe's army—tangible proof that Burgoyne's intention was to eventually open a line of communication with New York.[15]

Burgoyne's substantial German Division was commanded by Major-General Friedrich Adolf Riedesel, Freiherr zu (Baron of) Eisenbach.[16] Most of these units were from Herzogtum zu Braunschweig und Lüneburg (Duchy of Brunswick and Lueneburg), a natural choice since Herzog (Duke) Carl I's eldest son, Carl Wilhelm Ferdinand, was married to Princess Augusta, a sister of King George III. The Army from Canada's Infanterie (Infantry) Regiments Prinz Friedrich, von Riedesel, von Rhetz, and Specht were all new formations, albeit formed from existing multi-battalion Braunschweig regiments.

Paralleling the British procedure of combining grenadier companies into a single, cohesive battalion, all four Braunschweig regiments transferred their elite grenadier companies to serve in the Grenadierbattaillon Breymann (Grenadier Battalion Breymann). All officers of the five-company Leichtes

Infanterie Battaillon (Light Infantry Battalion) von Bärner were also drawn from preexisting Braunschweig regiments, but its men were new recruits, many of whom were inexperienced teenagers. This arrangement was meant to serve the dual purpose of having experienced military leadership and yet be the sort of fast-moving combat force that was a hallmark of a youthful corps of light infantry. While most of the battalion was armed with smoothbore muskets and bayonets, one of its hundred-man companies was a jäger company armed with rifles, and constituted the only riflemen in Burgoyne's army.[17] Together, the Grenadierbattaillon Breymann and Leichtes Infanterie Battaillon von Bärner formed the elite Braunschweig Reserve Corps, under Breymann's overall command. While all the Braunschweig battalions suffered from the same average lack of experience as did their British allies, most were nevertheless well drilled and consisted of many officers and soldiers who were noncombat military veterans.[18]

Probably the most unusual Braunschweig regiment in Burgoyne's army was the Dragoon Regiment Prinz Ludwig, a horseless cavalry corps. This arrangement was by design, though; the January 9, 1776, treaty between Great Britain

Braunschweig Infantry Musket
third quarter, 18th century
Michael and Joyce Barbieri collection; photograph by Miranda Peters

Braunschweig Wrist Plate (detail)
third quarter, 18th century
Michael and Joyce Barbieri collection; photograph by Miranda Peters

Like those of many other German nation-states, Braunschweig Musketen (muskets) were based upon the famed Pattern 1740 "Potsdam" *Muskete* made for Friedrich the Great's Kingdom of Prussia. A survivor of Burgoyne's army, this heavy, large-caliber (nearly .82) gun has a forty-two-and-one-quarter-inch-long barrel. Note the ducal coronet of Carl I, the Herzog zu Braunschweig und Lüneburg (Duke of Brunswick and Lueneburg), as well as his inverted double C monogram, both of which are engraved on the wrist plate. Solely made to engage in volley firefights, German muskets like this one were ineffective when used outside of that paradigm.

Braunschweig Musket Side Plate
third quarter, 18th century
Don Troiani collection
This brass side plate from a Braunschweig soldier's *Muskete* (musket)
was recovered from near Saratoga.

and Braunschweig und Lüneburg stipulated that the Herzog would provide "a body of Light Cavalry . . . but as his *Britannick* Majesty will not have occasion for the horses of this corps, the said corps shall serve as a corps of Infantry."[19] Unsurprisingly, the dragoon regiment drilled on foot intensely, and in his August 27, 1776, report to the regiment's commander, Lieutenant-Colonel Friedrich Baum, Riedesel stated that he was "satisfied as far as regards the Regiment of Dragoons" and found the regiment "in such a good condition on the whole, that all drill can cease excepting once a week, so that the men do not forget what they have learned."[20]

All told, the army's Braunschweig contingent numbered about 3,340 officers and soldiers.

There were Hessian corps in the Army from Canada as well, but unlike the thousands of Hessians serving in Howe's army who hailed from Landgrafschaft Hessen-Cassel, Burgoyne's Hessians were from the tiny state of Grafschaft (County) Hessen-Hanau. Its leader, Graf (Count) Wilhelm I, was a first cousin of King George III, and so here too the treaty between this state and Great Britain was a manifestation of familial relations.[21] The small size of the county allowed for the deployment of only a few corps to America, two of which were with Burgoyne. The 600-man Regiment Erb Prinz (Hereditary Prince) was one of Hanau's most elite, although, like most others in Burgoyne's army, was untested.[22] The 120-man Princely Hessen-Hanau Artillery Corps was a highly trained company which, unlike their infantry counterparts, trained with the British. Their longer, heavier cannons were replaced with shorter, lighter British pieces for use during the campaign.

With Burgoyne's army were two nascent corps of American royalists, the King's Loyal Americans and the Queen's Loyal Rangers ("Peters's Corps"). Both were composed of New England and New York refugees from places where loyalty to the crown was anathema to the vast majority of their neighbors, to say nothing of the newly constituted local and state Revolutionary governments. The plan was for these new corps to grow in number because of an anticipated groundswell of support for the king, and much hope was placed in these patriots for the crown. Burgoyne himself unabashedly claimed that these "provincial corps, acting zealously in the King's cause, must have great impression upon public opinion, and will . . . be of singular use to the ease and preservation of the regular troops."[23]

Canadien (French Canadian) assistance was difficult to procure, and never met the quota that government called for. Two *compagnies canadiennes* (Canadian companies), amounting to about 200 officers and soldiers, were formed, and while they were "officered by Seigneurs of the country who are well chosen," few men volunteered for the ranks and were instead "chiefly drafted from the Militia" rolls of the Québec and Montréal Districts.[24] While their officers met with Burgoyne's approval, the men did not:

> Those which I have yet seen afford no promise of use in arms—awkward, ignorant, disinclined to the service, spiritless. Various reasons are assigned for this change in the disposition of the natives [Canadiens] since the time of the French government. It may partly be owing to a disuse of arms, but I believe principally to the unpopularity of the Seigneurs, & to the poison which the Emissaries of the rebels have thrown into their minds.[25]

Sergeant, Hessen-Hanau Erb Prinz Regiment

Despite his ragged appearance, this *Unteroffizier* (noncommissioned officer) is easily identified by his *Kurzgewehr* (halberd) and cane—his leather gloves having been worn through and discarded. Although the Erb Prinz (Heir Prince) Regiment was one of Hanau's most elite, it was very poorly supplied, and its clothing was described as "extremely ragged" even before Burgoyne's campaign commenced. Because their yellow cloth breeches were particularly "in a very bad condition," they were replaced with linen gaitered trousers cut from old tents.

Von Gall to Wilhelm I, April 20 and May 16, 1777, in *An Account of the Hesse-Hanau Infantry Regiment*, trans. Ms. Raahage, U 55, U 60, Hessian Documents of the American Revolution, 1776–1783.

Increasing desertions within the ranks of the Canadien companies even before the expedition left Canada prompted the British general to ask Governor Carleton to call upon drafting "a Corvée of a thousand men to attend the expedition for a limitted time for the purpose of labour and transport." With Canadiens doing much of the labor work, claimed Burgoyne, his fighting regiments would "be properly full for their service in arms."[26] Carlton was unsurprised by the high desertion rate among the Canadiens, claiming they were "governed with too loose a Rein for many years, and had imbibed too much of the American spirit of Licentiousness and Independence." Yet, he added, "Ordering more would only tend to increase their Disobedience, and our Difficulties."[27]

In early June, Carleton ordered 500 corvée drafted from the Québec District to immediately repair to Burgoyne's army assembling at St. Johns to serve as laborers.[28] If the Canadiens of Burgoyne's army were perceived as "spiritless," it logically had more to do with the peculiar situation forced upon them. Canadiens had fought against the British during the Seven Years' War, barely fifteen years before. Predominantly conquered by the redcoats in 1759–60, they were now, in 1777, expected to assist them in putting down rebellious English colonists. It is not surprising that few Canadiens volunteered for this service, and the result was that they constituted the expedition's only draftees.

The Québec Indian Department, which coordinated British government policy with the province's Indians, worked to gain the support of chiefs and warriors for the expedition. These British allies would arrive in two distinct waves, the second of which was coming from the far shores of the Great Lakes over 1,000 miles away. The first wave of Indian allies, however, began to join Burgoyne in mid-June. These

Billhook

third quarter, 18th century

Don Troiani collection

Tools like these were a necessity for opening pathways for military travel in the wilderness. Billhooks were particularly made for cutting fascines, bundles of sticks which, when bound together, were used to augment field fortifications. Note the "King's Mark"—a broad arrow—which denoted government ownership. Recovered in the Lake Champlain Valley, this knife's wooden handle has long disappeared, exposing the iron tang.

Indian Trade Silver
second half, 18th century
Fort Ticonderoga Museum collection, MC-175, MC-173, MC-185, 2019.FIC.1; photograph by Margaret Staudter
The economies of Northeastern Woodlands Indians thrived on trade. Many items were produced by Europeans and Americans for bartering, including decorative wearing apparel such as sterling or silver plate armbands, moon gorgets, ear-wheels and bobs, brooches, rings, shirt-buckles, and the Catholic *Croix de Lorraine* (Cross of Lorraine). The elaborate cut ear-wheels are attributed to the Québec silversmith Joseph Schindler.

chiefs and warriors, accompanied by women and children, hailed from the Seven Nations of Canada. This multinational confederacy—consisting of the Bécancour (Eastern Abenaki), Caughnawaga (Mohawk), Lake of the Two Mountains (Mohawk, Nipissing, and Algonquin), Lorette (Huron), Oswegatchie (Onondaga, Oneida, and Cayuga), Saint-François (Sokoki, Penacook, and New England Algonquian), and Saint Regis (resettled Caughnawaga Mohawk) nations—added about 500 fighting men to Burgoyne's army by the end of June. With them were over a hundred British and Canadien officials, volunteers, and interpreters.

The noncombatant branches, including His Majesty's General Hospital, the Corps of Engineers, artificers, various commissaries, and waggoneers, added hundreds more people. As with most campaigning armies, Burgoyne's also had a number of followers. Hundreds of British, Irish, and German women, most of whom were the wives of the army's soldiers, and their children comprised the bulk of those following. All told, his army included about 600 women and children. As with most armies, sutlers—people licensed to sell alcohol, food, and a variety of dry goods to the army's personnel—were also present.

Most of the army was transported up Lake Champlain (south) by the Royal Navy. Thanks to the massive shipbuilding program begun the previous year, the British were well prepared for the advance, and even some of Arnold's boats captured in 1776 constituted part of the fleet. Commanded by Commodore Skeffington Lutwidge, the fleet consisted of H.M. Sloops *Royal George* and *Inflexible*,

British Army Soldier's Wife

"Women" was the common appellation given to the subset of "followers" who, married to soldiers, followed their husbands during the course of their military careers. Three women per company were allowed to attend the Army from Canada, and they performed paid laundering, sewing, and nursing duties; others could earn money as sutlers. This follower wears the ragged clothing typically resulting from long wear, including a silk bonnet, brown worsted English gown with stomacher and robings, blue worsted petticoat, and check linen apron.

Lieutenant-General John Burgoyne

Although called "Burgoyne, the Pompous" by British Whig politician Horace Walpole in 1777, the British general was never known by the moniker "Gentleman Johnny" until F. J. Hudleston's 1927 biography. Here, Burgoyne wears the plain frock of a British lieutenant-general, his rank displayed by the coat's button arrangement in sets of threes. Attending him are his senior engineer officer (Lieutenant William Twiss), junior aide-de-camp (Lieutenant and Captain Sir Francis Carr-Clerke, Bt., 3rd Regiment of Foot Guards), deputy quartermaster general (Captain John Money, 9th Regiment of Foot), and an assistant commissioner to administer oaths of allegiance (Lieutenant Andrew Philip Skene, 43rd Regiment of Foot).

Walpole to Mason, October 5, 1777, in *The Correspondence of Horace Walpole*, vol. 1, 316.

Brig *Washington*, Schooners *Maria* and *Carleton*, Cutter *Lee*, the Radeau *Thunderer*, Gondolas *Loyal Convert* and *Jersey*, 24 gunboats, and over 200 bateaux. All vessels were capably manned by nearly 700 Royal Navy personnel who were, incidentally, probably the most experienced military men in Burgoyne's entire force.

The Army from Canada began the process of advancing unopposed into New York in mid-June. Too large to move as a single body, the army's component brigades and corps moved south in stages. By June 25 the main body was collecting at the ruins of His Majesty's Fort of Crown Point in New York and Chimney Point on the lake's opposite shore. The sites were used as a staging area, and for the next week the army and its support fleet assembled for the opening of offensive military operations. On June 30 Burgoyne issued an inspiring general order to his forces:

> The army embarks to-morrow, to approach the enemy. We are to contend for the King, and the constitution of Great Britain, to vindicate Law, and to relieve the oppressed—a cause in which his Majesty's Troops and those of the Princes his Allies, will feel equal excitement. The services required of this particular expedition, are critical and conspicuous. During our progress occasions may occur, in which no difficulty, nor labour, nor life are to be regarded. This Army must not Retreat.[29]

Resistance

If they make an attempt upon us . . . I nothing doubt we shall be able by the smiles of superintendant Providence to give them as fatal an overthrow.
—Colonel Alexander Scammell, June 8, 1777[1]

A dozen miles south of Crown Point, Fort Ticonderoga was situated on a promontory jutting into Lake Champlain from the New York side. Originally called Carillon when constructed by the French in 1755 during the French and Indian War, the fort's purpose was to protect against British invasions north and facilitate French incursions south. The French could not have chosen a more strategic location for the task: The fort not only covered passage up the lake, but also protected the all-important outlet of the La Chute River, the rapid-chocked four-mile-long waterway that emptied the northern end of Lake George into Lake Champlain. Traditionally, all substantial land forces used this passage as their avenue of approach north or south, and 1777 was no different. Following a failed attack in 1758, the place was taken with ease by the British in 1759. Americans captured the fort from a hapless British garrison in May 1775 with nearly equal ease and held it ever since.

The square-shaped "old French Fort" itself was built of wood, stone, and earth and had fortified corner bastions and two ravelins. Stone barracks lay protected within the fort's walls, and for additional measure, most of the structure was surrounded by a star-shaped fortified log wall fronted with abatis. Located over a half mile northwest of this fortress were the "Old French Lines," a substantial network of continuous log and earthen walls built by the French to protect against any land-based approach from that quarter. Outbuildings such as huts, a bakery, sheds, and storehouses populated the area. For all of its strength, though, the fort had one major weakness: Because the peninsula's defenses were originally designed to ward off British attacks from the south or west, its primary defenses were thusly oriented. In order to shore up this inherent vulnerability, the nearly treeless peninsula was peppered with wood and stone redoubts and other strong fortifications, particularly north of the fort.

What had caught the British unawares in 1776, Mount Independence, was purpose-built to offset Ticonderoga's weakness. Mount Independence was sandwiched between Lake Champlain to the west and East Creek to the east, thereby forming a peninsula that jutted into Lake Champlain from the Vermont side of the lake, south-southeast of Ticonderoga. The mount was all but cleared of trees and a fort, named Fort Independence, was constructed on the height. Unlike most forts built in the region, it consisted of a large eight-pointed palisade wall fronted with abatis, which protected barracks, storehouses, and the powder magazine. Directly north of the fort was a U-shaped battery called the Citadel and, beyond that, an extensive fortified wall, both of which commanded the lake below. A hospital, workshops, ordnance laboratory, and sheds were spread across the hill. The entire peninsula was closed off by a wall "formed of rough Logs felled Trees &cᵃ" and fronted with abatis.[2]

Both peninsulas were connected by a one-third-mile-long floating bridge "made of large logs, loosely boarded over and strongly chained" to a series of large, sunken caissons "made of round logs pinned together and filled with stone."[3] A log boom spanned the lake directly below (north) of the whole, and although "feebly secured, for want of cables," this obstruction, as well as the caissons, were intended to serve as obstructions to prevent the British from advancing farther up the lake (south).[4]

In June 1777 both strongholds were under the command of the Northern Department's second in command, Major General Arthur St. Clair. Unfortunately for St. Clair, he did not enjoy the numerical superiority that Gates had at the posts the previous fall. Most of St. Clair's Continental Army regiments were newly formed in late 1776, with the majority of their personnel being appointed or recruited over the winter and spring. All three regiments of the New Hampshire line, consisting of Colonel Joseph Cilley's 1st, Colonel Nathan Hale's 2nd, and Colonel Alexander Scammell's 3rd New Hampshire Regiments, were present. Inspected in mid-June by the Northern Department's deputy muster master

14th Regiment of the Massachusetts Grand Army Button
1775
Private collection

Pewter buttons cast for the 1775 Massachusetts Grand Army employed a uniform motif. This regiment should not be confused with the 14th Continental Regiment of 1776 (a Massachusetts regiment) or Colonel Gamaliel Bradford's (14th) Massachusetts Regiment, which served in the Northern Campaign of 1777. This button was recovered from the lower Lake Champlain Valley.

10th Regiment of the Massachusetts Grand Army Button
1775
Don Troiani collection
Due to supply challenges, Massachusetts Grand Army buttons were issued to regiments regardless of whether or not the button's number matched the wearer's regiment. This regiment should not be confused with the 10th Continental Regiment of 1776 (a Connecticut regiment) or Colonel Thomas Marshall's (10th) Massachusetts Regiment, which served in the Northern Campaign of 1777. This button was recovered from the Lake Champlain Valley.

general, Lieutenant Colonel Richard Varick, Cilley's battalion was found to be "a pretty Good one & pretty well officered & armed, their Arms were neat & Clean the Clothing very indifferent." Scammell's was given a poorer review, described as "a very indifferent one having Many Young Soldiers, badly Clothed, the Arms were new, & Good & Clean." Another 1st New Hampshire Regiment, commanded by Colonel Pierse Long, present with the Northern Army was slated for disbandment in July.[5]

From Massachusetts, the garrisons included Colonel Michael Jackson's (8th), Colonel Thomas Marshall's (10th), Colonel Ebenezer Francis's (11th), Colonel Samuel Brewer's (12th), and Colonel Gamaliel Bradford's (14th) Regiments.[6] Likewise inspected by Varick in mid-June on the eve of the British invasion, Jackson's Regiment was identified as being "badly Clothed, tho pretty well armed. & Arms Clean," while Francis's Regiment was found to be "a pretty Good Corps both with Respect to officers & men, well armed & pretty well Clothed.—the Arms Neat & Clean." Brewer's was called out as "a small corps, indifferently armed & clothed, & not much better officered." Happily, Varick found their weapons to be "Neat & Clean."[7]

Colonel Seth Warner's Regiment was a small "extra" Continental Army battalion which, unlike most, was not under the auspices of a specific state. Personnel for this corps of "Green Mountain Boys" were predominantly drawn from the New Hampshire Grants, territory officially governed by New York but long disputed by a majority of the people living there. In early 1777 the Grants became a self-declared independent republic that was embodied as the State of Vermont in June.[8] Warner's Regiment was given a poor grade of being "indifferently officered & Clothed.—the Arms were very indifferent & they want Bayonets.—tho' Clean."[9]

The remaining Continental infantry units were small companies of rangers commanded by Captains Benjamin Whitcomb, George Aldrich, and Thomas Lee, all of whom were adept at ranging and scouting duties.[10] The army's Continental Corps of Artillery commanded by Major Ebenezer Stevens managed the artillery pieces spread throughout both peninsulas, further supplemented by infantry draftees. The noncombatant element of the army—including the quartermaster and various commissary departments; General Hospital; the armorer, carpenter, carriage-maker, and blacksmith artificer companies; bateaux companies; and waggoneers—provided the remainder of the Continental Army's personnel. Followers, including women, children, and sutlers, rounded out the garrisons. In all, the number of Continental Army fighting men under St. Clair's command was about 3,500 officers and men, of which nearly 430 were deemed sick but were nonetheless present with their regiments.[11]

St. Clair's Continentals were supplemented with militia, also drawn from New Hampshire and Massachusetts. Unlike Continental regiments, militia battalions, which were regulated and activated by their states of origin, were present for short, finite terms of service only.[12] Despite the forts' lack of personnel, militia battalions had come and gone as recently as early June; with

Matross, Major Ebenezer Stevens's Corps of Artillery
Stevens's artillery corps served as the Northern Army's primary artillery arm in 1777. These artillerymen were well clothed, constituting some of the Northern Department's few recipients of the massive amount of British clothing captured in 1776. Their purpose-built black coats, faced with red and adorned with "plain yellow buttons," were supplemented with "white waistcoats and breeches, with white buttons number[ed] 53" and "smart cocked hats with hair cockades and white tassels."
Independent Chronicle, Boston, March 13, 1777.

Private, Colonel Ebenezer Francis's (11th) Massachusetts Regiment
Along with other Massachusetts Continental regiments at Ticonderoga in the spring, Francis's was poorly shod, accoutered, and uniformed. Spears were issued to those who had no muskets. The regiment was rearmed with "Neat & Clean" surplus French arms shortly before Burgoyne's summertime attack. It was commanded by the only Continental Army colonel killed in the campaign, at Hubbardton, and was thereafter known as "Late Francis's Regiment" until October 25, when Gates promoted Lieutenant Colonel Benjamin Tupper to the colonelcy.

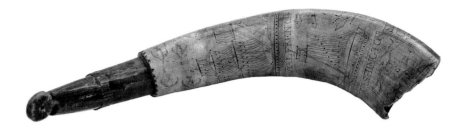

Cornelius Van Wormer's Powder Horn
1777

Fort Ticonderoga Museum collection, PH-027; photograph by Margaret Staudter
This beautifully decorated horn, dated Skenesborough, May 12, 1777, includes depictions of fish, birds, and six sailing vessels, two of which are identified as the *Lady Washington* and the *Royal French*. Van Wormer served as a private in Colonel Anthony Van Bergen's Regiment of Albany County, New York, militia.

French Model 1766 Infantry Musket
ca. 1766

Don Troiani collection
French muskets were built at one of three manufactories located at Saint-Étienne, Maubeuge, or Charleville, and each lock face bore the name of the musket's place of origin. When the French cargo ship *Amphitrite* entered harbor at Portsmouth, New Hampshire, on April 20, 1777, the vessel bore a trove of war matérial for the United States war effort: over 900 tents, 32,000 cannonballs, 10,000 tools, a boon of other weapons and military stores, and exactly 219 chests of arms containing over 6,000 French military muskets. This *fusil d'infanterie modèle 1766* (model 1766 infantry musket) was one of those pieces, and these arms were widely distributed among regiments that served in the Northern, Eastern, and Highlands Departments in 1777. Having smaller calibers (.69) than British infantry muskets, French muskets of this pattern also weighed less (about eight and a half pounds).

their enlistments expired, officers and soldiers of Colonel Benjamin Bellows's battalion of New Hampshire militia began to trickle away in mid-June, the last leaving as late as June 25. The remaining militia battalions, Massachusetts units commanded by Colonels David Wells and David Leonard, were only "raised to reinforce at Ticonderoga for the space of two months"; their enlistments were set to expire in early July. Numbering over 500 officers and soldiers, these battalions, like their Continental counterparts, had more than 100 sick men present in the ranks.[13]

The condition of most of the soldiers' muskets was somewhat problematic. Many of the Continental regiments were armed "very indifferent," although the three regiments of the New Hampshire line "had pretty good French arms, and chiefly bayonets."[14] The "majority of the other [Continental] regiments had not bayonets." The militia regiments had arms, "but very indifferent, but no bayonets," despite both Massachusetts and New Hampshire militia regulations demanding them. Neither the artillery battalion nor the artificer companies had arms to defend themselves with. What's more, the "lines and redoubts at Ticonderoga" were supplied with spears and "sharp pointed poles" which could be used for defense if necessary.[15] Less than a month earlier, many of those same polearms were in the hands of nearly a third of the Massachusetts Continentals due to the shortage of firearms at the time.[16] Even though polearms were no longer needed to arm soldiers by mid-June, Varick pointed out that many of the Massachusetts Continentals in particular "want Bayonets & Good Arms."[17] Many

Pike Head
second half, 18th century
Private collection
A lack of firearms at Forts Ticonderoga and Independence in spring 1777 forced many of the Massachusetts Continental Army troops there to be armed with pikes instead of muskets. These shortages were alleviated by the state shortly before the enemy's late June appearance. This iron pike head was recovered from an American campsite in the lower Champlain Valley.

14th Continental Regiment Button
ca. 1776

Don Troiani collection

Unlike their 1777 successors, uniforms of the 1776 Continental Army regiments bore numbered buttons. Disbanded in January 1777, the 14th Continental Regiment, a Massachusetts regiment commanded by Colonel John Glover, should not be confused with Colonel Gamaliel Bradford's (14th) Massachusetts Regiment. This enlisted man's pewter button was recovered from the Champlain Valley.

were in want of cartridge boxes, waist belts (used to carry bayonets), powder horns, bullet pouches, slings, and more. In some regiments, they lacked more of these than they had on hand.[18]

If the weapon situation wasn't optimal, the condition of the soldiers' clothing was worse. Because most of the regiments were nascent formations and deployed to the Northern Army before they were completely outfitted, the clothiers had little time to prepare uniforms for them. Clothing items such as shirts, trousers, overalls, waistcoats, jackets, and rifle shirts were doled in dribs and drabs by the states and the Continental Army's public stores, but in mid-June it was noted, "None of the troops have Uniforms & Consequently Make a very Awkward Appearance."[19] Upon his arrival at the forts, Schuyler admitted that he "expected to have had the pleasure of seeing the Troops . . . completely cloathed in uniform, and provided with the best arms, but was sensibly mortified to find it so totally otherwise."[20] Massachusetts and New Hampshire were not forthcoming with clothing, and the public stores were all but depleted "Except a few Oznabrig Shirts."[21]

The article most needed by the troops was footwear. Shoes were at a premium and wore out at a pace quicker than the soldiers received replacements. The situation was so bad that Colonel Marshall complained that the men going out on scouting missions in May "have been Obliged to Borrow the Shoes off the feet of those left in Camp.[22] The plight still hadn't been resolved by June, and Marshall begged for stockpiles of leather for making shoe soles, as it "would be a great Saving to Soldiers as for the want of it they throw by shoes that might be of Service & the greater part of them are barefoot, as there are none here."[23]

The soldiers themselves caused something of a stir among army command. When inspected in mid-June, Varick pointed out that there were "Many Very Young Lads" of which fifty were rejected, being "positively unfit for any kind of service," and sent home.[24] He planned to send off more underage males too, "had not the situation of our garrison forbid the measures" due to St. Clair's request that he "should not deal too strictly with the Young Soldiers, as his Garrisons were already too small."[25] Schuyler himself complained that too many of those who remained were "Boys or rather children." Conversely, Schuyler also complained that many in his army were "aged men that ought never to have been sent." In truth, Schuyler was difficult to satisfy. In an observation that exposed his racism, he also objected to the fact that the Northern Army was "composed of . . . negroes" that he claimed "disgrace our arms."[26] By 1777 freemen were legally and actively recruited by Massachusetts and New Hampshire Continental officers, and while enslaved men could not choose to join, they could be forced to serve in lieu of their drafted owners who refused to do so.

Brigadier General Enoch Poor
by Colonel Tadeusz Kościuszko, ca. 1777
New Hampshire Historical Society, 1907.016.02

Colonel Gamaliel Bradford
by Colonel Tadeusz Kościuszko, ca. 1777
Houghton Library, Harvard University, MS Am 2573
Described as "a beautifull limner" by the Northern Department's chief engineer, Colonel Jeduthan Baldwin, Kościuszko took to drawing portraits of the Northern Army's officers after arriving at Fort Ticonderoga in mid-May 1777. Because these sitters would not cross Kościuszko's path again after October, the portraits were probably drawn at Ticonderoga or Mount Independence on the eve of Burgoyne's assault, thus providing rare contemporary likenesses of some of the campaign's central participants.
Baldwin to Baldwin, May 18, 1777, Heritage Auctions, April 5, 2016, *Historical Manuscripts*, lot 49019.

Catastrophe

When, on July 1, Burgoyne departed Crown Point and Chimney Point to move against Forts Ticonderoga and Independence, he did not do so blindly. In March, Samuel MacKay and a party of Indians and Canadien volunteers made a secret trek to the area, gathering significant information on the conditions of the forts and their garrisons from a local royalist as well as from the twenty-two prisoners they took.[2] On June 17 a party of British-allied Indians set upon some unsuspecting Continental soldiers near the French Lines, and the small body of men sent in pursuit of the perpetrators were ambushed about five miles north of the fort. Most of the Americans escaped, but some men were killed, wounded, or captured, including the party's commanding officer.[3]

On the other side of the lake on June 22, Captain Alexander Fraser led an audacious reconnaissance of about 400 men drawn from his company of British Rangers, a detachment of British Light Infantry, two Canadien companies, and about 200 Indians up the Otter Creek valley into the Vermont countryside. After being out for about five days, his force returned and bivouacked near the Ticonderoga peninsula, but the Americans "did not Venture out of their Lines" to attack him.[4] Fraser rejoined the army on the 28th, bringing in significant additional intelligence and more prisoners. Area royalists provided additional intelligence on the area's landscape and forts.

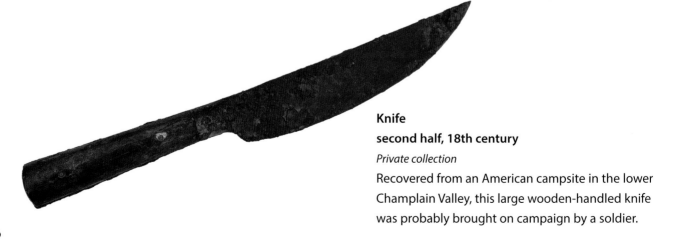

Knife
second half, 18th century
Private collection
Recovered from an American campsite in the lower Champlain Valley, this large wooden-handled knife was probably brought on campaign by a soldier.

Plan of Carillon ou Ticonderoga Which Was quitted by the Americaines in the night from the 5th to the 6th of July 1777

by Captain Michel Capitaine du Chesnoy, ca. 1778

The Library of Congress, 00557013

On the New York (west) side, Fort Ticonderoga guards over the point where the La Chute River empties into Lake Champlain. The thinly treed landscape was populated with a series of smaller log and stone fortifications that protected various approaches, while the massive "Old French Lines" dominated the main road to and from the fort. Note Sugar Loaf Hill (Mount Defiance), the bridge over the La Chute River, and the redoubt atop Mount Hope, located in the map's upper left corner. While the caissons are not depicted, the floating bridge is shown straddling both sides of the lake. On the Vermont (east) side of the lake is "Mount Independant," topped by Fort Independence, a star-shaped stockade surrounded by abatis. Separating the Mount on its eastern broadside is East Creek, although the manner in which it was drawn belies its substantial nature. Note the Mount's only road to and from the mainland, the Military Road, designated here as the "Road to hubbard town." One of many eighteenth-century maps depicting the area, this particular one simultaneously depicts the locations of British forces on July 6 and October 24, 1777.

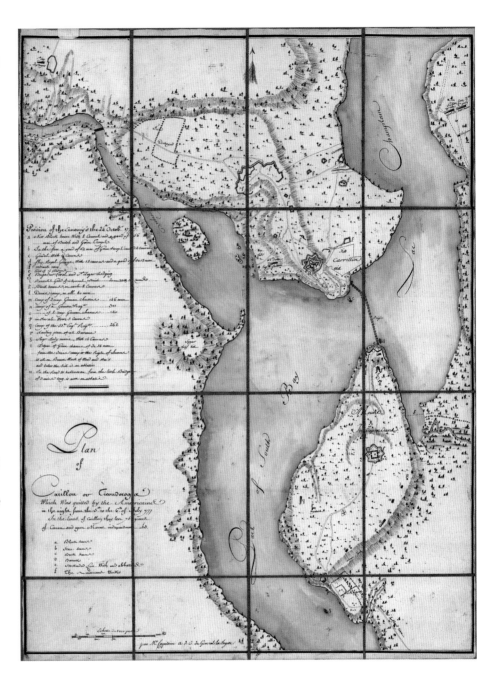

Broad Axe Head
third quarter, 18th century
Don Troiani collection
This large iron axe head (its haft is missing) with steel cutting edge would have been used to hew large trees. Note the "King's Mark" stamp—a broad arrow—which denoted government ownership. This piece was recovered from the Lake Champlain Valley.

Thusly informed, Burgoyne advanced his forces on both sides of the lake with the intention of cutting off both peninsulas from the mainland. On the New York side, Brigadier-General Simon Fraser's Advanced Corps drove south, followed by the army's two-brigade British Division and the Braunschweig dragoon regiment. The army's two-brigade German Division was tasked with cutting off Mount Independence on the Vermont side of the lake. Headed by Lieutenant-Colonel Heinrich Breymann's Reserve Corps, the German Division cut a road through the woods as it slowly proceeded to their destination.

The British and Germans made a steady, difficult advance south. It was "so very hot here," complained one German surgeon's mate, that many of the men, working in the hot sun to clear trees and brush, "who had taken off their clothes have been badly burned." They also waged "war against the flies that are torturing us during the day," and during the night, "the snakes (adders) visit us in the tents."[5] But they moved on. Heralding the onslaught to come, on July 1 British-allied Indians attacked a blockhouse guarding some sawmills on the La Chute River. The post, defended by two small cannons and twenty men from Colonel Thomas Marshall's Regiment, successfully kept them at bay.[6]

On July 2 a detachment from Fraser's Advanced Corps, with the addition of Indians, royalist Americans, and the Canadien companies, was unleashed upon the Ticonderoga peninsula. Operating west of the French Lines, a detachment of Fraser's troops cut farther west and took Mount Hope, a hill that was fortified in 1776 but dismantled and abandoned by the Americans due to a lack of personnel. Mount Hope's position was a crucial one, since it guarded the road that ran between Ticonderoga and the Lake George Landing. Nearby, the blockhouse attacked by Indians the previous day lay smoldering, the garrison having withdrawn to the French Lines by order of General St. Clair.

Fraser sent a detachment up the road to the Lake George Landing, where they attacked an isolated blockhouse garrisoned by Continental troops. Lacking artillery, the attackers were forced to fall back. Fearing the loss was inevitable, St. Clair ordered the place evacuated, and its Continental garrison retreated back to the French Lines "just in time, and without loss."[7] Several Indians struck east and attacked the French Lines' forward piquet. The skirmish was "Smart for about one Hour," and the piquet was called to the safety of the lines.[8] Pursued by the Indians, Fraser's Rangers, and Jessup's King's Loyal Americans, the British forces focused their attack on a portion of the lines but, after a few volleys and artillery fire from the defenders, withdrew. The Americans were bested in the skirmish, with one officer killed and fifteen men killed or wounded; British casualties numbered one officer wounded and nearly ten men killed, wounded, or captured.[9] It was this hour-long firefight that distracted the British operating in that quarter enough to allow the Lake George Landing blockhouse garrison to escape safely into the American camp. By evening, Ticonderoga was cut off from the mainland.

St. Clair's position was quickly becoming tenuous. The Northern Army's command anticipated such an eventuality, however. Although Schuyler remained in Albany while his Lake Champlain forts were undergoing the process of enemy envelopment, he had visited the posts in June and, on the 20th, hosted a council

French Model 1728 Infantry Musket
second quarter, 18th century
Don Troiani collection
Anglo-American victory in the French and Indian War (1754–63) secured thousands of French muskets, such as this *fusil d'infanterie modèle* 1728. Many of these leftover captured firearms were in the hands of militia and Continental troops at the beginning of the American War for Independence. These arms were also issued to Canadien militia and the *compagnies canadiennes* (Canadien companies) fighting for the British. The .72-caliber barrel measures nearly forty-six inches long.

Spearhead

third quarter, 18th century

Fort Ticonderoga Museum collection; photograph by Don Troiani

Even in the late eighteenth century, spears were sometimes used by European and American military forces, particularly in the defense of watercrafts or forts. At Ticonderoga in 1777, the peninsula's "lines and redoubts" were "furnished with some spears and sharp pointed poles" to be used in case of British attack.

Proceedings of a General Court Martial . . . for the Trial of Major General St. Clair, 25.

of war with his general officers. It was unanimously determined that the number of troops was "greatly inadequate to the defence of both posts," but, despite this, they were to be "maintained as long as possible, consistent with the safety of the troops and stores."[10] It was also decided that if wholesale abandonment became necessary, it should be effected by retreating up (south) Lake Champlain. Preparations were set in motion to repair and collect as many bateaux as possible for the purpose.

Unfortunately for St. Clair, they hardly had a chance to begin this work before Burgoyne arrived. There could be no retreat up the lake with the entire army now. The arrival of over 900 militia reinforcements at Mount Independence on July 3–4 (about 780 on the 3rd and 130 on the 4th) appeared to be a godsend for the defenders, particularly since most of the militia St. Clair had on hand were set to depart within days due to expiring enlistments. This optimism was short-lived, though, when the new arrivals informed the commander that they planned to remain only "but a very few days, as they had not a second shirt to their backs."[11]

On the New York side of the lake, the British arranged their formal camp, with artillery, as close as 900 yards from the French Lines, and prepared for the forthcoming siege against Ticonderoga. A simple survey of the area revealed an overlooked landscape feature: Located south of the La Chute River, over one mile southwest of Fort Ticonderoga, Sugar Hill—also known as Mount Defiance—lay undeveloped and undefended. The ever-astute General Fraser, who noted that the height "seemed to command everything," sent a forty-man detachment of British light infantry and some Indians to scale it on July 4.[12]

Informed that the hill formed "very commanding ground," Fraser and the army's senior engineer, Lieutenant William Twiss, mounted it themselves the following day. Not only did they find that the mountainous hilltop overlooked both American forts, but Twiss also determined that "it was very practicable to make roads for transporting of any ordnance to the top of it." Also amazed by the hill's military potential was one of the Indians who accompanied Fraser, who astutely "wondered [if] it never occurred to any person to occupy it before we did." Workmen immediately proceeded to clear a road up the hill in order to accommodate two medium twelve-pounders which, when positioned, would dominate the valley below. Unbeknownst to the British, the effort proved unnecessary.[13]

With the British swirling around the New York side of the lake and sightings of redcoats atop Mount Defiance, St. Clair called a council of war with his general officers, in which he noted that "the batteries of the enemy are ready to open upon the Ticonderoga side," and he fully expected "an attack on Ticonderoga and Mount Independence at the same time." His proposal to evacuate Ticonderoga's troops over to the Mount via the floating bridge was unanimously approved, but that wasn't all. The officers decided that the entire body would evacuate the Mount "as the enemy have already nearly surrounded us . . . a retreat ought to be undertaken as soon as possible, and . . . we shall be very fortunate to effect it."[14] Ticonderoga's forces crossed over the floating bridge to the Mount overnight, making as little noise as possible. In order to deceive the British into thinking no evacuation was taking place, a picket of over 300 New Hampshire and Massachusetts Continentals under the command of Colonel Ebenezer Francis was posted forward of the French Lines in order to keep

Massachusetts Drum
third quarter, 18th century
Colonel J. Craig Nannos collection
Drums were essential components of most eighteenth-century military units. Drumbeats helped keep cadence during weapons exercises, were used to communicate messages, and were used to play martial music. This particular wooden drum is painted with an eastern white pine—a popular seventeenth-century colonial Massachusetts and Revolutionary symbol—within a cartouche, surmounting a banner bearing the Latin phrase *Dulce et decorum pro patria mori*.

**"LIBERTY" Cartridge Box
ca. 1775**

Private collection
This beautiful small-capacity cartridge box, stamped with LIBERTY on its face, is of the type commonly used by northeastern Continental or militia troops during the war's early years. Unlike the British, who differentiated cartridge "pouches" from "boxes," Americans generally made no such distinction.

close watch on the enemy.[15] Intermittent artillery fire was kept up for as long as possible, proving to the British that the Americans maintained presence at their posts.

Although the men making arrangements to leave Mount Independence did so in relative silence, the process created plenty of chaos. Orders to evacuate came as quite a surprise to most, and there wasn't much time to make preparations. Clothing, food, drink, personal baggage, and military stores were scattered about, some of which were taken up by those soldiers with the stamina to carry them. The wooden home of Brigadier General Matthias de Roche Fermoy was accidentally set ablaze through a misunderstanding of St. Clair's express instructions that nothing was to be burned, a move which could signal to the enemy that they were preparing to abandon the place. Issuances of ammunition and provisions were erratic and irregular, with some officers and soldiers issued with as many as four days' worth of provisions and dozens of musket cartridges. Many received less.

General Riedesel's German troops, tasked with closing off the Mount Independence escape route, were nowhere in sight when St. Clair's exodus into Vermont began in the early morning hours of July 6. The landscape forced the Germans to make a substantial detour in their endeavor "on account of the many swamps" in the area of East Creek."[16] Thus, without opposition, St. Clair's troops "pushed out of Mount Independence without order or regularity, in a great deal of confusion," lamented one officer, as many of the militia aggressively started to march off before ordered to.[17]

The situation improved during the course of the march, which was along the military road that led southeast to Castleton, although some of the militia continued to behave "with the greatest disorder."[18] More often than not, the long, thin column marched in file (a two-man front) because the road couldn't accommodate a wider formation, but most of St. Clair's troops moved quickly despite the day's growing heat and humidity. Back at the forts, Francis's picket crossed the floating bridge, ripped up some of its planks in order to slow any British pursuit, and was the last unit to leave the Mount (at about 4:00 a.m.). This body served as a protective rear guard for the whole column and as such was also tasked with picking up all stragglers, including those who were lame or "others that were too heavily loaded [with stuff], and who had stopped to throw away a part."[19] Thus, not only was Francis the last to leave, but his troops made the slowest progress.

In the early afternoon, St. Clair arrived with the main body at Hubbardton, a tiny community located along the road to Castleton nearly twenty miles from the lake forts. There he stopped to rest his troops and wait for Francis to come up with the rear guard and stragglers. Hours later, Francis was still two miles away. Leaving Colonel Seth Warner to assume command of the rear guard once it reached Hubbardton, St. Clair marched off with the balance of his command to Castleton, located a further seven miles south. Warner was instructed to follow after the rear guard's arrival.

Except he didn't. With Francis's command arriving at Hubbardton late that afternoon, Warner, "tho' there were orders to march to Castle-Town, [said] he did not intend to go on any farther, because the men were much fatigued."[20] The body of troops then at Hubbardton consisted of Warner's 200-man Green Mountain Boys battalion, Colonel Hale's 2nd New Hampshire Regiment of perhaps 270, Francis's detachment of about 450 New Hampshire and Massachusetts Continental troops, and a couple hundred soldiers who fell behind during the march due to pains, heat exhaustion, or being overloaded with personal and plundered possessions. Warner was fully informed that the British were in pursuit, but nevertheless remained and planned to set off for Castleton early the next morning.

While the Americans were leaving Mount Independence earlier that day and marching off into Vermont, Fraser, whose Advanced Corps remained on the Ticonderoga peninsula, was woken by word that two American deserters had come in "and reported that the Enemy were abandoning Ticonteroga, and the works on Mount Independence." Immediate word was sent to Burgoyne, and Fraser ordered his soldiers to "accoutre without noise or delay." In anticipation of reclaiming the old French Fort, Fraser called for the 9th Regiment's colours to be brought to where the Advanced Corps soldiers were preparing to set off.[21] With a small party, Fraser set out in the dark toward the French Lines to personally investigate and

> found the report proved true, that they made a combined retreat by land towards Castletown, & by water to Skeenesborough . . . destroying nothing but the Bridge of communication between Ticonteroga & Mount Independence, I got planks, by means of which I cross'd my Brigade to the Mount leaving a sufficient number to guard the stores at Ticonteroga, having hoisted a Colour of the 9th Regiment in the old French redoubt, the Kings Colour was soon after displayed on the Mount, as there were many to plunder, it was with very great Difficulty I could prevent horrid irregularities.[22] I, however, so far succeeded, that about five o'clock I got everything tolerably well secured; I could not get any certain intelligence of the number of Rebels, who went by land; yet I believed their rear guard to be within four miles of me, I then formed a detachment of the Granadier & Light Infantry Battalions, with two Compys of the 24th Regiment, leaving an officer to acquaint the General, that I wished to be supported by the remainder of my corps, and some more troops, as I was resolved to attack any body of the rebels that I could come up with.[23]

Fraser set off from Mount Independence on the same hilly, wooded road St. Clair's troops had taken hours earlier. In total, Fraser had only 850 redcoats, of which about 730 were drawn equally from the British Grenadier Battalion, commanded by Major John Dyke Acland, and the British Light Infantry Battalion, commanded by Major Alexander Lindsay, Earl of Balcarres, with the remainder consisting of two companies from Fraser's own 24th Regiment of Foot. The same harsh, hot weather that St. Clair's troops endured dogged Fraser's, who, unlike St. Clair's, "were without an ounce of provision." They took up American stragglers, paused at a stream so the men could drink, and after having made about thirteen miles, stopped again by a creek in order to butcher "two fatt Bullocks" to refresh themselves.[24]

While eating their beef late that afternoon, Fraser received his reinforcements, but they were not what he expected. Instead of the remainder of his Advanced Corps, 180 Braunschweig troops arrived, including Riedesel himself. Riedesel informed Fraser that his Germans would bivouac in place overnight, too tired to continue, but Fraser wanted to

Brigadier-General Simon Fraser

by James Watson after James Scouler,
1778

Anne S. K. Brown Military Collection,
Brown University, bdr:227279

Simon Fraser of Balnain was one of
Burgoyne's most trusted generals
and confidants. A veteran of thirty
years of service in the British Army,
Fraser commanded Burgoyne's
most elite British troops—the
Grenadier Battalion, Light Infantry
Battalion, 24th Regiment of Foot,
and the independent company of
British Rangers.

proceed on the road towards Huberton, about three miles, or
untill I found a good post & running water for my men; I found both
near the distance I mentioned, I told Redeisel that I had discretionary powers to attack the Enemy where-ever I could come up with
them, & that I determined to do it, and for that purpose I would put
the British detachment in motion on the morning of the 7th at
3 o'clock, he said he would move early to support me, should I meet
with any opposition in my rout.[25]

Micah Hoit's Powder Horn
1775

Don Troiani collection

Hoit carried this horn in 1775–76 at the siege of British-held Boston, during which time he served as a subaltern officer in Colonel Samuel Gerrish's Regiment (1775) and the 26th Continental Regiment (1776). In 1777 Hoit was appointed the second lieutenant of Captain Caleb Robinson's company, Colonel Nathan Hale's 2nd New Hampshire Regiment. Because the company's captain and first lieutenant were both captured in the July 7 Battle of Hubbardton, Hoit, who survived the battle unscathed, commanded the company for the remainder of the year, including in both battles of Saratoga.

As planned, Fraser set off in pursuit of the Americans in the early morning hours of July 7. About two miles up the road shortly before 7:30 a.m., his "advanced Scouts descryed the Enemys' Centry's who fired and joined the main Body."[26] The Americans were in a very precarious situation to meet Fraser. Francis's detachment was formed and in the process of marching off on the road to Castleton, while Warner's, located almost a mile southeast of the rear guard near the cabin where their colonel had overnighted, were in the process of accoutering, slinging knapsacks, and forming ranks. Hale's men were cooking and eating their breakfasts near Sucker Brook. Francis's detachment immediately swung around to meet the British attackers, while Warner's battalion formed for battle; most of Hale's men scattered, retreating "back into the woods," because of their unpreparedness for the forthcoming British attack. Being most forward of the American troops, "a few" of Hale's men tried to form "in view of the enemy" but fell back.[27]

Fraser's column, formed on the military road, spread forth into line of battle, using the massive trees to cover their positions. Francis's troops "received a verry heavy fire from the enemy," and although his men were at a disadvantage, "being in the open field & our enemy in the woods in short shott," they "stood in the field and behind stumps to the value of 20 minutes or halfe an hour after which we were obliged by superior force to fall back into the wood."[28] The 24th Regiment's two companies surged forth to chase the retreating Americans, while Lord Balcarres's British light infantry, at the base of "a pretty steep hill," faced to their left and ran up it, with Fraser running behind them, atop which they "met the Rebels endeavoring to get possession of it." Acland's British grenadiers, held in reserve, went to support the hard-pressed 120 men of the 24th Regiment, whose commander, Major Robert Grant, was shot dead. The grenadiers were directed "to prevent, if possible the Enemys' gaining the road, which leads to Castletown."[29]

Private, Light Infantry Company, 53rd Regiment of Foot

Consisting of some of a regiment's shortest, youngest soldiers, light infantry companies were added to British infantry battalions, on both the British and Irish Establishments, in 1771. This light infantryman wears the regulation blackened tanned-leather accoutrement belting, chain-wrapped leather cap, hatchet, and round-cut red waistcoat decorated with regimental lace. He also wears a cartridge box around his waist, a small, innocuous item which became a subject of serious political contention after the campaign's conclusion.

British Light Infantry Powder Horn
ca. 1770s
Don Troiani collection

Regulations called for British light infantry companies to have small, nine-round-capacity cartridge boxes, bullet bags, and powder horns. While the seasoned light infantry companies in Howe's army replaced these ineffective accoutrements with higher-capacity cartridge pouches by 1777, the inexperienced companies with Burgoyne retained theirs. This particular piece has a brass charger nozzle and wooden plug.

Land Pattern Bayonet (Irish)
1770s
Erik Goldstein collection

This bayonet was issued to a soldier in Captain John Adolphus Harris's light infantry company, 34th Regiment, in 1776 on the eve of the regiment's embarkation for the relief of Canada. The soldier wielding it may have fought in the Battles of Hubbardton and Saratoga. The steel blade measures nearly seventeen inches long. Contrary to fiction, bayonet blades were dull along their edges and sharpened only at their points.

British Turnkey
ca. 1776
Don Troiani collection

Each British soldier was issued this multitool, which served as a screwdriver compatible with the dozen screw components of a musket. The threaded spoke could push the pins out of the stock in order to remove the barrel during cleaning; it would also have housed a threaded worm, which was used to clean the barrel's bore of black powder fouling. This piece was recovered near Hubbardton Battlefield.

On the left, the British light infantry eventually "beat the Enemy from the first hill and drove them to a hill of less eminence, which was their original post," centered upon "a strong barricade."[30] This barricade was "compos'd of large Trees, laid one upon the other," and as the British were "eager to be at them," the defenders "immediately fired and almost every shot took effect," by which the British light infantry fell back.[31] Warner's troops used trees, stumps, and fallen timber for cover, but the British were ready for this, having themselves trained at "treeing" tactics, and were thus able to hold their ground in the woods, fighting from behind the safety of the trees.

What the British were not prepared for, however, was a sustained firefight. The 24th Regiment's cartridge pouches carried only a meager number of rounds, perhaps as few as twenty-one, and the British light infantry troops, having only small-capacity cartridge boxes, bullet bags, and powder horns, were not equipped with much more.[32] Most Americans had more rounds of ammunition on hand, and thereby the ability to better endure a sustained firefight, particularly when hiding behind their obstructions. But, as the fighting progressed, Warner's men were worn down, and "pushed so warmly . . . that they left" their log defenses. Falling back, the Americans tried to withdraw south down the road to Castleton. This is exactly what Fraser had anticipated, and Acland's British grenadiers moved to cut the Americans off in their attempt to withdraw. But in cutting off the Americans' intended escape route, Acland's outnumbered grenadiers became the Continentals' prime targets. Fraser countered this weakness by sending Lord Balcarres with a detachment of light Infantry to Acland's support. With the strong British attack on their left, the hard-pressed Continentals "observed the weakness" of the now-depleted British light infantry facing them on their right and smartly "made some demonstrations to renew the attack," which "they began pretty briskly."[33]

Cartridge Pouch Device, Grenadier Company, 9th Regiment of Foot
ca. 1770

Don Troiani collection

This large cast-brass ornament in the shape of a flaming bomb was used by the 9th Regiment of Foot's grenadier company. The piece was recovered near Crown Point.

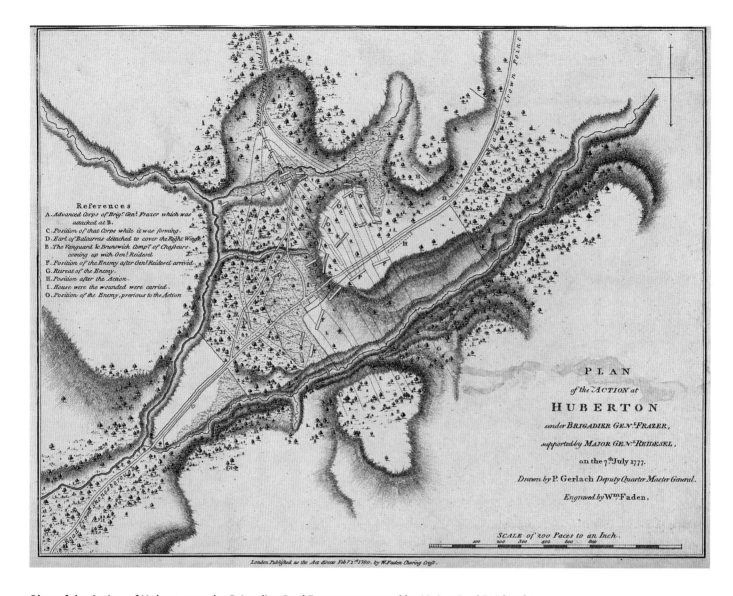

References

A. *Advanced Corps of Brigr Genl Frazer which was attacked at B.*
C. *Position of that Corps while it was forming.*
D. *Earl of Balcarras detached to cover the Right Wing.*
E. *The Vanguard & Brunswick Compy of Chasseurs coming up with Genl Reidesel.*
F. *Position of the Enemy after Genl Reidesel arrived.*
G. *Retreat of the Enemy.*
H. *Position after the Action.*
I. *House were the wounded were carried.*
O. *Position of the Enemy, previous to the Action*

PLAN
of the ACTION *at*
HUBERTON
under BRIGADIER GENL FRAZER,
supported by MAJOR GENL REIDESEL,
on the 7th July 1777.
Drawn by P. Gerlach *Deputy Quarter Master General.*
Engraved by Wm Faden.

SCALE *of 200 Paces to an Inch.*

London Published as the Act directs Feb 7t 1780, by W. Faden Charing Cross.

Plan of the Action of Huberton under Brigadier Genl Frazer, supported by Major Genl Reidesel on the 7th July 1777

published by William Faden, February 1, 1780

after Captain Johann Daniel Gerlach, ca. 1777

The New York Public Library Digital Collections, 57205669

The first pitched battle of the campaign, the Battle of Hubbardton was also the only battle fought within the independent State of Vermont during the entire war. As seen on this map, fighting in the battle occurred near the intersection of the Mount Independence Military Road and the road that stretched south to Castleton and north toward Chimney Point. The map's key, which identifies the various units and movements depicted on the map, uses the French (and preferred English) word for jäger—*chasseurs*—to label the company of German riflemen. This map, derived from a drawing made on-site after the battle by Captain Gerlach, the German Division's deputy quartermaster general, was published for Burgoyne's book *A State of the Expedition from Canada*.

Private, Jäger Company, Braunschweig Light Infantry Battalion von Bärner
The Leichtes Infanterie Bataillon von Bärner, consisting of four musketeer companies and one company of jäger, was raised in 1776 for service in North America. Because the company was expected to operate as woodsmen, the *Gemeine Jäger* (jäger privates) wore calfskin leather breeches—those of the *Sergeanten* (sergeants) were buckskin. Braunschweig jäger were equipped with specialized pattern *Hirschfänger* (deer-killers)—short-bladed swords that attached to their .62-caliber *Büchsen* (rifles) in order to be wielded as bayonets.

Braunschweig Hirschfänger
ca. 1770s

courtesy of James L. Kochan Fine Art & Antiques, Wiscasset, Maine

This brass-hilted *Hirschfänger* (deer-killer) doubled as a short sword and bayonet. In
a time when rifles capable of mounting bayonets were rare, this pattern *Hirschfänger*
could attach to the side of a *Büchse* (rifle) and be wielded as a double-bladed
bayonet by a jäger. The blade is engraved with the ducal coronet of Carl I, the
Herzog zu Braunschweig und Lüneburg (Duke of Brunswick and Lueneburg), as well
as his inverted double C monogram.

With casualties mounting on both sides, Fraser and Warner alike were in
immediate need of reinforcements. Having heard the shooting, St. Clair sent
word for Bellows's and Olcott's New Hampshire and Vermont militia battalions
"to march up and support" Warner.[34] Located only two miles from Hubbardton, these militia units were the nearest troops at hand and perfectly positioned
to offer much-needed assistance. Upon being ordered north to the fighting,
the militia promptly marched in the opposite direction, the commanding officers unable to "by any means prevail with the men to obey the order."[35]

Fraser was more fortunate. Having sent word back to Riedesel, Fraser's report
warned the German general that "he was at close quarters with the enemy, and
that the enemy were so numerous, that he feared he was not equal to them" and
needed immediate assistance. The Germans arrived in short order, and Riedesel
sent his hundred-man jäger company "to form the attack on the enemy's right
wing," while his eighty-man detachment of grenadiers and light infantry were
tasked with turning "the enemy's right flank on the left hand of the Jäger."[36]
Advancing by drumbeat so as to "frighten the enemy still more," the Germans
developed their attack just as Fraser's British light infantry were being swarmed
by Warner's counterattack. Warner's men attempted to make a stand, welcoming
the new arrivals "with a terrible fire," but it was all they could do.[37] Hemmed in
on both sides, Warner's entire rear guard fell back across the road to Castleton
and into the wooded hills beyond, "where they ran with the greatest precipitancy
to save their lives."[38] In less than an hour and a half, the battle was over.

Colonel Nathan Hale, 2nd New Hampshire Regiment

A merchant from Rindge, New Hampshire, Hale entered the war shortly after it began in April 1775. Appointed colonel of a regiment two years later, the experienced thirty-three-year-old was captured at Hubbardton on July 7. Taken to Ticonderoga, a German officer described Hale as having "formerly been a sutler [merchant]" and that he was "dressed in green regimentals with black facings." Released home on parole, Hale returned to British captivity after failing to secure an exchange for himself. He died as a prisoner of war on Long Island in 1780.

Prätorius, "Journal of Lt. Colonel Christian Julius Prätorius: 2 June–17 July 1777," trans. and ed. Helga Doblin, *Bulletin of the Fort Ticonderoga Museum* 15, no. 3 (1991): 66.

British Blanket

ca. 1776–77

Fort Ticonderoga Museum collection, FT-322.76;
photograph by Miranda Peters

This large woolen blanket, stamped twice with the GR and broad arrow denoting government ownership, has a provenance of being used at Hubbardton. Although the British brought no blankets to the battle, it may have been sent there to comfort the wounded under the care of British medical personnel. Thousands of barracks and hospital blankets were provided to the British Army during the war by John Trotter, owner of a firm that regularly fulfilled the military's camp necessary and hospital furnishing needs of the British military.

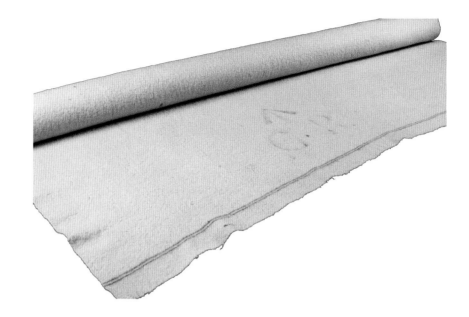

American rearguard casualties were substantial, with about 40 men killed, including Francis, nearly 100 wounded, and 240 captured, including Hale. Fraser's Advanced Corps casualties numbered nearly 40 killed and 130 wounded, while Riedesel's losses numbered about 10 killed and 15 wounded. Officer casualties for both sides were high, particularly among the Americans. Despite Fraser's victory, his truncated Advanced Corps was only barely able to defeat Warner's rear guard, and only because of Riedesel's timely reinforcement. Had Warner simply marched to Castleton on the 6th as ordered, Fraser probably would have pushed on, and in so doing would have come up against the entire Northern Army near Castleton. Fraser's only succor would have been Riedesel's 180 Germans. A more substantial, and sluggish, German reinforcement being led by Lieutenant-Colonel Breymann was too far behind, and "could not arrive . . . owing to the great distance."[39] Ironically, Warner's compassion for his exhausted men, and the rear guard's obstinate defense, gave Fraser (with Riedesel's indispensable assistance) his one chance to gain victory.

With the Battle of Hubbardton concluded, Fraser's troops remained to secure the establishment of an on-site hospital to care for wounded friends and foes alike. St. Clair decided to march his men to Rutland, Vermont, located about twelve miles to the east of Castleton. There, most of Warner's forlorn men joined him.

Flight

The fatigue of this day I believe I shall always remember.
                            —Captain James Gray, July 8, 1777[1]

While St. Clair withdrew with most of the former Ticonderoga-Independence garrisons through Vermont, the other arm of the evacuation, directed by Colonel Pierse Long of the 1st New Hampshire Regiment, made its way toward Skanesborough, located about 32 miles up the lake (south). His flotilla started out at about 3:00 a.m. on the morning of the evacuation, but its sheer size—five small armed vessels and over seventy bateaux—meant that the process would be long, drawn out, and slow. While most ordnance, provisions, clothing, and other stores were left behind, Long was tasked with transporting the army's followers, the sick, and whatever public stores and private baggage could be saved. Along with Long's regiment, most Continental units in the army provided detachments to assist with the processes of hauling and transportation.

While Long proceeded up the lake carrying away what little could be saved from the forts, the British began to inventory the captured stores. The take was remarkable, particularly considering these losses gutted the Northern Army. Ordnance stores taken at Ticonderoga alone netted the British 27 iron cannons (most of which were spiked) and nearly 400 cannonballs; implements and necessaries such as copper ladles, sponges, wad hooks, drag ropes, and slow match; over 100 rounds of grape, double-headed, and case shot; and 2,000 carbine balls, among other munitions. In a demonstration of the relative importance the Americans placed on Mount Independence, the war matériel captured there was greater. The Mount gave up 61 iron cannons (most of which were spiked), an iron howitzer, and substantial implements and stores, including additional copper ladles, sponges, fuses, tin, lead, and portfires. Counted among the munitions were over 10,000 prepared and loose artillery projectiles, including cannonballs; double-headed, grape, and case shot; dozens of barrels of gunpowder; and a substantial amount of small arms munitions. Unspoiled food losses were also substantial. At Ticonderoga, the British took 57 barrels of flour, 19 barrels of salt pork, 31 bushels of salt, and 50 barrels of biscuits. Substantially more was left behind at Mount Independence: 1,711 barrels of flour, 630 barrels of salted pork, 5 barrels of salted beef, 60 barrels of peas, and 120 barrels of rum. Additionally,

"Many hundred oxen and sheep were walking around" the Ticonderoga peninsula.[2] One German surgeon gleefully noted that the Americans also left behind "such victuals as wine, rum, sugar coffee, chocolate, butter, cheese, etc."[3]

It took half a day before Long's elongated fleet reached Skenesborough, which was gained by about 3:00 p.m. Upon arrival, the process of disembarking people and offloading baggage began in earnest; the enormity of the procedure would take time, but unlike St. Clair, Long fully expected to have the benefit of it. The log boom, floating bridge, and massive caissons would tie up the British fleet and prevent their immediate pursuit. This was especially important since their next destination, Wood Creek, required portaging above a falls to get to it.

Except it did not work as expected. To the Americans' surprise, Burgoyne's warships and gunboats descended upon Skenesborough less than two hours after all American shipping had arrived. Once it was realized that the Americans had escaped up the lake to Skenesborough, British gunboats went forth "and the boom and one of the intermediate floats [from the floating bridge] were cut with great dexterity and dispatch," and shortly after, "a passage was found . . . for the frigates also, through impediments [the stone-filled caissons]."[4] Now arrived, Burgoyne's gunboats began to engage the American vessels at South Bay—the *Royal George* and *Inflexible* were too big to get close enough to the action. Gunfire from the American vessels soon desisted, and the vessels were evacuated in the face of the inexorable British approach. With time expired, Long's troops set fire to whatever could not be carried away, including many buildings and the stockade fort, and he ordered an immediate retreat to Fort Anne,

New England Drum
1740

courtesy of Steve Rogers

This red-and-blue-painted drum includes a handwritten maker's label on the interior, reading "Made By Robt. Crosman of / Taunton Drum maker in New Eng[land] / Anno Domini 1740." Best known for his painted chests, Robert Crossman also built and repaired drums for the purpose of outfitting colonial forces ca. 1739–45. This piece is typical of an older but serviceable drum of the type still used by militia during the American War for Independence.

about fourteen miles south. Provisions and other ordnance stores were tossed in the water. Most of his troops and followers made their way along the singular, thin wooded road while the sick, invalids, and other noncombatants traveled up Wood Creek by bateaux. The shallowness of the creek, the presence of floating timber intended for milling, and the number of competing bateaux made the water-bound route a logjam.

With Long out of immediate reach, the British secured Skenesborough and set about to save whatever they could from the fires. About thirty Americans were taken prisoner, including two wounded officers and Colonel Cilley's fifteen-year-old son Jonathan, while British casualties numbered two killed, including an officer, and three wounded.[5] The five armed vessels, some of which served in the Battle of Valcour Island, were lost—the galley *Trumbull* and schooner *Liberty* were taken by the British, while the schooner *Revenge*, galley *Gates*, and sloop *Enterprize* were blown up or burned. Not only were the vessels and stores aboard them lost, but their forty cannons were taken by the British or destroyed. The men aboard those vessels had no choice but to jump ship and swim to shore, but in doing so, many were captured upon reaching it. Along the shoreline, "great numbers of Batteaux, laden with military stores, and powder," were "all burnt, or blown up by the Rebels."[6] While the larger vessels could never have been saved, the loss of even more stores, baggage, and people marked another severe blow to the United States.

With reports coming into Skenesborough that Long was making a slow, drawn-out retreat up Wood Creek, Burgoyne ordered Lieutenant-Colonel John Hill and his 9th Regiment of Foot to make pursuit on the morning of July 7. Because of the fragmented nature of the regiment at the time—the balance of the regiment was still back at Ticonderoga—only a small portion of it was present (about 190 officers and men) to set out on the mini expedition. This wasn't considered problematic, however. It was assumed, correctly, that Long would reach Fort Anne before Hill could catch up to the Americans. Hill's instructions were to secure what straggling boats and people he could during his sojourn and, when he got close enough, "take post near Fort Anne" in order to "observe" the motions of the enemy.[7]

Hill's truncated regiment set off, traveling up the little road toward Fort Anne, and eventually "overtook some boats laden with baggage, women, and invalids, belonging to the Americans rowing up Wood Creek, in order to escape to Fort Ann."[8] With the bateaux and prisoners in Hill's hands, he boldly detached a small party of his already small command back to Skenesborough to secure them. He pressed forth and took up additional stragglers, but not wanting to detach any more troops from his small force, decided to keep these captive

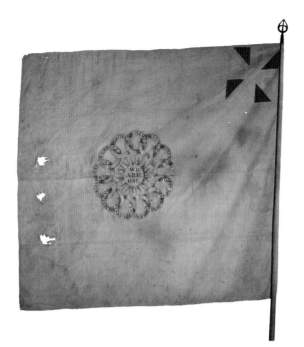 

National and Second (Regimental) Colours, 2nd New Hampshire Regiment 1777

New Hampshire Historical Society, 1913.002.01, 1913.002.02

These taffeta colours were assembled and painted in Boston for the 2nd New Hampshire Regiment. The buff colour, with WE ARE ONE emblazoned on a golden sunburst surrounded by linked rings bearing the names of the thirteen United States, was the regiment's national flag; the fringed light blue colour, with THE GLORY NOT THE PREY adorning a golden banner surmounting a red cartouche emblazoned with NH 2^{d} REG^{T}, was the regimental colour. These colours were separated from the regiment and taken with the baggage to Skenesborough by Colonel Long's flotilla, but lost to the 9th Regiment of Foot during the retreat to Fort Anne.

men and women on hand. With the bridges broken up and the road poorly maintained, the advance toward Fort Anne was difficult.

Late that morning, Captain James Gray of the 3rd New Hampshire Regiment was sent out from Fort Anne with nearly 170 troops to reconnoiter nearby Wood Creek in order to assist the stragglers of Long's flotilla, as well as scout for signs of any British pursuit. At about noon, about a half mile north of Fort Anne, Gray fell in with Hill's 9th Regiment. Gray's men "gave them fire, which was Returned by the enemy," who then fell back. Gray "pursued them with close fire till they betook themselves to the top of a mountain" about a quarter mile away.[9] Gray's troops remained at the foot of the height and kept up an intermittent fire with the redcoats on the hilltop. By evening, Gray received an additional 150 men but opted to withdraw back to the stockade fort because of oncoming nightfall. Gray's casualties in the fight were few—one killed and three wounded. Hill's, on the other hand, amounted to three killed and four wounded—losses that he could hardly afford in the face of a superior enemy.

Following Burgoyne's orders to the letter, Hill had his men lay on their arms overnight. On the morning of July 8, the British commander received accurate intelligence from a supposed American deserter that the Fort Anne garrison received reinforcements overnight and that they were now over 1,000 in number. Hill immediately sent a message to Burgoyne, informing the British Army commander "that the enemy had been reinforced in the night by a considerable body of fresh troops; that he could not retire before them with his regiment, but would maintain his ground." Burgoyne sent British reinforcements at once, but they were slogged down by a "violent storm of rain, which lasted the whole day," and thereby "prevented these troops from getting to Fort Anne so soon as was intended."[10] No redcoat reinforcements would be reaching the isolated 9th Regiment anytime soon.

In truth, Hill was in no position to hold his ground. The Americans had gained a sense of his capabilities and, more importantly, numbers the day before. Considering the detachment sent back to Skenesborough with the captured boats, baggage, and prisoners; the casualties sustained in the July 7 skirmish; and even the messenger sent back to Burgoyne, Hill's remaining strength amounted to only 160 officers and men, of which only about 130 were other ranks.[11] While his soldiers were well trained, they were never trained to fight in the manner that was now expected of them. Paralleling the predicament facing Fraser's Advanced Corps at Hubbardton, the obsessive need to pursue retreating Americans with only detachments resulted in Hill's eight companies numbering about twenty officers and men each—much less than half of their established strength. Even more challenging for the 9th Regiment was that the men were forced to move out of Skenesborough without their full allotment of ammunition—set at one hundred rounds per man—and instead had only what their cartridge pouches carried, perhaps twenty-one rounds each. Cartridges were certainly replenished from the dead and wounded, but Hill's men were left with limited, finite ammunition.[12]

9th Regiment of Foot Rank-and-File Button
ca. 1775
Don Troiani collection
Recovered near Hubbardton Battlefield, this pewter button would have come from the jacket of a soldier in the regiment's grenadier or light infantry company.

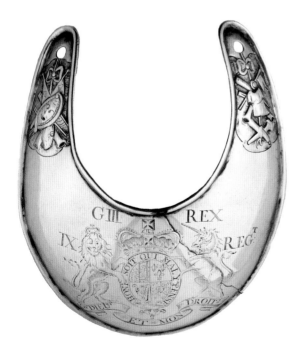

Silver Gorget, 9th Regiment of Foot
ca. 1770s
Don Troiani collection
British gorget metal matched the regiment's officer's metal—gold or silver—which was reflected in the officer's coat buttons, epaulet(s), and buttonhole lace or embroidery. Made of carefully hammered sterling silver, this gorget, marked with IX REG[T] and G III REX on its face, includes an engraved royal coat of arms and repoussé-worked ears adorned with martial trophies.

Commissioned Officer's Sash
second half, 18th century

Regulations called for British Army and marine officers to wear crimson-colored sashes. Woven with interlinked silk threads, this elastic garment could wrap tightly around the waist and was then knotted, allowing the corded, fringed ends to fall free. Geometric shapes, figures, and even dates could be built into the interlinked design. British Highland officers wore these sashes over the shoulder, as did some of the few Continental Army and militia officers who wore them.

Busk
1764

Jenna Schnitzer collection

This chip-carved wooden busk, dated January 9, 1764, on the reverse, would have been inserted in a purpose-built pocket stitched to the lining of a pair of women's stays. With a New England provenance, this busk is representative of those that would have been worn by many American Northern Army followers.

That morning, Long ordered Gray to move out with a large party of about 170 Continental troops to again engage Hill's redcoats. They marched directly to "the aforesaid mountain and attacked the enemy very warmly" at about 10:30 a.m.[13] Over the next hour and a half, neither side gained substantive advantage, but Gray had something Hill did not: a pool of reinforcements. Successively smaller parties—sixty, thirty, and twenty in number—bolstered the Americans' number and gave them the upper hand as the battle wore on past noon.[14] The last small party were New York militia under the command of Lieutenant Colonel Henry Killian Van Rensselaer, who, as the senior officer, took command of the attack.[15]

Corporal Lamb of the 9th Regiment recalled that the Americans' "numbers could not be seen, the woods being so thick, but it was soon found that they not only out flanked but were endeavoring to surround us."[16] To counter this, Hill ordered his battalion to withdraw to the hilltop in order to reposition to advantage. As the British rushed up the hill, they were forced to abandon some of their wounded as well as "a number of . . . people, men & women, who were the day before cut off," all of whom were scurried back to the stockade fort.[17]

Once the British arrived on the hilltop, they were arrayed in a long, single rank of not much more than a hundred soldiers so as to maximize their force-to-space ratio and cover the most ground against the numerically superior enemy. Hill's men "kept up a well directed fire" upon the Americans as they cautiously advanced up the wooded hill. Then the inevitable happened: The British ran out of ammunition. The Americans "observing that the firing ceased, was encouraged to press forward," but this didn't last long.[18] Van Rensselaer's men were beginning to have problems of their own, each soldier having come to the battle with a similar paucity of cartridges. The incompatibility of most weapon calibers provided little opportunity for the Americans to strip cartridges from the pouches of the numerous dead or wounded Britons.[19] With "none to be had" back at the fort, the American attackers began to conserve their ammunition.[20]

Suddenly, loud "Indian whoops" were heard from the woods north of the hill. Although unseen, no one failed to understand what they heralded, and Hill's men "answered with three cheers" in anticipation of the forthcoming reinforcement. Soon the hill's defenders were joined by Captain John Money and a large party of Caughnawaga Mohawk warriors with the Chevalier de Lorimier.[21] With the British thus buttressed by their allies, Van Rensselaer ordered his troops to fall back.

If casualty numbers resulting from an indecisive battle help to illustrate the combatants' respective fighting capabilities, the 9th Regiment was bested. Hill's redcoats sustained thirteen killed, twenty-two wounded, and four taken prisoner (including two officers), constituting nearly 25 percent of the men under his command. By contrast, Van Rensselaer lost ten killed and wounded; Van Rensselaer himself was wounded in the thigh. The proportionally high number of British casualties in the battle speaks well of American tactical competence, particularly considering their lack of training; that the British held their ground in the face of overwhelming numbers speaks laudably of their bravery. Importantly, for the second time in as many days, the British eked out another victory only barely, not from a superior capacity for battle but because they were saved by last-minute reinforcements, be they Braunschweig soldiers or Caughnawaga warriors.[22]

The 9th Regiment remained upon its conquered hilltop immediately after the battle. The aforementioned "violent storm of rain" hit hard that afternoon, drenching the redcoats alive and dead alike. Because the regiment's surgeon was taken prisoner in the battle, Lamb and a soldier's wife, "the only woman that was with us, and who kept close by her husband's side during the engagement," tended to those suffering from their wounds as best they could. The British

American Club Butt Fowler

ca. 1776–80

Richard Ulbrich collection; photograph by Don Troiani

This tiger-maple-stocked club butt fowler was made with a barrel from a captured British Long Land musket. As early as the seventeenth century, New England and New York colonial militia laws mandated firearm ownership for their militiamen. On the eve of the American War for Independence, many law-abiding Americans were readily armed with locally built muskets such as this one. These smoothbore muskets, often made for the purpose of hunting, were typically more accurate than British and German firearms.

Private, Battalion Company, 21st Regiment of Foot (Royal North British Fusiliers)
Because clothing for all British "redcoat" regiments in Canada was either captured by the Americans or not delivered on time, British units in the Canada Army cut their uniforms according to a regulated pattern. Coats were trimmed to jacket length, and the horizontal false pockets of most British infantrymen were turned vertically in order to emulate the slash-pockets that decorated light infantry jackets. Cocked hats were cut into caps and adorned with horsehair, with some regiments adding distinctive regimental devices, such as the thistle seen here.

reinforcement finally arrived later that day, and after assisting with carrying off the wounded to a "small hut" about two miles north, the British retired to Skenesborough.[23] The dead lay unburied.

Behind the safety of Fort Anne's stockade wall, Long called a council of war, during which it was decided that the best course of action was to evacuate to Fort Edward, located about thirteen miles south. Principal consideration for this retreat was due to the lack of ammunition on hand and the very credible report given by a Continental Army follower—one of the women released from captivity during the course of the battle—who warned of hearing about the aforementioned British reinforcement coming up from Skenesborough. Fort Anne was set on fire and destroyed, although the nearby sawmill and blockhouse were left "in good repair." Long's forces withdrew that afternoon during the storm.[24]

With the Battle of Fort Anne over, the British withdrawing back to Skenesborough, and the Americans falling back to Fort Edward, a definitive end to the whirlwind series of skirmishes, retreats, chases, and battles that marked the forepart of July was reached. Here were the first signs of the difficulties that would plague the Army from Canada for the remainder of the campaign: logistics. Simply put, Burgoyne's regiments pulled back to Skenesborough because there was no plan to support or sustain so many troops near Fort Anne. His army was overextended and scattered for upward of dozens of miles in the days following the capture of forts, leaving the whole in a precarious situation. However, when Burgoyne heard that the Americans destroyed Fort Anne, he was confident enough to send a single sixty-man company of the 21st Regiment (Royal North British Fusiliers) back to take the site. The company arrived at the smoldering ruins of the stockade fort on July 9, the day after the battle, and took possession of the blockhouse "without Opposition."[25]

Cap Device, 21st Regiment of Foot
1777
Private collection
This three-inch-long pewter ornament, recovered from an encampment site of the 21st Regiment of Foot (Royal North British Fusiliers), was made to decorate a soldier's felt cap. This predominantly Scottish corps was specially authorized to use the thistle as its royal device.

Waist Belt Clasp, 21st Regiment of Foot (Royal North British Fusiliers)
1774
Don Troiani collection
Although British Army battalion and grenadier company soldiers were issued waist belts, these were universally converted for wear over the shoulder for convenience in the Canada Army. This clasp was recovered near the Convention Army prison camp in Virginia, testimony to the fact that Burgoyne's British soldiers were allowed to retain their accoutrements after the surrender.

Fallout

The darkest Hour is just before the Dawn.

—Colonel Alexander Scammell, August 6, 1777[1]

All seemed hopeless for the Northern Army. Fallout following the losses sustained by the evacuations of Forts Ticonderoga and Independence, as well as losses in the Battles of Hubbardton and Fort Anne, left the evacuees open to further sufferings. Ever present in the mind of every American was the expectation that it would only be a matter of time before Burgoyne's army followed up on its victories and descended upon them. As if the tangible losses and psychological traumas weren't enough, the people in the Northern Army were beginning to experience severe privation.

Food stocks at the forts had been plentiful enough, but apart from the rations the troops were able to carry off, the army was for some time unprepared to victual them once their food was lost or ran out. St. Clair's officers suffered along with the men and were "almost totally destitute of any kind of provisions or any other necessaries of life."[2] The men were "oblidg'd to kill oxen belonging to the Inhabitants wherever we got them; before they were half skinned every soldier was obliged to take a bit and half Roast it over the fire, then before half done was obliged to March."[3] Once the army was finally able to provide essential provisions, the men only then received "some part of our Rations such as beef and

American Cocked Hat
ca. 1770s
Private collection
Cocked hats, popular wear for American and European males throughout much of the eighteenth century, were typically made of wool or fur felt. Their brims were often attached to the crown in three places with stitching, string, or cording. The style was a product of fashion; the term "tricorn hat" is a mid-nineteenth-century contrivance.

flour, without any kind of sauce save only once in a while a trifle of Pease, and that but only seldom."[4] "We draw nothing But fresh Beef and flower," confirmed Corporal Buss, "our men has had a very hard time Ever sence they left Ticonderoga."[5] Much lamented was the impossibility of acquiring "sugar or molasses, cheese, chocolate and divers other articles" of the sort at least at times previously enjoyed in garrison life.[6] The lack of salted meat had serious implications, since without it, commanders were prevented from "sending out any considerable parties of men on scouts, by which reason we have been deprived of intelligence from the enemy, except such as is very vague and uncertain."[7]

The Northern Army's clothing was in the same state of sparsity. St. Clair had "left all the Continental cloathing" behind in the wake of the fort evacuations, along with "every article that belonged to the army," lamented a Continental Army quartermaster. "Never was soldiers in such a condition without cloaths, victuals or drink & constantly wet. Caleb and I are just as our mothers bore us without the second shirt, the second pair of shoes, stockings or coats."[8] Most officers and soldiers had no spare clothes, and they were forced to wear the same shirt and breeches or trousers for weeks. Brigade Major James MacClure wrote to his wife, requesting that she acquire enough linen to make four shirts, since "as to Linnen Shirts I Have none old or new Except the won I have on."[9] He, like most in the army, had worn the same clothes for at least eighteen days, and would be forced to wear them longer.

"Clothing is a very material article; but none has ever come to us," complained some soldiers in the 1st New Hampshire Regiment who submitted a formal grievance. Their situation was so destitute that their brigadier general,

Leather Breeches
ca. 1775

Don Troiani collection

Because of their durability, leather breeches made of calfskin or deerskin were worn by European and American men of all classes. They were regularly issued to cavalrymen and German jäger, and were sometimes issued to Continental Army infantrymen. This pair of high-quality, American-made leather breeches has both leather-covered and brass buttons as well as a fob, a small pocket in the waistband that housed a watch.

Enoch Poor, had to borrow "a few frocks & trousers . . . wast-coats, stockings &c" from the Massachusetts stores, but the men were forced "to pay for them at the highest rate 22/6 for a single striped woolen wast-coat without sleeves; 18s for a paire mean sole-shoes & 18s for a tow-shirt &c." Adding injury to insult, many men lamented that they "lost all the clothing we had, and every other necessary, save only the cloaths on our back taken from us in the Battle with the enemy" at Hubbardton on July 7.[10]

"The officers lost all their Baggage, writings & all," Quartermaster Patrick Cogan admitted, since only that which could be carried was brought with St. Clair, and most which the army tried to save under Long's protection was lost or destroyed at Skenesborough.[11] This included not only personal effects but also most of the camp equipage, including tents, blankets, kettles, and entrenching tools. Without kettles, some decided to "mix our flour in our hats and bake it upon [stone] Chips before the fire."[12]

Without tents to cover themselves for over a month, and most having no blankets, the troops were forced to "ley in the woods without . . . covering" when barns weren't available.[13] Many soldiers acquired mill-sawn boards to sleep on, or under, or made huts out of "a little brush."[14] One staff officer, lucky enough to find and afford a blanket, found it "very useful—at Night I wrap myself in it & lay down upon the bare Ground & sometimes upon Boards, in the Morning my blanket is wet, cover'd with Dew." But, he lamented, few in the army had blankets and were wet with dew each morning, having only "a few Boards for Cover."[15] A significant amount of money, both public and private, was also snapped up by the British during Long's evacuation, such as the entire treasury (6,491 dollars) for the Engineer and Artificer Department.[16]

After leaving Ticonderoga shortly before Burgoyne's invasion manifested, Philip Schuyler returned to his mansion near Albany and immediately set to work. Writing to John Hancock (president of Congress), Washington, and heads of state governments, Schuyler kept military and civil leaders abreast of the situation (although his information was quickly out of date) and pled for reinforcements. On the morning of July 7, Schuyler received word that the forts were evacuated, and he immediately rode north for Fort Edward in order to take command of the situation. After overnighting at his country plantation at Saratoga (present-day Schuylerville, New York), he arrived at Fort Edward—almost fifty miles north of Albany—on the 8th.

Built in 1755 during the French and Indian War, Fort Edward once stood as a bastion of British strength in North America. Its location was critical: Built at the confluence of Little Wood Creek and the Hudson River, it guarded the southern access point to the Great Carrying Place, the fifteen-mile-long well-built portage road between the south-flowing Hudson River and north-flowing Lake George.

***Part of the Counties of Charlotte
and Albany, in the Province of New
York; being the Seat of War between
the King's Forces under Lieut. Gen.
Burgoyne and the Rebel Army***

published by Robert Baldwin, 1778
after Thomas Kitchin Sr., ca. 1778
The Library of Congress, 80693268

Published in the February 1778
issue of *The London Magazine, or,
Gentleman's Monthly Intelligencer*,
this map showcased the place-
names made famous by Burgoyne's
1777 campaign from Canada.
While difficult to see, the Charlotte
and Albany County boundary
(represented by a thin dashed line)
east of the Hudson extended along
Stoney Creek and the Batten Kill River
into Vermont. Royalist recruitment
in Burgoyne's army was complicated
by factious divides along county and
even district (county sub-divisional)
lines. This sectionalism expanded
the Army from Canada's two initial
royalist corps "in embryo" to over half
a dozen.

Burgoyne, *State of the Expedition*, 102

When the French and Indian War terminated and threats from New France came to an end, the fort fell into disrepair.

With the onset of the American War for Independence, Americans concentrated on repairing and expanding the defenses at Ticonderoga and building the stronghold on Mount Independence, thereby paying little attention to Fort Edward. By 1777 the enormous log, bastioned, moated structure, with its various barracks and infrastructure of outbuildings, was relegated to use as a supply depot and staging area. A small community of homes had sprung up around the fort, although most of these were being abandoned out of fear of the inexorable British approach. Now, the dilapidated fort constituted the Northern Army's northernmost defense against Burgoyne's invasion.

Schuyler's immediate task was to consolidate the Northern Army. Fort Anne's contingent arrived at Fort Edward that very night, which left only the main contingent under Arthur St. Clair (then located near Rutland) and the small Fort George garrison, located near the southern shore of Lake George, which guarded the other end of the Great Carrying Place. Construction on Fort George began in 1759, but was abandoned after only one bastion of what was to be a uniquely stone fort was nearly completed. Nearby, a smaller stockade fort (which took on the name of Fort George), a hospital, storehouses, barracks, a shipbuilding facility, and artificer workshops populated the sprawling site.

In late June, Schuyler instructed Major Christopher Yates, the Fort George commander, to build additional fortifications and arm the lake's vessels in order to better prepare the site for defense against any British attack.[17] But Schuyler's June expectation that these small measures would make the site "perfectly secure" changed once he arrived at Fort Edward.[18] Schuyler now ordered Yates to send all spare cannons, powder, musket balls and bullet molds, entrenching and artificer tools, salt, flour, and "all the rum that belongs to the suttlers" to Fort Edward with haste.[19] Yates was authorized to evacuate if necessary and, if so, he was to destroy the fort and buildings and remove the remaining stores to Fort Edward, along with "all the horses, horned cattle and carriages belonging to the inhabitants."[20]

In Vermont, St. Clair left Rutland and marched by a safe, circuitous route "between the [Green] Mountains" down to Arlington.[21] Detaching Warner's Green Mountain Boys over to Manchester, St. Clair then led his officers and soldiers directly west to the Hudson River, arriving at Saratoga, seventeen miles south of Fort Edward, on July 11. Leaving a cadre behind at Saratoga, he and the core of the Northern Army marched north to Fort Edward the following day. Simultaneously, Brigadier General John Nixon's brigade, recently transferred from the Highlands Department, arrived with Colonels John Greaton's (3rd), Rufus Putnam's (5th), Thomas Nixon's (6th), and Ichabod Alden's (7th)

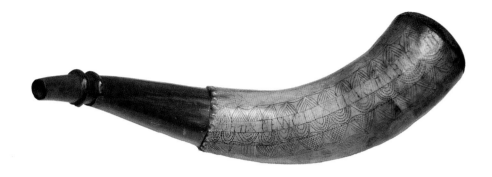

**John Elwell's Powder Horn
1777**
*courtesy of Skinner Auctioneers;
photograph by Don Troiani*
While many horns were engraved
with regional maps displaying
the owner's scope and breadth of
military service, others, like this
one, included fanciful imagery such
as animals and geometric shapes.
Unfortunately, if these designs once
held meaning for the owner, it is
now lost. This piece was owned by
John Elwell, a private soldier in the
Northern Army from Massachusetts.

Massachusetts Continental Regiments, adding another 580 troops to Schuyler's personnel pool. Small bodies of short-term service "alarm" militia began to arrive as well.

Despite the lack of troops under his command, Schuyler embarked upon an ambitious, proactive plan and sent his freshly arrived troops—Nixon's Brigade and a body of Massachusetts militia commanded by Colonel John Brown—north "as far as Fort Anne."[22] Nixon's responsibilities were to send out scouts north to gain intelligence of Burgoyne's movements, burn sawmills, "and then fall the trees growing on the banks of Wood Creek into the same." Causeways were obliterated, trees were felled across roads, and mills were rendered inoperable. Cattle and wheeled carriages were brought off, and inhabitants were encouraged to evacuate their homes. For those who chose to go, the military was instructed to help them leave. Forage was purchased from all inhabitants—forcibly, if necessary— not only to augment stores but also to deprive the British. While withdrawing, Nixon was further instructed to "break up all the bridges in your rear, that the enemy may be as much obstructed in their march as possible."[23] Given its isolated, precarious position, Fort George was evacuated on July 16; almost everything that could not be saved was set to flame, including vessels on the lake and those on stocks that were in the process of being built. This added most of the 1st New York Regiment and the remainder of Colonel John Bailey's (2nd) Massachusetts Regiment to the Northern Army.[24]

Another new addition to the growing Northern Army at Fort Edward was none other than Major General Benedict Arnold. Schuyler's panicked letters to Washington convinced the army commander in chief that "an active, spirited, officer" with a major general's rank should be sent to the Northern Department to work against the devolving situation. In his request to Congress for such an officer, Washington recommended sending the "active, judicious, and brave" Arnold, since he was well suited to lead the militia and was familiar with the upstate New York landscape.[25] Congress concurred, but there was a problem: Arnold, who toyed with the idea of resigning in 1776, submitted his letter of

Shoulder Belt
ca. 1770s

Don Troiani collection

Unlike most of their European counterparts, military accoutrements produced in America for the Continental Army and militias were commonly made of russet-colored harness leather. Such belts could carry scabbards, which sheathed bayonets, swords, or both. The lack of belts and scabbards in the Northern Army resulted in many Americans losing their bayonets.

resignation on July 11. Yet, on July 12, Congress voted to approve Washington's suggestion and ordered Arnold to repair to the commander in chief in order to receive further instructions.[26] Arnold immediately requested that a vote to confirm his resignation be postponed and, after meeting with Washington, made his way north, arriving at Fort Edward on July 21.

While the addition of Arnold, Nixon's Brigade, and the detachments from Fort George gave much-needed boosts to the Northern Army, there were some losses. Despite the crisis facing the defenders of the new United States, most of the army's Albany County, New York, and Berkshire County, Massachusetts, militia began agitating about returning "to their Habitations to harvest their crops."[27] A council of the general officers met at Fort Edward and consented to release half their numbers "lest the whole should go." Even worse, the remainder would "only remain a few days."[28] In anticipation of Burgoyne's impending advance, and with the drop in militia support, Schuyler began to evacuate the army five miles south of the dilapidated fort to the outlet of Moses Creek.

But where was Burgoyne? His troops still held the Fort Anne blockhouse since July 9, and parties of his Indians and other *petite guerre* troops were seen operating in the Lake George valley, Vermont, and observed scouring the woods north of Fort Anne, but there was otherwise no sign of the main enemy force. Given the overly aggressive British pursuits earlier in the month, the American command found this perplexing.

Repercussions

*[The] Rebels retreat very fast down the Country and [we] follow them as
fast as we can bring our provission and stores along with us.*

—Ensign Daniel Gwynne, August 26, 1777[1]

From his new headquarters at Skenesborough, Burgoyne had the pleasure of updating Germain on July 11 regarding his recent conquests, which happened with a rapidity that even he hadn't expected. Fraser's troops rejoined the Army from Canada at Skenesborough on July 10. There the Advanced Corps was joined by its other half, which remained behind at the newly captured Lake Champlain forts, and encamped near headquarters. The other British infantry battalions were likewise stationed there, excepting the 62nd Regiment of Foot, which was left behind to garrison Mount Independence. Most of the Royal Regiment of Artillery remained behind at the Lake Champlain forts.

With Fort Ticonderoga under garrison of the Regiment Prinz Friedrich, most of Riedesel's German Division was deployed throughout a large block of territory in Vermont south-southeast of Hubbardton, including Castleton, Wells, Tinmouth, and Rutland. There the regiments proceeded to acquire wagons, carts, and teams of oxen to assist with baggage transportation. They were also on hand to support the distribution of Burgoyne's manifesto. Publication and distribution of this document began in June and was written to shame, threaten, and bring to heel "disaffected" citizenry, particularly those living in Vermont. While the manifesto was doled out in Vermont by Philip Skene, Burgoyne's commissioner administering the oaths of allegiance, the Germans were instructed to be on their best behavior:[2]

> As General Burgoyne has issued a proclamation to the population, that they should declare their obedience to the King, the regiments must maintain their best discipline in order to show the best conduct toward those inhabitants in their homes, so that the most distant subjects might be influenced to declare for the King, and bring provisions to the camp.[3]

Burgoyne's Proclamation

1777

Massachusetts Historical Society, Bdses-Sm

1777 June 23

This was the first of a series of "manifestos" issued by Burgoyne during the first few weeks of the campaign. These broadsides were intended to communicate Burgoyne's intention of "re-establishing the blessings of legal government" to the people of New York and Vermont, but to many, his wordsmithed prose exuded a pomposity that Revolutionary Americans publicly derided and satirized.

By JOHN BURGOYNE, Esq; &c. &c.

Lieut. General of his Majesty's Forces in America, Colonel of the Queen's Regiment of Light Dragoons, Governor of Fort-William, in North-Britain, one of the Representatives of the Commons of Great-Britain in Parliament, and commanding an Army and Fleet in an Expedition from Canada, &c. &c. &c.

THE Forces entrusted to my Command are designed to act in concert, and upon a common Principle, with the numerous Armies and Fleets which already display, in every Quarter of America, the Power, the Justice, and, when properly sought, the Mercy of the King; the Cause in which the British Arms are thus exerted, applies to the most affecting Interest of the human Heart: And the Military Servants of the Crown, at first called for the sole Purpose of restoring the Rights of the Constitution, now combine with the Love of their Country, and Duty to their Sovereign, the other extensive Incitements, which spring from a due Sense of the general Privileges of Mankind. To the Eyes and Ears of the temperate Part of the Public, and to the Breasts of suffering Thousands in the Provinces, be the melancholy Appeal---Whether the present unnatural Rebellion, has not been made the Foundation of the compleatest System of Tyranny that ever GOD, in his Displeasure, suffered for a Time, to be exercised over a froward and stubborn Generation: Arbitrary Imprisonments, Confiscation of Property, Persecution and Torture, unprecedented in the Inquisitions of the Romish Church, are among the palpable Enormities that verify the Affirmative: These are inflicted by Assemblies and Committees, who dare to profess themselves Friends to Liberty, upon the most quiet Subject, without Distinction of Age or Sex, for the sole Crime, often from the sole Suspicion, of having adhered in Principle to the Government under which they were born, and to which, by every Tie divine and human, they owe Allegiance. To consummate these shocking Proceedings the Profanation of Religion is added to the most profligate Prostitution of common Reason! The Consciences of Men are set at naught, and Multitudes are compelled not only to bear Arms, but also to swear Subjection to an Usurpation they abhor.---Animated by these Considerations, at the Head of Troops in the full Powers of Health, Discipline and Valour, determined to strike where necessary, and anxious to save where possible, I, by these Presents, invite and exhort all Persons, in all Places where the Progress of this Army may point, and by the Blessing of God I will extend it FAR, to maintain such a Conduct as may justify me in protecting their Lands, Habitations, and Families. The Intention of this Address is to hold forth Security, not Depredation, to the Country; to those whose Spirit and Principle may induce them to partake the glorious Task of redeeming their Countrymen from Dungeons, and re-establishing the Blessings of legal Government, I offer Encouragement and Employment, and upon the first Intelligence of their Association, I will find Means to assist their Undertakings.---The domestic, the industrious, the infirm, and even the timid Inhabitants, I am desirous to protect, provided they remain quietly at their Houses; that they do not suffer their Cattle to be removed, or their Corn or Forage to be secreted or destroyed; that they do not break up their Bridges or Roads, or by any other Act, directly or indirectly, endeavour to obstruct the Operation of the King's Troops, or supply or assist those of the Enemy. Every Species of Provision brought to my Camp, will be paid for at an equitable Rate, in solid Coin.---In Consciousness of Christianity, my Royal Master's Clemency, and the Honour of Soldiership, I have dwelt upon this Invitation, and wished for more persuasive Terms to give it Impression; and let not People be led to disregard it by considering the immediate Situation of my Camp; I have but to give Stretch to the Indian Forces under my Direction, and they amount to Thousands, to overtake the hardened Enemies of Great-Britain; I consider them the same wherever they may lurk.---If notwithstanding these Endeavours and sincere Inclination to assist them, the Phrenzy of Hostility should remain, I trust I shall stand acquitted in the Eyes of God and Men, in denouncing and executing the Vengeance of the State against the wilful Outcast. The Messengers of Justice and of Wrath await them in the Field, and Devastation, Famine, and every concomitant Horror that a reluctant but indispensible Prosecution of Military Duty must occasion, will bar the Way to their Return.

J. BURGOYNE.

Camp at the River BONGRETT, June 23d, 1777.

By Order of his Excellency the Lieutenant General, ROBERT KINGSTON, Sec'ry.

With the thrill of the chase over, Burgoyne now had a critical decision to make. In order to continue on to the next phase of the expedition and get his army to Fort Edward, his next immediate target, the question was how to do it. No army had ever taken the twenty-seven-mile route between Skenesborough and Fort Edward via Fort Anne, since Wood Creek and the little cart road that paralleled it were too insubstantial to facilitate army-sized movement. Further, since Wood Creek did not connect directly to the Hudson River, a very inconvenient twelve-mile portage to the river over the insubstantial road would have to be made, and reports were coming in that the Americans were laying waste to it. Instead, armies traditionally used Lake George as their transportation avenue.

The lake was perfectly navigable for small vessels, and although the Great Carrying Place—the portage between Lake George and the Hudson River—was fifteen miles long, it was facilitated by a well-built highway that connected the two bodies of water.

This route had one major drawback, however: the La Chute River. The river flowed from the north end of Lake George and emptied into Lake Champlain at the foot of Ticonderoga. Although only about four miles long, nearly half of it was riddled with falls and rapids, making it impassable. The portage road that circumvented these rapids was about one mile long, but with an elevational difference of over 200 feet, movement between the lakes quickly exhausted draft animals and men alike.

Burgoyne settled on using both routes. His forces at Skenesborough would take the direct passage to Fort Edward, including some artillery, provisions, and the army's camp equipage. Most of the army's artillery, provisions, and ordnance stores, as well as the heavy baggage, were destined for the Lake George route. A primary reason for Burgoyne's determined advance against Fort Edward, despite the known obstacles in his path, was based more upon psychological factors: Withdrawal to Ticonderoga would encourage Revolutionaries and discourage royalists. Further, with British forces gaining Lake George and with the Germans in Vermont, Burgoyne could confuse the New England state governments into thinking that his ultimate goal might be the Connecticut River Valley. This fear alone could delay states from sending any substantial militia reinforcements to help Schuyler's Northern Department.[4]

Felling Axe Head
ca. 1770s
Don Troiani collection
As the name suggests, felling axes were particularly made to fell large tree, making them a necessary tool for military forces in rural New York. Stamped with a total of eight government ownership marks, no doubt was left to the handler that the axe was property of the crown.

Lieutenant Friedrich Wilhelm Ludwig Leopold von Geÿling

by Georg Carl Urlaub, ca. 1783

Museumslandschaft Hessen Kassel, LM 1935/209

Von Geÿling served as a *Leutnant* (lieutenant) in the elite Hessen-Hanau Erb Prinz Regiment. During most of the Northern Camapign, the regiment was relegated to serve as the Army from Canada's rear guard during its advance south. Note the tasselled silver loops embroidered to von Geÿling's coat, as well as the silver shoulder *Achselband* (aiguillette), features that denoted his station as an officer.

Laboring in the blazing summertime heat, workers immediately set out to clear the "fallen trees, sunken stones, and other obstacles" that formed the natural impediments on Wood Creek and the paralleling road.[5] While this was ongoing, enough provisions were brought up to sustain the troops in the short term, a process that caused a significant delay. On July 23 Fraser's Advanced Corps—the forward-most of the army's brigades—set off for Fort Anne, arriving there the following day. Royalist American work parties labored diligently to clear the roads of the destruction Nixon's Continentals and Brown's militia had committed. "The Rebels are exerting every nerve to make the very bad Road . . . [to] Fort Edward much worse, by felling timber [and] breaking up bridges," complained one of Burgoyne's aides-de-camp, adding they "mean to struggle hard to make our Progress difficult to the Hudson's River." Not only were the trees an obstruction, Wood Creek itself "turned so narrow" past the remnants of Fort Anne that it did "not allow more than one battow abreast."[6] In some areas, the bateaux had to be "pushed and pulled where the water is very scarce and shallow."[7]

Although the work was difficult, the British forces never wanted for food, clothing, blankets, or their basic camp equipage. With most bateaux utilized for public stores such as provisions, ammunition, and tents, few were available for the officers' belongings. Burgoyne admonished his officers for bringing too much, ordering them to return all baggage to Ticonderoga "that is not indispensably necessary to them." The British general informed his army's officers, most of whom never served on a military campaign, that officers in the French and Indian War often "took up with Soldiers' Tents, and often confined their Baggage to a Knapsack for months together," and that the like would serve in this instance as well.[8] Most officers were able to secure bathorses, upon which light baggage could be carried, thereby avoiding use of the disdainful knapsack. Many were enraged by this uncomfortable predicament and lamented the "poor care and orders" they received, being relegated to having "a private's tent and blanket, plus [having to eat] the salted meat, just like a private."[9] Another officer fretted over the indignity, complaining that they "cannot take more equipment along than their servants can carry. Most officer tents were left behind at Ticonderoga" and remained with the heavy baggage. Even worse, most officers had no horses to ride and "must march as the soldiers march."[10]

On July 17 a newly arrived canoe fleet made a spectacular appearance in South Bay near Skenesborough. Landed that day were about 400 chiefs and warriors and 170 Canadien volunteers. Unlike the Seven Nations of Canada men heretofore fighting with the army, these Indians were from the "far western" nations: Fox, Menominee, Ojibwe (Chippewa), Ottawa, Potawatomi, Sauk, and Winnebago. With them was the superintendent of the Québec Indian Department, Major John Campbell, as well as prominent Canadien leaders, many of whom fought the British in the previous war, including La Corne de Saint-Luc, Charles-Michel de Langlade, and Charles-Louis de Lanaudière. Burgoyne called a formal council, during which combat policy was defined: Prisoners should not be abused, the crown would compensate for prisoners, and scalps could only be taken from the dead.[11] After being issued with eight days, provisions per man, they set off south toward Fort Anne on the 20th.

It didn't take long for any Americans operating within the area between Fort Anne and Moses Creek to fall prey to Burgoyne's new reinforcement. On July 21 the British commander himself with a small guard accompanied by his "far western" Indian allies and Canadien volunteers ventured to Fort Anne to survey the situation there. A thirty-four-man detachment of Continentals from Nixon's Brigade happened to be scouting the area, and when spotted was "surrounded by about 200 Indians." The scout's commander and seventeen men were captured; the rest fled.[12]

Hessen-Hanau Spontoon
fourth quarter, 18th century
Don Troiani collection
This Hessian *Sponton* (spontoon) would have been carried by a commissioned officer as a symbol of his station. Unlike the British Army infantry officer corps, which readily exchanged their polearms for fusees early in the war, Braunschweig and Hessen-Hanau *Offiziere* (officers) retained theirs.

The following afternoon, two advance sentinels guarding the Nixon's Brigade encampment at Kingsbury, located eight miles south of Fort Anne, were attacked. Nixon responded by calling out most of his brigade to fend off the Indians and Canadien volunteers, and a "smart engagement ensued that lasted 28 minutes, very heavy fire on both sides." Colonel Thomas Nixon, commander of one of the regiments in his older brother's brigade, "had his horse at that time shot under him."[13] During this lengthy fight, Massachusetts militiaman Isaac Blackmer "shot and killed an indian who was lying in ambush and within fifteen or twenty minutes after we were ordered to charge with our bayonets" upon the enemy.[14] Captain Thayer crossed a nearby bridge with a party of men and charged the enemy's left "so hot [it] obliged them to retreat."[15] Casualties in the Kingsbury skirmish were slight for the attackers, with one Indian killed and fourteen Indians wounded, while the Americans suffered five men killed, nine wounded, and one taken prisoner.

Later that night, Nixon's troops were ordered back to Fort Edward, where, upon reaching it, they "made fires, laid down on the ground, without victuals or anything to cover" them.[16] There was one exception: Before setting off for the fort, Blackmer found the man he had killed and took his "Indian blanket and wampum belt," by which the militiaman was undoubtedly protected from the overnight dew.[17]

Indian Chief's Fusil
1777
Private collection
This brass-mounted English fusil was built by London gunmaker Richard Wilson for the purpose of trade with Indians. Note the arrow-filled quiver and bow engraved on the lock face, the ornamental serpentine side plate, and the brass tacks nailed into the stock that bear the date 1777 and *GG6*.

On the morning of July 24, Indians brazenly circumvented Fort Edward and went south, attacking a small party of Americans in the woods between the fort and Schuyler's Moses Creek encampment. There,

> Lieut. Jonathan Saywer [*sic*] and Samuel Rogers . . . was walking in the Road with tow [two] more with them Joshua White was one, Seven Endians ris up in the Bushes and fird they kild Samuel Rogers the first shot, Lieut Sayer run over the fence, the Endians all run after him and Catch him and the Rest Run Clear.[18]

With the shots fired, 200 men were sent from camp to investigate, but found the bodies of the slain only; both were killed and scalped. The party then set out "to scour the woods, but could discover none of them."[19] The Indians attacked again on July 26 but in greater force, hitting the twenty-man piquet stationed on a wooded hill located about a quarter mile north of Fort Edward. One of the men in the piquet, Private Samuel Standish,

> had not been there Long before he heard an Indian Scream and Instantly was fired upon by them—he [Standish] ran towards the River and Fort & before he arrived he met three Indians coming from the River between him and the Fort who all fired upon him, but missed him, where he was taken prisoner by them taken up the hill again near to a spring, was there striped of his hat coat & hand-kerchief and pillfered by them.[20]

Not everyone was as lucky as Standish. With the guard routed, the fleeing Americans became easy targets and six men were killed, including their commanding officer, Lieutenant Van Veghten.[21] Then, it struck. The sky darkened and burst forth with a heavy, short-lived summertime thunderstorm, which probably convinced many of the Indians—and everyone else—to seek shelter. For those Indians foremost in the attack, then located near the abandoned homes near the fort, the choice was obvious.

Found in one of the home's cellars was Jane McCrea, a young woman betrothed to a royalist American officer, and an older woman named Sarah McNeil, in whose house the pair were domiciled.[22] Why they remained there is no mystery: Both women were royalists and were, like some others, awaiting the forthcoming days when Burgoyne's army triumphantly restored crown authority, at which time McCrea could safely join her fiancé. The Indians saw an opportunity at hand: By taking the women to camp, they would be compensated and the prisoners released to British authorities.

Trade Knife
18th century
Don Troiani collection
This type of knife, with its plain wooden handle, was commonly traded to North American Indian nations. This example was excavated near Fort Haldimand.

As the storm subsided, the women, unknowing of the Indians' intentions, resisted helplessly as they were dragged out of the house. Standish, who still remained a prisoner nearby, "saw a party of Indians coming with two women they came up the hill to the spring and there they seemed to be in a quarrel, they shot one of the women and scalped her."[23] While Standish certainly heard the struggle and gunfire—memories of which he used to piece together his narrative to make sense of what happened—he had not seen it. McNeil's and McCrea's escorts separated, and as McCrea's gained the hill, a fight broke out between her captors. Either sensing heightened fear from this infighting or opportunity, she struggled to break free. One of the Indians attacked the young woman and mortally wounded her. When the Indians realized McCrea was still alive, she was scalped, given the coup de grâce, and partly stripped of her clothes.[24]

The Indians withdrew back to camp with a number of soldier prisoners and Mrs. McNeil. As for Standish, the "Indians then Led him away by the cord with which he was bound towards the British into an Indian Camp . . . he then saw four red coats with bayonets in their hands coming who came and took him before Gen[l] Frazier who asked him how he came there." After a brief interrogation, Standish and other prisoners were "sent under a Tory guard" to Ticonderoga, where, with those captured at Hubbardton, he labored to transport the Army from Canada's provisions.[25]

The following day, July 27, American patrols found both McCrea's and Van Veghten's remains and brought them down to the Moses Creek encampment. Private Luther Shaw recalled seeing McCrea "brought in, and the body laid out in an Officer's Marquee," noting that he "saw the body there, and the wound of the tommahawk that had been struck into the breast."[26] Chaplain Enos Hitchcock observed that McCrea had been "killed, Scalped & mangled . . . in a most inhumane man[r]," while Van Veghten "was killed, scalped" with his hands cut off "& otherwise mangled."[27] Another military chaplain, Hezekiah Smith, lamented that he "attended the Funeral of Miss Ginny Day and a Lieutenant in our Army [who] were killed and Scalped by Indians besides other abuses on their bodies."[28]

If anyone had hope that the death of a young royalist woman at the hands of Burgoyne's Indians would convince enraged militia to take up arms against the British and turn out to avenge her death, they were sorely mistaken. In fact, the incessant *petite guerre* attacks against American troops inculcated the very thing Burgoyne intended: fear. The Indians' tactics were not what soldiers of the Northern Department were prepared to fight against. In fact, with even more militia set to leave because of expired, short-term enlistments, Schuyler could only plead with state governments to send long-term service militia for support.

Jane McCrea, July 26

On a wooded hilltop north of Fort Edward, two Indians from a far-western tribe escort the prisoner Jane McCrea to Burgoyne's camp. They "disputed who should be her guard,"* and in a fit of rage against the one "from whose hands she was snatched," the offended warrior killed the young woman. McCrea wore a "light chintz frock"** and a black calamanco petticoat, recalled Dinah, an enslaved woman owned by Jane's brother, John, the local militia colonel. As such, the stripping of her obviously feminine clothing would have marked her killer as much as the scalp did. While her death was not a catalyst for vengeful militia to fight against the British, the myth of it having been so continues to be popularized.

*Burgoyne to Gates, September 6, 1777, Horatio Gates Papers, 5:470.

**"Charlotte Leslie of Salem," in *In the Path of War*, ed. Jeanne Winston Adler (Peterborough, NH: Cobblestone, 1998), 58.

Indian Peace Medal
fourth quarter, 18th century
Private collection

The British government gave silver medals to Indian nations for the purpose of cementing bonds of amity and loyalty. Made to be worn suspended around the neck, these medals typically bore a bust portrait of King George III on the obverse.

The situation was so acute, Schuyler thought it was finally time to speak plainly of the situation he faced when updating Washington on July 28:

> [T]he militia that are with me . . . are daily diminishing and I am very confident that in ten days . . . I shall not have five hundred left and altho I have entreated this [New York] and the Eastern States to send up a reinforcement of them, yet I doubt much, if any will come up, especially from the Eastern States, where the spirit of malevolence knows no bounds, and I am considered as a traitor.[29]

Schuyler indeed had a number of detractors, a majority of whom were New Englanders. However, he mistakenly exaggerated his own importance relative to the matter at hand, and thereby his reasoning as to why the states refused to turn out long-term service militia. The states retained their militias for more practical reasons, in fact, and these concerns overrode the needs of the Northern Army. Schuyler was right about one important point, though: Few militia would be joining the Northern Army any time soon.[30]

Burgoyne was furious. Informed that one of his Indian allies had "scalped a young lady, their prisoner," he ordered Fraser to have Campbell prepare a congress of the Indians. Meeting on July 27, Burgoyne "reprimanded them in very severe terms" for the attack on McCrea.[31] What's more, he demanded the execution of the Indian who killed her. The chiefs explained that the warrior, identified as a young Ottawa man, had fought with another over whose prisoner McCrea was. In the ensuing argument between the two, McCrea was killed. This did little to deter Burgoyne, but La Corne de Saint-Luc interceded. His argument was that if the young man was hanged, the Indians would certainly abandon the expedition and probably cause irrevocable damage to relations between the British government and a host of Indian nations. The British general acquiesced, but only after the chiefs promised to prevent similar incidents from happening again. The warrior apologized, and Burgoyne pardoned him.

The Indian and Canadien attacks against small numbers of American soldiers continued. On the 28th, one man was mortally wounded and scalped. On the 29th, "a man & Boy" were killed and another wounded in one quarter, while sentries were attacked (one was killed, one wounded) in another. Another sentry in a different part of camp was "wounded in the neck." An American scouting party encountered a large force of Indians and Canadiens; they "fired & killed one and ran" back to the American camp. Another American scouting party, operating near Argyle, located about five miles east-southeast of Fort Edward, reported finding the remains of eight civilians on a farm there. As with Jane McCrea, the victims of this "horrid murder" were another royalist, John Allen, along with his wife, her young sister, the Allens' three children, an enslaved man, and an enslaved girl.[32]

Facing the inevitable, American forces abandoned their meager foothold on Fort Edward and evacuated the Moses Creek camp in favor of Saratoga. On the 30th, the troops floated their sleeping boards downriver and marched south. During this withdrawal, troops on both sides of the river were attacked by Indians, Canadiens, and the King's Loyal Americans, resulting in about ten Americans killed, captured, or wounded; one royalist was killed.[33] On July 31, most of the Northern Army was in Saratoga.

With confirmation that Fort Edward was evacuated, Fraser's Advanced Corps captured the place on July 30. Apart from damaging buildings inside and outside of the fort, the retreating Americans left most structures intact. British forces operating on Lake George had captured the smoldering ruins of Fort George the previous day.[34] With both forts in Burgoyne's hands, he finally controlled the Great Carrying Place, which connected his supply line of provisions, ordnance stores, and heavy baggage on Lake Champlain with the Hudson River via Lake George.

McNeil's Ferry was the common Hudson River crossing point located about three miles north of Saratoga where, on August 3, Major

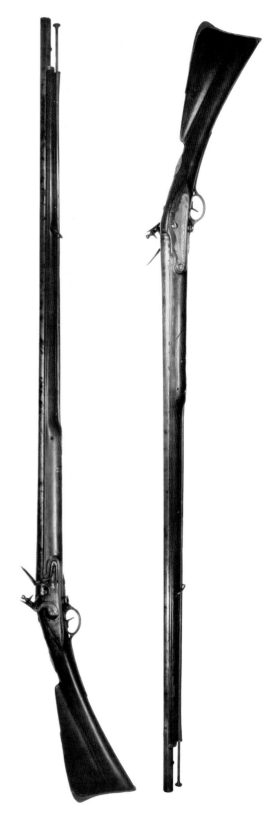

American Fusee

ca. 1775

Richard Ulbrich collection

Fusees, or fusils, were firearms commonly carried by British, royalist, Continental, and militia commissioned infantry officers during the Northern Campaign of 1777. Having a thinner wood stock and typically fit with a smaller-caliber barrel than a soldier's musket, fusees weighed appreciably less. Depending upon the regiment, uniform pattern fusees were purchased en masse for a British regiment's officer corps or procured independently by the officers themselves. Concerned with the consequences of having trigger-happy officers, Burgoyne set policy for the use of fusees at the commencement of the campaign: "The Attention of every Officer in Action is to be employed upon his men. To make use of a Fusil, except in very extraordinary cases of immediate personal defense, would betray an ignorance of his importance, and his Duty." This gun was made by Elisha Buell of Hebron, Connecticut.

June 20, 1777, Burgoyne, *Orderly Book*, 3–4.

Spike Tomahawk
second half, 18th century

Don Troiani collection

This austere iron tomahawk head was recovered near Fort Miller, New York, a small, abandoned French and Indian War fort that lay on the Hudson River's west side across from William Duer's estate.

William Hull was stationed with Schuyler's army's advance guard. Located on the western side of the Hudson, his 300 Continental and militia troops were tasked with guarding the place and keeping a watchful eye on enemy movements in that area.[35] Later that morning, Captain Alexander Fraser's company of British Rangers appeared. One Massachusetts militiaman remembered seeing the British

> descending a hill about 30 rods [165 yards] off at the bottom
> of the hill they displayed & fired a volley, when we were ordered to
> retreat. We fell back about 60 rods [330 yards] to a piece of woods,
> which we had hardly entered when the Indians rose up from the
> bushes on each side of us & fired upon our party. Each [militia] man
> then made his escape in the best way he could.[36]

Hull's choice to place the militia in his line of battle on the left flank, farthest from the river and closest to an enemy attack, had dire consequences, and being set upon by Indians, Canadiens, and royalists, they "retreated in some disorder." Amid the chaos, Fraser pushed forth along the front with his redcoats, while the flankers sounded "their hideous yells" in the defenders' ears.[37] Hull's men again retreated, nearly one mile fighting a running battle. They re-formed on a height and stood by as reinforcements came up from Saratoga, but by the time they arrived, Fraser and his attackers had withdrawn. British casualties in the McNeil's Ferry skirmish were light, if any. The Americans lost about twenty men killed and wounded, with seven captured.

Retiring to Saratoga later that evening, word was received that another party of forty men from Colonel Thomas Marshall's (10th) Regiment were ambushed earlier that day a few miles southwest of Saratoga. A full half of the men were killed or wounded, and the commanding officer was wounded mortally.[38] The Northern Army evacuated twelve miles south to Stillwater during a driving rain, arriving very early the next morning. Here the entire army was forced to bivouac "on the wet ground" while it continued to pour, "with nothing to cover most of us but the heavens."[39]

Back at Fort Edward, Burgoyne had a surprise awaiting him. La Corne de Saint-Luc and the chiefs of the "far western" nations informed the British general of their need to return home for the fall hunt. Given that they had to travel upward of 1,000 miles, they calculated that they would need to leave in early August. A council with his Indian allies was called on the afternoon of August 5, during which time Burgoyne beseeched them to remain and see the campaign through to conclusion—three weeks, Burgoyne told them. While some Indians from various nations departed, the vast majority elected to remain until Albany was taken. Given the brilliantly successful *petite guerre* tactics thus far employed by his Indian allies, Burgoyne needed them to keep pressure upon the retreating Northern Army. As one American officer at Stillwater happened to write on August 6, "One Hundred Indians in the Woods do us more harm than 1000 British Troops."[40]

Diversion

The fact that nothing is to be gained by this vast outlay of money is only to be ascribed to the exaggerated arrogance of the English gentlemen.
—First-Lieutenant Philipp Hildebrandt, August 4, 1777[1]

8th (The King's) Regiment of Foot Rank-and-File Button

ca. 1770s

Don Troiani collection

This British regiment had the perpetual duty of garrisoning outposts from the St. Lawrence River corridor west to Fort Michilimackinac, a frontier outpost guarding the Straits of Mackinac, which separate Lakes Huron and Michigan. The rank and file (corporals and privates) of this regiment bore buttons depicting the regimental number; because of the regiment's distinguished status, the buttons also bore the initial of its royal title.

With Burgoyne's continued successes north of Albany throughout July, the secret, secondary part of the two-pronged campaign from Canada was simultaneously gathering force. Lieutenant-Colonel Barry St. Leger, who held the rank of "acting" brigadier-general for the duration of the expedition, was handpicked by Burgoyne to lead the diversionary expedition.[2] The singular point that recommended St. Leger to the post of this independent command was his seniority: He was the senior field officer of the Canada Army, and the expedition required the command of a lieutenant-colonel. This was, of course, hardly a useful quality considering the enormously complex undertaking.

While St. Leger's command did not constitute anything close to an "army," the force preparing to plunge into New York's Mohawk Valley and meet Burgoyne at Albany did pose a serious threat to the revolutionary cause. St. Leger's largest cohesive body of troops was the King's Royal Regiment of New York (KRRNY), a royalist American battalion numbering about 250 officers and men. Nearly 130 from his own 34th Regiment of Foot comprised the largest British contingent, and an additional 100 were drawn from the 8th (The King's) Regiment of Foot. Two light six-pounders, two light three-pounders, and four small four-and-three-fifths-inch-diameter Coehorn mortars were manned by a forty-man detachment of the Royal Regiment of Artillery.[3] The German contingent—the only riflemen serving on either side of the forthcoming expedition—consisted of one ninety-man company of Hessen-Hanau jäger. A fifty-man company of Canadien militia draftees from the Trois-Rivières District rounded out the balance of his American-European combatants.

Per Germain's March 26 instructions, emphasis was placed upon recruiting Indian warriors for Burgoyne's and St. Leger's forces. With Québec Indian Department leadership focused on garnering support for Burgoyne's army, Six Nations Indian Department officials were tasked with recruiting men for St. Leger. Department officials called a series of councils with a variety of nations during the summer, and all told were able to secure about 600 warriors for the expedition. Foremost of these was a contingent of nearly 400 warriors from all

Seneca Nation War Captain

The Seneca were the first of the Haudenosaunee (Iroquois Confederacy) to formally accept the king's hatchet, which was done in July 1777. With about 200 warriors, the Seneca constituted the largest body of Indians to participate in St. Leger's expedition. This war captain wears a blue stroud matchcoat trimmed in red silk, draped over a printed calico shirt bedecked with a series of round trade silver shirt-buckles. Decorated silver ear-wheels hang from slit earlobes, a cultural characteristic practiced by many Eastern Woodlands Indian men.

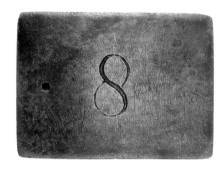

Waist Belt Clasp, 8th (The King's) Regiment of Foot
ca. 1770s

Old Fort Niagara Association; photograph courtesy of James L. Kochan

Like most waist belt clasps of this style, this cast-brass piece includes nothing more than the regiment's number, 8, upon the face. St. Leger's expeditionary force included nearly ninety rank and file (corporals and privates) drawn from this regiment, about three-quarters of whom were battalion company men who would have had these plates fastened to their waist belts. Like other British regiments, the soldiers of the 8th wore waist belts over the shoulder for the sake of convenience and comfort.

Private, Colonel Elias Dayton's 3rd New Jersey Regiment, 1776

Raised in New Jersey in early 1776, the 3rd New Jersey, then described as the "compleatest and best regiment in the Continental service," was dispatched to Johnstown in May with orders to arrest Sir John Johnson. The forewarned baronet and over 150 of his supporters fled, thus avoiding capture. The regiment remained in the Mohawk Valley throughout the summer and into fall, garrisoning German Flatts, building Fort Dayton (named for the regiment's colonel), and occupying and improving Fort Stanwix, which Dayton rechristened as Fort Schuyler.

Elmer, "Journal Kept during an Expedition to Canada in 1776," *Proceedings of the New Jersey Historical Society* 2:102.

six nations of the Haudenosaunee (Iroquois Confederacy)—Seneca, Mohawk, Cayuga, Onondaga, Tuscarora, and Oneida—the majority of whom were Seneca. About 150 Mississauga and St. Regis men from the Lake Ontario and St. Lawrence River valleys, as well as another 50 from the Lakes Nations near Detroit, including the Chippewa, Ottawa, Potawatomi, and Wyandot, rounded out the balance of warriors. Chosen as overall leaders were Sayenqueraghta (Old Smoke) and Gayentwahga (Cornplanter), who not only commanded the Indians but also coordinated efforts with the British, royalist, and Canadien officials of the Six Nations Indian Department.[4] Lastly, Captain Joseph Brant's Volunteers, over 200 American Indian (primarily Mohawk and Delaware) and royalist (primarily New York) rangers, increased St. Leger's American Indian contingent to about 800 total. Apart from Burgoyne's, no other military force assembled during the war was as ethnically varied as St. Leger's.

The core of St. Leger's secret expeditionary force set off from Lachine (near Montréal) in late June. Traveling by bateaux up the St. Lawrence River to Lake Ontario, the boats needed to be rowed, poled, and even sometimes pulled by ropes due to the intervening rapids. The work was difficult, but St. Leger himself arrived at Buck Island (present-day Carleton Island) on July 8. After most of the aforementioned units assigned to the expedition joined him there, the expedition set off onto Lake Ontario on July 19. The flotilla arrived at Fort Ontario, located near the outlet of the Oswego River where it empties into the Great Lake, on the 24th.

The little bateaux fleet continued its trek up the Oswego River, which caused such significant difficulties due to the various rapids that the men had to partially submerge themselves in in order to move the boats forward. Lieutenant Hildebrandt, commander of the expedition's ninety jäger, complained to the British commander on the 27th that his unit alone had to manage "fifteen bateaux laden with one hundred and forty-two barrels of provisions, not to mention the company's war chest, powder, lead, medicine cases, and baggage." He also complained that the arduous, submersive duty "completely ruined" his men's shoes, stockings, and feet, the latter of which was eased by their Indian allies wrapping the Germans' feet in alder tree leaves.[5] Summertime thunderstorms plagued their progress and affected not only their comfort but their food. Flour was a provision mainstay for the British forces, and when mixed with water was commonly baked on rocks "in a pit of hot ashes." An August 1 downpour destroyed their ration, "and so the men went hungry" that day.

Oneida Lake was attained on August 2. After crossing the massive body of water, the bulk of the expeditionary force (without its artillery, which was still in the process of catching up) arrived at its first target, a crumbling, poorly

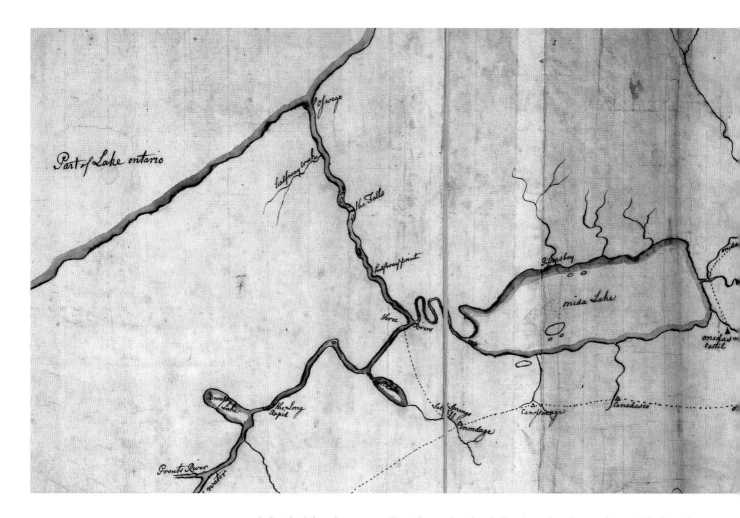

defended fort known as Fort Stanwix, the following day. It was from this fort that St. Leger planned to stage his descent into the Mohawk Valley.

Except the fort was neither dilapidated nor poorly defended. It was a fortress. While the 1758 building had fallen into disrepair after the French and Indian War, the massive structure was taken by American troops in 1776 and repairs begun thereafter. This was done at the suggestion of the Oneida Nation, its leadership suggesting that control of the fort would help protect the entry point into the Mohawk Valley, called the Oneida Carry, in reference to the portaging paths between the west-flowing Wood Creek (which flowed into Oneida Lake) and the east-flowing Mohawk River. Although there were no major threats in 1776, the fort remained garrisoned. Minimal repairs were made that year, but more money and personnel were poured into the project in 1777. The fort, originally named for British General John Stanwix when built in 1758, was officially renamed Fort Schuyler by its new owners.

Fort Schuyler was a solidly strong log and earthen fort built along a traditional European plan—"masterfully laid out," according to Hildebrandt.[6] Each

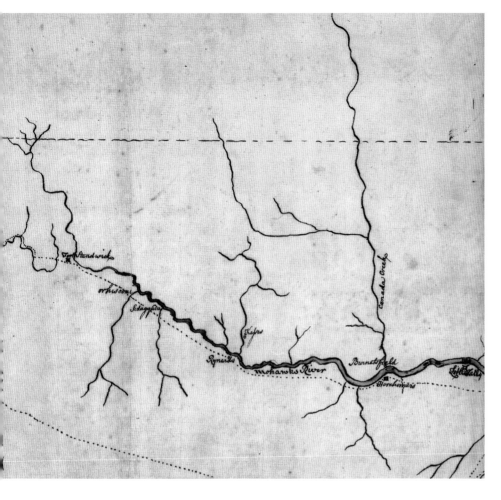

N.W. parts of New York, no. 156 (detail)

by artist unknown, ca. 1760
The Library of Congress, 75693009
This French and Indian War map effectively depicts St. Leger's arduous avenue of approach from Lake Ontario, the Oswego River, and Oneida Lake to "Fort Standwick" (Fort Stanwix / Schuyler), situated between Wood Creek and the Mohawk River. East of the fort lies the western third of the Mohawk River Valley, including "Orhiscani" (Oriskany) and "Herchimers"—Fort Herkimer—a French and Indian War fortification at German Flatts still in use during the American War for Independence. The dashed line located directly below the Mohawk River represents the main road between Albany and the Oneida Carry.

corner of the square-shaped post was defended by a diamond-shaped bastion and protected by artillery. Entrance to the fort was achieved by use of a drawbridge over a large ditch, which was defended by a fortified ravelin. The sally port—a small, alternative point of access to the fort—was located on the fort's east-facing side, offering more direct access to Technohat Creek, which provided the fort's fresh water supply, and, beyond that, the Mohawk River. Defending Fort Schuyler was the 400-man 3rd New York Regiment, supplemented by a 150-man detachment of Continental infantrymen drawn from Colonels John Bailey's (2nd) and James Wesson's (9th) Massachusetts Regiments. One forty-man detachment from Colonel John Lamb's (2nd) Continental Artillery Regiment rounded out the garrison, which was commanded by the 3rd New York Regiment's commander, twenty-eight-year-old Colonel Peter Gansevoort.[7]

The Oneida, ever mindful of providing intelligence and fighting assistance to the United States, brought word to Gansevoort in late June—more than a month before St. Leger's appearance outside the fort's walls—that the British were on their way. St. Leger's impending arrival became evident when it was reported,

Private, Colonel Peter Gansevoort's 3rd New York Regiment

Like most Northern Department Continental units, the 3rd New York was not uniform in appearance, although one company was issued "Coats blue with Red facings and white lineing." Most of the regiment was issued French arms, as well as American-made bayonet belts and cartridge boxes. This soldier wears a belted waistcoat—a round-cut vest which included an overlapping belt that tied in the back.

Gansevoort to Gansevoort, June 13, 1777, New York Public Library, Archives and Manuscripts, Peter Gansevoort, Jr., military papers, vol. 2.

and confirmed, that various people were being killed, wounded, or captured by Indians allied with the British. As early as June 25, a captain and corporal were attacked and scalped over a mile from the fort.[8] On July 3 a small party of one officer and seven men, tasked with "cutting sods for the Fort," was attacked; some were killed and scalped, but most were taken prisoner.[9] An attack that took place on July 27, however, took on a different form. After hearing the shots, Gansevoort sent some men to investigate,

> in the edge of the woods, about 500 yards from the fort. . . . The villains were fled, after having shot three girls who were out picking raspberries, two of whom were lying scalped and tomahawked, one dead, the other expiring, who died in about half an hour after she was brought home. The third had two [musket] balls through her shoulder, but made out to make her escape; her wounds are not thought dangerous. By the best discoveries we have made, there were four Indians who perpetrated these murders.[10]

On August 2 a welcome arrival of four bateaux laden with ammunition and food arrived at the fort, escorted by over a hundred Massachusetts Continental infantrymen. The stores were just barely whisked into the fort along with its soldier escort when the bateauxmen were attacked by St. Leger's advance party. The main body of the British forces arrived late in the afternoon the following day. The British general wasted no time and called for the garrison, numbering over 750 military personnel and civilians, to surrender but was summarily "rejected with disdain."[11] St. Leger's Indians and jäger spent August 4 firing at the fort's defenders with their small arms, and the Indians burned houses, barns, and other wood structures located nearby.

Most of New York's Mohawk River Valley was encompassed within Tryon County, and it was that county's militia that had to act against any incursions within its territory, large or small. On August 2 New York governor George Clinton wrote to Tryon County's militia commander, Brigadier General Nicholas Herkimer, to "raise a Reinforcement from the Militia in your Brigade." The "properly armed accoutered" militia would be drafted "by Ballot or other equitable Method" and officered by men who were "of approved Courage and if possible those who have seen some Service."[12] In truth, Herkimer was already assembling militia at Fort Dayton (located in present-day Herkimer, New York), situated in the Mohawk Valley about thirty miles from the surrounded fort. Schuyler had previously ordered Herkimer to send 200 militia reinforcements to shore up Gansevoort's garrison, but few were sent and none remained by the time of St. Leger's arrival. Herkimer claimed the militia were "dispirited," but

**American Musket
18th century**
Don Troiani collection
Typical of many American-manufactured muskets, this piece utilizes parts from an older European military firearm. This gun's lock and other parts were cannibalized from a French *fusil d'infanterie modèle* 1717 (model 1717 infantry musket).

**American Officer Hanger
third quarter, 18th century**

Don Troiani collection
This American officer's sword has a turned wooden grip and brass furniture, including a lion-headed pommel. The blade is engraved "God Bless the Province of New York." This particular sword has a Mohawk Valley provenance.

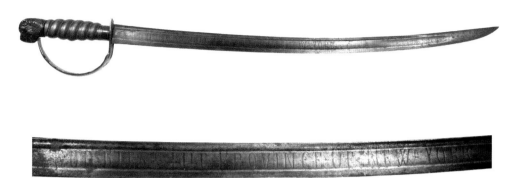

Schuyler reminded the militia commander that it was his "duty to keep up the spirits of the people and if they recover them they will be in no danger of any enemy from the westward."[13]

Schuyler's admonishment had the desired effect: Herkimer assembled an impressive force of perhaps 700 officers and men, which marched off from Fort Dayton on August 4. The troops had to cross to the south side of the Mohawk River, and on August 5 spent the night near Oriska, a small Oneida Nation settlement located near Oriskany Creek. There they were joined by perhaps sixty Oneida chiefs and warriors led by Hanyery Tewahangarahken (He Who Takes Up the Snowshoe), adamant supporters of the revolutionary cause.

On the morning of August 6, some of Herkimer's principal officers urged the general to form the column for its final push to Fort Schuyler, but Herkimer was reluctant. The day before, he cleverly dispatched some men to the fort with a message for Gansevoort, informing him that the militia were near at hand. Further, in case Gansevoort "should hear a Firing of small Arms" upon the militia's approach, he should "send a party from the Garrison to Reinforce" them.[14] Herkimer would know if the message came through by the discharge of three of the fort's cannons; no shots had been heard. Nevertheless, Herkimer acquiesced to his officers' demands, and the Tryon County militia brigade was arranged for the final leg of its march. The long, snaking column was fronted by Colonel Ebenezer Cox's 1st Regiment, followed by Colonel Jacob Klock's 2nd Regiment, Colonel Peter Bellinger's 4th Regiment, and in the rear with the brigade's fifteen baggage wagons, Colonel Frederick Visscher's 3rd Regiment. The Oneida and some of the militia deployed as van and rear guards. Fort Schuyler lay about eight miles away.

The column marched a couple miles west, down a substantial hill and over the Oneida Creek causeway. By 10:00 a.m. the column's wagons were in the process of crossing the creek when, from the high ground south of the road west of the causeway, shots were fired. Suddenly, "the Indians rose & with a dredful yell pored a destructive fire" against most of the militia column's southern broadside.[15] This was followed by the running onslaught of hundreds of Indians wielding tomahawks, knives, ball clubs, and spears. It was an ambush.

The previous day, St. Leger was informed by his Mohawk allies that Herkimer's militia were near Oriska and planned to advance in support of the fort on the 6th. Lieutenant-Colonel Sir John Johnson, St. Leger's second in command, coordinated a force to meet them en route, including the KRRNY light infantry company, Brant's Volunteers, and nearly half the jäger.[16] They were joined by hundreds of Indians, over a third of whom were Seneca, led by Sayenqueraghta himself. Despite Johnson's command authority, he deferred battle leadership to the senior Seneca chief, who, in the early morning hours of August 6, "immediately formed" the ambush force and "took the lead in the Action."[17]

Herkimer was severely wounded early in the fighting, but famously continued to command his men while propped up against a tree. Conversely, about 200 of Visscher's rear guard fled in a panic

Private, Colonel Jacob Klock's Regiment, Tryon County, New York, Militia

New York law required each militiaman "between the ages of 16 and 50" to provide themselves with "a good Musket or firelock & [a] Bayonet Sword or Tomahawk, a Steel Ramrod . . . a Cartouch Box to contain 23 rounds . . . and a knapsack." Noncompliance could be met with fines, payment of which might be taken from bounty money, wages, or the sale of requisitioned belongings. Captains were required to train their companies "at least four hours" once per month, while colonels had to "assemble and exercise" their regiments at least twice per year.

"The Militia Bill," August 22, 1775, in Berthold Fernow, *New York in the Revolution*, vol. 1, 31.

Eastern Woodlands Indian Ball Club
ca. 1770s
New York State Military Museum; photograph by Don Troiani
Indians wielded a variety of melee weapons in close-quarters combat, including tomahawks, knives, war hammers, and wooden ball clubs, such as the one seen here. This particular piece, owned by a warrior serving in St. Leger's expedition, was at one point taken during, or after, the siege of Fort Schuyer. It was presented as a gift to Colonel Peter Gansevoort, the fort's commander.

Indian Trade Musket
third quarter, 18th century
Colonial Williamsburg Foundation
This light musket, made by London gunmaker John Bumford II, is typical of those sent to the Hudson's Bay Company to be used as a trade item with North American Indians. Bumford worked as a company contractor from 1757 to 1775.

back down the road shortly after the battle began. The Indian melee weapons "made a shocking Slaughter" among the militia west of the causeway. Many militia fled north, through the woods and into the swampy ground in the direction of the Mohawk River, where many were chased down and killed. Private Henry Walrath, who fought in Klock's Regiment, later recalled that

> three of his companions were shot down by his side, [and he] fired nine times, & then the Indians rushed up and took him prisoner, tied a Rope around his neck & fastened him to a tree, that soon after the Indians had to retreat beyond where he was tied, & he was led off by his master the Indians who took [him] prisoner had plundered some of the baggage waggons.[18]

Treeing—fighting from behind the cover of trees—was employed by each side, but as many of the Indians lacked firearms, they had to wait for opportune moments to strike their foes. The Hessen-Hanau jäger kept their distance

Private, Hessen-Hanau Jäger Corps von Creutzbourg

This Hessian jäger appears as he would have upon the unit's arrival in Canada in summer 1777. Poorly supplied from home, their uniforms quickly devolved into "rags . . . the colors having faded to brown with not a shade of green noticeable." Their leather breeches became "stiff and cracked" from significant water and sun damage, and were eventually replaced with linen gaitered trousers. The company that marched with St. Leger did so without their *Hirschfänger* (deer-killers), hunting swords which weren't distributed to them before their departure.

Von Creuzbourg to Wilhelm I, October 3, 1777, *Diary of the Hanau Jäger Corps*, 40.

Battle of Oriskany, August 6

In one of the war's few battles defined by vicious melee combat, the serene, wooded approach to Fort Schuyler turned into a bloody battle near the Oneida village of Oriska. Seen here, soldiers of the Tryon County, New York, militia are directed by Brigadier General Nicholas Herkimer, shot in the leg and propped against a tree. Oneida Nation war chief Thawengarakwen (Honyery Doxtater), his wife Tyonajanegen, and Oneida warriors fight alongside Herkimer's militia against their British-allied Haudenosaunee (Iroquois Confederacy) kin. This battle marked the first time in which the divide growing between factions within the Haudenosaunee was manifested in battle.

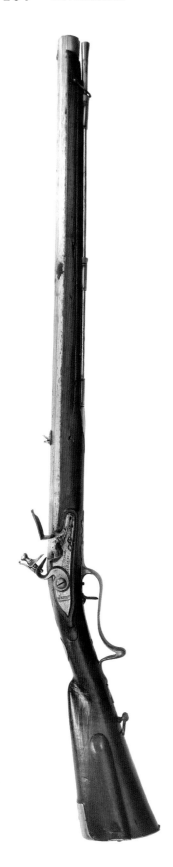

during most of the action, preferring to shoot long-range with their rifles. Lacking *Hirschfänger* (deer-killers)—they left Canada without them—they had no hunting swords with which to engage in hand-to-hand combat. As it was, their rifles were not particularly effective due to poor quality, and the entanglement of friends and foes alike, along with the intervening trees, significantly hampered their potency.[19] With casualties mounting on both sides, the Indian attacks lessened as the militia "recovered themselves" and "fell back to a more advantageous Ground" north of the road "& maintained a running fire for about an hour & a half."[20] Perhaps inspired by their sharp-edged-weapon-wielding allies, Sir John's royalist KRRNY light infantry made a formal deployment and attacked a pocket of militia with musketry and bayonets. After a sharp fight with the militia, they fell back.

After about three hours of fighting, the militia were thoroughly thrashed but had solidified their defensive position. A severe summertime thunderstorm poured down upon the battlefield early in the afternoon, which disrupted the battle and nullified gunpowder. The harsh storm also obfuscated everyone's view of the battlefield, making it too dangerous to proceed with melee weapons. After about an hour, the storm ended and the attack against the militia renewed. Reinforcements arrived in the form of about seventy officers and soldiers from the KRRNY, who, upon approach, supposedly altered their regimental clothing in order to be less conspicuous in their dress.[21] They approached the militia flank closely and at an opportune moment flooded forth with bayonets, renewing the battle once again in the crown's favor. Then, shots were heard to the west, toward Fort Schuyler. The renewed attack dwindled, and Sayenqueraghta's men gradually fell back. Eventually the British forces altogether departed in the direction of

Hessen-Hanau Jäger Rifle
second half, 18th century

Don Troiani collection

Begun as gamekeepers and foresters, Jäger (hunters) from three German nation states provided rifle support for all three British expeditions in the Northern Campaign of 1777; those serving with St. Leger were from Grafschaft (County) Hessen-Hanau and carried *Büchsen* (rifles) such as this. Made in Hanau, this .62-caliber firearm has a sliding wooden patch box in the stock. The British "openly" complained about the "poor marksmanship" exhibited by the jäger on St. Leger's expedition. The Hessen-Hanau jäger commander, Lieutenant-Colonel Carl von Creutzbourg, later opened an investigation and determined that the *Büchsen* of those jäger who served with St. Leger were, in fact, "not worth a shot of powder."

Von Creutzbourg to Wilhelm I, September 5, 1777, *Diary of the Hanau Jäger Corps*, 37.

the fort. Having been left masters of the battlefield, Herkimer's shattered militia retreated late that afternoon, carrying off what few wounded they could.

As the battle raged late that morning, Herkimer's messengers finally made their way into the fort. Unaware of the battle taking place, Gansevoort realized that either Herkimer was awaiting a diversion in his favor so as to safely approach the fort or he was in trouble. Either way, action was needed, and he ordered his second in command, Lieutenant Colonel Marinus Willett, on a daring mission in the face of the besieging British.

With 250 New York and Massachusetts Continentals and a three-pounder gun, Willett set out from the fort that afternoon south along the Albany road and struck at the all-but-undefended KRRNY encampment located about a half mile south of the fort near the Mohawk River. The few royalist defenders were swept aside, and Willett "ordered his Men to take as much of the Baggage as they could, and destroy the rest, which they effectively did, each one carrying with him as much as they could." The nearby Haudenosaunee camp was also set upon and plundered. A company of the 34th Regiment and some KRRNY troops were brought up to cut off Willett's inevitable withdrawal but proved ineffective, the redcoats' and green coats' fire being "very wild, and though [the Americans] were very much exposed, did no execution at all."[22]

Willett returned to the fort that afternoon, not having lost a single man. Not only had his troops destroyed some of the enemy's camp, but they also took a trove of clothing, kettles, weapons, camp colours, baggage, money, Indian packs, trade silver, and paperwork (including Sir John Johnson's personal papers), as well as some prisoners. Also recovered were four scalps, two of which were identified as belonging to two girls killed on July 27, "being neatly Dressed and the Hair platted."[23] Importantly, the papers and prisoner testimony yielded accurate intelligence on St. Leger's numbers, forthcoming artillery train, and positions.[24]

Back on the Oriskany battlefield, Herkimer's casualties were astonishing. Although estimates vary considerably, most concur that his losses were between 450 and 500, with as many as 350 to 400 killed or mortally wounded! Most of the wounded were left in the field to die; some men were carried away, including Herkimer, who died at his home after an unsuccessful surgery ten days later.[25] Oneida losses are unknown, but at least half a dozen were killed or wounded. Sayenqueraghta's losses numbered about ninety-five killed or wounded. Of this number, sixty-five were Indians, including Sayenqueraghta's son, Tocenando.

The Battle of Oriskany had significant repercussions. Although all but victorious, most of St. Leger's Haudenosaunee allies were intent on avenging their losses. The nearby Oneida settlement of Oriska offered the perfect target and, although it was abandoned by the time St. Leger's allies arrived, they laid waste to the community. With so much of the Tryon County militia establishment gutted

Private, Battalion Company, King's Royal Regiment of New York

The core personnel of the royalist American regiment of Lieutenant-Colonel Sir John Johnson, Bt., came from New York's Mohawk Valley. In 1777 Canadian militia clothing stockpiles yielded green jackets with red facings for the battalion, as well as buff-colored, round-cut waistcoats and breeches, the latter being replaced with linen trousers for St. Leger's expedition. Round hats "well Cocked" completed the ensemble. Their meager eighteen-round-capacity cartridge boxes were further supplemented with powder horns and shot bags.

May 22, 1777, *Orderly Book of Sir John Johnson*, 39.

from the battle, one of its officers reported that they "cannot . . . raise another Force to make any Stand" against the enemy.[26] If any relief was to come to Fort Schuyler, it would have to be in the form of Continental Army soldiers from Schuyler's army in the Hudson River Valley.

On the day following the battle, St. Leger's artillery train finally arrived, the movement of which was delayed by felled trees obstructing Wood Creek previously dropped by Tryon County militia. Since the fort had to be conquered before he could unleash his might onto the Mohawk Valley, St. Leger's artillery was key to forcing the defenders to surrender. The problem was that the artillery he had consisted of anti-personnel artillery, not siege artillery. After the British fired some small shells at the fort that did no damage, a cease-fire was imposed and Gansevoort was again called to surrender his garrison. As presented to Gansevoort, St. Leger's outrageous threats of what would happen if the fort wasn't surrendered only betrayed the desperation of his position. One of the garrison's officers recorded the gist of the verbal message:

> [The] Message from Gen[l] St. Leger was that the Indians having lost some of their Chiefs in a Skirmish with our party that sally'd out on the 6th Ins[t] were Determined to go down the Mohawk River and Destroy the Women & Children, also that they wou'd kill every man in the Garrison when they got in, that Gen[l] St. Leger had held a Counsel with them for two Days in Order to prevent them, but all to no Purpose unless we woud Surrender. The General therefore As an Act of Humanity, and to Prevent the Effusion of Blood, Beg'd we wou'd deliver up the Fort and promised if we Did, not a Hair of our heads shoul'd be Hurt.[27]

After St. Leger codified the demand in writing, Gansevoort responded that it was his "determined resolution, with the forces under my command, to defend this fort at every hazard to the last extremity, in behalf of the United American States who have placed me here to defend it against all their enemies."[28] Thus, on August 9 the cease-fire ended and the artillery siege began, but not before Gansevoort had cleverly dispatched Willett and another officer on a secret mission to garner help.[29]

St. Leger's four little Coehorn mortars began their bombardment, hurling explosive iron shells at the fort.[30] For days both sides exchanged scattering small arms shot and artillery fire. The rate of fire was not ad nauseam, however. Gansevoort had no need to waste ammunition against an enemy capable of doing only little damage, and St. Leger had such a limited supply of artillery shot that he needed to conserve what little he had available in the face of a prolonged

Waist Belt Clasp, 34th Regiment of Foot
ca. 1775
Private collection
These regimentally marked brass clasps were used to close the buff leather waist belts issued to the regiment's battalion and grenadier company soldiers.

Private, Battalion Company, 34th Regiment of Foot
All British regiments in the Canada Army, including those not serving with Burgoyne, trimmed their old coats and cocked hats in spring 1777 according to pattern, such as seen here. Most regimental colonels provided decorative brass devices for their cartridge pouches, and although nonfunctional, these badges provided a source of pride for the men who wore them. Along with one-third of the British regiments in Canada, the 34th received new Pattern 1769 Short Land muskets (Irish) from Dublin Castle before embarking for the relief of Canada in 1776.

siege. Still, sporadic shots were exchanged during most days and nights. As for effectiveness, both sides missed their marks far more than they hit, although Hildebrandt sagaciously admitted that the "garrison's guns greet us often with better effect than the damage we cause them. It has happened several times that the defenders loudly scold and laugh at us. It is too bad that our artillery cannot strike or . . . hit the fort." This was, he suspected, owing to the poor locations of the artillery batteries and the angles of the intersecting fire being "computed very poorly."[31]

Of further annoyance to Hildebrandt was "that combustible material had been forgotten," thereby limiting the possibility of setting fire to the fort or the wooden buildings within. To offset this challenge, the British tried another tactic:

> All the Indians received orders to close in on the fort to the maximum extent possible in order to scorch and burn. And, were they able to get near enough to set the place on fire, they would receive a reward. . . . To this the . . . Indians gave a smart answer: if we [St. Leger's Artillerymen] can't do it with a big cannon, how can they do so with their small arms![32]

Gansevoort's men removed their provisions from the wooden barracks to the open parade ground "for fear of the Shells Setting Fire to the Barracks and thereby destroying it." Public papers and money were transferred to the bombproof, an impregnable chamber located within the fort's thickly walled southwest bastion. Belatedly, the British altered the course of Technohat Creek, the Americans' freshwater stream, thereby drying it out. "This wou'd have done us much Damage," reported one of the garrison's officers, "had we not been able to open two Wells in the Garrison, which with one We had already proved a Sufficient

European Magazine.

Engraved by P. Roberts, from a Miniature Painted by
R. Cosway Esq.r R.A.

Col.l S.t Leger

Col.l S.t Leger
by P. Roberts after Richard Cosway, R.A., 1795
The New York Public Library Digital Collections, 422579
Narratives covering Barry St. Leger's diversionary expedition usually include this portrait, or ones like it, to represent the British commander. However, the subject of this engraving is Barry's nephew, Colonel John Hayes St. Leger. A favorite of the Prince of Wales, John Hayes St. Leger benefited from the future king's largesse and sat for portraits by Sir Joshua Reynolds, Thomas Gainsborough, and, as seen here, Richard Cosway (in ca. 1782). Unfortunately, no authentic portrait of Barry St. Leger is known to exist.

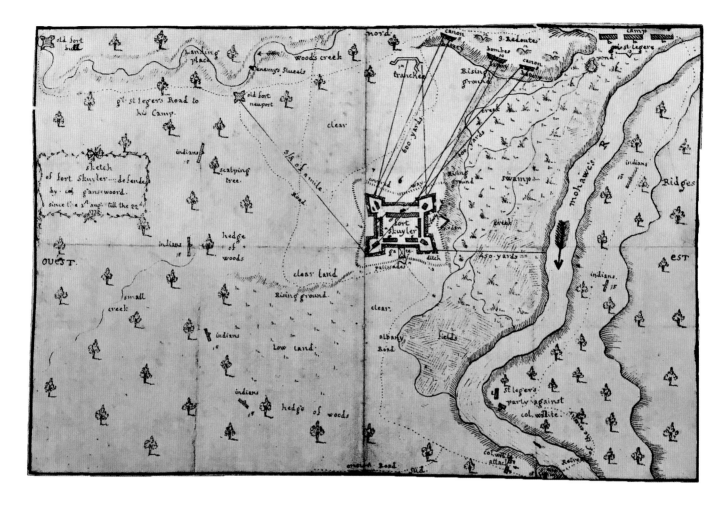

sketch of fort Skuyler . . . defended by col. Gansewoord. since the 1st aug. till the 22d 1777

by Lieutenant Colonel François-Louis Teissèdre de Fleury, ca. 1777

The New York Public Library, Emmet Collection

The very same continental divide (the Saint Lawrence River Divide) that forced portaging over the Great Carrying Place between Lake George and the Hudson River also made portaging necessary between Wood Creek and Fort Schuyler. Known as the Oneida Carry, this portage was the primary access point to the Mohawk River Valley from the west. Fort Schuyler (originally known as Fort Stanwix) was built to protect access to the Mohawk River; Fort Newport (seen northwest of Fort Schuyler), which lay in ruins in 1777, was one of a series of mid-1750s forts built to guard over Wood Creek. Note Technohat Creek, located between Fort Schuyler and the Mohawk River, which provided water for the garrison's sustenance until its flow was diverted by St. Leger's troops.

British Waist Belt Clasp

ca. 1770s

Fort Stanwix National Monument; photograph by Don Troiani
This unmarked clasp was recovered from the site of Fort Stanwix/Schuyler. Its form closely matches the type used by the British Third Regiment of Foot Guards—a regiment that did not serve in the Northern Campaign of 1777.

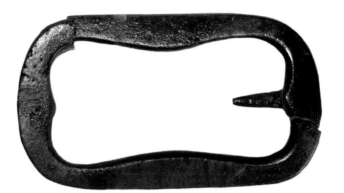

Supply."[33] Hildebrandt lamented that it was "a shame that so much time had been wasted in taking this measure."[34]

St. Leger was in a bind, and he knew it. With too few troops, a lack of siege artillery or incendiaries, and with his allied Indians displeased with the lack of competence and the lengthening duration of the siege, time was running short. He also received reliable intelligence that Gansevoort had sent for reinforcements. In order to fix his predicament, the British commander decided upon two new courses of action. First, he moved to garner support from New York royalists, for which purpose he sent Captain Walter Butler and a small party of royalist and British troops east into the Mohawk Valley.[35] Second, a new plan of attack against the fort was developed, consisting of the construction of a sap, a zigzagging series of interconnected trenches dug in the direction of the fort's northwest quarter. Not only could these trenches allow for a relatively safe approach to the fort, but the ultimate plan was to "run a Mine under their most formidable Bastion."[36]

Overconfidence

The Americans used to consider us invincible and did not believe they could capture our regular troops, but what will they now say about us!—will they keep on running away from us in the future?

—Surgeon's Mate Julius Wasmus, August 16, 1777[1]

While Schuyler successfully exchanged territory for time, Burgoyne's supply problem was acute due to the growing distance between his army and Lake Champlain. With the Army from Canada now anchored on the Hudson River, it was deemed that the best way forward was to immediately boost the number of provisions, wheeled carriages, and draft animals so that he could make up for lost time and make a final push to Albany, nearly fifty miles south.

The challenge was in acquiring these things quickly. Even though Burgoyne controlled the Great Carrying Place, the delay in getting everything necessary brought up from Lake Champlain was estimated at four weeks. A major cause of the delay was that most of the army's horses and wheeled carriages were brought from Canada up the Champlain Valley (south) by land, over "unbeaten roads—through mountains, woods and swamps, rivers, brooks, and lakes," for about 120 miles from St. Johns to Ticonderoga alone.[2] The original plan called for them to join the army as it besieged the Lake Champlain forts. But with St. Clair's

Hollow Silver "Egg"
ca. 1777

Fort Ticonderoga Museum collection, MC-119; photograph by Gavin Ashworth

Howe's July 17 note to Burgoyne received at Fort Edward on August 3 instructed the Army from Canada commander that once he took Albany, "the movements of the enemy will guide yours." The message was delivered by secret express, housed within a "small silver Egg and carried in the mans mouth," similar to this piece.

Napier, "Lord Francis Napier's Journal," 308.

unexpected evacuation, Burgoyne's s timetable was advanced in such a way that the Army from Canada's supply lines were incapable of catching up.

Serendipitously, Riedesel and Skene provided the answer: Their July operation in Vermont confirmed that it was all but abandoned of Revolutionary military activity and rife with food, livestock, and wheeled transport ripe for acquisition. The solution therefore was obvious, and based upon their recommendations, a detachment from the army would be sent into Vermont for the aforementioned purpose. Command of this expedition was settled upon Lieutenant-Colonel Friedrich Baum, commander of the Braunschweig Dragoon Regiment Prinz Ludwig. On August 9 Fraser's Advanced Corps and Baum's regiment marched eight miles south to seize the abandoned home of Senator William Duer in order to stage the forthcoming expedition.[3]

Baum's responsibilities were didactically laid out by Burgoyne in his "Instructions for Lieutenant Colonel Baume" and delivered to the German colonel on August 10 by Riedesel himself. The primary objectives of the expedition were to "try the affections of the country, to disconcert the councils of the enemy, to mount Reidesel's dragoons, to complete Peters's corps, and to obtain large supplies of cattle, horses, and carriages." Requisitioned cattle were to be sent to Burgoyne for slaughter; this was key to sustaining his army as it advanced on Albany simultaneously with Baum's foray. From Duer's estate, Baum was instructed to march south to Batten Kill and then cut east to Arlington, Vermont. From there he was to march northeast to Manchester then east, over the mountains, to Rockingham. From there Baum had to descend the Connecticut River Valley to Brattleboro and then immediately "return by the great road to Albany."[4] This was meant to be accomplished in two weeks.

The Braunschweig contingent of Baum's command consisted of the 230-man Dragoon Regiment. The only redcoat troops were the sixty men from Fraser's British Rangers. Superintendent John Campbell, with about 150 Seven Nations of Canada men and 60 Canadien volunteers, also attended. Over 150 men from the Queen's Loyal Rangers ("Peters's Corps") and a newly raised corps of American Volunteers went along to assist Baum with fatigue duties and to recruit from among the populace. The only Hessian contingent was twenty artillerymen operating two English light three-pounders configured as "grasshoppers."[5] Packhorses carrying bags of flour, along with oxen on the hoof, constituted the expedition's provisions, and carts carried the spare ammunition the soldiers could not. Language barriers were a potential problem. While many of the expedition's officers were multilingual, only a handful were capable of speaking any three of many the languages used—German, English, French, and Algonquian and Iroquoian dialects. Baum himself spoke only German. Inevitably, situations would

Private, Braunschweig Prinz Ludwig Dragoon Regiment

Named for Prinz Ludwig Ernst, a younger brother of the Herzog zu Braunschweig und Lüneburg (Duke of Brunswick and Lueneburg), this cavalry corps was trained and equipped to fight on foot. While their *Karabiner* (carbines) were modified to mount socket *Bajonette* (bayonets)—a necessary adaption for foot soldiers—they retained their long, brass-hilted *Pallasche* (broadswords). This *Gemeiner Dragoner* (dragoon private) has both a mustache and white shoulder aiguillette, marks of special distinction for the soldiers of this elite regiment.

arise in which three or even four languages would have to be used to translate a message from its source to the expedition's commander.

Baum's troops set out from Duer's house at noon on August 11 and moved south alongside the Hudson. They soon came to Batten Kill, where the men "had to walk up to their waists through the water, which was a most unpleasant and dangerous undertaking; for the current was so fast that one could hardly keep one's balance."[6] Once crossed, Baum's men bivouacked directly across from Saratoga and received a reinforcement of sixty Braunschweig light infantrymen and jäger. The next day, much to Baum's surprise, Burgoyne himself joined him and "talked a long time with . . . Baum, and returned to the army."[7]

Burgoyne ordered Baum to alter his route immediately and instead strike directly at the Continental Army supply depot located at Bennington, Vermont. The primary reason for the change was based upon a singular strategic consideration: Burgoyne received intelligence that the Northern Army was preparing to send troops to relieve Fort Schuyler. By sending Baum to southwestern Vermont instead of the northeast, he would still accomplish the original goal of garnering supplies and, by keeping closer to the Hudson Valley, prevent the Americans from "ventur[ing] to send the said corps against Lieutenant-Colonel St. Leger."[8] Ironically, it was Burgoyne who had to create a diversion to help St. Leger.

Baum set out for Bennington on the 13th, his snaking column taking the meandering road southeast to Cambridge, New York, located thirteen miles away. As he approached, Baum received word that nearly fifty cattle-guarding militia were located there, for which he sent thirty royalists and fifty Indians ahead to attack. The militia had advance warning of Baum's movements and most evacuated before Baum's men could arrive; only five who remained were captured. Baum's advance party continued another mile, where they "fell in with a party of fifteen men, who fired upon our people, and immediately took to the woods with the greatest precipitation," in which a soldier in Peters's Corps was wounded. Baum arrived in Cambridge at 4:00 p.m., where he learned from "the many people who came from

Braunschweig Cartridge Box, Prinz Ludwig Dragoon Regiment ca. 1770s

U.S. Army Center of Military History collection; photograph by Don Troiani
Trained to fight on both horse and foot, the Braunschweig dragoons were equipped with meager ten-round-capacity buff leather pouches. The narrow shoulder strap has two adjustments, allowing the trooper to wear it high when mounted and at hip level when on foot.

Bennington" that the Americans opposing him there numbered 1,800 troops. Writing to Burgoyne, Baum told the British general that he would "be particularly careful" on his approach to the Vermont town, located about eighteen miles southeast, and would continue to "be fully informed" of the Americans' numbers and location.[9] Captured cattle, wagons, and carts that fell into Baum's hands were sent back to Burgoyne according to plan.

Baum's little expeditionary force moved out early on August 14, taking the road to Bennington, which, due to the high hills southeast of Cambridge, delved directly south to the small community of St. Croix / San Coick (present-day North Hoosick, New York). Militia stationed there to watch over provisions and other stores located in a few mills withdrew east to Bennington upon Baum's approach, but in so doing "fired from the bushes" as they evacuated, wounding one Indian. The haul at St. Croix was impressive, amounting to "about 78 barrels of very fine flour, 1,000 bushels of wheat, 20 barrels of salt," and more.[10] A guard of thirty royalists were left to secure the spoils, while other royalists repaired the nearby bridge traversing Little White Creek.

Additional prisoners confirmed that up to 1,800 men were located at Bennington, but that they were "supposed to leave it"[11] on Baum's approach. With this intelligence, Baum confidently informed Burgoyne that he planned to attack them early on the 15th. Presumed royalists came to join Baum, seeking arms. Work on the bridge was complete by 9:00 a.m., and Baum set off east soon after. After marching about three miles, the British forces arrived at a bridge that crossed the Walloomsac River and made their bivouac there in the early afternoon. Baum was still in New York, but at seven miles distant, Bennington was within grasp.

Between evacuation of the Lake Champlain forts, roving British Rangers and Indians, the Battle of Hubbardton, and the presence of German detachments during the forepart of July, Vermont was in crisis. Apart from Warner's small regiment in Manchester, the Northern Army was in no position to support the nascent independent state, leaving open the "defenceless inhabitants of the frontier" to the enemy.[12] The new government's Council of Safety begged its neighbor, New Hampshire, for assistance.

On July 18 New Hampshire's legislature voted to draft a quarter of its militia from the 2nd Brigade and a quarter of the militia from three regiments of the 1st Brigade for "the Defence of this State & the Neighbouring States, to prevent the Encroachment & ravages of the Enimy thereinto."[13] With terms of service slated for two months, the whole was placed under the command of New Hampshire militia Brigadier General John Stark. Charlestown, New Hampshire, served as their staging point, and no time was wasted in sending small bodies of militia to Manchester as soon as they were outfitted.

Once in Manchester, Stark set out for Bennington with most of his brigade, arriving at the town on August 9. Days passed, and by the 13th Stark ordered his troops to join the Northern Army then at Stillwater. They had barely set off when reports were received that the enemy was in Cambridge. Lieutenant Colonel Gregg went with about 220 men to "make discoveries"[14]; his troops fired upon Baum's at St. Croix the following day.

After the St. Croix skirmish, Gregg withdrew and found that Stark was coming to his support. Defenses were erected over a mile east of the bridge where Baum's men were bivouacked, from whence Stark decided to mount an attack. Militia parties were sent out and an indecisive firefight ensued, but "the distance Being so far Did Little Execution."[15] After killing one Indian and wounding two others, the militia withdrew to their new defenses. Julius Wasmus, a German surgeon's mate who saw the fighting, noted with disdain that the militia would attack "either laying on the ground or standing behind trees, they load their guns and shoot. They run from one tree to another and then forward as circumstances demand."[16] They used houses and haystacks to shield themselves as well. As the attacks were dying down and the militia repulsed, an additional sixty-five Braunschweig grenadiers and musketeers joined the defenders.[17] That night, Baum's men "posted behind trees," but surprisingly, "no picket or even a guard had been posted" nor any sentinel to give warning in case of an attack.[18]

Thanks to a daylong torrential downpour, no fighting took place on the 15th apart from some morning skirmishing. But the rains didn't prevent the British and loyalists from building a series of fortifications to protect Baum's troops. The centerpiece of Baum's positions were two fortification lines built on the river's west side, which covered the bridge. Here the British Rangers, Braunschweig grenadiers, musketeers, jäger, and the two grasshopper guns were positioned, as was Baum with a cadre of his dragoons. Each grasshopper had three ammunition boxes containing a total of sixty rounds of ammunition, and two ammunition carts carried significantly more.

English Musket
ca. 1755–65
Don Troiani collection
English muskets built for commercial sale, such as this piece made by Richard Wilson, were imported to the American colonies before the outbreak of hostilities. As such, they were available for use by revolutionaries and royalists alike during the war. Note the American-made sheet-brass repair wrapped around the broken wrist.

British Light Three-Pounders 1776

Bennington Museum, A26

Saratoga National Historical Park, SARA 3725

The 1770s saw much design innovation in British and Irish light three-pounder technology. The most successful of these was invented by Royal Artillery Captain-Lieutenant William Congreve, whose streamlined, lightweight guns were cast at the Royal Brass Foundry in Woolwich. These guns were mounted on a pattern carriage capable of being pulled by one horse via a two-wheeled limber, disassembled and carried by men in pieces, or turned into a "grasshopper" by adding shafts capable of being pulled by one horse or a few men. Of the fifteen pieces brought with Burgoyne, nine were returned to Canada, two were captured in the Battle of Bennington (top), and four were surrendered at Saratoga (bottom).

On the other side of the river, the Indians and Canadien volunteers set up in houses located at the bridgehead. Also on the river's east side, precariously situated nearly 700 yards south-southeast of the bridge, was a fortification manned by the contingent's armed royalists. These volunteers had joined Peters's Corps or a brand-new unit, the American Volunteers, led by a prominent local man (and former British Army officer), Franz (Francis) Pfister.

Back on the river's west side, a large three-sided redan was built on top of a mountain located north-northwest of the bridge at the equally precarious distance of roughly 700 yards. Most of the dragoon regiment was posted here. The redan's open flank was covered by a small two-sided redan "built with big trees" on the hillside guarded by dragoons. The small Braunschweig light infantry detachment covered the wooded hillside as it sloped down to the river. Baggage, provisions, and the artillery and small arms ammunition carts, which held the balance of Baum's munitions, were tucked behind the foot of the mountain farthest from Stark's militia. While the German commander ordered the deployment of his troops, the British and royalist Americans built all fortifications, some of which were made of repurposed rail fencing, according to the dictates of the expedition's British engineer, Lieutenant Durnford.[19]

Americans flocked to Baum's camp, many swearing loyalty to the crown, and many with neither muskets nor ammunition asked to be armed. Otherwise indistinguishable from any opposing militia, those who swore oaths of allegiance were "given pieces of paper to stick in their hats" so that Baum's men "might recognize them in battle."[20] Baum received notice that Burgoyne had dispatched Lieutenant-Colonel Heinrich Breymann's Reserve Corps to join him at Walloomsac. Baum, abiding by the dictates of Burgoyne's didatic instructions, waited for the oncoming German relief in situ. Meanwhile, he never ventured forth up the hill or across the river to survey his disjointed defenses.

On August 16 Stark had perhaps 2,000 men under his command, including his New Hampshire Brigade, Vermont state troops and militia, a smattering of New York militia, and newly arrived militia from Berkshire County, Massachusetts. Determined to put an immediate end to Baum's incursion, Stark devised a brilliant multifold envelopment against the enemy positions. While engaging Baum's front with a diversionary force, Colonels Samuel Herrick and Moses Nichols, with 350 and 300 men respectively, would move to attack the wooded mountaintop defense.[21] Herrick was directed to attack from the west (achieved by a circuitous march around Baum's positions) and Nichols from the north. Simultaneously, 200 men commanded by Colonels David Hobart and Thomas Stickney would attack the royalist defense from the east and south.[22] The balance of the remaining militia, led by Stark himself, would hit Baum's center at the bridge after the flanking attacks developed. In order to best prepare for the hot oncoming fight, Stark's troops removed their coats or jackets and packs. Most soldiers were issued a small amount of rum mixed with water in order to sustain themselves for the oncoming fight, and many "chewed a bullet" to further stave off the day's thirst-inducing heat.[23]

While Stark's diversion successfully engaged Baum's bridge defenders, Herrick's and Nichols's troops meandered their way up the wooded slopes of the mountainous hill toward the German's two hilltop forts. At about 3:00 p.m.,

Bennington Drum
second half, 18th century
Massachusetts State Archives; photograph by Don Troiani
This maple drum has a provenance of having been used in the Battle of Bennington, although the painted name and date were added long after the battle. Militia companies, such as those that served at Bennington, typically included drummers and/or fifers.

The Battle of Bennington, August 16

Depicted here is the moment when Lieutenant Colonel Samuel Herrick's Vermont rangers and New England militia attacked the three-sided hilltop redan defended by men of the Braunschweig Prinz Ludwig Dragoon Regiment. Rittmeister (Captain-of-Cavalry) Carl von Reinking, seen on the left with *Pallasch* (broadsword) in hand, urges his men to hold their ground; he was "shot dead"* in the fight. As with the German soldiers defending the fort, the single British light three-pounder ran out of ammunition. "The day was very warm," recalled a Vermont militiaman. The Germans "were in full dress . . . and we in our shirts and trousers, and without our knap sacks, and thus had greatly the advantage."**

*Wasmus, *Eyewitness Account*, 73.

**Jesse Field, in *Gabriel, Battle of Bennington*, 52.

they attacked. The Americans "pressed forward & as the Hessians [Braunschweigers] rose above their works to fire we discharged our pieces at them," recalled a soldier with Herrick's attack force.[24] Wasmus noted in horror that the dragoons "fired up volleys on the enemy . . . and it did not take them long to load their carbines behind the breastworks. But as soon as they rose up to take aim, bullets went through their heads." One of the light three-pounder grasshoppers, pulled up the hill at the last minute and placed in the larger hilltop fort, shot cannonballs and case shot "into the brush," but was soon silenced after the Hessians manning it were killed or wounded.[25] The German dragoons fired slowly, only once "every half minute," in order to conserve the scant number of cartridges they had on hand, but this was not enough.[26] Then came the charge, as waves of militia surged forth from the woods to attack the shabby, open log defenses. The German defenders resorted to the bayonet; one Massachusetts militiaman later recalled that while he was "scaling of the brest work of the Enemy" on the hilltop with Herrick's column, he

> [p]ut his right hand upon the top of the breast work & threw his feet over but his right leg was met by a . . . Bayonet which held it fast and he piched head first into the Entrenchment and the [German] soldier hit him a thump upon the head but he was dispatched by the next man that came up & . . . [he] was thereby relieved and in the heat of feeling forgot his wounds.[27]

Braunschweig Belt
ca. 1770s
Massachusetts State Archives;
photograph by Don Troiani
This whitened buff leather Braunschweig Dragoon's waist belt was captured in the Battle of Bennington.

All this was too much for the Germans. Outnumbered nearly ten to one, out-flanked, and having expended their paltry ammunition—the dragoons' cartridge boxes held ten rounds—the Germans broke in a panic, rushing downhill in various directions through the woods, with the rangers and militia in pursuit.[28] After he "stormed the breastwork," Vermont militia Lieutenant Joseph Rudd

> snapped his gun at a stout built Hessian [Braunschweiger], and
> that from some cause, and for the first time on that day his gun
> missed fire, that he pursued to grapple with the Hessian to take
> him prisoner. The Hessian turned and raised his piece to fire, but
> Mr. Rudd said he was so near to him that by a spring and quick
> effort he knocked the Hessian's gun up, and he grappled with him
> drew the Hessian's sword instead of his own, and gave the Hessian
> a severe blow on his neck as he broke from him and turned to run.
> And that Mr. Herrick struck the hessian with the but of his gun and
> killed him.[29]

One of the last to attempt an escape from the death trap, Wasmus, who was busy tending to the wounded, took off after the fleeing Germans. But he didn't get far before he "stumbled over a big, fallen tree," behind which he scrambled to avoid the bullets "whistling over and beyond" his head. Before Wasmus knew

Braunschweig Broadsword
ca. 1770s
Massachusetts State Archives; photograph by Don Troiani
Following the Battle of Bennington, General Stark gifted captured Braunschweig weapons and accoutrements to the states of New Hampshire, Vermont, and Massachusetts as thanks for providing military support. Among the pieces sent to the latter was a "Hessian . . . broad sword," the very weapon seen here. Stark, like most Americans, was unconcerned with the Germanic origins of these trophies—they were Braunschweig, not Hessian. The Massachusetts General Assembly acknowledged receiving Stark's "acceptable present,—the tokens of victory at the memorable battle of Bennington." Still extant with this *Pallasch* (broadsword) is its original buff leather belt and iron-mounted, tanned-leather-covered wooden scabbard.
Powell to Stark, December 12, 1777, in Sparks, *Library of American Biography*, vol. 1, 94.

Private, Lieutenant Colonel Samuel Herrick's Regiment of Vermont Rangers

Although New York State still claimed authority over the New Hampshire Grants, Vermont's 1777 declaration of statehood effectively eliminated the former's authority over the territory. Anticipating the sweltering heat in the forthcoming August 16 Battle of Bennington, Stark's militia and rangers were instructed to remove their coats and jackets. Most fought with nothing on "but shirts, vests and long linen trousers, which reached down to their shoes; no stockings; a powder horn, a bullet bag, a flask [canteen] with rum and a gun—that was all they had on them."

Wasmus, *Eyewitness Account*, 72.

it, he was surrounded, upon which one American soldier "placed the bayonet of his gun with tightened trigger" on his chest. The soldier then asked Wasmus if he was "a Britisher or a Hessian":

> I told him I was a Braunschweig surgeon, shook hands with
> him, and called him my friend and brother; for what does one not
> do when in trouble. I was happy they understood me (*Freund und
> Bruder*) for that helped so much that he withdrew his gun. But he
> now took my watch, looked at it, held it to his ear and put it away [in
> his pocket]. After this, he made a friendly face and was so human
> that he urged me to take a drink from his wooden flask. He handed
> me over to his comrades, who started anew to search my pockets.
> One of them took nothing but my purse in which, however, were
> only 14 piasters (specie). He continued eagerly looking for money
> but then left, whereupon the third began searching my pockets. This
> one took all my small items [such] as my knife, my paper, my lighter,
> but he did not find the best; they were so dumb that they did not see
> the pocket in my coat. Thus, I saved my Noble pipe.[30]

Before the battle began, Stickney and Hobart positioned their troops opposite the royalist defensive line located on the other side of the river. The approach was easy; with neither hill nor river to traverse, the New Hampshire and Massachusetts militia formed about 300 yards in front of the fort, screened by "trees and corn intervening, which prevented our seeing each other."[31] From there, recalled Private Benjamin Bean, they

> crawled up as near their breast-works as we could without being
> discovered & there waited until the north wing [staging to attack the
> Germans on the hilltop] began the fire—our officers then said now
> my Boys is our time. [E]very man ran as fast as he can and made all
> the noise he can—we ran up within . . . shot of their Breast works &
> they then fired upon us.[32]

Lieutenant John Orr also recalled the noisy attack against the front of the royalist fort:

> We arose and with shouts marched rapidly to the attack. In the
> meantime, I remembered the fate of Col. Hale, who, about two
> months before [at Hubbardton], was overtaken in his retreat from

Private, Queen's Loyal Rangers ("Peters's Corps")

One of the nascent corps raised by refugee Americans in Canada, the Queen's Loyal Rangers and other royalist units formed part of Burgoyne's army with the intent of filling their ranks. Initially, royalist recruits received suits of clothing which included uniforms of "very common Red Stuff turn'd up with Green,"* stands of arms, and other necessaries. Many were never issued muskets, however, and fewer drew uniforms, in lieu of which they were "told to wear *White Papers* in their Hats,"** so as to be distinguishable from their Revolutionary counterparts.

*Gray to Carleton, January 11, 1777, British Library, Add. Mss. 21,818.

**Hadden, *Hadden's Journal and Orderly Books*, 132.

Ticonderoga, by the enemy, skulking in the beginning of the action
. . . and was degraded. Resolving that no one should have cause to
impeach me with cowardice, I marched on with the appearance
of a brave soldier. When we had passed through the wood and
cornfield, we came in sight of the enemy, at about fifteen rods [80
yards] distance. They commenced firing with muskets, at an alarm-
ing rate, so that it seemed wonderful that any of the attacking party
should escape.[33]

Orr escaped, but only just. Shot by one of the fort's defenders, he lay on the
ground until two men tried to carry him off to safety. But "the balls flew directly
at us," and the men had to "stoop so low" and drag the lieutenant on his back to
the cornfield, where he could rest "out of sight of the enemy."[34]

While the royalists held off the attack along their front, Massachusetts militia
suddenly appeared from behind. Colonel Joab Stafford, who commanded this surprise attack, had concealed his approach by marching his men along the low-lying
riverbank, spilling out directly behind the royalist position, which was located atop
a small eminence. One royalist soldier in Peters's Corps recalled that

the first we saw of the [militia] party coming to attack us they
made their appearance right under our guns. . . . I was standing at
the wall with my gun loaded in my hand, and several of us levelled
our pieces at once. I took as fair aim at them as ever I did at a bird in
my life, and thought I was sure of them although we had to point so
much downward [at Stafford's militia rushing up the eminence from
the riverbank] that it made a man a small mark. . . . [The militia] all
came jumping in upon us with such a noise that we thought of nothing but getting out of the way of their muskets as fast as possible, and
we scattered in all directions.[35]

As the royalists ran off, many threw down their arms to lighten their flight.
Peters, stabbed by a militiaman's bayonet in his ribs, escaped but barely. Pfister
lay mortally wounded.

Earlier in the day, when Stark's militia were in process of deploying for battle,
the Indians and Canadien volunteers recognized the movements for what they
were: The Revolutionaries were positioning to attack. The Chevalier de Lorimier
led his men and the Indians to "some high ground" from whence they hoped to
rout the militia before their attacks could manifest. The plan fell apart quickly,
however; their advance scouts were killed, and the Indians and Canadien volunteers fell back to the supposed safety of the dragoons' fortified hilltop. By this

time, the American attacks began in force. The Chevalier attempted to lead a counterattack, but instead

> fell into a fairly deep valley where I found myself face to face with the left-hand column of the enemy. I gave the war cry and we fired, but we got a volley in return from the American rear column that had come up to join the column on the left. Fortunately for us, the enemy wavered and in their confusion began firing at each other. Their fire went over our heads, but we were hemmed in on all sides and couldn't make our way back to our camp.[36]

Stark made his major push against the center at the bridge with perhaps 1,000 militia. Most soldiers guarding the position quickly burned through their ammunition, and the grasshopper that covered the bridge proved ineffective against Stark's approach. The Germans and British, including Baum himself, fled, mixing in with the torrent of Germans streaming down the hillside. At this point, with his dragoons' ammunition expended, Baum ordered his unmounted cavalrymen to "hang the guns over their shoulders and draw their swords," in order to hack their way through the militia.[37] This melee tactic didn't last long, and Baum and most of his men were forced through the open farm field southwest of the bridge. Forced against the river, and with Baum mortally wounded, the survivors surrendered. As with other prisoners taken into custody, Baum's possessions were plundered from his person; one Vermont militiaman recalled taking some of Burgoyne's "pompous proclamations out of Col. Baum's pocket as he lay on the field of battle."[38]

British Saber
third quarter, 18th century
Bennington Museum, A435a,b

Although this sword is traditionally identified as having been taken from Lieutenant-Colonel Friedrich Baum, its form and metallurgy reflect its British origins and usage. It was more likely owned by Franz (Francis) Pfister, a Braunschweiger who served as a subaltern officer in the British 60th (Royal American) Regiment of Foot, 1758–72. Living in Albany County's Hoosick District in 1777, he commanded a royalist corps in the Battle of Bennington. Baum and Pfister were both mortally wounded in the fighting, and as recognized leaders, they were taken to a nearby home, where they died soon after.

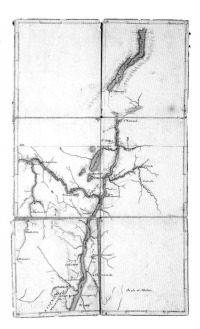

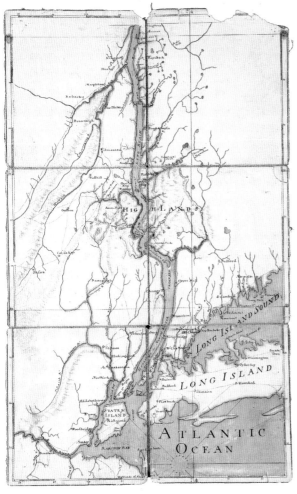

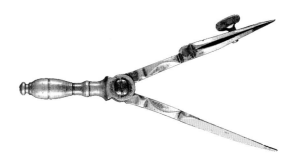

Map from New York to St John's
third quarter, 18th century
courtesy Morphy Auctions

These three maps, covering New York's eastern waterways extending from St. Johns, Canada, to Sandy Hook, New Jersey, were taken from Franz (Francis) Pfister's possessions in the aftermath of the Battle of Bennington. While serving as an infantry officer in the British Army from 1758 to 1772, Pfister became an assistant engineer tasked with surveying, drawing maps, and improving Forts Niagara, Ontario, and Stanwix. Large maps like these were often subdivided into smaller sheets and mounted to linen, allowing them to be folded and housed in cases such as the one these came in. Also taken was Pfister's brass drawing compass, an essential mapmaking tool.

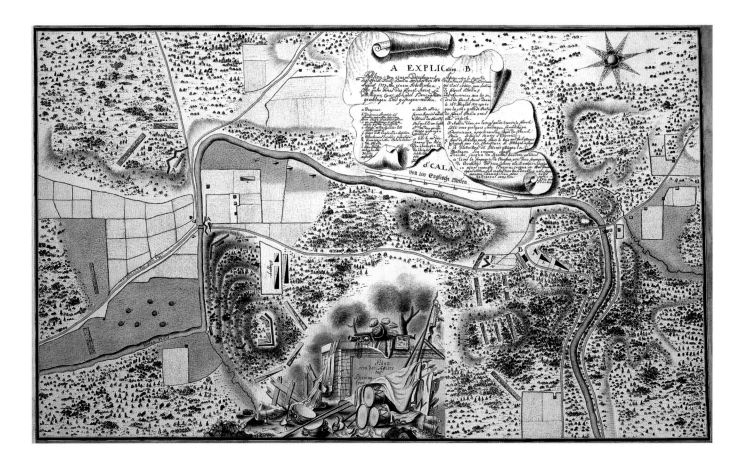

Plan von der Affaire beÿ Benning. town.

by "Vetter," n.d.

after Second-Lieutenant Johann Michael Bach, ca. 1778

Hessisches Staatsarchiv Marburg, WHK 29/54

Despite what's shown on the compass rose, this map is oriented with north on the bottom and east, the direction of Bennington, to the left. Baum's poorly fortified, disparate positions at the bridge, the high hill, and across the Walloomsac River are depicted (A), as is the baggage and ammunition park located at the base of the hill. Revolutionary and royalist Americans alike are represented by mottled-colored rectangles, reflecting their nonuniform appearance (excepting some of Peters's Corps). Note the large circles located in the open field northeast of Baum's bridge position—these represent the enormous haystacks used by Stark's militia for cover. Also depicted on the map is the battle's second phase, fought to the west (B). This highly stylized map was copied from one drawn by Lieutenant Johann Bach, who commanded the twenty-man detachment of Hessian artillerymen and the two new British light three-pounder "grasshoppers" in the first phase of the battle.

Brunswick Broadswords at Bennington, August 16

It didn't take long for Stark's militia and rangers to overwhelm Baum's positions and rout the defenders. Here, a wounded drummer beats to rally as many of the couple hundred fleeing German soldiers as possible. With their scanty ammunition expended and the militia coming on fast, Baum, *Pallasch* (broadsword) in hand, orders his dragoons "to hang the guns over their shoulders and draw their swords" in order to "hew a path" to escape. With panic-stricken dragoons and musketeers tumbling down the hill behind them, Baum and his men were soon chased by Stark's militia across open fields toward the Walloomsac River. It was there that Baum fell, mortally wounded. The survivors surrendered.

Cleve, *Journal of the Brunswick Troops*, HZ 270.

Braunschweig Broadswords
ca. 1770s

Don Troiani collection

These Braunschweig *Pallasche* (broadswords) were used by members of the Prinz Ludwig Dragoon Regiment. On the left is the *Pallasch* of a *Gemeiner* (private), with its heavy cast-brass hilt that includes the requisite ducal coronet and C monogram for Herzog (Duke) Carl I. On the right is a *Pallasch* for a commissioned *Offizier* (officer), which includes a lighter, more open-worked gilt-brass hilt, the coronet of which has been clipped. Captured from Baum's *Dragoner* (dragoons), these *Pallasche* were afterward issued to American cavalrymen. The blades alone are over thirty-six inches long.

Braunschweig Grenadier Cap, Regiment Specht
ca. 1770s

Massachusetts State Archives;
photographs by Don Troiani

Following the Battle of Bennington, Stark gifted trophies, including a Braunschweig "Grenadier's cap, taken on the memorable 16th of August," to the states of Vermont, New Hampshire, and Massachusetts. Only Massachusetts's cap is known to survive. This brass, die-struck *Grenadiermüze* (grenadier cap) is embellished with Herzog zu Braunschweig und Lüneburg (Duke of Brunswick and Lueneburg) Carl I's coronet, inverted C monogram, horse of Haus Hannover (House of Hanover), and motto, *Nunquam retrorsum*. The extant, white-trimmed red cloth cap is missing its three decorative brass flaming bombs, although ghosting on the cloth shows where they were originally located. The cap's pompom is also missing.

Stark to Massachusetts General Assembly, September 15, 1777, in Sparks, *Library of American Biography*, vol. 1, 93–94.

While Baum's troops fought for their lives, Burgoyne's army proceeded as planned. Fraser's Advanced Corps marched to Batten Kill on the 13th and crossed to the west side of the Hudson River the following day via a bridge of boats the British assembled, taking post at Saratoga. The wooden, two-story barrack buildings provided lodging for the conquering redcoats. Although Burgoyne sent Breymann's Reserve Corps to assist Baum on the morning of the 15th, this was only done as a measure of insurance. Baum had thus far repulsed all attacks against him, and with Baum and Breymann joined at Walloomsac, the Americans would certainly disperse ahead of the joint task force's march to Bennington. Therefore, with Baum bolstered, Burgoyne ordered the remainder of the Army from Canada to "make the crossing over the Hudson" at 6:00 a.m. on August 17.[39]

Breymann set out at 9:00 a.m. on the 15th and began the twenty-four-mile trek to Walloomsac. With him was his Reserve Corps, 670 officers and men consisting of the Grenadierbattaillon Breymann, the Leichtes Infanterie Battalion von Bärner, and two British light six-pounders manned by Hessen-Hanau artillerymen. Unlike Baum's dragoons who carried ten rounds per man, most of Breymann's soldiers had cartridge pouches containing forty rounds of ammunition; additional ammunition was housed in boxes placed on carts that accompanied them.

Problems began as soon as the column set off. Breymann was "detained a considerable time" by fording Batten Kill. What's more, the "number of hills, excessive bad Roads, and a continued Rain"[40] slowed his march to a crawl. The cannons and carts were dragged in tandem because the roads were too narrow to move anything side by side. An artillery cart spilled over, further delaying the advance.[41] Breymann's guide "lost his way," and it took time to find another. After a pileup of delays, the Reserve Corps reached St. Croix at about 4:30 p.m. . . . on August 16.[42]

Had Breymann been able to cover the twenty-four-mile distance in anything less than the nearly thirty-two hours that it took him, he might have been able to save Baum from disaster. That the very same commander who was unable to bring the German relief force to assist Fraser and Riedesel at Hubbardton in a timely manner was sent to help Baum is baffling. In the case of the former, Breymann's inability

Braunschweig Grenadier Company Cartridge Pouch ca. 1770s

New Hampshire Historical Society, 1974.501

This Braunschweig *Patronentasche* (cartridge pouch) is mounted with a large cast-brass ornament bearing the ducal coronet and *C* monogram of Carl I, the Herzog zu Braunschweig und Lüneburg (Duke of Brunswick and Lueneburg), as well as the horse of Haus Hannover (House of Hanover). Only one of the four decorative flaming bombs is still attached.

Private, Grenadier Company, Braunschweig Infantry Regiment von Riedesel

German grenadiers were the elite soldiers of German infantry regiments, easily identified by such distinctive features as *Grenadiermüzen* (grenadier caps), grenade-decorated *Patronentaschen* (cartridge pouches), and moustaches. In Burgoyne's army, Braunschweig grenadier companies from the Regiments Prinz Friedrich, von Riedesel, von Rhetz, and Specht were consolidated into the Grenadierbattaillon Breymann. This *Gemeiner Grenadier* (grenadier private) is dressed in marching order, with a *Tornister* (knapsack), *Feldflasche* (canteen), and *Brotbeutel* (haversack), which carried rations.

to move his Germans in a timely manner was rendered effectively moot due to the British forces' victory. The situation facing Breymann when he arrived at St. Croix was quite different: Stark's battle against Baum, three miles to the east, was all but over.

The few survivors of Baum's expeditionary force—particularly the Indians and Canadien volunteers who were able to escape the envelopment—fled toward Breymann's Reserve Corps at St. Croix. After being updated on the situation, Breymann immediately set off down the road toward Baum's position.[43] The Reserve Corps marched barely half a mile before encountering armed men approaching them on the wooded hills to the left of the road. Philip Skene, who survived Baum's fate and escaped to join Breymann, called out to them to identify themselves—royalist or Revolutionary. They responded "with no other answer than a discharge of fire-arms."[44]

Leaving their two light six-pounders on the road, the Germans lightened their load by dumping their *Tornister* (knapsacks) and *Brotbeutel* (haversacks) and immediately fanned out, with the light infantry to the high ground on the left and grenadiers and jäger on the plain to the right. The Chevalier de Lorimier proceeded ahead with his Indians and Canadien volunteers, skirting the mountainous hills to the left of the road, where, after climbing a high crag, they encountered armed men with white papers in their hats. Thinking they should be royalists, the Chevalier sought confirmation. "Friends" was the reply, upon which the soldiers started to shoot at the Indians and Canadien volunteers, who fled, enraged by the apparent betrayal.[45]

The main body of militia facing Breymann "at first withdrew" soon after their initial volley, which had the effect of instigating the Germans to push farther up the road.[46] The militia "kept up a constant fire generally from behind trees. The road appeared full of men, and it was like firing into a flock of sheep. The enemy [Germans] kept firing upon us, but we were greatly protected by the trees."[47] Breymann's Braunschweigers began outflanking the pressed militia, and the two light six-pounders easily kept the tired militia away. Here, the effectiveness of artillery shot was demonstrated by the fact that their projectiles didn't have to hit their targets directly in order to maim or kill. Private Daniel Gale, a New Hampshire militiaman, was a victim of such ancillary damage, when he was hit "between the Arch and Knee by a cannon ball passing through a hedge and throwing a cleft or splinter of wood which struck" his leg.[48]

Then, as if on cue, Colonel Warner's Continental Regiment appeared on the field. There they "opened right and left . . . and half of them attacked each flank of the enemy, and beat back those who were just closing around" the militia.[49]

Braunschweig Musket (details) third quarter, 18th century

Massachusetts State Archives; photographs by Don Troiani

Stark sent trophies to the states of New Hampshire, Vermont, and Massachusetts "taken from the enemy, in the memorable battle, fought at Wallomsac, on the 16th of August last." Among the prizes doled out to each state was "one Hessian gun and bayonet"; this is the Braunschweig *Muskete* (musket) gifted to Massachusetts in honor of its people's help in fighting the battle. Weighing eleven pounds, this musket has a .75 caliber and a barrel measuring over forty-one inches long.

Stark to Massachusetts General Assembly, September 15, 1777, in Sparks, *Library of American Biography*, vol. 1, 93–94.

Warner's attack was decisive and inspired many militia, albeit exhausted from the day's fighting, to join in. The Americans "ran towards the Enemy" and

> some with & some without bayonets followed suit & rushed upon the Enemy with all their might who seeing us coming took to their heels and were completely routed, as we came up to the Enemys line their field piece being charged a sergeant Luttendon knocked down the man with the port fire and caught hold of the Limber and whirled about the piece and fired it at the Enemy and the blaze overtook them before they had got ten rods [55 yards] and mowed down a large number of them.[50]

Braunschweig Bayonet
third quarter, 18th century

Massachusetts State Archives;
photograph by Don Troiani

Among the items taken in the Battle of Bennington was this Braunschweig *Bajonett* (bayonet), which, along with its matching musket, was given to the state of Massachusetts by General Stark. The blade is over thirteen inches long.

Braunschweig Brass Drum
ca. 1770s

New Hampshire Historical Society, 1966.544.01

This is the "brass-barrelled drum" that Stark gifted to New Hampshire in honor of his state's participation "in the memorable battle, fought at Wallomsac, on the 16th of August last." The Braunschweig *Trommel* (drum) has brass hoops instead of the usual wooden ones, suggesting it belonged to the Prinz Ludwig Dragoon Regiment.

Braunschweig Drum
ca. 1770s
Massachusetts State Archives; photograph by
Don Troiani
Taken in the Battle of Bennington, this brass Braunschweig *Trommel* (drum) was given by General Stark to the state of Massachusetts as a gift. It retains its original buff leather shoulder belt edged with regimental drummer's tape and brass scallop-shaped hook guard. The painted red and dark blue decoration on the wooden rims indicates it may have belonged to the Regiment Specht, the grenadier company of which fought in the battle. As with most militaria from the *Herzogtum* (duchy), this *Trommel* includes the ducal coronet and inverted *C* monogram of Carl I, the Herzog zu Braunschweig und Lüneburg (Duke of Brunswick and Lueneburg).

Isolated, with darkening skies signaling dusk, ammunition expended, artillery horses killed, cannons lost, and high casualties, Breymann, who was wounded, ordered a retreat. The Germans were not pursued.

Casualty returns from the Battle of Bennington were astonishing. Combined, Baum and Breymann lost over 900 officers and soldiers, of which about 670 were in American captivity.[51] Stark took a boon of war matériel, including Breymann's two light six-pounders, Baum's two light three-pounders, nearly 1,000 muskets and rifles, about 900 swords, accoutrements, and a great deal of camp equipage, including knapsacks. Stark's casualties were less than 100 killed and wounded. Beyond the obvious one-sided tactical victory, the battle's strategic ramifications were similarly astounding. News of Baum's and Breymann's losses forced Burgoyne to recall his forces from Saratoga and reverse plans to cross with the rest of the army on the 17th. In order to proceed to Albany, the Army from Canada was now forced to wait upon the lengthy supply train to the north, the very thing Burgoyne hoped to avoid. Of all the advantages gained from the battle, this gave the United States the one thing needed beyond anything else—time.

Routed

The chiefs desire the commanding officers of Fort Schuyler to exert them-selves in their defence—not make a Ticonderoga of it; but they hope you will be courageous.

—Thomas Spencer, July 29, 1777[1]

Victory in the Battle of Bennington was not the only good news heralded in the Northern Department in August.

With American forces in the department focused on Burgoyne and St. Leger, pockets of royalist Americans became emboldened enough to take up arms. Led by local leaders, hundreds began forming numerous small parties and companies within the rural reaches south and west of Albany. Most risings formed in expectation of St. Leger's anticipated, triumphant advance through the Mohawk Valley, and some marched off and joined St. Leger besieging Fort Schuyler. Some remained at home in order to garner support from other, like-minded Americans. Members of one such group, collecting around a farm in Hellebergh (present-day Guilderland, New York) about nine miles west of Albany, were captured or dispersed on August 12 by a task force of forty Massachusetts Continentals and sixty Albany County militia in a skirmish known as the Battle of Normanskill.[2]

The Schoharie Valley, located over forty miles from Albany and over seventy-five miles from Fort Schuyler, was the hotbed of these loyalist risings. Local leaders such as John McDonell, George Mann, and Adam Crysler were able to form upward of 150 men in the name of the crown. Their growing numbers empowered them to fan out through the valley and monitor the comings and goings of known Revolutionaries. They began to plunder and burn homes. The local Albany County militia commander, Colonel Peter Vroman, was able to gather only about twenty-five men, who barricaded themselves in a stone home, christened Fort Defyance, and await assistance.[3]

An ad hoc contingent under the direction of Colonel John Harper formed in Albany for their relief.[4] Consisting of "a small party" of Captain Jean Louis de Vernejoux's troop of the 2nd Regiment of Light Dragoons and "six French Men" hired at Harper's expense, they set out on horseback and quickly arrived in the valley.[5] They easily routed Mann's men, but Harper was unable "to inlist aney

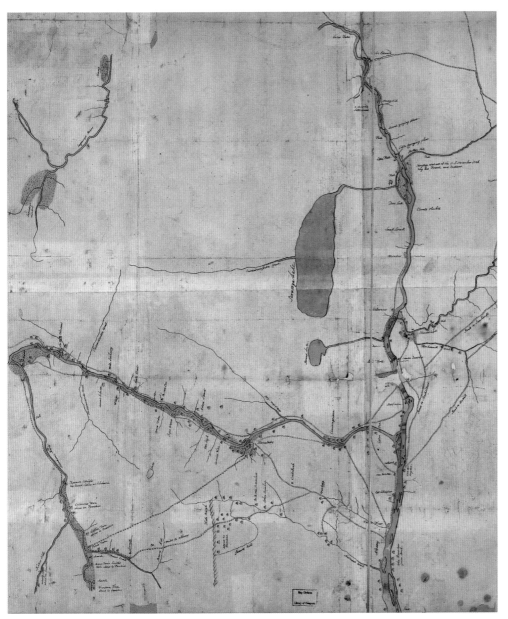

Map of the Northern Part of New York (detail)

by artist unknown, ca. 1758

The Library of Congress, 73691805

Drawn nearly twenty years before the Northern Campaign of 1777, this map depicts principal lakes, waterways, roads, and settlements along the upper Hudson River and the eastern third of the Mohawk River. Schoharie "River" (Creek) is depicted on the left, the outlet of which is located at Fort Hunter, which was then a Mohawk Nation settlement. "Kobes Kill" (present-day Cobleskill Creek) and Foxes Creek, tributaries of Schoharie Creek, are also shown. The Schoharie Risings occurred in Albany County's Schoharie District and were centered on the valley's many small communities, including Foxes Town (where George Mann resided), Smith's Town and Fountain Town (present-day Village of Schoharie), and Weiser's Town (present-day Middleburgh; this was located farther up Schoharie Creek). To the east the Battle of Normanskill was fought on a farm located along the road between Foxes Creek and Albany near the headwaters of Normans Creek, a tributary of the Hudson River south of Albany.

Squadron Colour, 2nd Regiment of Light Dragoons

ca. 1777

National Museum of American History, Division of Armed Forces History, 73540M

One troop of this regiment was with Gates's Northern Army, commanded by Lieutenant Thomas Young Seymour; the captain, Jean Louis de Vernejoux, deserted after the Battle of the Flockey for fear of being arrested and court-martialed on an unrelated matter. This pink (faded to cream) taffeta colour would have been carried by a squadron cornet. With the Continental stripes in the canton, the regimental device—a painted winged globe engulfed in a thunderstorm, with lightning bolts arcing above and below—surmounts a banner with the regimental motto, *Pata concita fulmnt nati.*

Considrabell number of [militia] men; and thos that Did ingage ware So Scatred" that he was unable to "Colect them as they had to go hom for their Nesacarys."[6]

De Vernejoux's cavalry pressed forward in search of the larger body of royalists and fell upon them near Crysler's farm (at present-day Fultonham, New York) on the 13th. The Battle of the Flockey was brief; de Vernejoux's troop suffered a few casualties and the royalists retreated through the wetlands and woods, which saved them from immediate pursuit.[7] Subsequent attempts to find them failed, and the remaining well-hidden royalists, about sixty in number, headed northwest to Fort Oswego.

These royalist risings constituted the sort of unsupported, local initiatives that rarely manifested in the north during the war. While they were put down with minimum force and effort, they nevertheless constituted growing, tangible threats to Revolutionary leadership. Despite this, neither state nor army leadership were poised to respond to the largest of these, which was only crushed by Harper's efforts. If left unchecked, growing royalist support could have dominated these rural local communities so completely that they could have constituted very serious threats behind the lines, particularly in the face of British military onslaught.

While there would be no more risings of substance, the concern over more of them incapacitated Schoharie Valley Revolutionaries for the remainder of the

American Horseman's Saber, Scabbard, and Belt
ca. 1770s
Don Troiani collection
This simple brass-mounted saber includes a turned-cherry grip. The scabbard, which includes an embossed wave motif, is still seated in its original whitened buff leather shoulder belt.

American Powder Horn
ca. 1758–70
Don Troiani collection
This carved powder horn is decorated with extensive mapping showing important place-names of the province of New York, particularly throughout the colony's Mohawk Valley. Seen from east to west are Albany, "Chinakety" (Schenectady), and Forts Hunter, Hendrick, "Halkiman" (Herkimer), Schuyler, and Stanwix. This Fort Schuyler, located about fifteen miles east of Fort Stanwix (named Fort Schuyler in 1776), was a French and Indian War fort that lay in ruins during the American War for Independence. The abandoned fort was unceremoniously renamed "Fort Desolation" during the war in order to differentiate it from Fort Schuyler (Stanwix).

campaign season. A week after the Flockey skirmish, a frustrated Vromen made an official complaint to the state, claiming that

> one half of this valuable settlement lyes in ruin & dselution, our Houses plundered, our Cattle destroyed & our well affected in Habitants taken prisoners and sworn not to . . . take up arms against the King of Great Britain or his adherents . . . and our whole Harvest (the best in the memory of Man) lyeing rotting in the Fields, and we see nothing but utter distruction before us.[8]

When the risings where at their peak, Schuyler was facing a major conundrum. His primary focus was on Burgoyne's invasion from the north, but the ever-present threat of St. Leger's from the west could no longer be ignored. Upon the unanimous advice of his generals, on August 12 Schuyler ordered Brigadier General Ebenezer Learned's Brigade at Stillwater, numbering about 950 troops and two artillery pieces, to march to Fort Schuyler and lift the siege.[9] Arnold offered to take personal command of the relief force, which Schuyler happily accepted "with great satisfaction."[10]

The Continental troops reached Fort Dayton on the 17th, but in an uncharacteristically cautious move, Arnold judiciously remained stationary in order to gather intelligence on the situation to the west. He would not make the same fatal mistake Herkimer had only two weeks earlier. On the 21st Arnold reported that

> a number of the Oneidas have arrived, several of whom have been at Fort Schuyler within these few days & say the enemies force is greatly superior to ours, this intelligence is confirmed by several prisoners and as Colonel Willet . . . is fully of opinion there is no danger of the Fort's surrendering for some time, a council of war are fully of opinion that we ought not to hazard our little Army until reinforced or a miscarriage would probably be attended with the most fatal consequences.[11]

Reports that St. Leger's force outnumbered his, and that Fort Schuyler's garrison was not in immediate peril, gave Arnold time to consider alternatives. Although Arnold now had about 1,500 Continentals and militiamen under his command, he requested an additional "one thousand light troops" from the Northern Army, then located near Albany, before continuing on to attack St.

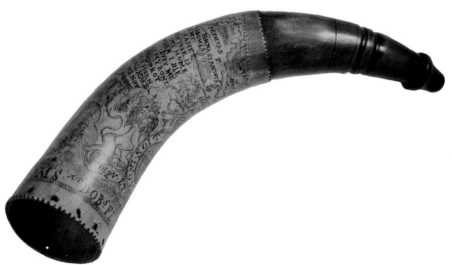

**John Addoms's Powder Horn
third quarter, 18th century**
Private collection
Engraved at Dobb's Ferry, located nearly twenty miles north of Manhattan, this American powder horn was engraved with the royal coat of arms and key geographical features located in northern New York. Included are Forts Stanwix, Edward, and Herkimer, the latter having been built at German Flatts, south of the Mohawk River.

Leger. The aforementioned "several prisoners" captured at nearby German Flatts who provided some intelligence of St. Leger's disposition were from the very same party sent by St. Leger into the Mohawk Valley under the direction of Captain Walter Butler. It was from within this party that Lieutenant Colonel John Brooks contrived a ruse with one of the more compliant captive soldiers, a Mohawk Valley royalist named Hanjost Schuyler.[12] Accordingly,

> Colonel Brooks proposed that he [Hanjost Schuyler] should be employed as a deceptive messenger to spread the alarm and induce the enemy to retreat. General Arnold soon after arrived, and approved the scheme of Colonel Brooks; it was accordingly agreed that Cuyler [Schuyler] should be liberated and his estate secured to him on the condition that he would return to the enemy and make such exaggerated report of General Arnold's force as to alarm and put them into flight. Several friendly [Oneida] Indians being present, one of their head men advised that Schuyler's coat should be shot through in two or three places to add credibility to his story.[13]

For Fort Schuyler's defenders, August 22 began like many others when St. Leger's artillery "bombarded verry smartley" and ceased shortly thereafter. After a long lull, a man claiming to be a deserter from St. Leger's camp approached the fort and informed Gansevoort that Burgoyne's army "was Entirely Routed and that three Thousand men was Coming up to reinforce" the garrison, "and, further, that the Enemy [St. Leger] was retreating with great precipitation."[14] Gansevoort ordered an artillery barrage, after which he sent a detachment of thirty men to investigate. Upon their return, they confirmed that save some few stragglers, the enemy camp was indeed evacuated. The British forces left substantial military stores behind, and broader searches revealed a number of bateaux and even St. Leger's abandoned artillery. The siege of Fort Schuyler was at an end.

Before the British forces fled from their camp that morning, Hildebrandt reported how an American

> lept over the breastwork in broad daylight and claimed to be a deserter. In order to make the occasion seem more genuine he was also shot at. In despair this loyalist told the most horrible lies—that three thousand men probably with artillery, were approaching, that the besieged were already making preparations to join them in wiping us out. Especially overhasty was the immediate order to break camp without even awaiting an advance troop or patrol of this [supposed] nearby army.[15]

Private, Colonel Michael Jackson's (8th) Massachusetts Regiment

Suffering from a serious wound received in 1776, Jackson's extended furlough left long-term command of the regiment to his lieutenant colonel, John Brooks. Like most Continental regiments in the Northern Department, Jackson's was issued a number of linen "rifle" shirts, so named in the north because of their association with the hunting shirt–wearing riflemen of the south. Despite the 1777 influx of surplus French muskets and bayonets, "many of the non commissioned officers and privates . . . [were] not furnished with Bayonet Slings," resulting in a number of bayonets being lost.

Varick to Gates, September 10, 1777, Horatio Gates Papers, 5:557.

St. Leger was made aware of Arnold's relief force, which the British estimated at about 1,000 troops. His Indian allies "complained of our thinness of Troops & their former Lossess," at which time a council of chiefs was called. The brigadier promised to "lead them on myself" in the forthcoming battle, and he agreed to reconnoiter the site intended for the battleground with the chiefs. Things changed when a man arrived, reporting that Arnold's force numbered 2,000. "Immediately after," a third man arrived, informing St. Leger that "General Burgoyne's army was cut to pieces & that Arnold was advancing by rapid and forced Marches with three thousand Men." Another council with the Indians was called so that the British commander could "know their Resolutions," upon which he was advised to retreat, else the Indians "would be obliged to abandon" the expedition.[16] The Indians had made their decision, and St. Leger could do nothing but follow suit. Hanjost and the Oneida men who offered corroboration of his story performed their task brilliantly.[17]

St. Leger's retreat was one of those rare wartime incidents in which a military force was routed by self-induced panic. Hildebrandt reported that in the chaos, "Huts and tents were set on fire" and "Wine and brandy kegs were smashed open." Many men, particularly the Indians, became drunk and some even became riotous and threatening. The fleeing body ran for Oneida Lake, which was gained the following day, and early on the 24th they began the process of crossing it. While on the lake and pondering recent developments, Hildebrandt reflected on how the "voyage was speeded up as if the whole of Canada were slipping away."[18]

Burgoyne learned of St. Leger's retreat on August 28.[19] He certainly did not welcome the news, but it had no impact on his strategy: The Mohawk Valley expedition was literally only a diversion, and had no tangible relevance on the British general's plan or capacity to reach Albany. Although the diversionary aspect of St. Leger's operation would be missed, his troops would not be. Consisting of little more than a regiment's worth of mostly royalist American troops, the men St. Leger was poised to bring could have no bearing on the success or failure facing Burgoyne's future. In truth, St. Leger's defeat was inevitable. Ironically, his small, mobile force was incompatible with heavy siege artillery, and yet it was the lack of siege artillery that prevented him from fulfilling his objective. Nevertheless, heavier ordnance alone would not have given the British brigadier wholesale victory, particularly as there was no considered plan to secure the fort afterward, to say nothing of the 750 captives that would have fallen into his hands.

Upon his return to Fort Oswego in late August, St. Leger summed up the reason for his inability to carry the fort as being the result of poor intelligence, and that what little he had before arriving at the fort was "the most erroneous that can be conceived." Instead of finding the fort in ruins or unfinished as "we were taught to expect," he "found it a respectable Fortress, strongly garrisoned with 700 men and demanding a Train of Artillery we were not masters of, for its speedy subjection."[20]

St. Leger was in no position to pass blame on to others for faulty data, however. Nearly a month before his forces arrived at Fort Schuyler, the British commander received up-to-date information on the disposition of American preparedness, including the shocking revelation that they were "working . . . towards repairing and finishing the old Fort which is a regular Square, and garrisoned by upwards of 600 Men, the Repairs far advanced, and the Rebels expecting us, and were acquainted with our Strength and Rout[e]." Upon being informed of this, St. Leger himself "owned that if they intended to defend themselves in that Fort, our Artillery was not sufficient to take it."[21] With this intelligence, however, the haughty commander did nothing. Ironically, the fort's successful defense was the very thing that probably saved St. Leger—had he been able to progress close to Albany, his isolated, unsupported band would have faced annihilation.

Arnold's reinforcement left Fort Dayton on the 23rd, but "excessive bad roads and necessary precautions in marching through thick woods" slowed his progress. While he had not received word of requested reinforcements from Northern Army command, Arnold nevertheless decided to wait no longer, "determined at all events to hazard a battle" against St. Leger's superior numbers "rather than suffer the garrison to fall a sacrifice." While the column cautiously made its way forward, an express from Gansevoort arrived with a letter from the fort commander, informing Arnold that the "enemy had yesterday left Fort Schuyler, with great precipitation."[22]

Arnold redoubled his efforts and forced-marched his 900 men in hopes of catching up with the fleeing British. On their approach to the fort, though, they encountered a devastating scene. One officer remembered:

> [W]e had to march over the ground where Herkimer's battle was fought, and as the dead had not been buried, and the weather warm, they were much swoln and of a purple colour, which represented the frailty of a man in a very figurative sense; we must have marched over and very near, about four hundred dead bodies.[23]

The troops arrived at Fort Schuyler on the 24th, eighteen days after the Battle of Oriskany. Arnold officially thanked Gansevoort and his garrison "for their Gallant Defense" of the post. An assessment of casualties among the defenders revealed that the sufferings among the overnumerous garrison during the siege totaled about twenty-five soldiers, followers, and refugees killed or wounded. Because of the pressing call to return to the Northern Army, Arnold re-formed

American Commissioned Officer's Epaulet
ca. 1770–80s
Don Troiani collection
Built from silver lace, sequins, and bullion fringe, this epaulet marked the wearer as a commissioned officer. It could have been worn on either shoulder or, as part of a pair, both. Use of commissioned officer epaulets in the Continental Army was not regulated until 1779; before then, the army used a system of colored hat cockades and ribbands to distinguish rank.

Learned's Brigade and set out for Albany two days later. The 1st New York Regiment was redeployed to various posts throughout the Mohawk Valley in order to further maintain order among its sometimes-despondent population.

One aspect of the siege rightfully became legendary—Gansevoort and his garrison successfully defended a fort. While it may sound simple enough, the feat was actually rare. The problem of Americans failing to successfully defend their forts (not only during the Northern Campaign of 1777) became so acute that John Adams himself spared no sentiments on the matter while writing to his wife, Abigail, only days before St. Leger's evacuation:

> [T]hey [the British] can maintain posts although we cannot. I think we shall never defend a post until we shoot a general. After that we shall defend posts, and this event in my opinion is not far off. No other fort will ever be evacuated without an inquiry, nor any officer come off without a court martial. We must trifle no more. We have suffered too many disgraces to pass unexpiated. Every disgrace must be wiped off.[24]

A manifestation of the rarity exhibited by Gansevoort's success is seen in Congress's (and Adams's) extraordinary response. That October the governing body of the new nation resolved that their thanks "be given to Colonel Gansevoort and the officers and troops under his command for the bravery and perseverance which they have so conspicuously manifested in the defense of Fort Schuyler." As a reward, Gansevoort was officially declared colonel-commandant "of the Fort so gallantly defended." Willett was likewise lauded by Congress "for a repeated instance of his bravery and conduct in the late successful sally on the enemy investing Fort Schuyler." In recognition of this, Congress awarded him with "an elegant sword . . . in the name of these United States."[25]

Galvanized

I speak with Confidence because our Army is truly respectable, & every thing wears the most flattering aspect.

— Major Robert Troup, September 14, 1777[1]

Continued losses of forts, ground, vessels, war matériel, and men left the Northern Department's senior generals exposed to growing criticism and concern for their competence and even their patriotism. With the shocking news of the losses of the Lake Champlain forts, Congress had sent Arnold (at Washington's request) on July 12. Ongoing reports of the devolving situation in the department, particularly with respect to the lack of militia turnout, prompted Washington to send Major General Benjamin Lincoln to help as well. Writing to Lincoln on July 24, Washington informed the former Massachusetts militia general that his "Principal view" in sending him was to aid Schuyler and "take the Command of the Eastern Militia, over whom I am informed you have influence and who place confidence in you."[2]

While these appointments were met with approbation, it's not surprising that there was increased clamoring for dismissals. On July 29 Congress ordered "an enquiry . . . into the reasons of the evacuation of Ticonderoga and Mount Independence, and into the conduct of the general officers who were in the northern department at the time of the evacuation."[3] Although the brigadier generals were spared, Schuyler and St. Clair were out.[4] On August 3 Congress instructed Washington to appoint a general to replace the beleaguered Northern Department commander. Washington demurred, however, and requested to be relieved from the responsibility. On the 4th, voting by secret ballot, eleven of the thirteen states chose Major General Horatio Gates to succeed Schuyler.

Most of the Northern Department's military men were happy to see Schuyler go, and news of his replacement was lauded, particularly from the New Englanders who formed a majority of the Northern Army. Chaplain Hezekiah Smith, who complained that his brigade was "harrased (besides Skirmishes) hungry, and ill treated by the Commander in Chief Schuyler," affirmed that news of his replacement was "to our great satisfaction."[5] In another brigade, Major Henry Dearborn thought that Gates's ascension would "Put a New face upon our affairs."[6] In yet another brigade, Corporal John Buss happily informed his parents that Schuyler had left the command, "and now I hope we shall have better doings."[7]

Since sending Arnold to the Mohawk Valley to raise the siege against Gansevoort's garrison, Schuyler's Northern Army continued to withdraw south. Leaving Stillwater on August 15, the troops marched six miles south to Half Moon, while a work party destroyed the bridges in their wake. After remaining a few days, the army finished the last few miles to the multibranch confluence of the Mohawk and Hudson Rivers. This confluence, known as the Sprouts because of the jumble of islands that lie at the outlet of the Mohawk River, was located nearly ten miles north of Burgoyne's ultimate target, Albany. Schuyler subdivided the Northern Army and deployed the brigades throughout the region. Enoch Poor's Brigade was deployed up the Mohawk River about five miles to Loudon's Ferry, the most likely place that Burgoyne intended to cross the Mohawk. John Nixon's Brigade lay at Haver Island (present-day Peebles Island) in the Sprouts. John Paterson's Brigade and the army's most recent arrival, John Glover's Brigade, encamped on Van Schaick's Island, located directly south of Haver Island.[8]

Gates assumed command of the Northern Department on August 19, setting up headquarters at Van Schaick's "Elegant" house on Van Schaick's Island.[9] When Gates assumed command, Arnold was in the Mohawk Valley, planning to move against St. Leger. Lincoln, who was sent into Vermont by Schuyler to coordinate forces in that independent state, continued there.[10]

Beyond the change of leadership and increased distance from Burgoyne's army, mid-August signaled more changes for the Northern Department. Reports of the Battle of Bennington arrived in camp the day before Gates assumed command, and news of St. Leger's flight to Canada followed shortly afterward. Ammunition and ordnance stores were replenished. After more than a month of bivouacking, most regiments that lost their tents during the retreat in early July received replacements, although many were still forced to live under boards or in huts built from the "Boughs of Trees."[11] Food stocks were on the increase, and officers and men could again enjoy delicacies such as rum, coffee, sugar, chocolate, and cheese, albeit at exorbitant prices.

More Continental regiments joined the army while it lay at the Sprouts. On August 22 the 2nd and 4th New York Regiments arrived from the Highlands Department and were sent up to augment Poor's Brigade at Loudon's Ferry. One week later, they were joined by Colonel Daniel Morgan's 400-man Rifle Battalion, composed of Virginia and Pennsylvania riflemen.[12] This corps was sent from Washington's main army in order to counter the incessant summertime *petite guerre* attacks practiced by Burgoyne's Indians and Canadiens. Before the arrival of the riflemen, the Northern Army had nothing to counter these strikes, and they wore heavily upon the army's morale. Not all the news on the personnel

American Officer Cuttoe
1775

Don Troiani collection

This silver-mounted cuttoe, or hunting sword, with a lion-headed pommel has a turned, green-stained ivory grip. American made, the blade is engraved "Drawn to Defend Inocence 1775." The sword's chain knuckle bow is missing.

Private, Colonel Henry Beekman Livingston's 4th New York Regiment

The 4th New York Regiment was one of the ten Continental battalions removed from Putnam's Highlands Department in order to bolster Schuyler's faltering Northern Army during its summertime retreat. Like most Continental regiments in the Northern Army, men of the 4th New York wore a variety of civilian and military clothing, including fringed linen "rifle" shirts issued from public stores. Because few felt hats were available, red and blue "Mill'd Caps" were doled out as "a very good substitute" in small quantities to most regiments.

Measam to Gates, September 5, 1777, Horatio Gates Papers, 5:459.

front was good, however. Colonel Long's 1st New Hampshire Regiment reached its sunset date in August, and despite the crisis facing the army at the time, "nothing" would induce its officers or soldiers "to stay one day longer."[13]

A major point of continued contention was the lack of long-term militia support. Only days before he was replaced, Schuyler complained to Washington that "not one militia man from the eastern states and under forty" from New York remained.[14] Ever since June, Schuyler continually begged and pleaded in vain with state governments for long-term militia assistance, and Gates continued to do the same immediately upon learning of his appointment to the command. Over the course of the next few weeks, only six militia units arrived to augment the army,: three infantry battalions from New York, and two infantry battalions and one light horse battalion from Connecticut (informally called "Arnold's Horse").[15] With New York tied down fighting a three-front war, the New England states were concerned that Burgoyne's ultimate goal was the Connecticut River Valley, or Boston, or that he intended to unite with the British at Rhode Island. By keeping his destination a secret, and by conducting operations in Vermont throughout the summer, Burgoyne cleverly ensured that the states retained their long-term militia for home defense. Until Burgoyne made a move leaving no ambiguity regarding his goal, Northern Army commanders could expect only ephemeral militia support.

With the army stabilized, strengthened, and emboldened by reports that the enemy remained stalled on the upper Hudson, Gates resolved to find more-advantageous defensive ground closer to the enemy. On September 8 the Northern Army reversed course and marched north, arriving at Stillwater the

Pennsylvania Rifle

ca. 1770s

Richard Ulbrich collection

In the hands of experienced marksmen, rifles exceeded smoothbore muskets in both distance and accuracy. Conversely, rifles were more expensive to produce and took longer to load. Because rifle making was all but unknown in New England and New York, any riflemen serving in the Northern, Eastern, or Highlands Departments had to be sent up from the "southern" states, such as Pennsylvania, Maryland, or Virginia. Made in Pennsylvania, this rifle is engraved with the famed Revolutionary motto "Liberty of Death" on the brass patch box. Rare features exhibited on this piece are the round barrel (most were octagonal) and truncated stock (most were stocked to the bore), both of which allowed the rifle to be mounted with a socket bayonet. Rifles capable of mounting bayonets were rare in the eighteenth century.

Private, Colonel Jonathan Latimer's Battalion, Connecticut Militia

All twenty-five of Connecticut's militia regiments provided draftees for the two provisional battalions that joined the Northern Army in mid-September. Terms of service were generous, including issuances of rum, sugar, and bounty money of forty shillings per month in addition to "the like pay, wages, allowances and refreshments, as the continental troops receive." State militia law required each man to provide a gun, bayonet, belt, knapsack, cartridge box, and blanket. Government provided them with canteens, kettles, tents, and ammunition.

Hoadly, *Public Records of the State of Connecticut, From October, 1776, to February, 1778, inclusive*, 375.

Asa Plank's Canteen
ca. 1777
Don Troiani collection

When two Connecticut militia battalions were formed in August 1777 to support the Northern Army, the General Assembly ordered towns to supply the men with canteens for the service. Plank, a corporal in Captain Isaac Stone's company, Colonel Jonathan Latimer's battalion of Connecticut militia, undoubtedly wore this canteen (inscribed "Asa Plank, Saratoga 1777") in both battles of Saratoga.

following day. There the army "took post on the Heights" and "began to open Communications and throw up a few small redoubts principally with a view of amusing the enemy."[16]

With work well under way, Gates's scouting parties reported on the 11th that Burgoyne's army, located about fifteen miles north, appeared to be "making every preparation to advance." Gates was now having second thoughts; with the British probably capable of attacking in a matter of days, the Northern Army commander wanted to ensure that his troops held the best possible defensive position. Believing that Stillwater "was not calculated for Defence," Gates, Arnold, and Colonel Tadeusz Kościuszko of the Corps of Engineers reconnoitered north in order to find something better.[17] Kościuszko found it immediately. About three miles north of Stillwater at Bemus Heights, the high bluffs overlooking the Hudson River Valley came very close to the river itself, squeezing the road to Albany in between. If the Northern Army held the position by blocking the natural defile and commanding the Bemus Heights bluffs, the British would not be able to pass.

Major General Horatio Gates
by Benoît-Louis Prévost, 1781, after Pierre-Eugène Du Simitière, 1777
The New York Public Library Digital Collections, EM3946

Major General Benedict Arnold
by Benoît-Louis Prévost, 1781, after Pierre-Eugène Du Simitière, 1777
The New York Public Library Digital Collections, EM5480

These portraits are the most realistic depictions of these generals on the eve of their entry into the Northern Campaign. Both men sat for the Philadelphia artist Du Simitière in 1777—Gates in March, Arnold in July. Du Simitière's drawings of these and other Revolutionary celebrities were sent to France, where they were engraved and published in the 1781 *Collection des portraits des généraux, ministres & magistrats qui se sont rendus célèbres dans la révolution des treize Etats-Unis de l'Amérique-septentrionale.* Note that both men wear their purple "ribbands," which signified their rank of major general.

"a feint Description of our Encampment"

by Lieutenant Colonel Richard Varick, September 12, 1777

The New York Public Library, Archives and Manuscripts, Philip Schuyler Papers, b.11 f.69

This map of the Northern Army's brigade arrangement at Bemus Heights and the surrounding high ground was drawn "by pencil" in a letter written to Philip Schuyler a few hours after the army moved there. Varick identified Gates's headquarters as being at "the Read House" of Ephraim and Anna Woodworth, while Arnold's and Poor's was located "on the highest part of the Hill at the House on the Road about north from Head Quars," in the home of John and Lydia Neilson. Despite the length of time the army was there, its size, and the significance of the moment, this map represents the only known contemporary depiction of the American camp. Unfortunately, it was drawn before any of the fortification lines were constructed, and thus they do not appear on the map.

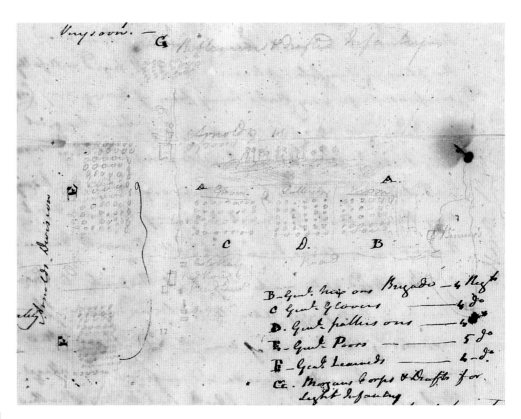

As this decisive landscape "fully answered his wishes," Gates ordered the army up to Bemus Heights on the 12th, where the men immediately began to clear ground for the brigade encampments and build fortifications. Over the next week, the "Americans intrenched to their Eyes" under Kościuszko's direction. There was "little or no Drilling" with their weapons in camp, since the soldiers were instead "on Fatigue and working very hard" to build their fortifications.[18] Major Robert Troup, Gates's senior aide-de-camp, exuded confidence for the future. In his letter to John Jay, he reported:

> Permit me to . . . [describe] the Strength of our post. There are two Roads only which lead to our Encampment. The one to our Flank by Saratoga Lake, thro a thick marshy swamp; and the other to our Front along Hudsons River. I am inclined to think they will advance on both in order to divide our attention. In the former their Artillery will be of little service; we have obstructed the Pass already by felling Trees, and shall secure it properly tomorrow by fortifying a commanding Eminence. The latter is also favorable to our Designs. Within Musket Shot of it, on the left, is a Ridge which extends very far. . . . In one word—if the action becomes general, they will be obliged to contend with Hills, Rocks, Gullies & Trees on *all sides*.[19]

Gates divided the Northern Army into three divisions. The Center Division, commanded by Gates personally, consisted of Nixon's, Paterson's, and Glover's Brigades. At Bemus Heights, Nixon's Brigade of four regiments encamped closest to the Hudson. Nixon's troops were "pretty well clothed" and "well armed, Except the want of a few Bayonets . . . their arms were clean & in such order as does Honor to the officers commanding them."[20] Paterson's Brigade, also of four regiments, encamped to the west of Nixon's. His men had "arms clean & in good order," but "many of them want Bayonets & most of the non commissioned officers & privates stand greatly in need of Clothing."[21] In the center of the army was Glover's Brigade, consisting of seven regiments; the quality of their arms, clothing, and disposition was the same as enjoyed by Nixon's men.[22]

Arnold's Division lay on the army's left flank, encamped west of Gates's. Located on a high hill called the Summit (the "commanding Eminence" that Troup referred to), Poor's Brigade's seven regiments (militia excepted) were in the same condition as Paterson's, which is not surprising considering their shared experiences since the beginning of the campaign.[23] Arnold made his headquarters in the Neilson House, a home that topped the Summit, which was, incidentally, the army's high ground. Learned's Brigade of four regiments encamped a half mile south of Neilson House, next to Gates's headquarters, which was taken up in the home of Ephraim Woodworth, the district's local militia captain. Learned's Brigade was "well armed, their Arms in very good order, but deficient in Bayonets," and their clothing was "tolerably good."[24] Arnold also had command of Morgan's Corps, which consisted of Colonel Morgan's Rifle Battalion and Major Henry Dearborn's Corps of Light Infantry. The latter was a newly formed battalion of 300 of the army's "most able, active, spirited Men," selected from the Northern Army's New England Continental Army regiments.[25] Serving with Morgan were Captain Abraham Nimham's "Stockbridge" Mohican Indians, who served as rangers and scouts.[26]

Major Stevens's Continental Army Corps of Artillery, supplemented with a detachment from Colonel John Crane's (3rd) Continental Artillery Regiment, was prepared to defend Gates's extensive fortified lines. While artillery losses earlier in July appeared insurmountable, Schuyler's efforts to acquire artillery from other departments and mount pieces saved from Forts Edward and George paid off. In all, Stevens's men managed twenty-two cannons, ten of which were French four-pounders mounted on carriages delivered to the Northern Army in late July.[27]

Gates's army at Bemus Heights was principally composed of officers and soldiers who were, by and large, experienced combatants. Although most of the regiments were formed less than a year prior, the service records of their personnel prove that most in the army had fought during the Lexington and Concord

Sleeve Links
second half, 18th century
Saratoga National Historical Park, SARA 13866
The sleeves of men's shirts and women's shifts often closed with a pair of metal sleeve links. Found at the Ephraim Woodworth house site, these octagonal links could have come from a member of the Woodworth family or from one of the many people who traversed the farm during the nearly four-week period in which it served as Gates's headquarters.

Le Corbeau

1761

New York State Archives,14297-87_3599

Cast in Strasbourg, France, this bronze four-pounder *a la Suédois* was named *Le Corbeau* (The Raven). In 1777 the French government gave tacit approval to the new United States by providing covert shipments of war matériel, one of which arrived at Portsmouth, New Hampshire, in April 1777. Included in the vessel's cargo were thirty-one cannons of the type seen here, ten of which were transferred to Schuyler's Northern Army in July. By the time of the Battles of Saratoga, these French guns formed nearly half of Gates's artillery train. This photograph was taken at Saratoga Battlefield in 1928.

alarm or in the Battle of Bunker Hill in 1775. Others had participated in the 1775 invasion of Canada and served in various actions including the Battle of Québec City, with additional fighting in Canada in 1776 adding to their military résumés. More so, those serving with Washington in 1776 experienced a whirlwind of fighting in battles such as Long Island, Harlem Heights, and White Plains. Many were the heroes of the decisive Battles of Trenton and Princeton. These officers and soldiers may not have been veterans in the strictest sense, but their collective military experience was in sharp contrast to the majority of enemy combatants then staging to complete their campaign to Albany.

All told, Gates commanded about 6,900 Continental Army infantry, cavalry, and artillerymen; 1,300 militia infantry and cavalrymen; dozens of Stockbridge Mohican, Munsee, and Wappinger war captains and warriors; and hundreds of army support personnel and followers, including women, children, and sutlers. Gone were the days of the demoralized, panicked, and deprived Northern Army.

Stymied

We shall try the Countenance of Mr. Gates; they pretend to be in spirits and threaten us a drubbing, but on the approach of the red Coats I rather believe it will be as usual.

—Captain Sir Francis Clerke, Bt., September 10, 1777[1]

One month. That's how long Burgoyne's Army from Canada was delayed collecting supplies on the eastern side of the Hudson River following Baum's and Breymann's defeats in the Battle of Bennington. Scouting missions continued, hundreds of British "additional company" and German infantry recruits arrived, and the 53rd Regiment of Foot was sent back to Ticonderoga while the 62nd was brought up to join the army. About 150 Haudenosaunee Mohawk men, women, and children, who fled their settlement at Fort Hunter, made the nearly fifty-mile trek in order to join Burgoyne's army as refugees.[2] More royalists joined the army and enlisted in any one of the growing number of fractious royalist corps. Also joining Burgoyne at this time were the wives and children of some of the army's officers, including the German commander's wife, Lady Frederica Riedesel, Freifrau zu (Baroness of) Eisenbach, and their three young daughters.[3]

But not everyone was joining Burgoyne. Immediately following the Battle of Bennington, the Indians were "astonished" to learn that the British commander

British Additional Company Musket Wrist Plates 1770s

Saratoga National Historical Park, SARA 1722, 33930

On September 3 Burgoyne received much-needed redcoat reinforcements in the form of additional companies— provisional companies that served as hosts for transferring recruits to their designated regiments. The additional company men were armed with English Pattern 1769 Short Land muskets. These wrist plates, engraved with the company number (11) over an issuance number (in this case, 21 and 27), probably came from their muskets.

Pipe Tomahawk Head
second half, 18th century
Private collection
Pipe tomahawks were often given to Indian nation chiefs as gifts by British, French, and American officials. As the name suggests, these were meant to be smoked; the end of the hollow wooden haft (no longer extant) would be smoked as a pipe, and the smoke would exit through a hole in the tomahawk's head. Some pipe tomahawks could also be used as weapons. This engraved brass piece was recovered from Fort Haldimand, a 1778 fort built on Buck's Island.

had no plans to send a corps to "collect the remains of the two scattered detachments at Bennington, and to succor those that were wounded, and . . . perishing." This lack of concern for his men, and "indifference toward the Indians" who served with Baum, prompted many to reconsider their part in the campaign. A council was called, which included both the "far western" nations with La Corne de Saint-Luc and the Seven Nations of Canada men with the Chevalier de Lorimier. The conference did not go well for Burgoyne; the Indians "were so greatly dissatisfied, that they immediately departed" en masse on August 20 and over the days that followed.[4] By the end of the month, fewer than eighty Canadien volunteers and Seven Nations of Canada men remained under the command of war chief Tehoragwanegen (Thomas Williams).

For weeks, provisions and military stores were transported to the Army from Canada over Lake George via the Great Carrying Place. Bateaux and scows were portaged overland and laid in the Hudson River. This trickling, "scanty and difficult delivery of the provisions" was unavoidable in the wake of the Battle of Bennington.[5] Corvée, Royal Navy, German, British, and royalist personnel worked as fast as they could, but the great distance between Ticonderoga and the Batten Kill camp—about sixty-two miles—was a logistical challenge that Burgoyne was unprepared for.

Finally, by mid-September, the army accumulated five weeks' worth of provisions, along with the bateaux needed to convey them. The army's heavier baggage, sent back to Ticonderoga during the summer in order to lighten the army's load, was brought to an island in Lake George, positioned to be brought up at a future date. Scuttlebutt circulating in camp that Burgoyne's lavish lifestyle was supported by "about thirty Carts on the Road" between Forts George and Edward "loaden with Baggage, said to be the Lieutenant General's," was summarily quashed in general orders. Burgoyne's personal baggage train, like those of Major-Generals Phillips and Riedesel, consisted of six carts (per the army's regulatory plan) and no more.[6]

Burgoyne's army began crossing the Hudson on September 13 over a bridge of boats, built of bateaux laid parallel to the flow of the river, roped and chained

Landsman, Royal Navy

From beginning to end, Burgoyne's army moved by the tireless labor and skill of its Royal Navy contingent. While most naval personnel did not pass Lake Champlain, 150 landsmen, sailors, and officers continued on to row bateaux, forward provisions, and construct the boat bridges used to traverse the Hudson River. Although seamen had no pattern uniform, this landsman wears the blue jacket with slash cuffs and trousers commonly worn by mariners. Burgoyne's boatmen "had to drill daily for several hours" with muskets in order to defend their boats.

The Specht Journal, 84.

together, and topped with plank boards. For three days men, women, children, dogs, horses, cattle, carts, wagons, and artillery pieces traversed this bridge and gained the river's western shore, about eleven miles north of Bemus Heights, after which the bridge was broken up and floated beside the army as it advanced. Burgoyne marched from Saratoga to Dovegate (present-day Coveville) on September 16 and encamped at Swords's house, located three miles north of Bemus Heights, on the 17th. The British advance was accomplished without hindrance, apart from the threat of an American attack force commanded by General Arnold, which showed itself near the British camp on September 18 but never initiated battle.

Having gained intelligence regarding the American positions and strength, Burgoyne settled upon a plan of attack. With the cannon emplacements overlooking the Hudson Valley from atop Bemus Heights, a full march down the River Road would not do. Instead, most of the army would advance into the wooded interior and strike at the American fortifications at their weak points, located west of Bemus Heights. Conveniently, one of the area's few royalists, John Freeman, was a soldier in Jessup's King's Loyal Americans and knew the interior avenues of approach south.[7]

On the morning of September 19, the Army from Canada was divided into three columns. The western, or right-hand column, consisting of Brigadier-General Fraser's stalwart Advanced Corps, which included the army's combatant royalists, Canadiens, and Indians, had 2,400 officers, soldiers, and warriors. Marching behind them was Lieutenant-Colonel Breymann's Reserve Corps with 530 additional troops. This column marched due west from their Swords's house encampments until it reached the Quaker Springs Road, located about two and a half miles inland from the river, and turned south. The army's center column, which Burgoyne himself attended, consisted of Brigadier-General James

Fusee Bayonet
second half, 18th century

Eric Schnitzer collection

With most British and American commissioned infantry officers utilizing fusees—lightweight, small-caliber smoothbore muskets—bayonets became an essential armament. With a blade measuring only eleven and a half inches long, this lightweight English-made piece is representative of those used in the Northern Campaign.

Folding Knife
ca. 1770s

Saratoga National Historical Park, SARA 205

Folding knives were recovered from various British encampment sites within the Saratoga military corridor.

Hamilton's Brigade, with 1,700 officers and soldiers. This column advanced south along a wooded cart path which dipped into the cavernous Great Ravine, crossed Kromma Kill, and scaled its southern slope. The army's eastern, or left-hand column, marched south along the Hudson River in the valley. Commanded by Major-Generals William Phillips and Friedrich Riedesel, it consisted of the army's two-brigade German Division of 2,200 officers and soldiers. The 47th Regiment of Foot, two Royal Artillery companies, His Majesty's General Hospital, baggage wagons and carts, the Royal Navy contingent, other noncombatant military personnel, and all followers, including American royalist and Mohawk Nation refugees, constituted an additional 1,500 people. This column's soldiers guarded the army's food supplies, all of which were conveyed in the army's boats.

Each soldier was issued a hundred rounds of ammunition, and was therefore well prepared for the upcoming battle. Because no cartridge pouch or box could carry that many rounds, British soldiers placed overages, "carefully packed up . . . in paper or linen . . . in the top of the knapsack."[8] The Germans relied on ammunition carts to carry any overages. All soldiers were in marching order and wore slung knapsacks packed with spare clothing, necessaries, and other personal belongings (and, for the British, the balance of their ammunition). Each soldier carried a blanket, a linen haversack filled with three days' worth of rations (nine pounds of food), and filled tin water flasks. One man from each mess (four to six men) carried a bagged tin cooking kettle slung over his shoulder. Compared to the soldiers, officers had a much easier time of it. Light baggage lay on the backs of packhorses, negating the need for knapsacks. Even canteens were carried by their servants, men who also served as soldiers in the companies to which the officers belonged.

While Gates allowed the British to begin their advance unfettered, he made sure to gain intelligence on their disposition. Burgoyne's intentions were

British Officer's Saber

1775

Don Troiani collection

This sword, with turned green-dyed ivory grip, has ornate sterling silver mountings hallmarked to 1775. Small, light swords like this were favored by British commissioned officers on most military expeditions. In Burgoyne's army, most British officers opted to leave their swords behind with "their baggage in Canada" or sent them back with the heavy baggage to Ticonderoga in the summer, opting to carry bayonets and fusees only.

Anbury, *Travels Through the Interior Parts of America*, vol. 2, 79.

Private, Grenadier Company, 20th Regiment of Foot

Consisting of most of a regiment's tallest men, British grenadiers represented the stalwart elite of the British Army long before the American War for Independence. In preparation for Burgoyne's expedition, their famed, foot-high, black bearskin caps were replaced with felt caps, the fronts of which bore pewter bomb decorations. Note the private's laced shoulder wings, marking the wearer as an elite British soldier. With a knapsack, haversack, and canteen, this soldier is in full marching order such as he would have appeared while marching toward Bemus Heights on September 19.

revealed when the British camp was packed up that morning, and the signal guns that coordinated their advance further alarmed Gates's camp. Gates was intent on a defensive approach for dealing with the advancing enemy—this was to be his first battle command in the war—but Arnold had a different idea. He had marched out with his division the previous day in order to fight the British, if an opportunity presented itself, but the British never bit. He returned to camp later that evening, having taken only a few dozen unarmed, foraging British soldiers, women, and children prisoner. While the mini expedition hadn't resulted in much, the strategy's potential efficacy wasn't lost on Arnold, who requested that the same be allowed as the British were advancing. Gates consented by instructing Arnold to send Morgan's Corps (consisting of his 400 riflemen and Major Henry Dearborn's 300 light infantrymen) to "observe their Direction, and harrass their advance" north of the camp.[9]

Morgan's Corps of picked men was well suited for making initial contact with Burgoyne's advancing troops, particularly in the woods. The landscape was a maze of farm clearings, most of which were enclosed with wooden rail fences, each of which included a number of now-abandoned dwellings and outbuildings. Innumerable cart paths meandered across farm fields and throughout the mostly wooded terrain, which was heavily cut with creeks and ravines both deep and shallow. It was through this terrain that Morgan's Corps marched toward John Freeman's farm, north of which shots were being exchanged in the woods between British and American sentinels. Because of the thin cart paths they had to march upon, Morgan's 700 troops had to advance in a very long, thin, drawn-out column, the van of which arrived on the south side of Freeman's farm after 12:30 p.m. The few American sentinels were falling back onto the open field from the north, having been pushed out of the woods skirting the north side of the farm.

At about 12:45 p.m. the British center column's hundred-man picket, commanded by Major Gordon Forbes, advanced out of the woods and onto the Freeman farm clearing, tasked with ensuring the location was devoid of American resistance.[10] As the British maneuvered up the low-rising hill topped by Freeman's log house and fencing, they saw Morgan's riflemen rushing up from the south, a few hundred yards away. Forbes's British soldiers "gave them a Shot," but with little effect, and the American riflemen "rushed on & obliged them to Retreat" back into the woods north of the farm from whence they came. The riflemen, "being rather a head" of Dearborn's Light Infantry, gave chase, but their extended, unsupported formation left them vulnerable.[11]

As the foremost company of riflemen surged into the woods, a well-timed reinforcement from Fraser's column, consisting of two companies of the 24th Regiment, a light three-pounder grasshopper, and Seven Nations of Canada

Cartridge Pouch Device, Grenadier Company, 20th Regiment of Foot ca. 1773

Don Troiani collection

These large, solid brass, flaming grenade devices were often issued to grenadier companies of regiments garrisoned in the Kingdom of Ireland in the 1770s. This ornament was recovered in the Mohawk Valley.

Morgan's Rifles, September 19
This scene depicts Morgan's Rifle Battalion marching to Freeman's farm at about 12:30 p.m. The corps, with Captain Van Swearingen's Pennsylvania company in the van, marches in a column of files as Morgan, wearing his white linen "hunting shirt," urges them on. Behind Morgan is Lieutenant Colonel Richard Butler, wearing the red cockade that marks him as a field officer. Morgan's blue-coated aide-major, Captain the Chevalier du Bouchet (a former French infantry officer who volunteered his services to the United States), watches with anticipation. Flanking the column are Captain Abraham Nimham's Stockbridge Indian volunteers, serving as scouts for the corps.

Morgan's Retreat, September 19
Having routed the hundred-man piquet of the enemy's center column, the front of Morgan's Rifle Battalion, consisting of riflemen from the 8th Pennsylvania Regiment commanded by Captain Van Swearingen, surged into the woods after the fleeing redcoats. Overextended, the riflemen were in turn outflanked by a detachment from Fraser's column. The riflemen were scattered, and Swearingen was captured. Brought before Brigadier-General Simon Fraser for interrogation, Swearengin, "with the most undaunted firmness," refused to provide intelligence to Fraser—even while threatened with being hanged.

Anbury, *Travels Through the Interior Parts of America*, vol. 1, 412.

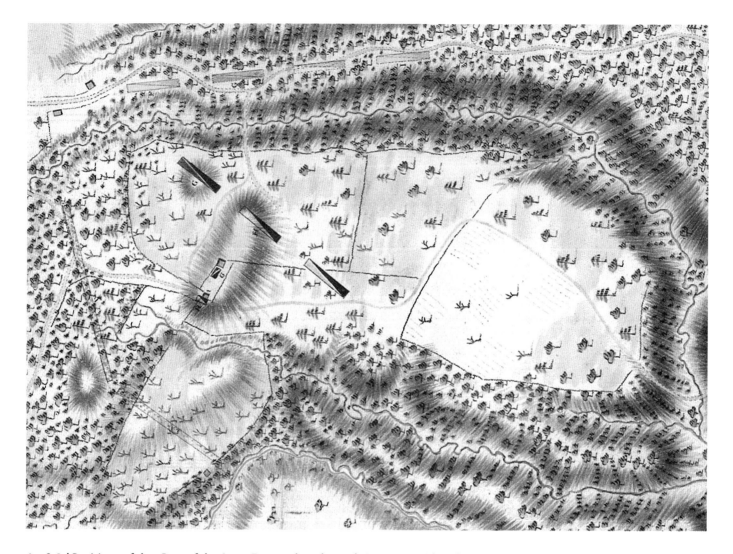

1st & 2d Positions of that Part of the Army Engaged on the 19th Septr 1777 (detail)

by Lieutenant William Cumberland Wilkinson, ca. 1778

The Library of Congress, gm71000664

Freeman's farm was the focus of discord for one of the longest land battles of the war. Once the Americans were scattered following the opening skirmish, the four British infantry regiments of Hamilton's center column marched onto the field and deployed in line of battle. The 9th Regiment of Foot (F) was shortly thereafter sent back to form a reserve, leaving the 21st (Royal North British Fusiliers) (G), the 20th (I), and the army's junior British Regiment, the 62nd (H), seen in the center. Although not shown on the map, the brigade's Royal Regiment of Artillery detachment of four light six-pounders, arranged in two pair, were also on the field. Freeman's house and barn are shown as yellow squares on the field's northernmost hill. American forces are depicted as mottled formations, most of which are shown taking cover behind tree lines. Note the creek-cut ravines surrounding the landscape, split-rail fence lines, and the cultivated field on the eastern side of the farm, most of which was devoted to wheat and rye. Also depicted on the map are the farm's girdled trees—standing dead trees that had their trunks partially stripped of bark and cut in preparation for clearing. The map's maker was a lieutenant in the 62nd Regiment of Foot, as well as an acting assistant engineer, who fought in the Battle of Freeman's Farm.

Abenaki warriors, attacked the riflemen's unprotected left flank, sending the unsuspecting Americans reeling. Fraser's men came on so fast and unexpectedly that Morgan's entire rifle battalion was thrown into chaos and dispersed, with most of his troops retreating deep into the woods south of the farm. Dearborn's Light Infantry was unable to come to the riflemen's assistance in time, but the major judiciously retired to an extended wooded hill located near the southern end of the farm, about 275 yards southwest of Freeman's log house.

With the skirmishing at an end and the open field cleared of Americans, at about 2:00 p.m. Hamilton's Brigade moved through the woods and formed on the northern end of Freeman's farm in line of battle. The 9th Regiment of Foot—the brigade's only regiment whose personnel had any recent combat experience—was sent off the field and eventually took up their original position in the woods north of the farm in order to form a reserve (which was never employed). The 21st Regiment of Foot (Royal North British Fusiliers) now formed the right of the line and the 20th the left, while the 62nd, the army's junior British regiment which also had the highest percentage of new soldiers, held the middle. The Royal Regiment of Artillery detachment paired its four light six-pounders, two with the Fusiliers and two with the 62nd.[12] Dearborn's men were plainly observed about 300 yards away, and the British prepared for the forthcoming fight. Following army regulations, the British piled their knapsacks, blankets, haversacks, tin water flasks, and bagged kettles behind them.[13] There they waited, anticipating a renewed American attack, but it never materialized.

21st Regiment of Foot (Royal North British Fusiliers) Commissioned Officer Button ca. 1775

Don Troiani collection

Made of higher quality than those of the other ranks, commissioned officer buttons such as this were often made of silver repoussé and wrapped over a bone form, while crossed catgut was used as a shank. For regiments requiring gold metal plating, the buttons were gilt. This fine commissioned officer's button, from the 21st Regiment of Foot (Royal North British Fusiliers), includes the regiment's authorized crown and Scottish thistle motifs.

British Tin Water Flask second half, 18th century

Don Troiani collection

Tin canteens were issued to most campaigning British regiments annually as part of their camp equipage. As part of their marching order ensemble, regulations called for British soldiers to pile knapsacks, haversacks, kettles, and even canteens behind their battalion formations at the commencement of battle. This piece retains its rare, original hemp "string."

British Haversack
second half, 18th century

Colonel J. Craig Nannos collection

Osnaburg linen haversacks were issued to campaigning British regiments annually with their camp equipage. Stamped with the "King's Mark"—a broad arrow—and the *GR* monogram of George III, soldiers carried their rations—usually salt pork and flour—in these bags. Multiple days' worth of rations were usually issued at once and thereby carried therein.

The British didn't wait long. At about 2:30 p.m. Major George Forster, commanding the Fusiliers, and Lieutenant-Colonel John Anstruther, commander of the 62nd Regiment, ordered their battalions forward toward Dearborn's position. The regiments passed by Freeman's house and barn, then meandered through the farm's many girdled trees. These trees were by no means difficult to move around, since the British lines were formed in "open files," allowing about eighteen inches between each soldier, thereby affording the redcoats with greater maneuver flexibility.[14] Although this was the first opportunity the officers and soldiers of either regiment had to prove their mettle in the campaign, they were both well equipped for the occasion. Most of the Fusiliers were armed with newly issued Pattern 1756 Long Land muskets, and their pouches, issued in 1774, probably held near thirty rounds of ammunition. The 62nd had the best the military had to offer: Pattern 1768 Short Land muskets and cartridge pouches that carried thirty-six rounds each, both of which were issued in 1776. No regiments in Burgoyne's army were better armed or equipped.

Suddenly, Colonel Joseph Cilley's 1st New Hampshire Regiment appeared out of the woods, and "the engagement

Cartridge Pouch with Shoulder Belt, 62nd Regiment of Foot
1776

Don Troiani collection

Made in Ireland and issued to the 62nd Regiment of Foot in 1776 shortly before embarkation for the relief of Canada, this pouch was a technological achievement. Its singular, removable wooden block held eighteen cartridges on each side (thirty-six total) and could therefore carry twice the amount of ammunition of other, similar-sized pouches. Iron buckles mounted to the pouch's bottom allowed the whitened buff leather shoulder belt to be adjusted for length. This particular piece was issued to a soldier in company "D," commanded by Captain George Marlay.

**Captain, Colonel Alexander Scammell's
3rd New Hampshire Regiment**
Unlike their British infantry officer
counterparts, most of whom purchased
at least one of their commissions to gain
promotion, those of the Continental
Army were usually appointed by state
governments. Cockades provided the
only formal identification for regimental-
level Continental Army officers, the
colors of which determined rank: green
for ensigns and lieutenants, yellow
or buff for captains, and red for field
officers. Infantry officers in the Northern
Department, including colonels, fielded
on foot and carried fusees, bayonets,
and often swords.

The 62nd Regiment of Foot, September 19

This scene depicts the 62nd Regiment of Foot charging into the woods bordering Freeman's farm in order to close in with the 3rd New Hampshire Regiment. Seen here is Major Henry Harnage, seriously wounded in the abdomen from a shot through his left side, being tended to by a drummer and his soldier-servant, Private John Pruit, while eighteen-year-old Lieutenant Gonville Bromhead looks back to his fallen commander. Lieutenant Thomas Reynell, shot in the head, lives his last moments against a tree. In the distance is the green-coated lieutenant colonel of the 3rd New Hampshire Regiment, Andrew Colburn, encouraging his men forward; he was mortally wounded in the action.

began very closely, and continued about twenty minutes," during which Cilley "lost so many men, and received no reinforcement," and the regiment was "obliged to retreat."[15] Countermoves happened quickly. Both pairs of light six-pounders were dragged up to support their respective British regiments. Dearborn "Ran to [Cilley's] assistance with the Light Infantry," but the decision was made too late to be of use.[16]

While the 1st New Hampshire withdrew through the woods back toward camp, Colonel Alexander Scammell's 3rd New Hampshire Regiment marched in their direction, sent by Arnold as a reinforcement. Cilley turned his men around and returned to the field of battle. With the 3rd New Hampshire Regiment on the left and the 1st New Hampshire on the right, the American line of battle formed along the wood line on the farm's fence-bordered southern side. Soon after, Colonel Thaddeus Cook's battalion of Connecticut militia joined them, and formed on their right flank. Being that they were from his home state, and probably because they were also militia, Arnold "first addressed" these men in particular before they marched out to Freeman's farm.[17] The American line of battle thus reinforced, the fighting was "renewed, with great Warmth and Violence" at about 3:00 p.m.[18]

The 62nd Regiment of Foot bore the brunt of the revived American attack. Commanding his two light six-pounders, Second-Lieutenant James Murray Hadden placed his guns within the regiment's battle line, which was "drawn up . . . on a more open field," while the Americans "fought under cover of a wood." The 62nd fired into the forest, but the "fire of their . . . musketry was very ill directed," with most of their shots impaling the large tree trunks. Using the tree-scape for cover, the Americans loaded their guns and took aim at the British,

**Major Henry Harnage's Pistol
ca. 1775**

Don Troiani collection

This elegant piece is one of a brace (pair) of brass-mounted holster pistols that belonged to Major Henry Harnage of the 62nd Regiment of Foot. As the regiment's major, he was expected to be mounted during general reviews, exercises, and field maneuvers but not in battle.

Silver Gorget, 62nd Regiment of Foot
ca. 1770s

Don Troiani collection

In the British armed forces, only commissioned officers in the Foot Guards, marching regiments of foot, and the Corps of Marines were authorized to wear gorgets; those serving in the ordnance branches (regiments of artillery and corps of engineers), cavalry regiments, Royal Navy, and staff offices were not. This gorget sports simple engraved ears, and the regimental designation 62^d REG^T flanks the engraved royal coat of arms. Silk ribbon was fastened through the two upper holes, which allowed the piece to be suspended around the wearer's neck. Ribbon color usually reflected the officer's coat's facing color, but not always—for the 62nd Regiment in 1777, theirs was pink, not buff.

who, protected only by the girdled trees that peppered the open field, took heavy casualties. Such a firefight would inevitably break the 62nd Regiment, and Anstruther ordered his men to charge forth into the woods

> with the "national weapon" [the bayonet], and furiously too, quitting their position each time: the conflict was grievous to behold; the contest was unequal; the rebels fled at every charge deeper still into the woods; but when the British troops returned to their position, they were slowly followed, and those who had been the most forward in the pursuit were the first to fall.[19]

During the course of the multi-hour battle, the 62nd Regiment performed these unsuccessful bayonet attacks four times, but the Americans—most of whom had bayonets—kept their distance. With dominant numbers, the Americans were easily able to turn the tables in the woods and chase the British out each time. As the battle grinded on, the New Hampshire and Connecticut men were able to force the British to break and retreat. The Americans advanced, and despite the temptation to plunder the dead of valuable items, they did so only "when their guns or ammunition failed them. They would swoop down and pick up the enemy's who lay thickly scattered upon the ground," from which the British were driven.[20] For their part, the British had no such problem. While each American went into battle with a couple dozen rounds of ammunition per man, the British were able to repair to their equipage piles on the northern end of the field and replenish their rounds. Conversely, the Americans were unable to use British

French Model 1763 Infantry Musket (detail)

ca. 1763

Don Troiani collection

French military arms delivered to Portsmouth, New Hampshire, aboard the *Amphitrite* in April 1777 included a variety of infantry models, particularly those authorized in the 1760s. One-third of the ship's store of over 6,000 muskets were acquired by the state of New Hampshire, and in May famed Exeter silversmith John Ward Gilman was paid two pennies for "marking & numbering" each gun. Stamped on the barrel near the breech, each musket was struck with state, battalion, and individual number markings. This particular piece, issued to a soldier in Colonel Nathan Hale's 2nd New Hampshire Regiment, was probably used in the Battles of Hubbardton, Freeman's Farm, and Bemus Heights.

May 10, 1777, *Collections of the New Hampshire Historical Society*, vol. 7, 96.

cartridges found among the dead and dying because most of the bullets within were too large for the guns they carried.

As the fighting on Freeman's farm ground on toward evening, Cook's militia received so many casualties that they were forced to return to camp. Colonel Nathan Hale's 2nd New Hampshire Regiment, commanded by Lieutenant Colonel Winborn Adams, was sent to the field, and General Poor appeared to take personal command of the fighting. Arnold even wrangled a small body of volunteers drawn from one of his division's piquets, commanded by Major William Hull, and Poor ordered them to replace the withdrawn militia. Poor's numerical superiority allowed him to extend his battle line, a move that threatened the 62nd Regiment with being outflanked. In response, the 62nd refused its left wing's grand division (two companies) in order to better protect itself. Four additional "heavy guns" were brought up from the river valley and positioned on the northern side of Freeman's farm. Able to fire large-caliber balls with greater force and at longer distances, the ranging shot helped keep the Americans at bay.[21] What started out as a battle in which the British failed to close in and defeat the Americans in the woods was turning into a fight in which the British were trying to keep the Americans out of the field.

Hadden's Royal Artillery detachment serving with the 62nd Regiment was in serious trouble. While his two light six-pounders were well suited for blasting into an open field, attempts to shoot into the woods were of little use, "except among the limbs of trees."[22] With most of his artillerymen killed or wounded, the guns were silenced, and an attempt to bring the guns back into action with a reinforcement failed. The 62nd Regiment, "being worn down had begun to get into confusion," and Hadden and his remaining men tried to pull and push the guns

Bombardier, 1st Battalion, Royal Regiment of Royal Artillery
Identified by a gold epaulet on his right shoulder, this "blue boy" bombardier rests upon a T-shaped linstock wrapped with slow match which, when lit, would ignite artillery fuses. In addition to the ordnance they operated, Royal Artillery soldiers were armed with carbines, bayonets, and cartridge pouches containing eight or nine rounds of ammunition. Although the Royal Artillery companies in Canada received new clothing for 1777, it was laid aside and the old clothing, modified according to the universal Canada Army pattern, was worn instead.

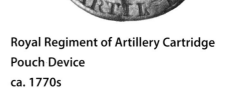

Royal Regiment of Artillery Cartridge Pouch Device
ca. 1770s
Colonel J. Craig Nannos collection
The Royal Regiment of Artillery was a single regiment constituting four battalions of ten companies each (including two invalid companies). Backed with red leather, these devices adorned the buff leather pouches worn by the regiment's carbine-carrying soldiers. This piece is engraved with markings identifying it with the regiment's 1st Battalion, from which two companies served with Burgoyne.

Pattern 1756 Royal Regiment of Artillery Carbine
second half, 18th century

Don Troiani collection

Regulations called for this pattern carbine of .65 caliber to be issued to the private men (matrosses, gunners, and bombardiers) of the Royal Regiment of Artillery. This was expanded in the Canada Army when orders for the regiment dated July 6, 1776, instructed "Serjeants and Corporals . . . to use Carbines instead of Halberts when on Duty." This particular piece is marked to the regiment's first battalion. With a thirty-seven-inch barrel, the piece weighs about seven pounds.

Hadden, *Hadden's Journal and Orderly Books*, 210.

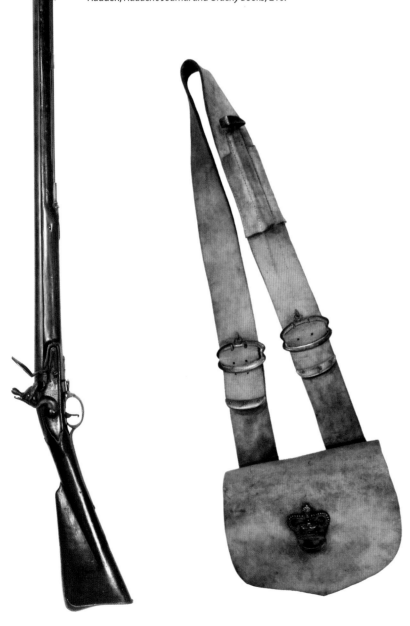

Royal Regiment of Artillery Cartridge Pouch and Shoulder Belt
ca. 1770s–80s

Private collection; photograph by Don Troiani

These cartridge pouches were worn by the carbine-carrying matrosses, gunners, and bombardiers in the Royal Regiment of Artillery. Unlike those used by their British infantry counterparts, the pouch's flaps were made of buff leather which, like the shoulder belt, had to be whitened with pipe clay. Because Royal Artillery soldiers were supposed to use their carbines only for the purpose of defending their artillery pieces, the blocks within held a meager eight or nine rounds. Note that the forepart of the shoulder belt includes a buff leather keeper, which typically housed a pick (used to prime artillery charges), a spike (used to spike an artillery piece in case it had to be abandoned), and a hammer, seen here, which was used to beat the spike into the vent. While the pouch's priming horn, used to prime an artillery charge in case of emergency, is missing, the three brass rings used to keep the horn's cord in place remain.

to safety—all the horses were killed early in the action—but to no avail. The 62nd "were forced to abandon the Hill & on it" Hadden's two cannons. Their route was followed by the retreat of the Fusiliers, which also "quitted the height," and the Americans "following the retreating troops."[23] The British rallied and retook the hill, but the back-and-forth fight over the field continued and both sides engaged in "several smart struggles" over the artillery throughout the battle.[24]

Hamilton's left-hand regiment, the 20th Regiment of Foot, lay within Freeman's flat, cultivated farm field located directly east of the heights upon which the main battle was being fought. Stationed to protect Hamilton's left in case Poor attempted an envelopment, the regiment remained until it was fired upon from the woods directly south of their position. Morgan, who was finally able to re-form his riflemen, deployed his troops in the woods on the Americans' extreme right, which happened to be behind the 62nd Regiment and in front of the 20th. From this strong position, the riflemen shot at the rear of the hapless 62nd, and the 20th, likewise exposed in the open field, was ordered south into the woods to attack Morgan's troops.

Lieutenant-Colonel John Lind led his men into the woods with fixed bayonets, but soon found the maneuver futile. There, the British found the riflemen "strongly posted in a wood, with a deep Ravine in their front," along with a makeshift abatis on the other side.[25] These unexpected, wooded ravines—there were a few of them in the woods—were too deep to overcome, and Lind's men

Case Shot
ca. 1776–77
Saratoga National Historical Park, SARA 846
Case shot consisted of small iron balls that, when packed together in a cylindrical tin container and discharged from a cannon or howitzer, could kill or maim significant numbers of enemy soldiers. These, measuring about three-quarters inch in diameter, were shot by the Royal Regiment of Artillery during the September 19 Battle of Freeman's Farm.

Officer's Gorget, 20th Regiment of Foot
ca. 1770s
The Colonial Williamsburg Foundation, Acc. No. 2005-13
British infantry officers were expected to wear gorgets while on most duties, including in battle. This silver gorget includes the regulation royal coat of arms of King George III, below which is engraved the regimental designation, XXth REG[T]. Repoussé-worked ears adorned with martial trophies complete the decor.

withdrew. The blatant futility of fighting in the woods against Morgan's riflemen forced Lind to more directly support Anstruther's struggling 62nd Regiment on the hill to the west. There, the 20th joined in the fighting over Hadden's pair of cannons, over which they "contested with small arms and at the point of the bayonet . . . with alternate slaughter on both sides." One 20th Regiment soldier remembered that, as the hours passed, the "ground flowed with English and American blood, and the dead bodies of friends and enemies covered each other" on the contested field.[26] Part of the Braunschweig Leichtes Infanterie Bataillon von Bärner was sent from Fraser's column in order to help the redcoats and blue boys fend off the American assault.

As for Fraser's column, it remained nearly stationary so as to maintain contact with the army's center. Most of Fraser's troops were centered on or near the Micajah Marshall farm, located a couple hundred yards west of Freeman's. The 24th Regiment of Foot was posted in the Marshall farm clearing itself, while the British and German grenadiers deployed in the woods to the west, thereby forming the army's extreme right. The British and German light infantry, royalists, Indians, and Canadiens were spread thinly across the entire area. As the battle

Pattern 1769 Short Land Musket (Irish) ca. 1776

Don Troiani collection

British regiments on the Irish Establishment received muskets from Dublin Castle, where their component parts were assembled from pieces supplied by private contractors. Constituting the newest pattern weapon available, this musket was issued to the 20th Regiment of Foot on the eve of its embarkation to Canada in 1776. In 1777 half the regiment carried these muskets while the other half used older, English-made Long Land muskets issued in 1773. Weighing about ten pounds, this pattern musket has a .75-caliber forty-two-inch-long barrel.

20th Regiment of Foot Rank-and-File Button ca. 1775

Don Troiani collection

Button designs for British marching regiments of foot varied considerably. Unlike most regiments, the 20th commonly used Roman numerals (XX) for its regimental designation.

progressed, shots were fired from the woods between Freeman's and Marshall's farms in the direction of the 24th Regiment, by which

> Major William Agnew with [five companies of] the 24th Regt advanc'd into the wood, in order to flank them; on the first onset the Rebels retired in confusion, but the fire from the line having abated considerably at this time, and the Rebels finding their left Flank in danger, poured a strong force upon [the 24th] Regt which caused them to retire about one hundred yards behind an inclosure in a grass field [the Marshall farm].[27]

The Americans who remained in the woods were Dearborn's Light Infantry. Agnew, however, would not be deterred. He ordered the 24th Regiment to "file off by the left," by which "they took the wood, before them firing after their own manner from behind Trees, and twice repuls'd" strong American attacks "without any assistance."[28]

Colonel Latimer's Connecticut militia and the 2nd and 4th New York Regiments were sent forth and, as ordered by Poor and Arnold, moved against Fraser's column. Colonel Philip Van Cortlandt maneuvered his 2nd New York Regiment through the fields and woods and "discovered their advance far from their Main Body," which he "determined to attack." The few dozen Braunschweig jäger of Breymann's Reserve Corps were no match for the few hundred New Yorkers and the Germans fell back, but were "Instantly supplied by the British Light Infantry." The ensuing firefight in the woods lasted for "upwards of an hour," during which the German Leichtes Infanterie Battaillon von Bärner struck Van Cortlandt's left flank, forcing him to fall back. The New Yorkers fell back

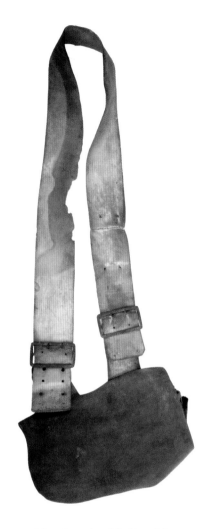

Cartridge Pouch with Shoulder Belt, 20th Regiment of Foot ca. 1760s

Don Troiani collection

This soft-leather pouch contained a wooden block that held only nineteen cartridges. Its large size, meager carrying capacity, and brass-buckled belt stitched to the pouch body are features prevalent in pouches of the 1760s and early 1770s. The buff shoulder belt is marked to the 20th Regiment of Foot.

British Buckle ca. 1770s

Saratoga National Historical Park, SARA 34163

This brass buckle was recovered from where the British Light Infantry Battalion and a detachment of the 3rd Battalion, Royal Regiment of Artillery, were positioned at the start of the Battle of Freeman's Farm. Similar buckles have been found at other British Army campsites.

Cartridge Pouch Device, 24th Regiment of Foot
ca. 1770

Don Troiani collection

Waist Belt Clasp, 24th Regiment of Foot
ca. 1770

Don Troiani collection
Very rare among British marching regiments of foot, the 24th had matched-design openwork brass devices for its clasps and pouch ornaments.

Edward Lounsbery's Cartridge Box
ca. 1776

Don Troiani collection
This bag-style leather cartridge box includes a wooden block drilled with nineteen holes for carrying that many rounds of ammunition. In 1777 Edward Lounsbery was the junior captain of Colonel Philip Van Cortlandt's 2nd New York Regiment. With this box, a fusee, and a bayonet, Lounsbery would have fought in both battles of Saratoga.

to a "favorable . . . footpath," located on a reserve slope covered by a three-foot ledge. With the onset of dusk, Van Cortlandt ordered his troops not to fire "until the Enemy did and then directly below the flash of the Enemies fire," which was done effectively.[29]

Colonel Jackson's (8th) Massachusetts regiment was ordered to go "to the left of all the American troops, so as to outflank the British," against which he formed his line of battle. Commanded by Lieutenant Colonel John Brooks, the Massachusetts men could not identify the troops formed in front of them "because of the lateness of the evening, and the dusk being increased by the trees." The darkened line fired in their direction, and Brooks ordered a return fire, noting they were German grenadiers from the glints of their "brass cases on their breasts, for containing lighted match." Having no way to sustain a nighttime battle in the woods, Brooks's troops retired back to camp.[30]

The men of Colonel Thomas Marshall's (10th) Massachusetts Regiment had a similar experience. The last regiment sent to the battle, Marshall's reached the woods in "the dusk of the evening," where "distinguishing the regimentals" was proven difficult. Upon noticing a body of troops nearby, Marshall cautiously ordered his men to prepare to fire. Once the darkened soldiers' "grenadier-caps" were discerned, the Americans fired upon the enemy grenadiers; after a firefight in the dark, Marshall's regiment sought "its safety in a retreat."[31] The British grenadiers likewise had difficulty "On its turning dusk,"

Private, Musketeer Company, Braunschweig Light Infantry Battalion von Bärner

The Leichtes Infanterie Bataillon von Bärner, consisting of four musketeer companies and one company of jäger, was the only new Braunschweig battalion raised from scratch in 1776 for service in North America. While its commissioned and noncommissioned officers were drawn from preexisting Braunschweig corps, young men and boys were newly recruited for its ranks. This *Gemeiner Musketier* (musketeer private) is dressed in marching order, with a *Tornister* (knapsack), *Feldflasche* (canteen), and *Brotbeutel* (haversack), which carried rations.

Private, Colonel Thomas Marshall's (10th) Massachusetts Regiment

As with most Continental battalions in the Northern Army, Marshall's Regiment received spurts of inadequate amounts of nondescript coats, jackets, "rifle" shirts, breeches, overalls, hats, and other necessary clothing. In early September enough brown and green broadcloth, serge, large and small buttons, thread, and sticks of mohair (used to bind buttonholes) were issued to uniform a portion of the regiment. The spectacular color combination inspired an enemy officer to note these unique-looking "brown coats with ocean green facings and turn-ups."

The Specht Journal, 101.

as they were "near firing on a body of our Germans, mistaking their dark clothing for that of the enemy" Americans.[32]

Back in the American camp, Gates was concerned that the enemy's left-hand column might attack Bemus Heights, and he therefore ensured that the defenses there were well manned. In fact, Gates had prepared for every eventuality: He allowed Arnold to attack Burgoyne, he was prepared to defend the lines in case of attack, and, as a precaution, he had earlier in the day ordered the "tents . . . struck and baggage loaded . . . to secure a retreat if it was necassery."[33] Having deployed all his troops to the battle, Arnold returned to camp, seeking permission from Gates to send additional men from the army's Center Division. But his request for "a reinforcement . . . was overruled by the Commander in Chief [Gates] & on the former urging it, the latter drew his Sword & said he commanded & would be obeyed or something to that purpose."[34] There would be no further reinforcement to support Arnold's attack.

As for Riedesel's left-hand column, it slowly lumbered down the Hudson Valley since morning. Although unhindered by Americans, its advance was slowed by a series of wrecked bridges that crossed the many creeks that flowed into the Hudson River. It took half a day alone to repair the bridge that traversed Kromma Kill, the large creek that cut through the Great Ravine. Once repaired, the column continued, but for only 500 yards before encountering another ruined bridge. Once repaired, the column advanced, only to be held up by a third destroyed bridge. While the laborers toiled away and the afternoon hours passed by, the sounds of gunfire to the west only grew louder. This concerned Riedesel a great deal: Because the battle was clearly coming from the same area, it could only mean that Burgoyne's battle wasn't going well. In the absence of any direction from the army commander, Riedesel took the initiative to stage some of his forces in such a way that they would be well positioned in case Burgoyne requested assistance.

Pattern 1770 Sergeant of Grenadiers Carbine (British) ca. 1775

Don Troiani collection

Regulations called for British Army grenadier, light infantry, and fusilier sergeants to carry carbines of this pattern, which were shorter, lighter, and of a smaller caliber (.65) than the muskets carried by the rank and file (corporals and privates). This particular piece, assembled at the Tower of London, was issued to the 21st Regiment of Foot (Royal Northern British Fusiliers). This pattern carbine has a thirty-nine-inch barrel and weighs about seven pounds.

Drummer, Braunschweig Infantry Regiment von Riedesel

This *Tambour* (drummer) wears the distinctive yellow coat with light blue lapels, cuffs, and collar associated with the Infanterie Regiment von Riedesel. *Tambour* coats in this regiment were edged with white lace "mixed with black and yellow," colors that were also reflected in the painted wooden hoops of their brass *Trommeln* (drums) and belts. As with all Braunschweig soldiers in the 1777 Army from Canada (excepting dragoons and jäger), this *Tambour* wears striped linen gaitered trousers in lieu of woolen breeches.

Tabelle nach welcher des General Major von Riedesel Regiment im Jahre 1776, trans. Claus Reuter, Staatsarchiv Wolfenbüttel, Acta Militaria (ältere), 234, Part 2, Mondirungs-Anschlag.

Finally, an officer brought orders for Riedesel to strengthen his positions in the floodplain for defense and "fall on the enemy's right flank at Freeman's Farm with all the troops he possibly could spare."[35] The baron immediately set off with his own regiment, two companies of the Infanterie Regiment von Rhetz, and two light six-pounders managed by Captain Georg Päusch and his Hessen-Hanau artillerymen. Their progress along the wooded cart path that cut due west toward the farm went unhindered. Near dusk, his reinforcement of over 700 troops covered the one and a half miles and reached the eastern end of Freeman's farm. Once arrived, Riedesel could see that

> [t]he enemy were stationed at the corner of a wood, and were covered on their right flank by a deep swampy ravine, whose steep banks covered with bushes had moreover been made quite insurmountable by means of an abatis. There was an open space in front of this corner of the wood, in which the English Regiments had formed into line. The possession of this open piece of ground, on which Freemann's [*sic*] Habitation was situated, was the apple of discord during the whole of the day, and was now occupied by the one party now by the other. . . . There was nothing but dense forests round the place where the English Brigade had formed into line.[36]

With his troops fresh and poised to make a flanking maneuver against the Americans, the question was in how to execute it. The field before them was open enough, but such a movement might simply drive the Americans into the woods and thereby give them the advantage that they enjoyed for most of the battle. The preferred option—deploying in the woods to their left (the Americans' right)—would be difficult not only because of the deep ravines therein, but also because German maneuvers were incompatible with the wood fighting tactic of "treeing." Before Bennington, at least. One of the repercussions of the Battle of Bennington—the only one that benefited the Germans—was a reassessment of tactical doctrine. Riedesel finally realized that his men's predisposed, traditional

Braunschweig Polearms
ca. 1770s

Don Troiani collection

The commissioned and noncommissioned officers of German infantry regiments, except those serving in the light infantry or jäger, carried polearms. While British commissioned officers and noncommissioned officers replaced their polearms with fusees and carbines during the war, their German counterparts did not. On the left is a sergeant's *Kurzgewehr* (halberd), and on the right, a commissioned officer's *Sponton* (spontoon). Note that the engraving on the *Sponton* is gold-filled.

General Riedesel, September 19

This is when thirty-nine-year old Major-General Friedrich Riedesel arrived on the eastern end of Freeman's farm at the head of 730 Braunschweig and Hessen-Hanau reinforcements. With the battle being played out before them on the other side of the field, Riedesel considers his deployment options. Surrounded by some of his general staff, including his deputy adjutant-general, Captain Julius August von Pöllniz, and aides-de-camp Captain Samuel Willoe (8th Regiment of Foot) and Lieutenant and Captain Archibald Edmonstone (1st Regiment of Foot Guards), Riedesel expresses his desire to send the bulk of his infantry into the woods on their left in order to outflank the Americans.

approach to fighting the Americans by slow, plodding marches, open-field linear formations, and carefully coordinated volley fire could hinder battlefield success. In order to implement some necessary changes in fighting style, Riedesel instructed his Braunschweig soldiers, when necessary, to

> seek trees or other cover behind which they can hide, and run from behind one tree to another. Then each soldier has his own defense. This is the only means which puts us in a position to be able to attack and dislodge the enemy in a wood without great loss. It is to be noted that no soldier must shoot except when he is behind a tree or another cover so that he can take a sure aim at the enemy; otherwise, a soldier would shoot off his cartridges in less than half an hour without the least effect. . . . I believe it my duty to issue an order which will perhaps save the lives of many men, at a time, when, at any moment, we can be put in a position where one battalion or another can engage the enemy in the woods and cannot act against it in any other manner than that described above.[37]

The baron immediately deployed his troops onto the Freeman clearing, after which his 700 infantrymen were sent into the woods to work their way west in order to outflank the American right. Päusch's two cannons were dragged along a path across Freeman's cultivated field and, with difficulty, unlimbered and dragged up the towering hill by British and German soldiers alike. The horses were left behind the hills out of harm's way, and the artillery "cartridges were carried up in the men's arms and placed beside the guns" so that Päusch's men could quickly fire "twelve to fourteen shots, one after the other, at the enemy standing under a full fire at about a good pistol shot distance" away.[38] The British rallied with this new German reinforcement, while the Braunschweig infantry in the woods forced "their way through the ravine no matter what it cost."[39] Without a similar reinforcement, the Americans' fire "faded in the distance" as the troops retreated into the dark forest.[40] Having lasted about eight hours, one of the longest land battles of the war was over.

British casualties numbered 550 officers and soldiers killed or wounded, with another 41 captured by Arnold's troops. Losses were heaviest among Hamilton's three regiments, particularly the 62nd (over 210 casualties) and the 20th (over 115 casualties). Considering the heavy, daylong firefight, it's notable that not a single one of the thirty-four commissioned officers killed or mortally wounded were above the rank of captain, and the Americans were able to take only a few low-ranking officers into captivity.[41] Displeased with the performance of the

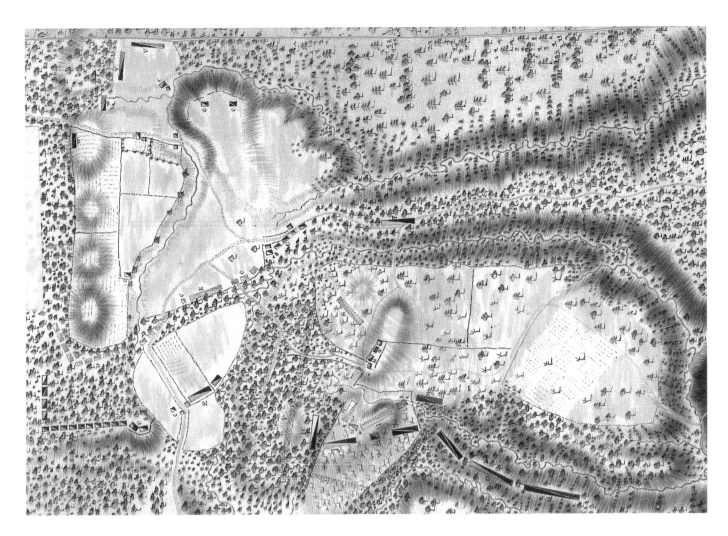

3d & 4th Position 19th Septr 1777 (detail)

by Lieutenant William Cumberland Wilkinson, ca. 1778

The Library of Congress, gm71000664

As the Battle of Freeman's Farm grew throughout the afternoon and wore on into evening, the fighting expanded to the smaller Marshall farm and the adjoining woods to the west. The Braunschweig Grenadierbattaillon Breymann (N) and the British Grenadier Battalion (D) formed the army's defenses on the British right wing (west, or left) within the woods. Fraser's 24th Regiment of Foot (E) is arrayed on the Marshall farm, and the wooded span between that farm and Freeman's was heavily fought over by that regiment. On Freeman's farm, Hamilton's three British regiments (represented by G, H, and I), joined by part of the German light infantry and jäger (M and L), are shown in some of the positions they took in the fighting during the latter course of the battle. Riedesel's infantry reinforcement, which consisted of the five-company Braunschweig Infanterie Regiment von Riedesel (O) and two companies of the Regiment von Rhetz (Q; miscolored and not shown proportional to size), are shown charging through the ravine-cut woods south of the farm. As is usual with British-generated maps, the American forces (Y) are incompletely depicted as mottled blocks. Also not shown by the artist were the more than 850 people of both armies killed or wounded who covered the ground by day's end.

Lieutenant Stephen Harvey

attributed to Sir George Chalmers, Bt.,
ca. 1775/1778

Trustees of the Goulburn Settled Estates

Nephew to Lieutenant-General
Edward Harvey, adjutant-general
of the forces, Stephen served
as a teenaged lieutenant in the
62nd Regiment of Foot. Although
wounded in the Battle of Freeman's
Farm, "his heroic ardor would not
allow him to quit the battle, while
he could stand and see his brave
lads fighting beside him." A mortal
wound, however, sealed his fate.
With death fast approaching, "he
had one request, which he had just
life enough to utter 'Tell my uncle
I died like a soldier!'" This portrait
is probably the one Chalmers
showed at the 1778 Royal
Academy of Arts exhibition titled
An Officer of the 62nd Regiment,
lately killed in America.

Anbury, *Travels Through the Interior Parts of*
America, vol. 1, 423–24.

infantry regiments in Hamilton's Brigade, Burgoyne felt the need to admonish them for their poor performance in general orders two days after the battle:

> [T]he impetuosity and uncertain aim of the British Troops in giving their fire, and the mistake they are still under, in preferring it to the Baynotte, is to be much lamented. The Lieut. General is persuaded this error will be corrected in the next engagement, upon conviction of their own experience and reason, as well as upon that general principle of discipline *never* to *fire* but by the *order of an officer*.[42]

Despite the claim, the aforementioned "experience" was not applicable to most of those in Hamilton's Brigade. None of the three British regimental commanders had commanded battalions in battle before, and most of the commissioned officers had never served in battle. As for the redcoats, most were likewise completely inexperienced at combat, and with the influx of non-English-speaking German recruits—the 62nd Regiment's rank and file were nearly 25 percent German—any lack of cohesive combat experience is not to be wondered at. As for the Royal Artillery blue boys, they fared little better, since half of those who fought were recent recruits from the Royal Irish Regiment of Artillery who, like most of their redcoated brethren, had no combat experience. The decimation of his redcoat regiments was so severe, Burgoyne authorized a unique scheme: two days after the battle, 120 royalist American men "of tried bravery and fidelity" were drafted into the army's British infantry ranks.[43]

American losses numbered over 300 officers and soldiers killed or wounded, with an additional 23 taken prisoner by the British. The New Hampshire line and Cook's battalion of Connecticut militia bore the brunt of the army's casualties, particularly the 1st New Hampshire Battalion (sixty casualties). The army's officer corps sustained a high number of casualties in the battle, having lost twenty-seven killed or wounded and an additional three captured.[44] Of those killed or mortally wounded, two held the rank of lieutenant colonel.[45] Arnold was so shocked by the high number of officer casualties that he noted in the following day's divisional order that "two [*sic*] many officers, that Zeal & Spirit push'd on" led from "the front of their companies" instead of taking up their "proper stations" in the rear.[46] The riflemen certainly made effective combatants and caused a significantly disproportionate number of casualties on the enemy. But their easy dispersal early in the action and the complete lack of coordination with Dearborn's light infantry both demonstrate an ineptitude reflective of the reality that the corps had never fought a pitched battle as a cohesive body nor previously trained together.

Freeman's Farm Battle Souvenir
ca. 1890s
Saratoga National Historical Park
The First Battle of Saratoga lasted for nearly eight hours, with most combat taking place on and around Freeman's farm. With thousands of soldiers firing thousands of muskets across the forest-bound clearing, over 150,000 lead musket balls were discharged, most becoming imbedded in the ground and in tree trunks, such as seen here.

Trooper, Major Elijah Hyde's Detachment of Light Horse ("Arnold's Horse")

In August, Connecticut ordered one-half of four of its light horse regiments to join the Northern Department for two months' service. Portions arrived at the Sprouts shortly thereafter and the remainder at Bemus Heights in September. There the men received orders "to Look out for our Selvs," upon which they found "Good Pastter for our horsis" as well as "a few board [to] make a lettel hut out in [the] field." This unit's primary duties included patrolling, gathering intelligence, escorting prisoners, and providing express services for Generals Gates, Lincoln, and Arnold.

NARA, Revolutionary War Pension Files, Robert Treat (R.10,691).

Although the Battle of Freeman's Farm was a British victory, it was so only on a tactical level, measured by the fact that they held the field of battle at the end of the day. Strategically, however, it was an American victory, measured by the stymied British advance. Not only had the British won a Pyrrhic victory for themselves, but they had not even seen the Bemus Heights defenses let alone removed Gates's army from them. Arnold's strategy of attacking the British before they reached the defenses was proven to be the correct one, as was the calculated deployment of his division's regiments. Arnold successfully managed the Battle of Freeman's Farm from afar—his aides-de-camp and troopers from "Arnold's Horse" acted as his eyes and ears for most of the battle—and while he was close enough to observe the action at times, he did not micromanage it. In stark contrast, Burgoyne did just that, and his myopic focus on the fighting at Freeman's farm caused him to all but ignore the management of his army. But, once again, Burgoyne was lucky: Just like in the Battles of Hubbardton and Fort Anne, the British redcoats eked out their victory only with last-minute reinforcements. Notably, for the second time, it was Riedesel and his Germans who saved the day.

Interregnum

Since the Battle we have been fortifying and suffering the enemy to do the same Very few in the army but sees the absurdity of it.
—Colonel Henry Beekman Livingston, October 4, 1777[1]

The British used the day after the battle to rest, reorganize, and replenish ammunition. Despite the necessity of these precautions, no one then could have anticipated the enormous implications of this daylong respite. Early the following day, Sunday, September 21, fate intervened when a courier entered Burgoyne's camp and delivered a cryptic letter from Lieutenant-General Sir Henry Clinton, commander of British forces in the city of New York:

> You know my good will and are not ignorant of my poverty, If
> you think two thousand men can assist you effectually, I will make a
> push at [Fort] Montgomery in about ten days, but ever jealous of my
> flanks. If they make a move in force on either of them, I must return
> to save this important post. I expect reinforcement every day. Let me
> know what you would wish.[2]

The above message was incorporated within an otherwise mundane letter that was supposed to be deciphered by use of a precut paper "mask." The challenge was that Burgoyne no longer had his copy. Without the overlay on hand, it took some time to puzzle out the letter's true meaning, which, when revealed, presented Burgoyne with the unexpected proposal. Burgoyne's reply, sent back with the currier, was simple:

> I have lost the old Cipher, but being sure from the Tenor of your
> Letter, you meant it to be so read, I have made it out.
> An Attack or the Menace of an Attack upon [Fort] Montgomery,
> must be of great Use, as it will draw away a part of this Force and I
> will follow them close. Do it, my dear friend, directly.[3]

This changed everything. Clinton's unanticipated offer of support, in the form of a potent diversion in Burgoyne's favor, was exactly what the Army from

196

Braunschweig Buttons
ca. 1776
Saratoga National Historical Park, SARA 1561, 1687, 34159, 34192, 34203, 34208, 34218
These brass German soldier buttons came from the fortified camp garrisoned by Breymann's Reserve Corps, 80 percent of which wore uniforms bearing brass buttons. Having plain, slightly domed faces with indented edges, the large coat and waistcoat buttons measure three-quarters inch in diameter while the small button measures one-half inch.

Braunschweig Buttonhook
third quarter, 18th century
Saratoga National Historical Park, SARA 1625
This four-and-a-quarter-inch-long iron "gaiter key" was owned by a Braunschweig officer or soldier in Breymann's Reserve Corps camp at the time of the Battle of Saratoga. It was used to draw buttons through the holes of woolen gaiters or linen gaitered trousers.

Canada commander needed. With Clinton's "push" north from the city of New York, it was expected that Gates would have to divide his force so as to see to Clinton's threat south of Albany, allowing Burgoyne to pounce upon his weakened adversary. All he needed to do was wait.

Over the next two weeks, Burgoyne's troops built an intricate system of fortifications in order to protect their encampments and supplies, stretching for one and a half miles west from the Hudson River. Covering the line's southwestern corner, located at Freeman's farm, was the British Light Infantry Redoubt, a substantial, enclosed log and earthen fortification, which guarded Fraser's Advanced Corps's camp. North-northwest of the British Light Infantry Redoubt was an open-worked fortification complex that guarded the camp of Breymann's Reserve Corps, as well as the east–west road that ran behind Burgoyne's entire encampment. Because these two forts were separated by about 500 yards, two fortified cabins located in the vale between them were garrisoned by the army's two companies of Canadien militia draftees. Collectively, the enormous British redoubt, Breymann's fortified lines, and Canadien cabins were purpose-built to complement each other if they fell under attack, despite the substantial gap and limited line of sight between them.

Officer, Braunschweig Infantry Regiment Prinz Friedrich

The premier Braunschweig musketeer regiment in Burgoyne's army was named after Prinz Friedrich Augustus, a son of the Herzog zu Braunschweig und Lüneburg (Duke of Brunswick and Lueneburg). Braunschweig officers in Burgoyne's army were armed with swords and wore rich silver-and-yellow-mix sashes and sword knots, leather gloves, silver or gold aiguillettes, and canes; *Ringkragen* (gorgets) were worn by infantry officers. Despite the nature of the campaign, *Sponton* (spontoons) were carried by most German infantry officers in the Army from Canada.

Before Gates's army moved north from the Sprouts with his Center Division and Arnold's Left Division on September 8, the Army's Right Division, commanded by Major General Benjamin Lincoln, was coalescing in Vermont. Shortly after he took command of the Northern Department on August 19, Gates met with his second in command at headquarters, and the two hashed out plans for future operations. Lincoln immediately returned to Bennington on August 25 and sent messages to the Councils of Massachusetts and New Hampshire to have them direct their militia to "assemble in the Grants [Vermont], where, probably, they will act for a time."[4] Flour and beef cattle were stockpiled in anticipation of the military buildup, as was ammunition, although the initial supply of musket balls were of too large a caliber for most of the troops to use. As planned, once Gates moved north to Stillwater, Lincoln and his growing Right Division moved north to Pawlet, Vermont, about forty miles north of Bennington. Scouts gathered intelligence on the disposition of Burgoyne's forces left behind at Lakes George and Champlain, by which an ambitious, multifold operation was conceived. Lincoln had over 2,000 men.

On September 12, the very day that Gates moved his forces to Bemus Heights, Lincoln instructed Colonel John Brown to take 500 men and move on the Lake George Landing. There, he was to free any prisoners reportedly located nearby, destroy any enemy war matériel encountered, and, if Ticonderoga itself appeared vulnerable to attack, he was to attempt it. Above all, Brown was given discretionary powers to do everything he could that would "most annoy, divide, & distract the enemy."[5] On September 13 Lincoln gave a similar order to Colonel Samuel Johnson to take 500 men and move against Mount Independence, where, "without risking too much," he would attack the post if he deemed it efficacious.[6] Lincoln also instructed Colonel Benjamin Woodbridge to take 500 militia to cut directly over to Skenesborough, then down to Fort Anne, and strike at Fort Edward with the similar caveat that the place was to be taken only if it could be done without unnecessary risk.[7] All three operations were planned to take place simultaneously.

On the Mount Independence side, Johnson's men, with a detachment of the Green Mountain Boys and Massachusetts and Vermont militia, marched on the same road that St. Clair

Braunschweig Gorget
third quarter, 18th century

Don Troiani collection

Like their British counterparts, non-jäger Braunschweig commissioned infantry officers wore *Ringkragen* (gorgets) while on most duties; commissioned officers of the Prinz Ludwig Dragoon Regiment, serving as infantry, wore them as well. Larger and heavier than British gorgets, Braunschweig *Ringkragen* were made to a uniform pattern. The gilt, repoussé-worked ducal coronet surmounting war trophies, the whole of which surrounds a porcelain-enameled representation of the rearing white horse of Haus Hannover (House of Hanover) on a red ground, is screwed to the silver plate.

*Project for the Attack of
Ticonderoga, proposed to be
put in Execution as near as the
circumstances and ground will
admit of*

by William Furness Brassier, May 29, 1759

The Library of Congress, gm71000611

Although this map was drawn in
1759 during the French and Indian
War in preparation for a British
attack on the French, it nevertheless
provides an excellent period
depiction of the La Chute River. The
four-mile-long waterway empties
Lake George into Lake Champlain,
and in so doing, drops over 200
feet during its short course. This
extreme elevational change
created a series of "Rifts and Falls"
in the shallow river, making most
of it unnavigable. When Brown
attacked on September 18, 1777,
the barn housing the American
prisoners and the encampment
site of the two companies of the
53rd Regiment were located on
the open plain between the road
("Carrying place for the boats &ca")
and the paralleling ridge to the east
of it. Also attacked was the Lake
George landing place (depicted),
the blockhouse being built on
Mount Defiance, the single bridge
that crossed the river, and two
blockhouses on the Ticonderoga
peninsula (not depicted).

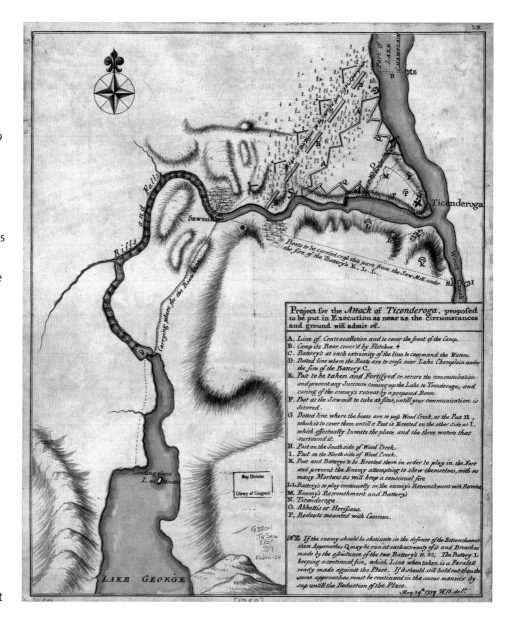

retreated on in July. Joined by Brigadier General Jonathan Warner, who took overall command of the threefold operation, an advance party engaged the Mount's sentries on the 17th. A "Small Spattering Fire began," but Johnson's men kept their distance.[8] The following day, the Mount's garrison, composed of the Braunschweig Infanterie Regiment Prinz Friedrich and half the 53rd Regiment of Foot, "immediately hurried to the alarm place[s]" behind the Mount's extensive fortifications.[9] The Americans, unable to observe weakness in the defenses, maintained their distance while the defenders poured a "Heavy fire all day to no purpose."[10]

On the Ticonderoga side, Brown's troops had a significantly different experience.[11] At daybreak on September 18, they struck at an encampment where two companies of the 53rd Regiment lay, located on the unguarded plain between the Lake George Landing and Mount Defiance. The British officers, soldiers, women, and children were easily taken; Brown's men, being "favour'd by a fog,"[12] were able to surround the British camp before they were discovered. Flushed with success, Brown's men fanned out across the area to strike at multiple targets. One body cut west and freed nearly 120 American prisoners, most of whom were captured at Hubbardton, from the barn they were imprisoned in, and the dozen redcoats guarding them were taken prisoner in turn. They continued on to

Private, Colonel John Brown's Battalion, Berkshire County, Massachusetts, Militia

Although Massachusetts militia served with the Northern Army since the beginning of the campaign, at issue were the terms of their "alarm" services, which typically ran for only a few days or, in the case of Brown's battalion in September, twenty. Massachusetts required its militia to have a "fire-arm, with a steel or iron ramrod . . . a bayonet . . . a cutting-sword, or a tomahawk or hatchet, a . . . cartridge-box that will hold fifteen rounds of cartridges, at least, a hundred buck-shot, a jack-knife . . . a knapsack and blanket, a canteen . . . sufficient to hold one quart."

"An Act for Forming and Regulating the Militia within the Colony of the Massachusetts Bay," January 22, 1776, in the *Acts and Resolves, Public and Private, of the Province of the Massachusetts Bay*, vol. 5 (Boston: Wright and Potter, 1886), 448.

Waist Belt Clasp, 53rd Regiment of Foot
ca. 1775

Don Troiani collection

This sheet brass clasp, cast with the regiment's number and laurel branches, is stamped COLLINS on the reverse, signifying the name of the brass founder who made it. Most British Army soldier clothing, arms, and accoutrements were made under contract with private firms at the behest of regimental commanders.

53rd Regiment of Foot Rank-and-File Button
ca. 1775

Don Troiani collection

It was not until 1767 that British regiments were ordered to bear identifying numbers on their buttons. Made of pewter, other ranks' buttons cast with a higher lead content, such as this one, would have resulted in a heavier coat. A typical British soldier's coat had about forty buttons.

the Lake George Landing, where a number of Royal Navy officers, sailors, and Canadien corvée lay, and Brown's men snapped them up along with an armed sloop.[13]

To the east, Brown sent a detachment to scale Mount Defiance, where they captured an unfinished blockhouse, another dozen 53rd Regiment soldiers, and some artificers. In order to access the Ticonderoga peninsula, Brown proceeded north to cross the singular bridge that spanned the La Chute River. The four British sentinels watching over the bridge "permitted a small party of rebels to approach too near, mistaking them . . . for Canadians," and the Americans captured them with ease. This exposed another barn where another company of the 53rd Regiment was lodged and captured, again with the assistance of the thick morning fog. The only substantive resistance offered by the British was at another blockhouse, located west of the aforementioned barn. Its small garrison, commanded by Lieutenant Simon Lord, was now alerted to Brown's handiwork and put up a defense "till the rebels brought a six pounder against him, on which he surrender'd."[14] Brown then turned his sights east, took the undefended French Lines, and called upon the commander to surrender both forts.

The British commander of the forts and their dependencies was Brigadier-General Henry Watson Powell.[15] With the surprise loss of a substantial portion of his 53rd Regiment, all that remained on the Ticonderoga peninsula was the hundred-man garrison of the fort itself, a mixed British and German body commanded by Captain William Thomas Taylor.[16] Most everyone else, including Powell himself, was on the Mount. After receiving Brown's surrender demand, Powell's response was immediate: "The garrison intrusted to my charge I shall defend to the last."[17]

For days, Johnson and Brown remained in their respective positions. Using a captured medium twelve-pounder atop Mount Defiance, Brown's troops fired at Fort Ticonderoga and even across the lake at Mount Independence, but with little effect. The defenders returned cannon fire with similar ineffectiveness. Johnson's troops fired musket shots at the Mount's defenders, who in turn would open up with musket and artillery barrages into the woods. With limited

Tomahawk Head
18th century
Don Troiani collection
This diminutive, round pole tomahawk head was recovered in the Lake Champlain Valley. It is typical of those carried by American soldiers serving in the Northern Department.

ammunition and provisions and his regiment's enlistments set to expire, Brown proposed that further operations against the forts be abandoned. General Warner concurred, and the besiegers withdrew south on the evening of September 22.

With the loss of fewer than 10 men killed or wounded, Brown captured a dozen British commissioned and staff officers, 140 British soldiers, 120 Canadien corvée, 20 artificers, a sloop, dozens of bateaux, and 2 gun boats, and freed nearly 120 American soldiers from captivity.[18] Brown sent his British prisoners up Lake Champlain to Skenesborough, which Woodbridge had handedly retaken. Although thwarted in his hopes to take the forts on Lake Champlain, Brown set his sights on another prize: Lake George's Diamond Island. With his sloop, 2 gunboats, 17 bateaux, and about 420 officers and soldiers, Brown set off from the Lake George Landing in the early morning hours of September 22. By 9:00 a.m. on September 24, he advanced his vessels to make the attack.

Diamond Island, a small island located about three miles north of the ruins of Fort George, was garrisoned by about 200 British and German troops under the command of Captain Thomas Aubrey.[19] On the island lay much of the Army from Canada's baggage, collected there from Fort George for easier protection in the event of an American attack. Unlike the British at Ticonderoga, Aubrey was alerted to Brown's plans, having been forwarded by some men, including a paroled sutler, that the armed flotilla was on its way.

Brown sent his gunboats to test both ends of the island in order to see if it was practical to land his troops. Aubrey's few cannons cannonaded Brown's little fleet, and Brown's eight-gun sloop returned the favor. After nearly two hours, Brown's flotilla was bested, and they "retreated to the shore" and "burnt their boats" before evacuating inland.[20] Brown's casualties in this fight were about one dozen killed or wounded; Aubrey had none. For Brown, the Battle of Diamond Island marked an inauspicious end to an otherwise brilliant expedition.

Nail-Driven Musket Balls
second half, 18th century
Don Troiani collection
Undoubtedly designed to inflict maximum carnage, use of lead balls driven with wrought-iron nails appears to have been very rare, considering how few have ever been found. These .70-caliber projectiles were recovered near Fort Ticonderoga.

John Brown's Sword (detail)
ca. 1770s

Fort Ticonderoga Museum collection;
photograph by Don Troiani

This fine gilt-hilted sword was
owned by Colonel John Brown.
Small swords such as this
were worn more as a symbolic
representation of authority and
stature than as a fighting weapon.
The underside of the counterguard
is engraved "Colonel John Brown
Slain by the British on his 35th
Birthday, October 19, 1780 at the
battle of Stone Arabia, N.Y."

When word of Brown's raid reached Bemus Heights on September 21, Gates
ordered the firing of thirteen cannons, upon which "a genl. Whooray" was heard
"throo all our camp."[21] Lincoln, and most of the Massachusetts militia arm of
his right wing, started to arrive over the following days and added considerable
strength to Gates's Northern Army.[22] In fact, during the weeks after the Battle of
Freeman's Farm, Gates's camp was practically overrun by thousands of Massachusetts, New York, Connecticut, and New Hampshire militia reinforcements. Because
New England was safe from Burgoyne's grasp, Massachusetts and New Hampshire
finally released substantial numbers of long-term service militia to assist Gates, and
New York's Albany County activated its strongest wave of reinforcements yet. The
additional militia ballooned Gates's army from 8,200 to 12,500.

Also joining the army were over a hundred Oneida and Tuscarora men,
women, and children, some of whom, like Hanyery Tewahangarahken and his
wife, Tyonajanegen (Two Kettles Together), fought in the Battle of Oriskany.
Their arrival in camp on September 20 was auspicious, since they had just
attended a weeklong conference held in Albany at the behest of Philip Schuyler,
serving in his role as president of the Board of Commissioners for Indian Affairs
in the Northern Department. While in Albany, the Oneida and Tuscarora officially recognized the independence of the United States—the first nations to do
so—and, upon hearing news of the fighting at Freeman's farm, many decided to
immediately repair to Bemus Heights. Their scouting parties went out "every day
and lay in the woods and bushes near the enemy's camp, and take more or less
prisoners every day, and give us intelligence of all Burgoyne's movements." While
these Haudenosaunee allies left by the end of the month, one Continental Army
officer praised them for being "of great service to us." [23]

Because of the massive numbers of reinforcements, Gates's army was on the
brink of collapse on one important front: food. In September and into October,
Northern Army people at times enjoyed a great variety of provisions, including
fresh beef, flour, rice, peas, beer, and milk. Even chocolate, sugar, and rum were
available as limited army rations for some of the troops, or from sutlers. Despite
this boon of sustenance and treats, a secret known only to a few in Gates's army
was that provisioning the troops at these levels was unsustainable. While the army
was "Tolerably well off for Beef," they were for "Nothing else," particularly flour.[24]
Flour rations were being consumed by the people of Gates's enlarging army at
over seventy barrels per day, and military officers were dispatched far and wide to
find additional sources and ensure that as much flour was being forwarded to the
army as possible. "Provisions have been extremely scarce," wrote Jonathan Trumbull Jr., "sometimes not more than two or three days on hand. Once not one. .
. . Bread is most wanted. Fresh beef is plenty, but at a very great price." Despite
the burdensome challenge of feeding the troops during the weeks following the

**American Accoutrement Set
ca. 1770s**

Don Troiani collection

Worn by a soldier from Connecticut, this rare matched accoutrement set was suspended over the shoulders by woven linen shoulder belts. The bayonet belt's russet-colored leather frog still houses the original bayonet and scabbard.

Battle of Freeman's Farm, Trumbull later happily reported that "the prospect on this head grows much better." Never once were rations cut or not distributed when the army faced off against Burgoyne.[25]

Weighty issues facing army commanders aside, something more personal was coming to a head in the American camp at Bemus Heights: Benedict Arnold was in crisis. Shortly after his arrival at Fort Edward in July, a congressional friend warned him that an impending vote to backdate his commission would probably fail. Despite the heightened calamities facing the army at that time, Arnold immediately asked Schuyler's permission for "leave to retire," upon which the Northern Department commander "advised him to delay it for some time."[26] Although chagrined, Arnold remained. The congressional vote on Arnold's career advancement came on August 8:

> A motion was made, and seconded, that a new commission be made out, and sent to Major General Benedict Arnold, giving him the rank of major general in the army, from the nineteenth day of February last [backdated from May 2, 1777]:
> After debate, a motion was made to amend the motion by adding "On account of his extraordinary merit and former rank in the army":
> Question put, carried in the negative.
> Question put on the original motion. Carried in the negative.

Oneida Nation Warrior

The Oneida contingent of Haudenosaunee (Iroquois Confederacy) warriors who joined Gates's army after the Battle of Freeman's Farm served with Morgan's Corps as scouts and spies, during which time they wore army-issue red woolen caps so as to avoid friendly fire. Fascination with the Haudenosaunee caused Gates to forbid his soldiers "from crouding around the Indians Encampment." Wary of the potential for displays of discrimination against their new allies, Gates also stipulated that "the first person detected in abusing them will be severely punished."

September 25, 1777, *Orderly book of Capt [sic] Thaddeus Cook.*

The vote was not even close, with six in favor of Arnold and sixteen against.[27]

Word of this resolution reached Arnold simultaneously with Schuyler's preparations for relieving Fort Schuyler—convenient timing for anyone wanting opportunity to secure the interests of his country and prove his worthiness. Rather than redouble his threats, Arnold volunteered to lead that expedition (which otherwise already had a general, Ebenezer Learned, leading it), and did so successfully.

Once Arnold returned to the Sprouts and received command of the Left Division, his cordial relationship with Gates continued as it had in the Champlain Valley the previous year. The amiability between the two was challenged, however, since Arnold continued to surrounded himself with Schuyler sycophants—the "New York gang," Gates's own partisans called them—such as Majors Matthew Clarkson and Henry Brockholst Livingston, and Lieutenant Colonel Richard Varick.[28] The tangible break in the relationship came when Gates penned his report on the Battle of Freeman's Farm to John Hancock, president of Congress, three days after it was fought. It was short on details and even shorter on compliments; neither Arnold nor his division were named or particularly acknowledged as having participated. Gates claimed that "to discriminate in praise of the officers would be injustice, as they all deserve the honor and applause of Congress."[29]

This breach of protocol infuriated Arnold, and he wasted no time confronting the Northern Army commander about it. An argument erupted between them, after which Arnold wrote a seething letter to Gates. He accused his commanding officer of slights real and perceived, and cited his anger over a September 22 order that transferred Morgan's Corps from Arnold's Division to headquarters command. He raged over the lack of credit received for himself and his division in the Battle of Freeman's Farm. Despite the fact that all the regiments, but one, deployed to the fighting were from his division, Arnold noted that Gates's report stated that they were merely a generic "Detachment from the Army."

Adding to the laundry list of complaints, Arnold also claimed that he had "been received with the greatest coolness at Head Quarters, and often huffed in Such a manner as must mortify a Person with less Pride" than he had." He called Gates out for claiming that once General Lincoln arrived, Arnold's command would be removed from him, since Gates thought Arnold "of little Consequence to the Army." Lincoln had arrived, in fact, and although Arnold was not removed from command, he requested a pass to leave and, with his two aides-de-camp, "Join General Washington," where he might "serve my Country altho I am thought of no Consequence in this Department."[30]

Gates replied immediately. While the army commander may have been satisfied with Arnold's departure, he was thrilled to be rid of his aides-de-camp and the rest of the "New York gang." Gates granted his request to leave, but in

General Gates Creamware Mug
ca. 1778

Richard Ulbrich collection

The American War for Independence garnered great interest among English consumers for pictures of the war's famous personages—even Americans. As with most likenesses produced for the purpose, this mug's portrait of Horatio Gates was contrived to meet market demand.

the unusual form of an open letter to Hancock, in which Gates informed the president that Arnold's "reasons for Asking to leave the Army at this Time shall with my Answers be transmitted to Your Excellency."[31] Infuriated by this breach of protocol, Arnold ratcheted up the tension by responding to Gates:

> I thought myself Intitled to an answer, and that you would at least have condescended to acquaint me with the reasons which had induced you to treat me with affront and indignity, in a public manner, which I mentioned and which has been observed by many Gentleman of the Army, I am concious of none but if I have been guilty of any Crimes deserving such treatment I wish to have them pointed out that I may have an Opportunity of Vindicating my conduct.[32]

Arnold again requested a pass to leave the army. Gates again immediately replied, claiming he had given "such Answers" to Arnold's "Objections" as he thought were "Satisfactory." Claiming he knew of no "Insult or Indignity," Gates provided Arnold with a "common Pass" to leave the Northern Army.[33] Once again, Arnold had the means to act upon his threat to leave. Once again, he didn't do it. General orders of September 25 officially appointed Lincoln commander of the army's consolidated center and right divisions but left Arnold's left division intact.[34]

Gates and Arnold continued to write sparring letters back and forth, as did their teenaged and twentysomething staff officers. Schuyler couldn't help but add gossipy fuel to the fire, which helped justify Gates's paranoia over the existence of the "New York gang." The army's deputy adjutant general, Lieutenant Colonel James Wilkinson, did what he could to debase Arnold, who he called a "pompous little fellow."[35] With the enemy army located close at hand, this infighting was the last thing that anyone in the Northern Army needed.

Enterprise

Joining Burgoyne is Certainly there first & Chieff Object.
—Major General Israel Putnam, October 8, 1777[1]

Like his Canada Army counterpart, Henry Clinton spent the winter of 1776–77 in England, during which time he met with Lord George Germain and discussed the strategic situation facing the British Army in America.[2] Clinton, like Burgoyne, did not enjoy his subordinate role in the war, but he had no proposal for an independent expeditionary command of his own. In one of his meetings with Germain, Clinton voiced concern over Howe's overland campaign to take Philadelphia. Taking the Revolutionary capital, Clinton stated, would be part of such a massive, slow, methodical expedition that it would prevent Howe from returning to New York in time to support Burgoyne if needed. Germain assured Clinton that Howe's orders to assist Burgoyne were clear enough, and that the commander in chief would undoubtedly fulfill this obligation.

Newly knighted, Sir Henry set sail for New York. On May 8—only days after Clinton's departure—Germain received a momentous update from Howe, one that would have significant repercussions on the outcomes of both Howe's and Burgoyne's campaigns. In his April 2 letter, Howe informed the secretary that he proposed "to invade Pensylvania [*sic*] by sea."[3] On April 5, three days after Howe's letter to Germain was penned, he wrote a more blatant piece to Carleton, informing the Canadian commander in chief that he had

> but little expectation, that I shall be able, from the want of suffi-
> cient strength in this army, to detach a corps in the beginning of the
> campaign, to act upon Hudson's River, consistent with the operations
> already determined upon, the Force your Excellency may deem expe-
> dient to advance beyond your frontiers after taking Ticonderoga will, I
> fear, have little assistance from hence to facilitate their approach, and
> as I shall probably be in Pensylvania [*sic*] when that corps is ready to
> advance into this province [New York], it will not be in my power to
> communicate with the officer commanding it so soon as I could wish;
> he must therefore pursue such measures as may from circumstances
> be judged most conducive to the advancement of his Majesty's service
> consistently with your Excellency's orders for his conduct.[4]

Howe's letter—which Carleton shared with Burgoyne before he began his invasion—was not written in response to knowledge of Burgoyne's expedition from Canada. Rather, it was based upon an expectation that an army from Canada would advance from Québec, such as was done in 1776. Germain informed Howe of Burgoyne's expedition to Albany in the form of a copy of the same March 26 instructions Germain had sent to Carleton. Incidentally, Howe received his copy of Burgoyne's instructions on July 5, the day before Burgoyne captured Forts Ticonderoga and Independence. So, while Howe always expected the Canada Army to commit to an invasion of northern New York, the details of the plan, including Burgoyne's appointment as commander, were received months after Howe had already eschewed the concept of facilitating any operation from Canada.

With Burgoyne's instructions in hand, in which it was made clear that both Burgoyne and St. Leger were to proceed to Albany without physical assistance, Howe's sea-bound expedition was a fait accompli. After informing government of this radical departure from the preapproved overland route to take Philadelphia, Germain responded to Howe on May 18—ten days after receiving Howe's letter—with the king's approbation. Despite the approval, however, Germain warned Howe that "the King trusts, whatever you mediate may be executed in time to cooperate with the army ordered to proceed from Canada."[5]

Enter Sir Henry Clinton. When he arrived in New York in early July, Clinton was shocked to learn that Howe's overland campaign would be abandoned for one taken by sea. Clinton was incensed, complaining that the sea route would not only delay the opening of the campaign against Philadelphia, but the change would remove Howe from being able to communicate with Burgoyne. Howe had his reasons, and they were good ones. Incessant fighting against Washington's forces in New Jersey during the 1777 wintertime "forage war" demonstrated that an overland campaign against Philadelphia was untenable. Unable to secure a safe avenue of approach to Pennsylvania by land, Howe wisely altered his route. His strategy to take Philadelphia by sea was sanctioned by the king, although formal approval for the change was only received by the British general after his fleet set sail on July 23.

Howe's fleet ascended Chesapeake Bay and encamped in Maryland at the mouth of the Elk River, about seventy miles southwest of the United States capital. There, at the end of August, Howe finally admitted the obvious in a letter to Germain—he would not "be able to act up to the King's expectations" and cooperate with the Northern Army.[6]

Despite his apparent apathy, Howe had made a singular provision to help Burgoyne, albeit a last-minute, impractical one. On July 30—seven days after his fleet departed New York—the commander in chief decided to give Clinton, who

Clinton's Letter to Burgoyne, with Cypher

August 18, 1777

University of Michigan, William L. Clements Library, Henry Clinton Papers

Messages sent between Burgoyne and Clinton or Howe were concealed by a variety of means, such as within clothing linings, double-walled wooden canteens, hollow buttons, silver eggs, and feather quills. Some, like this one, required use of a cut paper "cypher" to reveal the message's true meaning. Although it never reached Burgoyne, this one informed the Army from Canada general that Howe "is gone to the Chesapeak bay."

**King's Colour (detail), 7th Regiment of Foot
(Royal Fusiliers)**
1771

West Point Museum; photograph by Don Troiani
As a royal regiment, the 7th (Royal Fusiliers)
displayed its royal device on the center of
its colours, which, according to regulations,
consisted of "the rose within the garter, and the
crown over it." In January 1771 Robert Horne
was directed to provide materials and labor for
making a pair of colours for the regiment, which
included "Embroidering on the two Colours the
Rose within the Garter and Crowns." This colour
was taken at Chambly during the Americans' 1775
invasion of Canada. Although a replacement set
was ordered in 1777, no colours were brought on
Clinton's Highlands expedition.
The Commander of the 7th Regt of Foot to Robt Horne, January
20, 1771, Berkshire Record Office, Berkshire, England, Downshire
Papers, D/ED.

was left behind to command in the city of New York, allowance to
"make any diversion in favor of General Burgoyne's approaching
Albany," as long as he could ensure the security of New York.[7]
However, with the New York garrison sapped to populate Howe's
expedition against Philadelphia, Clinton lacked the soldiers
necessary to make any diversion. Further, on August 22, American troops launched three simultaneous attacks against Long
Island, King's Bridge, and Staten Island, which, while unsuccessful, reminded Clinton that he was on the defensive. Conveniently,
Burgoyne's sanguine August 6 report written from Fort Edward,
stating that the Army from Canada was preparing to make its
final push on Albany, proved that no diversion was necessary.

Bennington ruined Burgoyne's plan to descend on Albany in
August. With official confirmation arriving in New York by late
August, Clinton grew very concerned for Burgoyne's situation.
Thanks to reinforcements set to arrive from Europe, and confirmation that Burgoyne remained stalled on the upper Hudson,
Clinton now had the impetus to act. It was with this in mind that
he wrote his coded September 11 letter, which Burgoyne received
on September 21, two days after the Battle of Freeman's Farm.

Clinton's expected reinforcements arrived on September
24. With Burgoyne's "Do it, my dear friend, directly" response
received five days later, Clinton prepared an impressive force for
his ambitious diversionary expedition to the Hudson Highlands.
His British units were the 7th (Royal Fusiliers), 26th, 52nd, 57th,
and 63rd Regiments of Foot; one company of the 71st Regiment
of Foot; and one dismounted troop of the 17th Regiment of
(Light) Dragoons. Also included was the "Detached Corps," a
rare combined British-German fighting unit.[8] The Hessen-Cassel
Infanterie Regiment von Trümbach and two companies of newly
raised Jäger rounded out the European portion. The expedition's
royalist American arm ("Regiments of Greens") included the
Loyal American Regiment, King's American Regiment, New York
Volunteers, King's Orange Rangers, Emmerich's Chasseurs, and
the Corps of Guides and Axmen.[9]

Taking neither knapsacks nor tents, Clinton's more than
3,000 troops were well prepared for the sort of lightning-strike
enterprise they were embarking upon. Starting off on the evening of October 3, one-third of his troops floated upriver and
landed by daybreak at Tarrytown, about twenty-four miles north

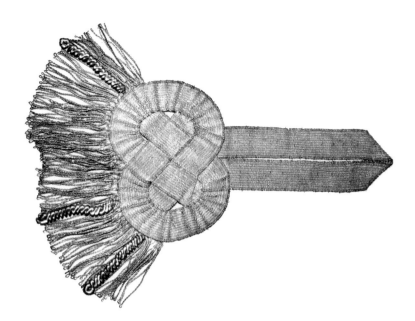

Silver-Laced Epaulet
ca. 1770s
Private collection
Continental Army officer uniform standards did not regulate use of epaulets until 1779, although they were commonly employed before then. Laced epaulets of this form were popular with the officer corps of American and British regiments in the 1770s.

Connecticut Drum
ca. 1776
Museum of Connecticut History; photograph by Don Troiani
This wooden drum bears Connecticut's colonial and statehood coat of arms, which includes three grapevines and the Latin motto *Qui transtulit sustinet*. Note the flanking Continental flags, consisting of only red and white (and sometimes blue) alternating stripes. This design served as the unofficial flag of the new United States until the congressional resolution of June 14, 1777. On that date, nearly one year after independence was declared, the "flag of the United States" was determined to be "thirteen stripes, alternate red and white: that the union be thirteen stars, white in a blue field, representing a new constellation."
Journals of the Continental Congress, 1774–1789,
vol. 8, 464.

of Manhattan, with ease. There they were joined by another third, which marched overland up from King's Bridge, and the final third, which came up in another flotilla. The whole assembled fleet, commanded by Commodore William Hotham, moved north about fifteen miles and landed Clinton's troops at Verplanck's Point, where the Americans on the beach quickly dispersed.[10] Clinton's targets, Forts Clinton and Montgomery, were located less than seven miles north.

Commanded by Major General Israel Putnam, the Highlands Department was the smallest territorial region of the Continental Army.[11] Sandwiched between the hard-pressed Northern and Main Departments, regiments from the Highlands Department were transferred to the north and south throughout the summer in order to reinforce both Schuyler and Washington. What little remained was spread on both sides of the Hudson. On the eastern side of the river, Putnam planted headquarters at Peekskill. Given the importance of the post, a majority of the department's battalions, including the 2nd, 3rd, and 6th Connecticut

Private, Colonel Lewis Dubois's 5th New York Regiment
The junior regiment of New York's Continental Army establishment, Dubois's battalion was the sole Continental infantry regiment tasked with defending both Forts Montgomery and Clinton in the fall of 1777. Partially uniformed in brown coats faced with blue, the men wore a variety of head coverings and smallclothes, including deerskin breeches. DuBois's men, like many others throughout New York's Continental line in 1777, were armed with surplus French muskets (without slings), bayonets, scabbards, belts, and nineteen-round-capacity cartridge boxes. A knapsack, such as seen worn by the soldier here, would have been worn while on a march.

Regiments, Colonel Samuel Webb's Additional Continental Regiment, and newly raised New York and Connecticut militia, were stationed on that side of the river.

The Highlands Department's two strongest posts, Forts Montgomery and Clinton, were located on the western side of the river. Fort Montgomery was begun in early 1776 for the express purpose of providing an impregnable defense against British forces coming up the Hudson. It was a strong, irregular-shaped, bastioned fort built upon a rocky promontory overlooking the Hudson. Fort Clinton, built less than a quarter mile to the south, was likewise constructed upon a promontory overlooking the river. It was a star-shaped fort, which included an extenuated defensive curtain and a large satellite redoubt and stone wall that covered the road approaching the complex from the south. Separating the neighboring forts was the outlet of Popolopen Creek, over which a bridge facilitated movement and communication between the two.

If all this wasn't enough, an iron chain and a log boom were stretched across the Hudson River between Fort Montgomery and Anthony's Nose, which provided the ultimate protection against any enemy attempt to surpass the forts. Above the chain and boom, a pool of five armed vessels were available to give further check to any British attempt upon the defenses.[12] The forts, festooned with artillery, were further defended by rings of entangled abatis laid out across the open fields along their fronts. Defense of the forts was left to the 5th New York Regiment, two companies of Colonel John Lamb's (2nd) Continental Artillery Regiment (one in each fort), and four battalions of New York militia.[13] All told, about 700 officers and men were stationed at the forts, which were under the overall command of Brigadier General George Clinton—Fort Clinton's namesake—who held the title of Commandant of the Forts in the Highlands. He was also New York State's governor.

At Verplanck's Point, a royalist officer from Burgoyne's army arrived bearing unexpected news for Sir Henry. Unlike the unassuming response Burgoyne sent on September 23, this verbal update—the information was too sensitive to be left in writing—was anything but. The officer, who left Burgoyne's camp on September 28, painted a dire picture of Burgoyne's predicament.[14] Furthermore, Clinton was told that Burgoyne

> wished to receive my orders whether he should attack or retreat to the Lakes. That he had but Provisions to the 20th of this Month [October], and that he would not have given up his Communications with Ticonderoga, had he not expected a cooperating Army at Albany. That he wished to know my positive Answer as soon as possible whether I could open a Communication with Albany, when I should be there. . . . That if he did not hear from me by the 12th Instant, he should retire. [15]

Private, King's American Regiment
Unlike the American royalist units serving with Burgoyne, the royalist battalions of Howe's army were generally well armed, accoutered, and uniformed. One of six royalist American corps to participate in Sir Henry Clinton's October Highlands expedition, Colonel Edmund Fanning's King's American Regiment was deployed to the Hudson River's eastern bank at Verplank's Point in order to serve as a distraction from Clinton's intended targets. Note that, per Fanning's orders, this soldier wears his eighteen-round cartridge box above his larger-capacity cartridge pouch.

The message exemplified the definition of being blindsided. Burgoyne's September 23 note never suggested that the Army from Canada was in such dire straits. Further, Burgoyne's demand that Clinton should give him any commands was a curious development, since Burgoyne understood the chain of command. He and Clinton held the same rank, and Burgoyne's independent command meant that only Howe had authority to give him instructions. Clinton sent the officer back with his verbal reply, exclaiming (in the third person)

> [t]hat not having received any Instructions from the Commander in Chief [Howe] relative to the Northern Army, and unacquainted even of his Intentions concerning the Operations of that Army, excepting his Wishes, that they should get to Albany, Sir H Clinton cannot presume to give Orders to General Burgoyne. General Burgoyne could not suppose that Sir H. Clinton had an Idea of penetrating to Albany with the small Force he mentioned in his last Letter [dated September 11]. What he offered in that Letter he has now undertaken.[16]

Despite the necessarily terse response, Burgoyne's update gave new speed to Sir Henry's Highlands operation, and he arranged for the immediate desolation of Forts Clinton and Montgomery. Leaving the King's American Regiment and Orange Rangers behind at Verplanck's Point, Clinton's troops were transported across the river at King's Ferry, located directly north of Stoney Point, on the morning of the 6th. The troops then marched inland along a long, meandering road, over "hills and cliffs" which were "steep and rough."[17] The march was exhausting, and the early October heat caused many men—who had only biscuits and rum, no water—to drop out of the ranks. They pressed on for miles, rounding the imposing Dunderberg Mountain. Once arrived at Doodletown Brook, the column split in two. The troops destined to attack nearby Fort Clinton remained in place while the Fort Montgomery attack column continued on for miles along a circuitous route before reaching their destination. Once in place, both forces planned to attack the forts simultaneously.

Major-General John Vaughan commanded the column staged to strike against Fort Clinton, which included the 26th and 63rd Regiments of Foot, Hessen jäger companies, the troop of dismounted 17th Regiment of (Light) Dragoons, the company from 71st Regiment of Foot, and the Detached Corps. As they were coming out of the woods and spilled out onto the sprawling open space before the stone wall, an artillery barrage "came flying so thick that tree-limbs were falling on us," followed by musket fire that "came like hail." The British and Germans

Plan of the attack of the Forts Clinton & Montgomery, upon Hudsons River, which were stormed by His Majestys forces under the Command of Sir Henry Clinton, K.B. on the 6th of Octr 1777

published by William Faden, June 1, 1784

after Second-Lieutenant John Hills, ca. 1783

The Library of Congress, gm71002205

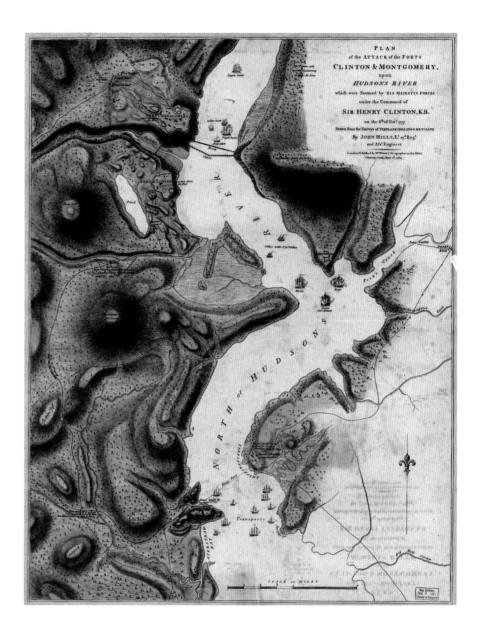

Just as the United States maintained two forts guarding against any British attack up Lake Champlain, Forts Clinton and Montgomery protected against any British attacks up the Hudson River. Both forts, built on high bluffs overlooking the river, were separated by "Peploaps Kill" (Popolopen Creek). Apart from the diversionary body landed at Verplank's Point, Sir Henry Clinton's troops were landed at King's Ferry, a primary river crossing site located directly north of Stoney Point. This map shows most of the meandering, mountainous British approach lines taken in order to attack the forts simultaneously. Note the location of Fort Independence on the east side of the river; built in 1776, the place was abandoned by Putnam's troops during the course of the British Highlands campaign. The large "Pond" later became known as "Hessian" or "Bloody" Lake after ridiculously exaggerated stories of heavy "Hessian" casualties sustained during the expedition against Fort Clinton. Instead, according to one non-Hessian German soldier journalist, it was the American dead who were "thrown in the water with a rock tied around their neck in proportion to their weight."

pressed forward but tumbled into the sprawling abatis. The attackers were able to force their way to the stone wall, but

> the fort began firing canister so heavily that we thought Heaven was falling. We stopped and took cover behind rocks and let the enemy fire over us until more troops arrived. Man after man had to crawl through the abatis so that when [all of Vaughan's troops were] in position, orders were given to storm the fort. Every man had to find the best and safest way to get there, certainly there were many deaths here. The canister could have done much damage here but was absent.[18]

There was, in fact, "much damage" to the assault force's leadership. The commanders of the 63rd Regiment and the Detached Corps were killed even before the fort itself was assaulted, and even Vaughan's horse was "dashed to pieces by a cannon-ball."[19] Nevertheless, with the signal given, Vaughan's men regrouped and pressed the attack and "began climbing the rocks in order to storm the fort." Assault on the fort proper was swift and decisive. The 7th Regiment of Foot (Royal Fusiliers) was brought up to bolster Vaughan's attack, upon which

> the bloodbath only began, those still in the fort were not pardoned, but dispatched with the bayonet. Fortunately most of the Rebels were so scared by the sight of the bayonets they panicked and discarded their arms, fled. This gave impetus to their anger at losing their brave officers, so that those who were not killed were driven into the North [Hudson] River. We would have killed more had we been able to get closer. The men had to crawl through the gunports to get in.[20]

Fort Montgomery's assault force, commanded by Lieutenant-Colonel Mungo Campbell, consisted of the 52nd and 57th Regiments of Foot, the Loyal American Regiment, New York Volunteers, and Emmerich's Chasseurs.[21] Having finished their extenuated march in order to approach Fort Montgomery from the west, the van, "advancing with hasty Strides," ran up against a fieldpiece and about 120 American troops. The Americans "made great Havock" among Campbell's men and were "repeatedly driven back 'till filing off thro' the Woods upon the right and left with a View of surrounding" the Americans, who withdrew back to the fort, leaving the gun spiked behind them. Campbell's men moved forward against a hail of grapeshot and began the attack against the fort, "which

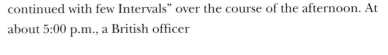

continued with few Intervals" over the course of the afternoon. At about 5:00 p.m., a British officer

> appeared with a Flag. [Governor Clinton] ordered Lt Colo. Livingston to meet him without the Works and know his Business. Colo¹ Livingston having demanded his Rank and Business, he was told by the Bearer of the Flag that he was Lieut. Colo¹ Campble, and that he came to demand a Surrender of the Fort to prevent the Effusion of Blood. Colo¹ Livingston replied he had no authority to treat with him, but if they would surrender themselves Prisoners of War, they might depend on being well treated, and if they did not chuse to accept of those Terms they might renew the Attack as soon as he should return within the Fort, we being determined to defend it to the last Extremity. As soon as Lt Col. Livingston returned the Attack was renewed with great Violence.[22]

Fort Montgomery's defenders had no chance. By dusk, the British cannonade from vessels on the river and the attackers' "Superiority of Numbers" on land "forced the Works on all Sides"; the defenders who could save themselves scattered. Governor Clinton was "so fortunate as to effect an Escape under cover of the Night,

Private, Battalion Company, 57th Regiment of Foot
Most British regiments of foot consisted of a single battalion with ten fighting companies. Eight of these were common "battalion" companies, while the other two were the elite "grenadier" and "light infantry" companies. As a participant in Clinton's expedition in the Highlands, this battalion company soldier wears the regiment's regulation uniform, consisting of a cocked hat, skirted coat, and woolen breeches. Half-gaiters cover the tops of the soldier's shoes. His loaded musket is held at the "recover," a position often used when advancing to attack.

after the Enemy were possessed of all the Works."[23] One of the garrison's armed artificers recalled that the enemy "succeeded in mounting the wall before we discovered them, all the principle officers & a few privates . . . made our escape by a passage out of the Fort next to the River this was a place unknown to the British, the rest were made prisoners."[24]

Clinton's October 6 attacks against Forts Clinton and Montgomery were a resounding success. Overall, British forces lost 7 officers, including Campbell, and about 35 men killed, and an additional 11 officers and about 130 men wounded.[25] American losses were about 80 killed and wounded; 28 officers and about 240 Continental and militia soldiers from the two garrisons were captured.[26] Also taken were 67 cannons, over 12,000 pounds of loose gunpowder, nearly 40,000 rounds of prepared cannon and musket cartridges, and over 5,400 pounds of loose cannonballs, grapeshot, case shot, and musket balls, as well as additional war matériel and provision stores. Only one American vessel escaped; most others were run aground, abandoned, and burned.[27] The ten-gun sloop *Camden* fell into Sir Henry's hands.

Continental Army Officer's Shoulder Belt Ornament
ca. 1770s
Don Troiani collection
Buckled shoulder belts sometimes included metallic ornaments that protected the belt's leather end tip and helped to weigh it down. These useful devices were often decorative as well. This simple brass piece includes a "liberty" cap atop a pole, a popular motif employed by revolutionaries in Europe and America.

"LIBERTY" Sleeve Link Glass
second half, 18th century
Fort Montgomery State Historic Site, Fort Montgomery, NY, New York State Office of Parks, Recreation and Historic Preservation, A-FM-1967-1795
Found within the broken remains of Fort Montgomery, two of these decorative pressed-glass ornaments were set within a pair of sleeve links. Whether made in England in support of Whig politician John Wilkes and his drive for British constitutional liberty or in America in support of the American Revolution, the message would have resounded with the man who wore them at Fort Montgomery.

Private, Colonel Samuel Webb's Additional Continental Regiment

Composed primarily of Connecticut men, Webb's was one of the few Continental battalions remaining in the Hudson Highlands in the fall of 1777. The men wore unmodified British 20th Regiment of Foot clothing captured at sea the previous fall, giving them the outward appearance of being British soldiers. This confused Daniel Taylor, a royalist tasked by Sir Henry Clinton to deliver a message to Burgoyne, who was captured when he "accidentally [met] with some of our Troops, in British Uniforms" and "was thereby deceived, and discovered himself to them."

General Court Martial of Daniel Taylor, October 14, 1777, in *Public Papers of George Clinton*, vol. 2, 443.

With the forts now under British dominion, Sir Henry planned to follow up his victory by taking another. Located only six miles to the north on Martelaer's Rock, an island connected to the Hudson's east shore by marshland, Fort Constitution was easy prey. Begun in 1775, the fort was left unfinished, but still maintained a small garrison and supply depot. After a few hours' work on the morning of October 8, Royal Navy personnel cut through the chain and log boom at Fort Montgomery, clearing the way for about 1,500 troops to sail north without opposition. The small, abandoned, thirty-six-gun fort was captured without incident late that afternoon. Before evacuating, its garrison burned what they could, including the barracks, store-houses, and most of the supplies.

On October 9 Clinton sent Major-General and New York Governor William Tryon with the 7th Regiment of Foot (Royal Fusiliers), Infanterie Regiment von Trümbach, a detachment of jäger, and Emmerich's Chasseurs to attack Continental Village, located on the Hudson's east side about four miles north of Peekskill.[28] Tryon's troops moved in without opposition and burned the expansive Continental Army depot, which included barracks, storehouses, a mill, and wagonloads of supplies. After his whirlwind successes—capturing three strategic American forts in as many days—Clinton triumphantly wrote to Burgoyne from Fort Montgomery on October 8:

> *Nous y voici* and nothing now between us but Gates. I sincerely hope this little success of ours may facilitate your operations. In answer to your letter of the 28th Sept[r] by C.C. [Captain Campbell] I shall only say I cannot presume to order or even advise for reasons obvious. I heartily wish you success.[29]

The next day, yet another officer from Burgoyne's army arrived, bearing similar bad news as before but with an additional twist. If Burgoyne was "to get to Albany," explained the officer, "he [Burgoyne] does not think he could be supplied with Provisions for the Winter, the

Cartridge Pouch and Waist Belt Fragment, 7th Regiment of Foot (Royal Fusiliers)
ca. 1771

Don Troiani collection

This twenty-nine-hole British cartridge pouch, which is missing its shoulder belt and the two iron buckles that fastened it, has a fragment of the buff leather waist belt crudely stitched to the pouch's back. Still attached to the belt is the sheet-brass regimental waist belt clasp. Sets of pouches and waist belts, including "new Plates" (waist belt clasps) purchased by the regiment's colonel in 1771, were worn by the men in 1775 while garrisoned in the province of Québec. These accoutrements were probably captured during the 1775 American invasion of Canada, and at some point the waist belt was stitched to the pouch body by an American soldier so as to be worn around the waist.

Buff Accoutrements &c Provided, with Repairs, & Alterations done by Jon Hume, for the 7th Regiment of Foot, November 8 1770–July 12 1771, Berkshire Record Office, Berkshire, England, Downshire Papers, D/ED.

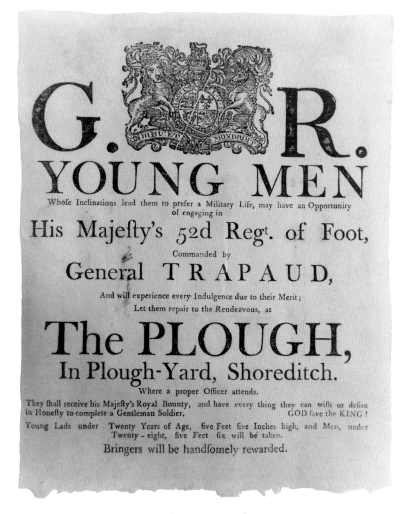

Recruitment Broadside, 52nd Regiment of Foot

ca. 1778

Eric Schnitzer collection

After the successful attack on Fort Montgomery, the 52nd Regiment returned to New York, where it remained for the winter. This rare wartime broadside bears testimony to the reality that regiments in the British Army were principally recruited from citizens who joined voluntarily, not men drafted into service nor convicted criminals opting to serve in lieu of punishment.

Country there, & on the Mohawk River, being much drained, unless the Communication is opened between Albany and New York."[30] Despite having brilliantly fulfilled even the most extreme interpretation of Howe's off-the-cuff allowance to make a diversion in Burgoyne's favor, his late achievements would still not be enough to help Burgoyne's situation. With Howe gone, and Burgoyne's fortunes souring, only Clinton was positioned to make a difference at this critical time.

Sir Henry immediately returned to New York and prepared "small vessels, such as could go within a few miles of Albany, [loaded with] provisions sufficient to supply General Burgoyne's army for six months," which would alleviate the Army from Canada's inevitable food shortages after it reached its destination.[31] After making these arrangements, Clinton returned to the Highlands and dispatched Vaughan with the Advanced Squadron, along with over 1,600 British troops, north. Vaughan's task was to cause further distraction south of Albany and, if possible, join the Army from Canada.[32] If he reached Burgoyne, he was instructed to send immediate word back to Sir Henry, who planned to follow up with the balance of the expeditionary force and the food stores. Vaughan set off on his northbound journey on October 14.

Ascendancy

No man in the army has known anything of all this, and the expedition about to be undertaken has even today remained a secret to all the brigadiers.
—Second-Lieutenant Anton Du Roi, October 7, 1777[1]

Apart from the message received on the morning of September 21, Burgoyne knew nothing of Clinton's progress, or if Clinton's expedition had even begun. As September turned to October, the British commander came to realize that he could no longer wait in his fortified camp in expectation of succor from the South. Reports that Gates's army was increasing in number juxtaposed with Burgoyne's situation, in which attrition from daily skirmishes and desertions was becoming acute. In fact, the situation was so bad among the German ranks that Riedesel ordered the following on October 2:

> Since it appears that the desertions are increasing, Major General von Riedesel commands that the pickets be increased . . . by as many men as will double the outposts. . . . You must also order the men that one is to keep close watch on the other. Major General von Riedesel promises ten guineas to those who seize their comrades. Should it be impossible for a man to have the culprit in his possession, he is permitted to shoot him, and, in the event that he shoots him dead, he will receive five guineas as emolument.[2]

**Scissors and Thimble
third quarter, 18th century**
Saratoga National Historical Park, SARA 1718, 1720
Recovered from the 21st Regiment of Foot (Royal North British Fusiliers) encampment site from the time of the Battles of Saratoga, these iron and steel sewing tools speak to the need of military men and women followers to make and repair clothing.

Comb
third quarter, 18th century

Saratoga National Historical Park, SARA 1738
Combs were sometimes listed among a regiment's necessaries, being seen as essential for the purposes of maintaining health and uniform hairstyles. While combs varied, this particular piece from a British camp includes a lead ridge that holds a series of iron teeth in place.

Traveling Cellaret
fourth quarter, 18th century
Lined with paper and green baize, this lockable chest houses four case bottles that were used to hold alcoholic beverages, such as Madeira, claret, rum, or porter. General officers sometimes brought portable liquor chests like this one with them on service but, unable to bring such weighty pieces on campaign, most officers instead bought refreshment directly from sutlers.

While Burgoyne's fighting men were on the decline, royalist American refugees were on the increase. Strong-arm tactics practiced by area Revolutionary authorities, particularly militia commanders and district Committees of Safety and Protection, resulted in the displacement of significant numbers of men, women, and children who were loyal to the crown. While Revolutionary Americans saw Burgoyne as an invader, royalist Americans saw him as their hope for restoring colonial government by which, eventually, they could safely return home.

The number of refugees combined with the unplanned stagnation following the Battle of Freeman's Farm caused a worsening provision shortage. During the course of the campaign, the people of Burgoyne's multinational force enjoyed one and a half pounds of bread (leavened), biscuit (unleavened), or flour (from which "flour Cakes without ovens, which are equally wholesome and relishing with the best Bread," were made) and one and a half pounds of salted pork (or, on rare occasions, beef) per diem.[3] Women and children (younger than age ten) received proportionally less. The army's increasing rate of provision depletion caused Burgoyne to order on October 3 that "the Ration of bread or flour is for the present fixed at one pound." Sutlers were running out of stock, and many items "could no longer be had for money."[4]

On October 4, the day after Clinton began his movement northward, Burgoyne called a council of war with his two major-generals "in order to get their counsel as to what should be undertaken under the present circumstances."[5] During the meeting, Burgoyne made a bold proposal for action. He would leave 800 men behind to guard the entire camp, while the balance of the army would push south to attack Gates's left and rear. However, Phillips and Riedesel argued that they were, as yet, unfamiliar with the approaches to the American camp. Further, because the Americans had such overwhelming numbers, they would easily be able to commit a portion of their army to conquer the 800 men left in camp and capture the army's supplies.

Concern was also expressed over the quality of the army's defenses, "especially since the redoubts, that had been put up for covering our supplies [located in the Hudson River Valley near the river], were spread much too far apart; moreover, they defended each other quite badly." Word of this inspired Burgoyne to inspect the defenses the following day, upon which he confirmed the poorness of the valley's fortifications. These observations quashed Burgoyne's proposal for a major attack on Gates's positions. Action was essential, yet an all-out attack was now seen as unadvisable. In effect, this left only two options open to the British commander. Burgoyne, Phillips, Riedesel, and Fraser convened on the evening of October 5 to hash out further plans,

> and after the situation of our army had been minutely examined, it appeared that if we could not set out against the enemy very shortly . . . it would be more advisable to re-cross the Hudson and take possession of our former position on the other side of the Batten Kill, as we should then not only be in communication with Lake George again but might also await what movements General Clinton would make on the other side of Albany. . . . These sentiments, which were so fitting in our present position, were approved of by all, partly aloud and partly in silence. But General Burgoyne looked upon a retrograde movement as too hard, and declared that he himself would make a reconnaissance as close to the rebel left wing as possible on the 7th, so as to see whether same could be attacked or not, and would then either attack the enemy with the whole army on the 8th, or retreat behind the Batten Kill on the 11th. This was his decision, and at the same time his order.[6]

The mission's reconnaissance-in-force formed on the morning of October 7. Numbering about 1,500 officers and men, it consisted of troops drafted from across the army. Most personnel were drawn from Fraser's Advanced Corps (about 700) and Breymann's fortified camp (about 300). Because the force would set off from between these forts, it was deemed safe to sap their garrisons rather than take more personnel from Burgoyne's other defensive positions. A growing number of small American attacks across the fronts of the defenses in the valley and the main camp convinced Burgoyne that taking too many troops from those quarters would be unwise. Since the reconnaissance force was expected to be out for only a few hours, the soldiers were instructed to leave

Iron Barrel Hoop Broiler ca. 1777
Saratoga National Historical Park, SARA 1770
Britain's Victualling Office, which oversaw the production of casks meant for storing military provisions, used broad arrow-marked iron hoops to bind its barrels. One clever soldier from the 21st Regiment of Foot (Royal North British Fusiliers) took a hoop from an empty cask and folded it to make a meat broiler.

**Belt Clasp, 20th Regiment of Foot
ca. 1773**

Don Troiani collection

This brass belt clasp would have secured a whitened buff leather belt either around the waist or over the shoulder of the wearer. Because battalion company men of the regiment were issued standard rectangular plates bearing the same "XX" designation, these more ornately shaped pieces may have been issued to the regiment's grenadiers or drummers and fifers. This clasp was recovered in Virginia.

their haversacks (which stored their food) and blankets behind. With updated, eyewitness intelligence of the American positions on the American left flank, Burgoyne could intelligently determine if an all-out attack on the 8th was possible. Captain Alexander Fraser's reconstituted British rangers, royalists, Indians, and the Canadien militia draftees, over 200 men in all, were dispatched in advance of the 1,500-man reconnaissance-in-force, purposed with distracting the Americans' attention by gaining their rear near the Summit.

At about 11:00 a.m., Generals Burgoyne, Phillips, Riedesel, and Fraser moved out with the reconnaissance-in-force, which included ten artillery pieces. Divided into three columns of 500 officers and soldiers each, the troops marched upon roads in a southwesterly direction toward the American left. Moving through the open fields and woods, the columns spilled out onto two adjacent wheat fields less than one mile from Burgoyne's camp and about one mile from the main American lines. The clearings, separated by woods and connected by a traversing dirt path, were surrounded by a wall of canopy trees. The most dominant feature was a high, wooded hill located west of the westernmost clearing, which offered a commanding view of the field below.

As the three columns entered the adjacent fields, the small American advance picket posted there was easily brushed aside by the Braunschweig jäger, which were then sent forward to reconnoiter the woods to the south with Braunschweig light infantry and grenadiers. The British light infantry detachment established a position on the western clearing near the base of the wooded hill. The 24th Regiment formed to their left, on the wooded road between the clearings. The Braunschweig and Hessen-Hanau musketeers from the German Division formed the centerpiece of the line in the eastern clearing, left of the 24th Regiment. Left of the Germans, the British grenadier detachment, most of which was posted in the woods, protected the probing force's left flank. Four pairs of cannons were placed at key points through the fields in order to deter an American attack.

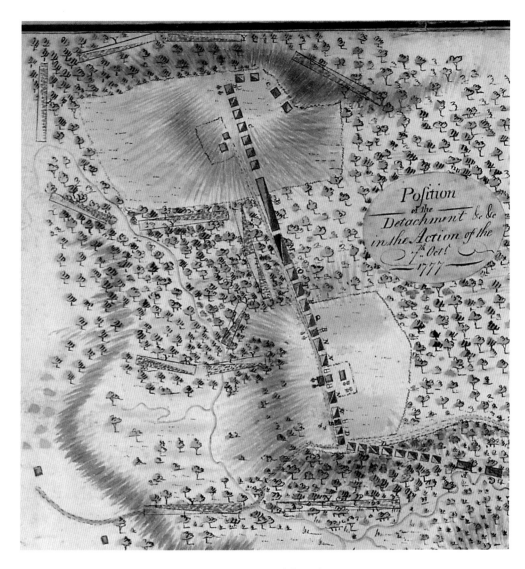

Position of the Detachment &c &c in the Action of the 7th Octr 1777

by Lieutenant William Cumberland Wilkinson, ca. 1778

The Library of Congress, gm71000664

With north on the right and west at the top, this map shows the British reconnaissance-in-force's order of battle arrayed throughout the adjacent wheat fields on October 7, including the particular locations of all ten artillery pieces. Located below a wooded hill, one pair of light six-pounders served with the British light infantry in the western field. On the western side of the larger field was a pair of light six-pounders, commanded by Captain Georg Päusch, while another pair of light six-pounders were placed with the British grenadiers on the field's eastern side. In the center, located directly in front of "Weisser Haus," was the pair of medium twelve-pounders. Behind them, resting next to the building (a ruined barn) located north of the house, was a pair of limbered royal howitzers. These were never deployed in the battle.

Officers climbed on the roof of the eastern field's "Weisser Haus" in an attempt to observe the Americans' left-wing defenses at the Summit, but the tall trees to the south obstructed their view.[7]

Although the primary objective of Burgoyne's probing force—to reconnoiter the American left—was temporarily stalled, another, much needed opportunity presented itself in the form of substantial amounts of wheat available for the taking. This offered the perfect, short-term solution for Burgoyne's acute food shortages. Word was sent to camp to have the carters proceed to the fields in order to collect the grain. The process would take a long time to complete; the soldiers sat on their arms.

The short skirmish between the retreating Americans and the Braunschweig jäger, whose rifle shots reverberated loudly in the woods, was enough to give alarm in the American camp. At headquarters, General Gates and some of his principal officers, including General Arnold, were eating dinner together. Despite the fact that the two generals had recently feuded, their break was repaired well enough to again enjoy a working relationship. This dramatic alteration was probably reflective of their professionalism and a mutual consideration of serving the greater good. Lieutenant Colonel John Brooks particularly recalled that when the British forces made contact with the Americans' sentinels at the wheat fields, that

> we all rose from table; and General Arnold, addressing General Gates, said "Shall I go out, and see what is the matter?" General Gates made no reply; but, upon being pressed, said, "I am afraid to trust you, Arnold." To which Arnold answered, "Pray, let me go: I will be careful; and, if our advance does not need support, I will promise not to commit you." Gates then told him he might go, and see what the firing meant.[8]

Morgan's Corps, along with detachments from others Continental and militia units, had only lately returned from a reconnoitering expedition sent out the day before. With the two-and-a-half-week standstill having apparently no end in sight, Gates had sought to initiate a break in the status quo by sending simultaneous flanking forces against the British on October 6. One was sent directly up the valley against the enemy lines, while the other, commanded by Morgan, circumvented Burgoyne's camp and proceeded about seven miles north to Saratoga.

While the valley force engaged in a very sharp running battle with the enemy and was repulsed with significant loss, Morgan's troops became lost in the woods. They bivouacked all night in a cold rain, having to remain quiet "being just by the enemy." Morgan's troops finally returned to camp late in the morning of

Private, Colonel Daniel Morgan's Rifle Battalion

Washington's June 1777 order to form the provisional rifle corps stipulated that only men who were "known to be perfectly skilled in the use of these guns [rifles], and who are known to be active and orderly in their behavior" could be drafted. Commanded by Colonel Daniel Morgan of the 11th Virginia Regiment, the battalion was organized into five "Virginia" and three "Pennsylvania" companies. Clothing varied due to the men's various regimental origins, but most wore the fringed linen "hunting" shirt stereotypically associated with riflemen.

June 1, 1777, in Washington, *Writings of George Washington*, vol. 8, 156.

October 7, having captured a dozen enemy soldiers and followers. With only a few hours to rest and refresh, Arnold ordered Morgan's Corps to "file to the left and ascend the eminence and then advance in a direction to meet any part of the enemy that might be moving in that direction." Horatio Gates decided to deploy troops as well, and sent Colonel Alexander Scammell's 3rd New Hampshire Regiment forth, which "advanced and moved on in front of the Enemies main line."[9]

Adjutant Nathaniel Bacheller was in the perfect position to be "eye & ear witness" to a remarkable event in the American camp that afternoon. General orders for October 7 assigned his and another New Hampshire militia battalion to Learned's Brigade, which formed part of Arnold's Division, and the militia marched there. After arriving in camp, Bacheller proceeded to Arnold's Neilson House headquarters to copy the day's divisional orders—Arnold's orders—during which time

> General Arnol Soon went out in to the woods on horse Back with his adecamp to View the Enemy which were then Ingaged with the Riffell men . . . General Gates Soon arived to our Lines & Inquired for General Arnol & was Told he was out of the Lines to View the Enemy he soon ordered an officer on horse Back to go to General Arnol to order him to give orders to the Riffell men not to fire on Coll Scammells Regiment For he had ordered that to march.[10]

Arnold, observing the deployments of Morgan's Corps and Scammell's battalion, as well as that of the enemy at the wheat fields, rode back to his headquarters at Neilson House, where he found Gates waiting for him. Arnold then

> [t]old General Gates that the Enemy Design was To Take Possession of a hill about a Quarter of a mile To the west of our Lines where we were then Posted the Enemy were within three Quarters of a mile of us about north the [British] cannon Began to sound in our ears & some small armes, General Arnol says to General Gates it is Late in the Day but Let me have men & we will have some Fun with them Before Sun Set upon which the Briggades Began to march.[11]

True to form, Arnold wasted no time to assemble his attack force, which consisted of the balance of Poor's Brigade and Learned's Brigade. Other regiments were added as well, including battalions of Massachusetts and New Hampshire militia. They marched out in good order toward the fighting at the wheat fields, arriving there at about 4:00 p.m. Their timing could not have been better;

upon their approach, the New Hampshire Continentals, being "much inferior to . . . the enemy . . . gave ground about sixty rods [330 yards]." Arnold's arrival reversed the fortunes of battle, the American attack was renewed, and the fire becoming "violent and incessant."[12] Morgan's Corps moved forth toward the westernmost wheat field, where they encountered Lord Balcarres's British light infantrymen. After a short firefight, Morgan's men moved west and "March'd out far Enough to the Left to flank their flank we tack'd abo[ut] and march'd [back] towards" the British.[13] This maneuver took time, but, returning east, they ascended "the woody hill to a small field about 500 yards to the right of the enemies main line," below which Lord Balcarres's British light infantrymen were "handsomely posed on a ridge 150 yards from the edge of the wood" where Morgan's men were.[14]

By the time Morgan's men were scaling the height on the British right, Arnold's reinforcement was battling against the British left and center. The intensity of the attacks were such that the 24th Regiment, located in the woods between the two fields, was ordered to leave their ground to support Major Acland's British grenadiers, the grenadiers having fallen back against the pressure. Some had even "broke their ranks, but on some aid du camps calling to them for shame, to continue their rank, they marched to their station in good order"[15] With the 24th's arrival, the left flank was solidified, and the pairs of cannons on the eastern field kept the American attackers back. The pair near the British left "were taken as booty" by the Americans. The pair of light six-pounders on the other side of the field, commanded by Captain Georg Päusch, had to be withdrawn to the "Weisser Haus," since his German infantry support "had all run [away] across the road into the field and thence into the bushes, and had taken refuge behind the trees."[16] They were re-formed with difficulty and brought back into the fight closer to the house, where Päusch's guns were brought. The Hessian artillerymen kept up a constant fire

> with balls and with case [shot], without, however, being able to discriminate in favor of our men who were in the bushes; for the enemy, without troubling them, charged savagely upon my canons, hoping to dismount and silence them. But in this attempt, they twice failed, being frustrated each time by the firing of my case [shot].[17]

With the two fields cut off from each other, Morgan could not have been in a better position to attack. His rifle and light infantrymen "determined to make a dash" against the British light infantry below them, "and endeavor[ed] to force our way on to the rear of the Enemies main body." Morgan's men ran down the hill, "jump[ed] over the fence, rais[ed] a shout and [ran] upon the Enemy

Grenadier Bomb
1770s
Saratoga National Historical Park,
SARA 650
This small brass ornament would have been one of two mounted to the back of a British grenadier's cartridge pouch shoulder belt, between which a strand of decorative twisted slow match was wound. This bomb was recovered where the British grenadier battalion detachment deployed at the wheat field on October 7.

Hessen-Hanau Artillery, October 7

Utilizing British cannons during Burgoyne's expedition, Captain Georg Päusch's Hessen-Hanau artillery company was a highly trained corps capable of firing their guns at least one dozen times per minute. Shown here is a point during the fighting at the wheat field when Royal Artillery Second-Lieutenant William Smith asked Päusch to abandon his pair of light six-pounders in order to bring two medium twelve-pounders into action. "I could not grant that request," Päusch wrote, since his smaller cannons could fire three times faster and were successfully keeping attacking Americans at bay. Despite their best efforts, the Hessians were forced to flee with the rest of the reconnaissance force, abandoning their cannons.

Päusch, *Georg Päusch's Journal*, 87.

Subaltern, Colonel Nathan Hale's 2nd New Hampshire Regiment

A Light Infantry corps was formed in late August by drafting one officer and seventeen men from each of the Northern Army's Continental regiments (the Rifle Battalion excepted), including Second Lieutenant Ebenezer Light of the 2nd New Hampshire Regiment. The 2nd New Hampshire's officer corps suffered disproportionally high casualties during the campaign; of the thirty-four officers serving in arms, fourteen were killed, captured, or wounded, including Colonel Hale (captured), Lieutenant Colonel Adams (killed), and Major Titcomb (wounded and furloughed).

Royal Artillery Pocket Pistol
second half, 18th century
Private collection

This brass half-barreled pocket pistol, engraved ROY^L ARTILLERY, would have been carried by an officer of the regiment. Because general orders of 1770 instructed Royal Artillery officers to carry swords only, this diminutive firearm would have given the officer additional protection.

Private, Colonel Nathan Hale's 2nd New Hampshire Regiment

Being the only American regiment that fought in three of the campaigns battles, the 2nd New Hampshire sustained severe casualties in 1777. The men also endured clothing shortages and were only issued uniform coats and waistcoats, as seen here, in late October. A lack of pay and food caused further strife, resulting in about forty enraged men, led by a private of the regiment, to mutiny at Fishkill, New York, on November 6. The revolt dissipated after the ringleader and a captain from the 3rd New Hampshire Regiment sent to stop them ended up killing each other.

without firing." Lord Balcarres's troops "gave way and ran in disorder without firing a shot," withdrawing from the field with their two light six-pounders.[18] Lord Balcarres's departure was not a panicked retreat, but by purposeful command.

At this point in the fight, "all was in disorder," and Burgoyne had had enough.[19] Followed by Phillips and Riedesel, he rode back to camp "in order to take proper measures for its defence" in the face of the inexorable American wave.[20] Burgoyne's aide-de-camp, Captain Sir Francis Clerke, was instructed to alert all commands down the line that "the whole of the detachment" was to return to camp. In so doing, however, he was shot off his horse, mortally wounded, and captured. With overwhelming numbers, the Americans, joined by Dearborn's Corps of Light Infantry, were enveloping the eastern wheat field, during which the British and German defenders broke. Päusch tried to bring off his guns, but his plan

> proved delusive, and was totally dispelled . . . I found the road
> occupied by the enemy. They came towards us on it; the bushes
> were full of them; they were hidden behind the trees; and bullets in
> plenty received us. Seeing that all was irretrievably lost, and that it
> was impossible to save anything, I called to my few remaining men
> to save themselves. I myself, took refuge through a fence, in a piece
> of dense underbrush. . . . Here I met all the different nationalities of
> our division running pell-mell.[21]

In order to stave off complete disaster, Fraser pulled together a rear guard consisting of any of the probing force's survivors able to maintain cohesive discipline. They formed on the Marshall farm, the open, cultivated field located between the wheat fields and Freeman's farm. There they were attacked by Arnold's overwhelming onslaught, which crashed through the woods and hit Fraser's line of battle. After a short firefight, "Fraser received a mortal wound, and the fire of [the American] Troops instantly compelled" the British forces to retreat in disorder.[22]

The British and Germans retreated to the closest fortification at hand, the British Light Infantry Redoubt. The Advanced Corps camp behind the redoubt was alarmed, and the women, children, sutlers, and horses evacuated into the woods for safety. The other half of the British Light Infantry Battalion populated the redoubt's walls and Royal Artillerymen manned the fort's eight artillery pieces.[23] Hundreds of British and German troops, remnants of the shattered reconnaissance, entered the fort, bringing the mortally wounded Fraser with them.

Although the Americans thus far controlled the battlefield and had the initiative, the immediate pursuit was called off. General Poor, having been ordered by

The Encampment & Position of the Army under His Excy. Lt Gl Burgoyne at Swordss and Freeman's Farms on Hudsons River near Stillwater 1777 (detail)

by Lieutenant William Cumberland Wilkinson, ca. 1778

The Library of Congress, gm71000664

Built upon Freeman's farm, the British Light Infantry Redoubt was an enormous fortification festooned with eight artillery pieces. The open field to the east (toward the bottom of the map) was populated by a number of redans overlooking the deep ravine fronting the southern broadside of the farm. This is where Fraser's Advanced Corps encamped. The British Grenadier (D) and Light Infantry (C) Battalions are shown arranged in their grand-divisional orders of battle. The corps's eight-company 24th Regiment of Foot (E) is located between them, and its Royal Regiment of Artillery Company (B) is encamped near its ten artillery pieces. To the northwest were two fortified cabins garrisoned by the army's two companies of Canadien militia draftees (W), and north of these lay the poorly conceived and constructed defenses of Breymann's Reserve Corps. The Braunschweig Grenadierbattaillon Breymann (N), Leichtes Infanterie Battaillon von Bärner (M and L), and Loyal Volunteers (V) garrisoned the line, along with two light six-pounders (S) managed by the Hessen-Hanau Artillery Corps. When attacked on October 7, Breymann's German infantry were at 50 percent strength, and the Canadien and royalist defenses were all but left unmanned.

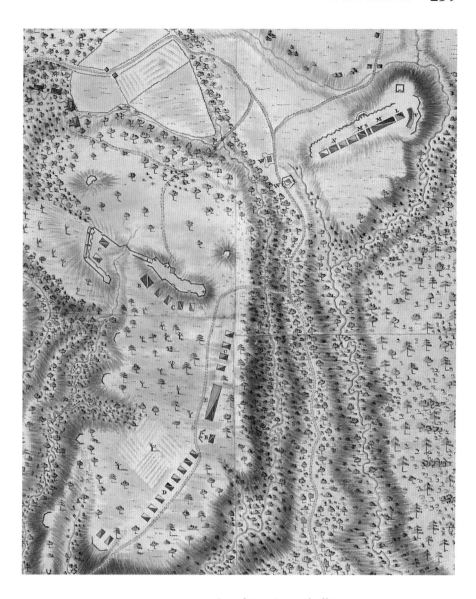

Royal Howitzer Shell Fragments 1770s

Saratoga National Historical Park, SARA 33874, 33875

When Arnold's troops struck the British Light Infantry Redoubt on October 7, the fort's cannons and howitzers rained a hail of case shot and explosive shells upon his men. These shell fragments, recovered from the American position during the attack, bear testimony to the accuracy of the Royal Artillerymen's fire.

British Light Six-Pounder
1761

Rutherford B. Hayes Presidential Library & Museums at Spiegel Grove, 1914.801.1

This cannon was cast during the Seven Years' War by Richard Gilpin in order to meet the British Army's ordnance needs in lieu of the underperforming government-run Royal Brass Foundry at Woolwich. In 1777 it formed part of the Hessen-Hanau artillery detachment assigned to Lieutenant-Colonel Heinrich Breymann's Reserve Corps. During the October 7 Battle of Bemus Heights, this piece and another British light six-pounder defended Breymann's fortified camp, at which time the guns were captured. This cannon was memorialized in 1783–84 with the inscription "Taken at the Storm of the British-Lines near Saratoga by _____ Oct. 7. 1777"; the blank cartouche, reserved for Benedict Arnold, simultaneously acknowledged and admonished the former American hero.

Arnold "to bring his men into better order," halted the advance, which "arrested our progress and prevented our taken the British Battery [Light Infantry Redoubt] in less than ten minutes as we should have Intered it almost as soon as the British."[24] Once Poor's Brigade formally deployed to attack the redoubt, it had no more success than taking two small satellite outposts in advance of the fort. With their position under fire, particularly from the shelling of the fort's howitzers, Poor's troops withdrew to a safer distance.

While the attack on the British Light Infantry Redoubt was losing potency, other American forces moved on the fortified camp of Lieutenant-Colonel Breymann's Reserve Corps. The flimsy fort, consisting of little more than two discontiguous log walls and two light six-pounders, was undermanned. Half the Reserve Corps garrison was sent on the reconnaissance earlier in the day and never returned. With little more than 200 Reserve Corps officers and soldiers and a few dozen royalist troops from Captain Samuel MacKay's Loyal Volunteers, the isolated fortification complex made a tempting target.[25] With Poor commanding the troops fighting against the British Light Infantry Redoubt, Arnold coordinated an assault against Breymann's post.

Most of Morgan's Corps ran across the open field far in front of Breymann's main fortified wall, outside the reach of most of the defenders' weapons, and immediately took position behind a large hill that was inexplicably, and conveniently, located directly in front of the fortification. The blind spot caused by this large hill to the immediate front of Breymann's main line was only one of the fort's ridiculous, but very real, weak points. Colonels Rufus Putnam's (5th) and Thomas Nixon's (6th) Massachusetts Regiments arrived and formed at distance from the fort's front, arrayed for battle.

More American troops swept through the vale against the fortified cabins, which lay nearly unoccupied—their Canadien garrisons had gone out with Captain Fraser's party earlier that day. The cabins were captured without incident, a move that completely exposed Breymann's open left flank. There the hapless German defenders were attacked first, by which "Gen[l] Arnold was the first who Enterd, one Major Morris with about 12 of the Rifle men follow[d] him on the Rear of [the enemy] flank." That was the signal. With Arnold leading the attack against the Germans' left, American troops along the fortified wall's front rushed forward. The defenders had only enough time to give "one fire," after which, overwhelmed, they "fell back from [their] works to [their] line of tents," in confusion.[26]

The Americans—pouring through the artillery embrasures, lapping around the fort's two open flanks, and even climbing over the fort's log wall—formed on the other side, facing toward the downsloping camp. Arnold rode near, demanding that the Germans and royalists lay down their arms; he was met by gunfire

Breymann's Redoubt, October 7
During the decisive dusk-time fighting
that ended the Battle of Bemus Heights,
a major American attack took place
against the left flank of Breymann's
Reserve Corps's fortified camp. Arnold,
seen here with purple ribband displayed,
joins Major Joseph Morris of the 1st New
Jersey Regiment, sword in hand, and
the dozen Continental infantrymen who
front the massed assault. With half its
garrison extracted for Burgoyne's probing
force, the defenders were left isolated
and unprepared. Here, the Regiment von
Rhetz's grenadier company, commanded
by First-Lieutenant Wilhelm Helmcke,
begins to flee the untenable defenses.

from the Braunschweig grenadiers, which killed his horse and shattering his left leg, near the ankle. The defenders scattered through their camp and into the woods on the other side, dispersing toward the direction of Burgoyne's main camp, "Except here and there a Scatering one behind a Tree."[27] Breymann was dead, reportedly "killed by his own grenadiers after he had killed four of them," while fighting to keep them at their posts.[28] Twilight ended the battle.

Later that night, Lieutenant-Colonel Ernst von Speth received orders to retake Breymann's camp, for which task he set out, in the dark, with fifty-five Braunschweig officers and soldiers. The party got lost in the woods and came upon a German-speaking man, claiming to be from MacKay's Loyal Volunteers, who promised to show them the way. Their guide did just that; von Speth and two of his officers, leading at the head of the column, were snapped up by American troops stationed near the captured fort, and the remaining Germans fled into the darkened woods.[29] For the British, von Speth's blunder marked a sorry end to one of the more strategically important battles in world history.

Gates's Northern Army lost about 150 officers and soldiers killed or wounded, the latter of which included the incapacitated Arnold, who was whisked away to the General Hospital at Albany. Burgoyne's casualties were much greater, with about 450 officers and soldiers killed or wounded, and an additional 180 captured. In stark contrast to the Battle of Freeman's Farm, losses among Burgoyne's principal officers were substantial; not only was Fraser mortally wounded and Breymann dead, but many other senior officers were taken captive.[30] Breymann's fortified camp was lost to the victorious Americans, along with the camp equipage and personal effects of the Reserve Corps. The Americans also took a trove of ordnance and stores, including two medium twelve-pounders, six light six-pounders, hundreds of rounds of round and case shot, two ammunition wagons, five ammunition carts, and a barrel of gunpowder.

Thwarted by his reconnaissance-in-force gamble, Burgoyne now faced the very thing that in June he promised his army he would never do: retreat.

Endgame

*The most wanton Barbarity marks the Retreat of our magnanimous
Enemy, who seek with a vindictive malice to desolate a Country, the Inhabitants whereof they cannot conquer.*

—Lieutenant Colonel Richard Varick, October 12, 1777[1]

Possession of Breymann's fortified camp exposed the rear of Burgoyne's entire defensive network. The post guarded the very road that traversed the camp's rear, sloped down the Great Ravine, and met with the River Road at the foot of the Great Redoubt, the largest of the three hilltop fortifications overlooking the Hudson River Valley. This route provided direct access to the British General Hospital, artillery and baggage parks, and provision stores. With no hope of reclaiming Breymann's camp, Burgoyne ordered the withdrawal of his troops from the British Light Infantry Redoubt and the main British and German lines. With tents left standing in place, the troops and followers were relocated that night to the Hudson Valley and along the nearby bluffs. The next morning, preparations were begun to facilitate a wholesale retreat.

On October 8 Gates dispatched patrols north to investigate the British positions, at which time it was confirmed that the enemy had evacuated and were crammed into the valley and on the bluffs. General Lincoln himself

British Spade
third quarter, 18th century
New Hampshire Historical Society, 2013.500.018
Consisting of an iron-wrapped wooden core, this spade includes the inscription that it "was used . . . in digging the British intrenchments at the battle of Saratoga and was picked up after Burgoyne's defeat by an American soldier named Andrew Todd." Todd was a private soldier in Captain Daniel Runnels's company, Colonel Moses Nichols's New Hampshire militia battalion.

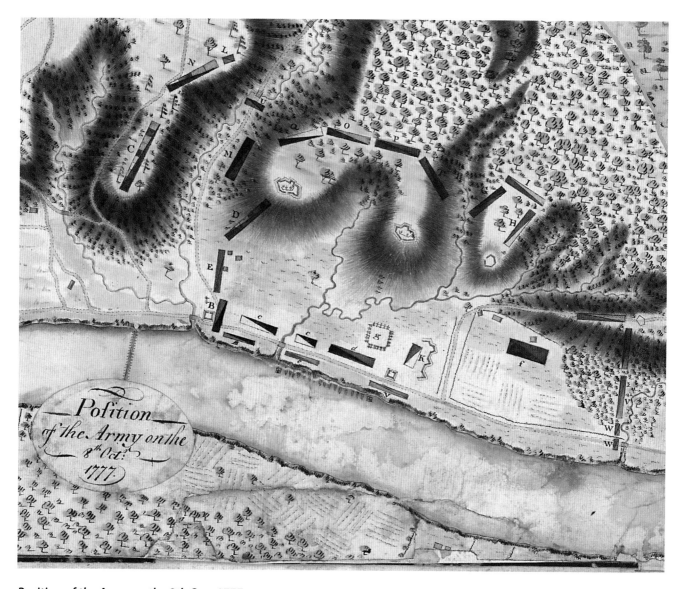

Position of the Army on the 8th Octr 1777

by Lieutenant William Cumberland Wilkinson, ca. 1778

The Library of Congress, gm71000664

This map depicts the positions of Burgoyne's consolidated Army from Canada following the Battle of Bemus Heights. Military units are identified by colored blocks, most of which reflect each unit's coat or jacket and facing colors. Note that the individual facing colors for the companies that comprised the British (D) and German (N) Grenadier Battalions and the British Light Infantry Battalion (C) are all accurately reflected in their correct sub-divisional orders of battle. The largest block (f) represents His Majesty's General Hospital, removed up the valley away from American artillery fire (hospital physicians, surgeons, and mates wore scarlet coats faced blue). Kromma Kill is the squiggly creek that flows from the west (on top of the map) into the Hudson River. Notice the three hilltop redoubts located on the high bluffs overlooking the valley—the southernmost one (nearest Kromma Kill) was the Great Redoubt, in which General Fraser was buried.

The funeral of General Fraser, who was shot after the action at Saratoga, October 7, 1777

by John Graham, 1791

courtesy of James L. Kochan Fine Art & Antiques, Wiscasset, Maine

Exhibited at the Royal Academy of Arts in 1791, this painting exemplifies the lasting impression that Fraser's death made upon the British public. Among those who attended the funeral were Burgoyne (left, deep in thought), Phillips (to Burgoyne's right, in blue), and Riedesel (right, in blue). In the foreground, Captain Alexander Fraser, General Fraser's nephew and commander of the elite company of British Rangers, takes his deceased uncle's hand. The artist's patron, the Earl of Harrington (styled Viscount Petersham in 1777), who served as Burgoyne's acting aide-de-camp, stands behind Fraser with hands clasped, lamenting the poor general's demise—and the impending doom awaiting the whole army. Fraser was one of only two British generals killed or mortally wounded in battle during the entire eight-year-long war.

Cartridge Pouch Device, Grenadier Company, 21st Regiment of Foot ca. 1774

Don Troiani collection

While British grenadiers were issued the same cartridge pouches as the battalion company men in their regiments, their pouch ornaments often differed. Consisting of the universal flaming bomb motif associated with grenadiers, this device also includes the regimental number and the GR monogram for King George III.

reconnoitered that day, and while riding on "an open cart path"[2] that ran through a thick wood, he rounded a corner and saw a body of men. Unable to "distinguish them by their dress," he rode "so near as to perfectly discover" his mistake. While turning his horse to flee, two of the redcoated men aimed and fired at the American general, the "ball from one of their pieces" entering his right leg. Upon his return to camp, he was, like Arnold the day before, sent to the Northern Army's General Hospital in Albany. If Gates was to take further action against Burgoyne, it would be without a major general to assist him.

American artillery was brought up the valley and began to cannonade the British forces' positions and, particularly, the floating bridge. Missing their floating marks, some of the balls fell near the British General Hospital tents, which were then relocated up the valley, away from the fire. The British returned the favor by shelling the Americans in the open valley with howitzers. Throughout the course of the daylong artillery duel, each side sustained a few casualties. At 6:00 p.m. Burgoyne and some of the army's principal officers set off in a solemn funeral procession up into the Great Redoubt. General Fraser succumbed to his mortal wound that morning, and his very particular last request was to be buried in the Great Redoubt that evening, at 6 o'clock. Although this delayed the army's retreat, Burgoyne made sure to honor his most trusted general's final request. While Fraser's burial ceremony took place, American artillerymen directed artillery fire at the redoubt. Some shots even "flew around and over the heads of the mourners."[3]

After Fraser was laid to rest, the Army from Canada made its very slow trek north along the River Road. Officers, soldiers, and followers took as much of their personal baggage as they could, but much was left behind in the abandoned camp. The bateaux bridge was broken up, and with the army's other bateaux and scows, they immediately set off upriver, carrying most of the army's provisions. The army's artillery, along with wheeled transports piled with as much of the public and ordnance stores that could be loaded, accompanied the long, drawn-out column. The British Grenadier Battalion formed the rear guard, departing their camp in the early hours of October 9.

By about 6:00 a.m. the retreating column became mired in a torrential October downpour. While the troops were slowed in their march, anything on wheels became bogged down, resulting in the column becoming elongated and diffused. Burgoyne ordered his army to halt at Dovegate (present-day Coveville, New York) "to give time to the bateaux, loaded with provisions, which had not been able to keep pace with the troops, to come a-breast."[4] There the army remained. Six days' rations were issued to the troops, and officers were warned that "no great consideration would be given" to their baggage and that "they would do well to take their best possessions along on their own horses." Looking to expedite the

Lady Harriet Acland during the American War of Independence

by Robert Pollard, ca.1783

© *National Trust Images, 78033; photograph by John Hammond*

This painting shows Lady Harriet Acland and her retinue traversing the Hudson River during Her Ladyship's October 9 mission to join her wounded husband, Major John Acland, in American captivity. Burgoyne later claimed the American sentinel "apprehensive of treachery . . . threatened to fire into the boat if it stirred before day-light," forcing Acland's entourage to wait overnight in the cold, open boat until morning. Dearborn refuted the story, stating that he received Lady Acland with hospitality, without delay, and housed her and her party overnight. Note the red-and-white-striped Continental flag flying in the American camp; this was changed to the Stars and Stripes when Robert Pollard published this painting as a print in 1784.

Burgoyne, *State of the Expedition*, 129.

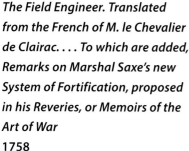

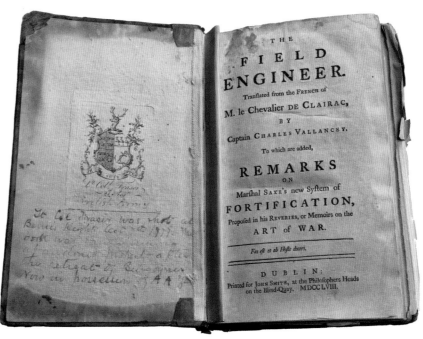

The Field Engineer. Translated from the French of M. le Chevalier de Clairac. . . . To which are added, Remarks on Marshal Saxe's new System of Fortification, proposed in his Reveries, or Memoirs of the Art of War
1758

Fort Ticonderoga Museum collection, MC-154; photograph by Gavin Ashworth

This military text was translated into English by Charles Vallancey, longtime officer in the Irish Corps of Engineers, whose son served in Burgoyne's army as an officer in the 62nd Regiment of Foot. This volume was owned by Simon Fraser, whose printed bookplate pasted within includes his coat of arms. Fraser brought this book on the expedition, and the handwritten inscription reveals that it was "found among abandoned property—after the retreat of Burgoyne."

retreat, "Various officers cared so little for their equipage that they voluntarily destroyed or burned part of it."[5] The downpour continued. Americans were spotted moving north on the other side of the river.

While Burgoyne's forces spun their wheels on October 9 during the muddy, stalled retreat north, Gates's remained in camp at Bemus Heights. American troops captured Burgoyne's old camp and His Majesty's General Hospital. Consisting of over 400 wounded and sick officers and soldiers, complete with a surgeon, mates, and nurses, Burgoyne had left it behind.[6] On October 8 Gates had sent Brigadier General John Fellows's Brigade of 1,300 Massachusetts militia up the east side of the Hudson opposite Saratoga, where they forded the river and began to entrench. Burgoyne's army approached Saratoga on the night of October 9, and Fellows's militia immediately retreated back to the Hudson's east shore, where they entrenched along the crest of the hills, covering the river ford over which the eastbound road crossed.

Although Gates's Northern Army was still located ten miles south at Bemus Heights, his October 9 general orders instructed his troops to "hold themselves in Readiness to march at a moment's Warning With Blankets and Provisions only the Gen[l] Expects every man Will be Ready for action Compleat With 30 Rounds."[7] After being issued provisions and ammunition, the Northern Army set off in pursuit of Burgoyne's early on October 10.[8] During this northerly march,

Field Bedstead
ca. 1775

Saratoga National Historical Park, SARA 3767

In order to pass nights more comfortably, foldable wooden field bedsteads, complete with curtains, were often brought by the high-ranking officers of both armies. A mattress, bolster, pillow, blankets, coverlet, and bearskin or goatskin usually completed the ensemble. Tradition holds that this bedstead was taken from Burgoyne's abandoned camp during the British retreat to Saratoga.

Camp Stool
ca. 1770s

Concord Museum; photograph courtesy of Joel Bohy

This folding stool has a provenance of having been used by a British lieutenant in Burgoyne's army. While officers of higher rank often brought field bedsteads on campaign, lower-ranking officers, lacking both the funds and an accommodating transportation allowance, sometimes brought three stools and arranged them as a bed.

the Americans were shocked by the devastation left in the wake of Burgoyne's retreat. Ensign Blake noted that the British had "burnt most of the buildings as they went, and cut away the bridges; and whenever their wagons or tents or baggage broke down, they knocked the horses on the head and burnt the baggage."[9] General Walcott lamented that the British "in their Progress have burnt the House of every Man who has been reported friendly to his Country" and that they "burnt Gen¹ Schuyler's House, Barn, Mills," as well as the barracks in Saratoga that morning.[10] Barrels of gunpowder, flour, salt pork, and even some abandoned bateaux were taken by the Americans, as were piles of unburned and littered war matériel and personal effects. Gates's advance guard reached Fish Creek in the afternoon, having covered in four hours what it took Burgoyne's army about twenty-four hours to do.

Earlier in the day, while Gates's troops marched north and Burgoyne's settled in Saratoga, a British-royalist work party was dispatched north above Saratoga in order to "reconnoitre, and repair the roads and bridges, in order to facilitate the retreat of the army from Saratoga towards Fort Edward." The work proceeded well, and the party arrived within a few miles of Fort Edward. But with the arrival of Gates's forces near Saratoga that afternoon, Burgoyne immediately recalled most of the workmen's guard, consisting of the 47th Regiment of Foot and Fraser's Rangers, leaving only Captain MacKay's Loyal Volunteers behind to cover the

Private, Colonel Samuel Brewer's (12th) Massachusetts Regiment

As with most Northern Army Continental corps in 1777, the soldiers of Brewer's Regiment wore a disparate mix of coats and "rifle" shirts, shoes and moccasins, neck stocks and rollers, and breeches, trousers, and overalls. While some recruits received "new French Arms" and some were issued "Gun Slings & Knapsacks," half the regiment's arms were returned as "Bad" on the eve of the enemy's invasion. Because of the army's continual lack of haversacks, provisions were often wrapped in blanket rolls when knapsacks were unavailable or ordered left in camp.

Sewell, April 25–26, 1777, *Journal*, n.p.

Captain Joseph Stebbins's Cocked Hat

ca. 1775

Pocumtuck Valley Memorial Association, 1927.28

Stebbins commanded a company in Colonel David Wells's battalion of Hampshire County, Massachusetts, militia and served during the final month of the Northern Campaign. This rare wartime survivor is made of felted beaver hair. The hat's brim, which was attached to the crown at three points, has since become detached.

Pattern 1756 Long Land Musket and Bayonet (British)

ca. 1775

Don Troiani collection

Although Long Land muskets were outdated by the time of the American War for Independence, they were still issued to many regiments needing new arms. Assembled at the Tower of London and issued to the 47th Regiment of Foot as part of a 1775 arms augmentation, this musket and its matching bayonet were surrendered at Saratoga in October 1777. The musket's stock was branded with "United States," indicating its post-Saratoga Continental Army ownership. Weighing over ten pounds, this pattern musket has a .75-caliber forty-six-inch-long barrel.

workmen. Shortly after, MacKay's isolated 180-man party was attacked by about 500 militia, upon which the royalists retreated "some little distance into the adjoining woods to the west."[11] Having sustained over forty casualties, MacKay and his remaining party made their way through the woods to Fort George.

With Gates's arrival at Saratoga on the afternoon of October 10, the siege of Saratoga had begun. Both sides cannonaded each other as the British entrenched in and around the small settlement and the Americans began the careful process of enveloping enemy positions. Gates's forces on both sides of the river expanded on a daily basis thanks to Massachusetts, New Hampshire, and Vermont militia reinforcements, and over the next few days grew to exceed 17,000 officers and soldiers present and fit for duty. Another 3,900 troops were stationed at posts in Vermont and between Fort Edward and Skenesborough.

Operating under the belief that the main body of Burgoyne's army had continued its evacuation north, Brigadier General John Nixon, General Gates's senior officer, was charged with making a major multifaceted advance over Fish Creek on the morning of October 11. Covered by the sort of thick fog that

Officer, Battalion Company, 62nd Regiment of Foot
Uniforms of the British Army's commissioned officer corps did not include a means by which to identify rank, resulting in junior subaltern and senior field officers appearing indistinguishable from one another. Paralleling the men of their regiments, British officers in the Canada Army modified their uniforms in spring 1777 by having coats trimmed and hats cut into caps and decorated; sashes, and usually gorgets, continued to be worn on duty. Spontoons, and often swords, were laid aside in favor of fusees and bayonets for use on Burgoyne's expedition.

prevailed in the valley on cool October mornings, portions of Nixon's attack force, which consisted of his and Glover's brigades and Morgan's Corps, began to ford across the creek into Saratoga that morning. Morgan's Corps proceeded west along Fish Creek, skirting the heights of Saratoga where Burgoyne's most massive fortification lay (present-day Victory Woods). The fog completely obscured their view, and before Morgan's men knew it, they "fell in with the Enimys guards in a thick fogg," located "Close to the Enimy works." Morgan's Corps hunkered down in their position while the British "Began a Brisk Canonade" upon them. In a reverse of the usual outcome, Morgan's Corps lost about a dozen men killed or wounded; the British lost none.[12]

To the east, part of Glover's Brigade had greater success. Their target was the mouth of Fish Creek, where the British lodged their bateaux and scows, and a store of some provisions and war matériel that had yet to be brought up to Saratoga's defenders. Captain Goodale led the van of the attack, whereby most of the royalists and Royal Navy personnel fled, but a nearby platoon of the 62nd Regiment of Foot was not so lucky. Upon hearing the shouting and commotion, the

> British guard were all paraded, the [British] officer gave the
> word, make Ready, they all cocked their pieces, in this situation Capt
> Goodale had the command to prevent his own men from fireing to
> give the alarm to the Enemy who could not see him on account of
> the Fogg, and such boldness of address as to Deter the British officer
> out of his fire, and the whole to ground their arms.[13]

Having taken one British officer, thirty-six soldiers, and some sailors without firing a shot, the Americans carried off significant stores, destroyed what they could not take, and even rowed some of the captured bateaux downriver to the safety of the American lines.

Nixon's and Glover's Brigades hardly had time to develop their main attack. Deployed in columns south of the creek, both brigades were halted in the fog when reports were received that the British remained in Saratoga behind their defenses. But because the fog obscured all views across Fish Creek, Nixon and Glover halted operations until they could get confirmation from Gates on how to proceed. As the morning wore on and the fog lifted, the British began a cannonade of the awaiting Americans. Glover's troops took to the safety of the wooded heights. Nixon's men, exposed on the open River Road, surged north toward Saratoga, sliding down the very steep southern bank of Fish Creek, and remained there, covered from enemy artillery fire in the high-walled creek bed. After about an hour, Nixon's and Glover's troops withdrew out of cannon range.

Iron Six-Pounder Cannonball
ca. 1776–77
Saratoga National Historical Park,
SARA 181
Cannonballs were solid iron projectiles that smashed through enemy defenses and soldiers. Many objects produced for the British or Irish Boards of Ordnance were stamped with the "King's Mark"—a broad arrow—which denoted government ownership. This particular cannonball was found in Burgoyne's October 1777 camp in Saratoga.

Braunschweig Cartridge Pouch Device

third quarter, 18th century

Don Troiani collection

This heavy cast-brass ornament adorned the *Patronentasche* (cartridge pouch) of a Braunschweig musketeer soldier in Burgoyne's army. The device includes the ducal coronet and inverted *C* monogram of the Herzog zu Braunschweig und Lüneburg (Duke of Brunswick and Lueneburg), Carl I. This piece was found near the Lansing/Marshall House in Schuylerville at the turn of the twentieth century.

Over the followings days, conditions in Burgoyne's entrenchments devolved fast. Without tents, men, women, and children suffered overnight in the frigid fall air. Access to running water was limited due to its proximity to the American lines.

> All things in this camp became sadder and sadder for us. Our poor sick and wounded crept around in the camp to look in part for safe places of refuge, in part for compassionate surgeons who could dress their wounds or provide them with medicines. A regular hospital could not be established. Loyal provincials [royalist Americans] walked around sadly bemoaning either the fate of their families left behind or their own, if they should fall into the hands of their enemies. The horses began to die for lack of forage they became living skeletons.[14]

Followers suffered as well, even those of the upper classes. A number of men, women, and children, including Lady Riedesel and other officers' wives and their families, sought safety in the cellar of Peter Lansing's home (present-day Marshall House), the army's designed hospital. Located at the northern end of Burgoyne's camp, the house was exposed to American artillery fire, on account of which "the women and children, afraid to go outside, had polluted the entire cellar." Lady Riedesel had the cellar evacuated so it could be swept and "fumigated with vinegar."[15] On the southern end of camp, royalist refugee Elizabeth Fisher complained that "provisions were scarce, and not to be had for money" from the sutlers. Few in the British entrenchments dared "to kindle fire for fear we should be observed from the other side of the river, and they may fire on us, which they did several times." They "suffered cold and hunger" and for many days had "nothing but a piece of raw salt pork, a biscuit, and the drink of water."[16]

Corporal George Fox, who with the 47th Regiment encamped at the edge of the woods in the Saratoga valley, also lamented that the cooking fires created firing points for the American cannonade, which "killed several of our men so that we put out the fires and lay upon the ground all night." As for those rations, they consisted of "4 biscuits per man per day and then we had some flour served out to us which we made dumplings of. We durst not go to our bateaus for the little beef and pork in them."[17]

With the siege in full swing, Burgoyne called together a council of war with most of his general officers, during which a variety of military options were explored. After considered discussion, it was decided that evacuation under cover of darkness was the best course of action, before the Americans completely cut off the route north out of Saratoga. Preparations were put in

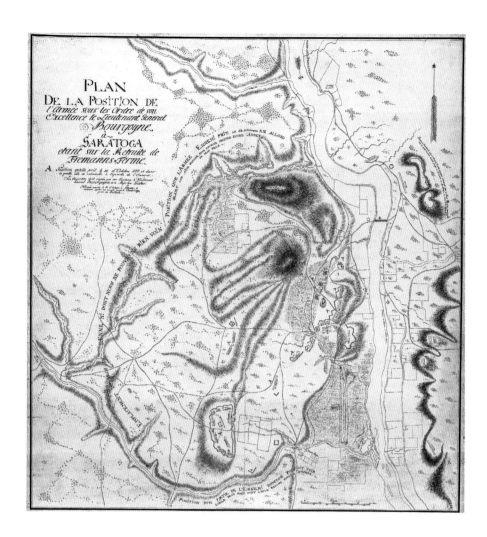

Plan de la Position de l'armée sous les Ordre de son Excellence le Lieutenant General Bourgoyne à Saratoga etant sur la Retraite de Fremanns Ferme [Plan of the Position of the Army under the Orders of His Excellency Lieutenant General Burgoyne at Saratoga on the Retreat from Freeman's Farm]

by Captain Johann Daniel Gerlach, ca. 1778

The New-York Historical Society, M006834

Saratoga was a small community of about thirty homes, outbuildings, military barracks, and storehouses. It was also the seat of Philip Schuyler's plantation, which consisted of mills, barns, and the dwellings of enslaved people he owned. Burgoyne's troops summarily burned most of these buildings on October 10. The majority of Burgoyne's British and royalist troops bivouacked within an enormous entrenched redoubt located on the heights (present-day Victory Woods) overlooking Fish Creek and the river valley below. To the north, shallow subsoil prevented the German Division from digging deeper than one and a half feet into the ground for their fortifications. Peter Lansing's home (present-day Marshall House), in which the army's ladies, their children, and many other followers and wounded sought refuge, is marked as "Hospital General"—the army's General Hospital. Note the bevy of British boats located at the mouth of Fish Creek as well as the ruins of Fort Hardy, a dilapidated French and Indian War fort.

Lieut^t Genl John Burgoyne Col^l of the 16th Re[giment] of Light Dragoons & Governor of Fort William.

attributed to Luke Jackson, 1777

Eric Schnitzer collection

Inspired by Burgoyne's sanguine July report of the campaign's whirlwind successes, this triumphant print accompanied a front-page biography of the general in *The Hibernian Magazine: or, Compendium of Entertaining Knowledge, for October 1777.* Readers were updated on the campaign's conclusion in the magazine's December issue. Prints like this one, made for a wide audience and not derived from original painted portraits, resulted in inaccurate representations of the subject's likeness and uniform.

Lieut. Gen. John Burgoyne Col. of the 16.Re of Light Dragoons & Governor of Fort William.

motion, but shortly before midnight, Burgoyne "decided differently and ordered the army to stay put."[18]

At 3:00 p.m. on October 13, Burgoyne called together a second council of war, consisting of his generals and regimental commanders. He spoke plainly of the devolving situation facing the Army from Canada, that he "considered it impossible to attack the enemy," and even if such resulted in British victory, they "could not make use" of it. The army's provisions were running extremely low—there now remained only enough to last through October 18. Only "One sole possibility remained: that each one for himself would seek his own way through these desolate woods as well as he could and to get to Carillon [Ticonderoga] in this manner." After the council rejected the concept, Burgoyne then asked if it was

Drummer, Battalion Company, 21st Regiment of Foot (Royal North British Fusiliers)

Drummers of royal infantry regiments in the British Army—units authorized to wear blue "Royal Facings"—wore scarlet coats faced with blue; drummers of nonroyal regiments wore coats in the opposite colors of the men of their regiment. As with their soldier counterparts in the Canada Army, British drummers' coats were shortened and their black bearskin caps were replaced with horsehair-crested caps. Drummers' lace was usually distinctive from that worn by the men of their regiment, typically designed with a different pattern and woven with a loop pile.

"dishonorable to capitulate in such a situation" as the one they were in, which was answered with a resounding "No!" After Burgoyne posed additional questions related to the efficacy of a capitulation, the Army from Canada commander revealed a "final draft of a document of surrender which, in case of acceptance by the enemy, would save the whole army for the King, who then could use it for other purposes."[19]

Burgoyne's ten-point proposal for surrender was unanimously approved by the council's officers. That night a British drummer was sent to deliver a message to the American camp, requesting that Gates meet with a British field officer in the morning, who would come bearing a "Message . . . upon a Matter of high moment to both Armies."[20] Gates agreed, and a cease-fire was immediately declared.

Considering his army's terminal situation, Burgoyne's terms for his own army's surrender were audacious. Included among his ten proposals was that his troops would be allowed to march out with the honors of war. After they surrendered their arms and artillery, they would march to a port and receive "free Passage . . . to Great Britain upon Condition of not serving again in North America during the present Contest." Officers, soldiers, and followers would be allowed to retain their personal belongings and

**British Document Trunk
third quarter, 18th century**

Bennington Museum, 1963.22
This small, beautifully embossed leather-covered trunk displays the crown and *GR*—the Latin initials of *Georgius Rex* (King George)—on the dome. Lined with printed legal papers, it was probably used to house official military documents. This piece, which belonged to an officer in Burgoyne's army, was acquired by the prolific nineteenth-century historian-illustrator Benson J. Lossing, author of the famed two-volume set *Pictorial Field-Book of the Revolution.*

such would not be "molested or searched," with Burgoyne "giving his Honour that there are no Public Stores Secreted therein." All "Canadians and Persons belonging to the Establishment in Canada" would be "permitted to return there."[21]

On the morning of October 14, Burgoyne's blindfolded deputy adjutant-general, Lieutenant-Colonel Robert Kingston, was led to Gates's headquarters, located a little over one mile south of Fish Creek. Kingston barely had time to submit Burgoyne's proposal when Gates presented a copy of his own, a seven-point proposition that demanded, among other things, that Burgoyne's troops surrender as prisoners of war. Leaving Burgoyne's terms with Gates, Kingston brought Gates's back to Burgoyne, upon which a third council of war was convened. Every officer flatly rejected Gates's articles by unanimously declaring that "they would rather die than accept such dishonorable conditions." What's more, Burgoyne upped the ante by asserting "never to agree to any other proposition than the one that he . . . had offered."[22]

The following morning, Gates sent a message to Burgoyne in which, "To everyone's surprise," the former agreed to all of Burgoyne's original terms, with only some minor revisions. Gates's primary stipulation was that the final treaty must be agreed to by 2:00 p.m. that afternoon, and that Burgoyne's capitulation must occur at 5:00 p.m. Burgoyne convened a fourth council of war, suspicious of Gates's newfound willingness to accept terms so readily and of the puzzling short deadline for the capitulation. The council agreed that 2:00 p.m. was too soon, and that the terms arranged by Burgoyne (which Gates had already signed, further throwing suspicion upon his eagerness) were only meant to be preliminary. With many details and "secondary articles" still needing to be worked out,

Burgoyne replied by proposing that two commissioners from each army, with full authority to finalize the formal treaty, should meet. Gates concurred.[23]

The commissioners met late that afternoon near General Schuyler's unburned "upper sawmill" located on Fish Creek. Representing Burgoyne was Lieutenant-Colonel Nicholas Sutherland and Captain James Henry Craig, the latter officer being the army's deputy judge advocate. Gates sent his deputy adjutant general, twenty-year-old Lieutenant Colonel James Wilkinson, and Brigadier General William Whipple, a New Hampshire militia general and sitting delegate of the Second Continental Congress.[24] They worked until about 8:00 p.m. and, in the end, the resultant document looked little different from Burgoyne's October 13 proposal.

With the commission dissolved, Sutherland and Craig promised to return their copy of the *Articles of Capitulation Between Lieutenant-General Burgoyne and Major General Gates*, with Burgoyne's signature, the following morning. A few hours later, a note from Craig was delivered to Gates's headquarters, admitting that while Burgoyne agreed to every one of the thirteen provisos of the treaty, there was one major error "of a term in the title," which was "very different" from Burgoyne's intentions. While a change in title had no bearing on the treaty's contents, Burgoyne was thinking ahead toward the political fallout. Burgoyne's demand—it was not a request—was to exchange the word *Capitulation* with *Convention*, a more lighthearted word that might suggest to some that the treaty was an innocuous agreement between army commanders on equal footing instead of a document of surrender between victor and vanquished. Gates promptly admitted to "the alteration required."[25]

In the dark, early hours of October 16, royalist Joseph Bettys secreted his way into Burgoyne's camp.[26] He was sent south in early October to gain intelligence of Clinton's movements in the lower Hudson Valley, and now returned to report that he had "heard . . . General Clinton had taken the fortifications in the Highlands, and had arrived with the troops and fleet at Esopus a week ago [October 8], so that he would probably be at Albany by now."[27] Expectedly, the British commander was "delighted" with this admittedly "uncertain piece of information." Bettys's testimony was the only intelligence that Burgoyne had of Clinton's movements since receiving his offer on September 21. Although Bettys's report was only a thirdhand rumor, it energized the British general to continue playing the endgame against Gates in hope of gaining additional beneficial Convention provisos.

What Burgoyne did not know was that Vaughan's foray up the Hudson River had, in fact, ascended to Esopus and beyond, but not according to the timeline that Bettys described. Having successfully navigated past the cheval-de-frise laid between Pollepel Island and New Windsor, the British Advanced Squadron

British Staff Officer Epaulet ca. 1770s

Private collection

While regimental officers wore epaulets according to patterns set by their respective regimental commanders, staff officer epaulet patterns were regulated by the crown. This pattern, consisting of silver-thread embroidery, was particular to army-level quartermasters and adjutants general.

Cartridge Pouch Device, 26th Regiment of Foot ca. 1770s

Fort Ticonderoga Museum collection; photograph by Don Troiani

The 26th Regiment of Foot garrisoned various outposts in Canada and northern New York in 1775, including Fort Ticonderoga when Ethan Allen and the Green Mountain Boys captured it. The regiment also participated in the October 1777 attack on Fort Clinton and in the destruction of Kingston and Clermont. This piece was recovered at Fort Ticonderoga.

anchored about six miles below Esopus Landing by the evening of October 15. The landing, located on the Hudson River's west shore, constituted the beachhead for Esopus, a large village that rested alongside Esopus Creek, about three miles inland from the river. Located about fifty-five miles south of Albany, Esopus—also known as Kingston—was the seat of New York State government and the state's Council of Safety.[28] American defenses at Kingston Landing were deemed too dangerous to leave in the Advance Squadron's wake, and Vaughan made plans to attack.

Shortly after 10:00 a.m. on October 16, two small forts at the landing manned by Ulster County, New York, militia cannonaded the Advanced Squadron, setting off an artillery duel. The Royal Navy vessels returned fire, forcing most of the defenders to retire toward Kingston, and Vaughan deployed his infantry—the 7th (Royal Fusiliers), 26th, and 63rd Regiments of Foot—at 3:00 p.m. They met with little opposition at the landing, easily overran the small forts, and "spiked & destroyed their Guns."[29]

The British marched inland and attacked Kingston's militia defenders "drawn up, with Cannon," which Vaughan's troops easily defeated. Although a few Americans supposedly remained to shoot at the British "from their Houses," the village was all but deserted, and Vaughan's redcoats and Royal Navy personnel promptly worked to "reduce the Place to Ashes." Not only were the storehouses, mills, and magazine destroyed, but nearly every home and outbuilding was torched that evening, numbering about 250 buildings in all.[30] Despite the fact that most of the houses were made of stone, the flames had the desired effect and obliterated the community. All American vessels found within reach were likewise destroyed.

Few on either side were casualties in the fighting, although a Royal Navy officer, master, and three sailors were severely wounded when they were setting fire to gunpowder stores.[31]

On the evening of October 17, Vaughan's troops landed a few miles north at Red Hook, on the Hudson's east side, and burned more houses, barns, and mills belonging to Revolutionary sympathizers. On the 18th he landed his troops at Clermont, located about twelve miles upriver from Esopus Landing. There the British found what they were undoubtedly looking for: estates belonging to New York's powerful Livingston family. The head of the family, Robert R. Livingston, was a former delegate to the Continental Congress and a member of the new nation's five-member committee that drafted the Declaration of Independence. Although Livingston was safe—he was not there—and his family, workers, and enslaved people evacuated the properties, Vaughan's redcoats burned the magnificent estates of Clermont and Belvedere late that afternoon. Other homes likewise suffered British wrath, as Vaughan unleashed forces on both sides of the river to destroy more property, possessions, and food stores.

There Vaughan remained. His reasoning was not solely to spite the crown's enemies, but was grounded upon more practical considerations. The pilots "absolutely" refused "to take charge of them further," citing the river's increasingly difficult navigability.[32] Vaughan took the opportunity to send two spies northward to seek out Burgoyne's army. Reporting back days later, they admitted to not being able to make contact, but heard rumors of Burgoyne's situation. Further complicating Vaughan's hopes were reports that thousands of Americans were forming on both sides of the Hudson. Foiled on all fronts, Vaughan decided that it was "impractical to give [Burgoyne] any further assistance" and withdrew on October 23.[33] As it was, Vaughan's return downriver was well timed—Sir Henry had received orders from Howe to send thousands of reinforcements to Philadelphia, thereby nullifying Clinton's capacity for any further operations in the Hudson Valley.[34]

Back at Saratoga on October 16, Burgoyne again called his council of war together. The general asked whether or not it was appropriate to renege on his promise to sign the Convention in consequence of Bettys's report. This time, the vote was fourteen to eight against the measure, the majority of officers stating that "it would be contrary to the honour of the nation and all *raison de guerre*."[35]

Despite the vote, Burgoyne was not about to be thwarted by his own officers. Operating under the assumption that Betty's timeline was accurate and that Clinton had gained Albany, Burgoyne wanted to buy more time. His officers concurred that he could write to Gates, claiming that the American general detached "a considerable force" during the Convention negotiations, which invalidated Gates's "great superiority of Numbers" and therefore negated the

Articles of Convention Between Lieutenant-General Burgoyne and Major General Gates; October 16, 1777

1777

Saratoga National Historical Park, SARA 683

This is one of many handwritten copies of the Articles of Convention drafted for the purpose of spreading word of the Saratoga victory to the American public. This particular version was secured by Giles Jackson, who served as first major in Colonel John Ashley's battalion of Berkshire County, Massachusetts, militia.

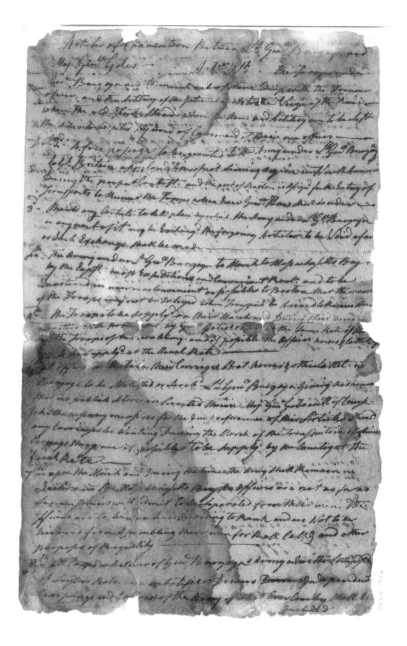

essential reason why Burgoyne engaged in the negotiations in the first place. Burgoyne then requested that two of his officers "be permitted to see that the strength of the Forces now opposed to him is Such as will convince him that no such Detachments" were sent.[36] Gates responded immediately, claiming that no such "violation" had taken place and that Burgoyne's request was "inadmissible."[37] A final council of war was called, and "Neither General Burgoyne himself nor the council of war . . . could object to General Gates' declaration, and General Burgoyne at last signed the treaty, although he could hardly bring himself to do it."[38]

Surrender

It may I think be reckoned among the extraordinary events history furnishes us with.

—Lieutenant Colonel Dudley Coleman, October 28, 1777[1]

While Burgoyne and Gates signed off on the Articles of Convention on October 16, the Army from Canada's physical surrender took place the following day. In Burgoyne's camp, preparations began in earnest to ensure that as much could be saved from loss to the Americans. Burgoyne's representatives very cleverly ensured that the Convention stipulated that only "arms" were to be surrendered, a detail that passed by Wilkinson, Whipple, and

Braunschweig Saber
third quarter, 18th century
Colonel J. Craig Nannos collection
Infantry soldiers of nearly every German nation-state, including Braunschweig, were armed with brass-hilted *Säbel* (sabers) of a form like this. This blade includes an engraving of Herzog (Duke) Carl I's coronet surmounting a cartouche that includes the running horse of Haus Hannover (House of Hanover), testifying to the shared lineage of Herzog Carl I and King George III.

Braunschweig Commissioned Officer's Sword
third quarter, 18th century
Private collection
Unlike most of their British commissioned officer counterparts, German officers retained their swords during the Northern Campaign of 1777. This *Degen* (small sword) has a gilt-brass hilt and a wire-wrapped grip. The straight blade includes gold-filled engravings depicting martial trophies and the running horse of Haus Hannover (House of Hanover), as well as the Latin inscription *Nun quam retrorsum*.

The Siege of Saratoga, 1777

by Colonel Tadeusz Kościuszko, ca. 1780
courtesy of the Richard H. Brown Revolutionary
War Map Collection

Traditionally identified as a map depicting the Battles of Saratoga, this piece actually shows the American and British forces' positions during the October 1777 Saratoga siege. Despite its cartographic flaws (the map was not drawn from surveys), Fish Creek is clearly visible, as is the Americans' floating log bridge, which was brought up from Bemus Heights and reassembled across the Hudson. Generalized positions for the various military forces are written in Polish and include the *Wojsko Amerykanskie* (American Army—marked "A"), *Millicja Amerykanskie* (American Militia—marked "a"), and *Wojsko Angielskie* (English Army—marked "B"). Kościuszko, the Northern Department's Corps of Engineers second in command, drew this map himself—it is the only known map drawn by a Revolutionary participant depicting a military engagement from the entire Northern Campaign of 1777.

Gates. According to British military culture, "arms" were specifically defined to include soldier muskets and polearms, bayonets, drums, fifes, and "cartridge boxes"—small, eighteen-round-capacity wooden blocks covered with simple leather flaps. "Accoutrements," such as waist belts (which housed the scabbards that sheathed bayonets and, sometimes, swords) and cartridge pouches with shoulder belts (the large-capacity pouches that retained a soldier's ammunition), were privately owned by regimental colonels and therefore not subject to being given up.[2] All officers would keep all their own weapons.

Colours, however, were a different matter. Although an "accoutrement," colours were subject to being taken as trophies by the victors.[3] Burgoyne's officers covertly worked to subvert this expectation, and orders went out the night of October 16 for "the flags of all the regiments in the army" to be "made away with, so as not to surrender any trophies to the enemy, which were too beautiful for them."[4] This was accomplished by removing the silk colours and metallic-and-silk-mixed tasseled cords from their wooden staves, the latter of which were summarily burned in the nighttime fires. The colours and tasseled cords were

King's Colour, 62nd Regiment of Foot ca. 1770

Eric Schnitzer collection (photograph); courtesy of Martin McIntyre

Each British infantry battalion had a stand (pair) of silk colours—a King's (or First) and a Second (regimental). The King's colour consisted of "the great Union throughout," upon the center of which was painted or embroidered the regiment's "Royal Device" or "Ancient Badge." As most regiments had neither, they otherwise had their number emblazoned on a gold-framed rococo cartouche, interwoven with "the Wreath of Roses and Thistles on the same Stalk." British and German colours brought with Burgoyne's army in 1777, such as this one, were hidden away from the Americans in advance of the surrender and were afterward secretly returned to Europe.

**Royalist Accoutrement Ornament
ca. 1776–77**

Don Troiani collection

These brass devices were probably
mounted to leather shoulder belts
issued to royalist troops. Some
have been recovered in Army from
Canada royalist encampment sites.
The face is marked with the script
GR monogram—the Latin initials of
Georgius Rex (King George).

stashed in personal baggage which, according to the Convention, was off-limits
from being searched. Lady Riedesel herself participated in this deception:

> I had to conceive some means now for bringing the flags of our
> German regiments into safety. We had told the Americans in Sara-
> toga that they had been burned, which annoyed them very much
> at first, but they said nothing more about it. In fact, only the staves
> had been burned, and the flags themselves had been hidden. My
> husband entrusted me with this secret and assigned me the task of
> keeping the flags concealed. I got a trustworthy tailor, locked myself
> up in a room with him, and together we made a mattress, in which
> we sewed up all the flags.[5]

With the accoutrements saved on a technicality and the army's thirty British
and German colours saved by a breach of faith, there only remained the crown's
treasury. The army's military chest consisted of a hefty trove of silver and gold
specie, and it was vital that this did not fall into American hands. Shortly before
the surrender, the military chest was emptied and its contents doled out to the
army's command and staff officers and regimental paymasters. "Not a shilling"
made its way into the hands of the victors.[6]

Finally, there were the American royalists. Although the Convention stipulated that all people of Burgoyne's army would be treated equally and "compre-
hended in every respect as British subjects," there remained particular concern
for their safety.[7] John Peters, commander of the Queen's Loyal Rangers, received
from Burgoyne "a written permission to retire" from camp. With authorization in
hand, Peters and dozens of others from his corps "whose safety on any terms was
doubtful" set out at night on October 14 and made a successful escape north to
Fort George.[8]

Peters and his men were not the only ones to make their escape. Captain
Munro of the American Volunteers, and many others, were advised by General
Phillips to "make our Escape as soon as possible, lest we, perhaps might not be
able to effect it in case of great Hurry, and so fall into the Hands of our inveterate
Enemies."[9] Despite the Revolutionary American envelopment of Saratoga, they
also effected nighttime escapes to Fort George, as did most of those who made the
attempt. Some sneaked off for home, hoping for fair treatment from their Revolutionary neighbors. Some elected to remain with Burgoyne, even into captivity. But
in the end, most who remained were, in fact, released to Canada by Gates.

On the morning of October 17, the officers and soldiers of both armies prepared to meet each other for the first time without trying to kill each other. With
the wooden bridge crossing the high banks of Fish Creek in ruins, the auxiliary

road that forded Fish Creek near its mouth would host the forthcoming ceremony. The road ran south through Schuyler's burnt country estate and met up with the main River Road, upon which two very long lines of American Continental and militia troops were drawn up on each side as it meandered south. Late in the morning, Burgoyne and his military family rode out of their camp. Private Elisha James, who, with others, came up from Albany to see the surrender take place, described the momentous meeting he had seen in a letter to his wife, Sarah:

> Lieu^t Generall Burgoyne & all the Genarell officers Rid out in the Road from their Lines into ours . . . after that I Saw Genarall Gates & others Riding Towards the . . . Church that Stood near where I Stood & then he halted & Generall Burgoyne & his generll officers Rid To meet him came up To Generall Gates with his hatt of[f] & Shook hands & then took the Left hand of Generall Gates.[10]

When they met in person for the first time, the words exchanged between the two generals near the Dutch Reformed Church were somewhat surprising. Chaplain Hezekiah Smith, who was with Gates's entourage of officers, recorded what was passed between the two generals at that moment:

> [A]t the meeting of Gen. Burgoyne and Gen. Gates, Gen. Burgoyne addressed himself thus, "The Fate of War has put me into your Hands." Gen. Gates replied, "If Enterprize, Courage and Perseverance would have given you Success the Victory would have been yours."[11]

Private Henry Hallowell recalled that the generals and their scores of attending officers then "Dind together with genl gates on a small hill, there being awning taken from vessels placed some like a marquee."[12] The dinner, according to a contemporary report, consisted of "a ham, a goose, some beef, and a boiled mutton. The liquor was New England rum, mixed with rum, without sugar." After dinner, Gates "filled a bumper, and, in a most polite and liberal manner, drank *his Britannic Majesty's health.* Gen Burgoyne would not be outdone in politeness: he filled a bumper, and drank *General Washington's health.*"[13]

While Burgoyne and his entourage dined, his famished army was finishing the process of surrendering ordnance, stores, and arms near and in the decrepit remnants of Fort Hardy, an old French and Indian War fort located north of the outlet of Fish Creek. After the British stacked their arms and the Germans grounded theirs, the regiments formed in columns and marched off. In all, the Army from Canada yielded 1 lieutenant-general, 2 major-generals, 3 brigadiers, 350 commissioned and staff officers, 5,900 other ranks, and about 600 women

**Stock Clasp, 29th Regiment of Foot
ca. 1776–81**

*Fort Ticonderoga Museum collection, 2017.F.7;
photograph by Gavin Ashworth*

This is the hook portion from a set of brass clasps that were used to close a soldier's stock behind his neck. Black stocks, which were usually made of stiffened velvet or horsehair fabric, and clasps were part of a soldier's necessaries; many regiments, such as the 29th, engraved their stock clasps with regimental information.

**Joseph Eliot's Canteen
1776**

*courtesy of Skinner Auctioneers;
photograph by Don Troiani*

Eliot served as a twenty-eight-year old corporal in Captain Moses Knapp's company, Colonel William Shepard's (4th) Massachusetts Regiment. A veteran of the 1775 Lexington Alarm and the 1776 New York–New Jersey campaign with Washington, Eliot served in the Northern Campaign of 1777. He returned home on furlough after Burgoyne's surrender, having "been sick in the Hospital . . . & died on the fifteenth of December AD 1777."
NARA, Revolutionary War Pension Files, Joseph/Joanna Elliot (W.14,677).

and children.[14] A large number of ennobled officers—including a Scottish earl, an English viscount, a German count, and many Scottish and German barons—were among the captives, as well as a few members of Parliament, including Burgoyne himself.[15] Most of the army's royalist combatants, Royal Navy contingent, Canadiens, waggoneers, and American refugees, numbering over 500 additional people, were released to Canada.

Never before had American armed forces taken in such a haul of arms and war matériel. Although private baggage and personal belongings were off-limits, all government arms and public stores had to be given up. This included 30 artillery pieces, nearly 5,500 rounds of artillery shot, 12 kegs of flints, 17 boxes of musket balls, 72,000 prepared musket cartridges, 60 wagons and ammunition and powder carts, 2 traveling forges, over 200 sets of dragropes and harnesses, and 2 boxes of signal rockets, among other items. Over 4,600 muskets and rifles, 3,400 bayonets (without scabbards), 1,500 swords (without scabbards), 640 cartridge boxes, 110 drums, and 100 polearms were also included among the spoils.

That afternoon, the British column set off down the road, forded the creek, and proceeded through Schuyler's estate. With the German column behind them, the surrendered troops threaded their way through the two long lines of American troops flanking the road. The Germans were particularly fascinated with the Americans, noting that they

> stood straight and in orderly lines under arms. There was absolute silence in those regts. as can only be demanded from the best disciplined troops. . . . [N]ot a single man gave any evidence or the slightest impression of feeling hatred, mockery, malicious pleasure or pride for our miserable fate. Their modesty rather filled us with amazement.[16]

Braunschweig Woman and Child

A follower of the Regiment von Riedesel, this woman wears her deceased husband's old regimental coat, paid for via stoppages extracted from his wages. She and her daughter's hair are covered with caps, a long-standing custom of Euro-American society. German women earned money by working as nurses, seamstresses, laundresses, sutlers, and butchers, and their daughters often labored alongside them. As with soldiers, women had to carry all their personal possessions with them in their hands, over their shoulders, and on their backs during a march.

While the Americans were excited to see the professional European soldiers marching between their lines, nothing was more fascinating to them than the surprising number and appearance of the followers. Elisha James described the enemy's children as "tyd on a hors & Some in Knapsacks & others in Baskits on the womens Backs."[17] Teenaged drummer Daniel Granger recalled seeing "Women, who wore short Petty coats, bare footed, & bare Leged, with huge Packs on their backs, some carrying a child & leading an other or two, They were silent, civil, and looked quite subdued."[18] Hannah Winthrop, a Massachusetts women who saw the German followers in particular, thought they

> seemd to be the beasts of burthen, having a bushel basket on their back, by which they were bent double, the contents seemd to be Pots & kettles, various sorts of Furniture, children peeping thro gridirons & other utensils. Some very young Infants who were born on the road, the women barefoot, cloathd in dirty raggs Such Effluvia filld the air while they were passing, had they not been smoking all the time, I should have been apprehensive of being Contaminated by them.[19]

As the troops marched past the hill, the auspicious moment arrived. It's unclear if this was formally planned or not, but it doesn't appear to have been, particularly since such a surrender was without precedent. Private Isaac Quackenboss, who stood near the dining tent while performing duty as "one of the Life Guard of General Gates," vividly recalled seeing "General Burgoin deliver up his sword too General Gates who gave it back to him as a present." Apparently, Gates was handed another sword that day, as Quackenboss also observed that as "Colonel . . . Skeins delivered his sword to General Gates he Skeins looked very sour at General Gates who kept his sword."[20]

Apart from observing that the surrendered soldiers wore a mix of "smiling countenances, others with sour," Private Samuel Harris Jr. was fixated on the fact that the surrendered soldiers were, unexpectedly, marching into captivity while retaining their military accoutrements and even carrying musket parts. "They came out with their cartridge boxes [pouches] and bayonet-belts on; others having their iron ram-rods for walking-sticks," he wrote with surprise.[21] He wasn't the only one. Gates was nonplussed as well, which is all the more surprising since, as a former British Army officer, he should have been more careful regarding the nomenclature used in the Articles of Convention.[22] As the vanquished troops passed by the hilltop, Gates brought the question to the forefront:

Surrender of General Burgoyne at Saratoga, October 16, 1777
by John Trumbull, ca. 1820s
Yale University Art Gallery, Trumbull Collection, 1832.7

At the convention of Saratoga . . . when the troops marched with their accoutrements, General Gates asked me, if it was not customary for arms and accoutrements to go together. Replying, that the accoutrements were the colonels, and private property, General Gates said, very true; they are yours as such, and because we have not mentioned them in the convention.[23]

Both armies overnighted together at the old British camp at Freeman's farm. On October 18 Gates forced-marched the Northern Army to Albany upon fear that Clinton was ascending the Hudson and positioning to attack the city. After an exhausting trek, most of the army's wearied troops arrived in Albany that night; the next morning, they were deployed to make the best defense of the city. There they remained for about five days, after which most of the Northern Army

Connecticut artist John Trumbull, whose artistic skills were honed in England during and after the war, created eight epic history paintings depicting some of the Revolution's most important moments. Like most history paintings made at the time, focus was placed on capturing participant likenesses above historical accuracy. Lauded as the war's turning point, *Surrender of General Burgoyne* commemorates the first time in world history that a British Army ever surrendered.

Captain, Colonel Rufus Putnam's (5th) Massachusetts Regiment

Typically, after an officer died, his possessions were valuated and sold in camp at "vendue" (auction), with proceeds benefiting the deceased's family. An inventory for the effects of a dead officer of Putnam's Regiment, taken at Albany shortly after Burgoyne surrendered, included a coat; greatcoat; hat; black handkerchief; knapsack; powder flask; cartridge box; two stocks; two woolen jackets (waistcoats); a pair each of boots, shoes, buckles, and trousers; two pairs of leather breeches; three pairs of stockings; and two shirts—one white, the other striped.

was marched down the Hudson on October 23. The troops arrived at Clermont on October 26, only days after the last of Vaughan's vessels withdrew down the Hudson. They remained for three days there, without food, drenched from a continual cold, driving rain. Most of the long-term militia were released at this time, and the Continental troops continued their march south, eventually joining Washington's army in time to winter at Valley Forge, Pennsylvania.[24]

As for the Convention Army—the moniker given to Burgoyne's captive army—its officers, soldiers, and followers set out for Cambridge, Massachusetts, on October 18. According to the Articles of Convention, the port of Boston was chosen as the place where the Convention Army would embark upon Royal Navy vessels and be allowed to return "to Great Britain, on condition of not serving again in North America during the present contest."[25] Split into manageable bodies, the officers, soldiers, women, and children were led east to Cambridge, where most arrived on November 6–7. They were set up in huts atop nearby Prospect and Winter Hills, fully expecting that arrangements were being made to fulfill the obligations set forth in the Articles of Convention.

While news of the Convention spread fast, Congress did not receive official word of it from Gates's sluggish deputy adjutant general, Wilkinson, until November 3. Burgoyne's surrender was of course received with welcome, but when the terms of the Articles of Convention were scrutinized, congressional members started having second thoughts. Most notable among the objections was that the Europeans would be given free passage home. Reports of apparent breaches in the Convention—notably the absence of colours and money, the shortfall of muskets and bayonets surrendered, and sightings of Convention Army soldiers wearing accoutrements—provided Congress with the impetus to intercede.

With regard to the accoutrements Congress demanded from Burgoyne's troops, at the heart of the argument was a simple disagreement over military material culture nomenclature. The British Army had long defined government-issued "arms" to include eighteen-round "cartridge boxes," while colonel-purchased "accoutrements" included "cartridge pouches with shoulder belts." The new Continental Army did not make such a distinction, however, and Americans generically referred to any cartridge-carrying container as a "cartridge box." Congress's refusal to acquiesce, understand, or even acknowledge the difference provided the governing

Watch, Chain, and Key
third quarter, 18th century
Longfellow's Wayside Inn; photograph courtesy of Schuyler Selden
Once Burgoyne surrendered, the former belligerents immediately replaced combat for capitalism. This silver English-made verge fusee watch, key, and chain were purchased by Colonel Ezekiel How, commander of a battalion of Middlesex County, Massachusetts militia, "from an officer in Burgoyne's Army at Saratoga for 30 silver dollars." The officer, according to How, was "out of money [and] sold it under price."

British Cartridge Box, Bayonet Frog, and Waist Belt
second half, 18th century

Don Troiani collection

Muskets and bayonets issued from the Tower of London or Dublin Castle included this ensemble, which consisted of little more than a thin leather flap (often with an embossed, gold-filled GR3 and crown monogram) nailed to a wooden block and a small removable bayonet frog. The block, capable of carrying eighteen cartridges, affixed to a very thin belt that precariously buckled around the waist, making the block prone to flipping upside down. Because of this design flaw, they were "by most regiments left in Canada as less convenient than pouches"; the 47th Regiment of Foot and the light infantry companies alone retained them for the expedition. Interpretations of the words "box" and "pouch," as well as questions of private versus public ownership of these pieces, caused a ruckus between Congress and Burgoyne after the Saratoga surrender. This seemingly insignificant difference in interpretation of military material culture constituted a principal reason why Congress broke the terms of the Convention.

Burgoyne to Laurens, February 11, 1778, in *Parliamentary Register*, vol. 11, 208.

Sergeant's Pouch, 62nd Regiment of Foot
ca. 1776

Colonel J. Craig Nannos collection

Although regulations called for British Army battalion company sergeants of non-fusilier regiments to carry halberds, those conspicuous polearms were commonly laid aside during the American War for Independence and replaced with muskets (often carbines) and pouches. This small, crudely made pouch was issued to a sergeant in company "B," Lieutenant-Colonel John Anstruther's company, of the 62nd Regiment of Foot.

body an opportunity to undermine the Convention.[26] As for the colours, however, Congress was on firm ground. When asked about them, Burgoyne "declared upon his Honor, that the Colours of the Regiments were left in Canada."[27] This was a blatant lie, and Congress's initial investigation provided proof of their presence with the Army from Canada during the 1777 campaign year. With these points in mind, on December 27 Congress resolved to suspend the Convention Army's departure until a "distinct and explicit ratification of the Convention shall be properly notified to these States by the court of Great Britain."[28]

This put a period to the Articles of Convention. The British government would never ratify the document, since such an act would be tantamount to recognition of United States legitimacy. Held in limbo for years, the Convention Army became de facto prisoners of war. Apart from the few officers, like Burgoyne, who secured exchanges or paroles of honor, the majority of officers, soldiers, women, and children remained in America. They were bounced back and forth between "Convention Camps" in New England, Virginia, Pennsylvania, and Maryland, some remaining imprisoned until the end of the war. Over the years, thousands of soldiers made their escape from the prison camps. Many British soldiers returned to the British Army. Most escapees chose to remain in America.

Legacy

The great news of Burgoyne's defeat and surrender . . . occasioned as much general joy in France as if it had been a victory of their own troops over their own enemies.

—Benjamin Franklin, Silas Deane, and Arthur Lee,
December 18, 1777[1]

The first surrender of a British Army in world history was bound to have significant repercussions on an international scale. The British might surrender forts, lose battles, or win Pyrrhic victories, but the loss of an entire army was different. What's more, the British even abandoned Forts Ticonderoga and Independence on November 8, thereby conceding all of Burgoyne's 1777 territorial gains. In Britain, King George III "fell into agonies" upon hearing of Burgoyne's surrender.[2] Parliamentary debates raged, with its members particularly looking to cast blame on Germain, Howe, and, of course, Burgoyne. With the advantage of hindsight, Whig politician Charles James Fox proclaimed that the entire plan was nonsense to begin with:

> This expedition was not a plan of diversion in our favour, but a diversion against ourselves, by separating that force which ought to have been united to one point, that of dispersing the rebel army; instead of which, it left general Howe too weak . . . and sent general Burgoyne, with a still lesser army, to a place where the enemy were much stronger.[3]

Revelations like this were easily observed after the fact, but Fox's observation did touch upon the principal underlying cause of the campaign's failure: Gross miscalculation. Overestimation of the importance of European military professionalism. Underestimation of American military nascency. Overestimation of the level of support for the crown among the northeastern American populace. Underestimation of logistics. Whoever or whatever was to blame, another Parliamentarian foresaw the significance of the loss:

> The event of the expedition . . . [from] Canada, has not only annihilated the idea of the conquest of America, but has lost an

army of 8,000 men; has cost this country an infinite sum, and the lives of many thousands of its best subjects. It is the blackest page in the English history; it is a disgrace which this nation never can recover.[4]

Hyperbole aside, Burgoyne's surrender at Saratoga was in fact the touchstone for a major shift in the American War for Independence, one from which the British nation could never recover. Moving with speed, two men—Jonathan Loring Austin and Captain John Paul Jones—separately set out for France in order to share news of Burgoyne's momentous surrender.[5] Once arrived, they sought out the three ministers plenipotentiary operating on behalf of the United States of America, namely Benjamin Franklin, Silas Deane, and Arthur Lee. Bad news came with the good. Washington's forces were soundly trounced by Howe's in the September 11 Battle of Brandywine, decimated in the September 20 Battle of Paoli, and defeated in the October 4 Battle of Germantown. Howe took Philadelphia, and Congress was exiled to York Town, Pennsylvania.

Austin delivered the news first, but Jones brought eyewitness testimony of Burgoyne's surrender and a copy of the Articles of Convention. Addressed to Franklin, Deane, and Lee, the letter borne by Jones was written by John Langdon, a former member of the Continental Congress who arrived at Bemus Heights shortly before Burgoyne evacuated to Saratoga. Langdon admitted that while the British were "in Possession of Philadelphia," he "had the Happiness to be one of those to whom the great Burgoyne with all his Army were Oblige[d] to submit." Langdon exuberantly added:

> [T]hat Glorious prospect we had in seeing the Polite and able General Burgoyne with his whole Army marching out of their lines and laying down their Arms at the feet of the Generous Yankees, who were marching in, and takeing Possession of the Enemies lines, Steping off with a tolerable good grace at the old favourite Tune of Yankee Doodle this was truely pleasing.[6]

Franklin, Deane, and Lee immediately spread word of the victory to France's elite. King Louis XVI, who certainly supported Revolutionary America's fight against Britain conceptually, was now convinced that the time had come to make his nation's support official. On February 6, 1778, on behalf of the United States of America, Franklin, Deane, and Lee signed the Treaty of Amity and Commerce and the Treaty of Alliance, with France's Council of State Secretary Conrad-Alexandre Gérard signing on behalf of the king. With France's recognition of the United States, Britain declared war on the ancien

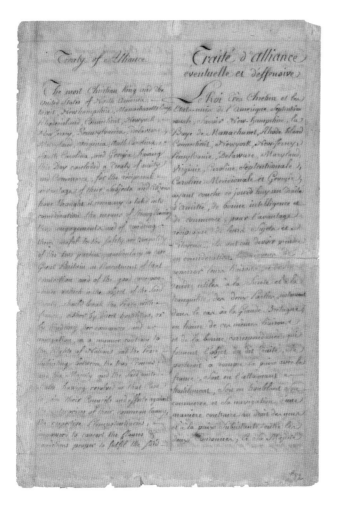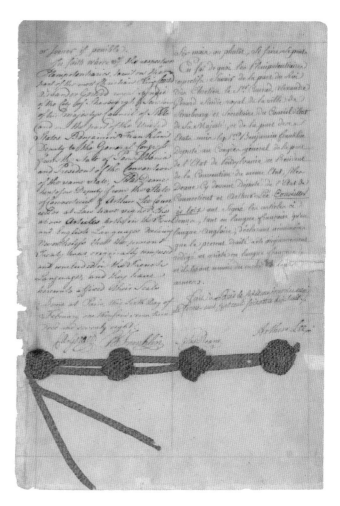

Treaty of Alliance
February 6, 1778

U.S. National Archives and Records Administration, Record Group 11, General Records of the United States Government, International Treaties and Related Records, 1778–1974, Treaty of Alliance with France, 1778
Gates's victory over Burgoyne at Saratoga set off a chain of events that ultimately resulted in United States victory in the American War for Independence. Meeting in Paris on February 6, 1778, representatives of France and the United States signed copies of the Treaty of Amity and Commerce, the Treaty of Alliance, and an Act Separate and Secret Between The United States and France. The latter document consisted of a proviso in which Louis XVI noted his "intimate union" with the King of Spain, Carlos III, and that an assurance of "equality, reciprocity & friendship" must exist between the three nations. Members of the Continental Congress ratified all three unanimously while in session at York Town, Pennsylvania, on May 4; after receiving official verification of France's move to recognize United States sovereignty, Great Britain declared war on France on March 17. The war thus widened to international waters, Spain's declaration of war against Britain on June 21, 1779, expanded global warfare even farther.

"Act Separate and Secret," in *Treaties and Other International Agreements of the United States of America 1776–1949*, vol. 7 (Washington DC: Department of State, 1971), 781.

régime shortly thereafter, with the first battle in this new international conflict being the indecisive naval Action of June 17, 1778, off the French coast.

In America, the first two major Franco-American joint military operations—the 1778 Battle of Rhode Island and the 1779 Siege of Savannah—were disasters for the new allies. The third endeavor, the 1781 Siege of Yorktown, Virginia, was executed with brilliant success, forcing yet another British Army to be "Burgoyned." Since a majority of the besieging military personnel at Yorktown were from the French armed forces, no one could fail to see the significance of the alliance. Victory at Yorktown triggered the lengthy process that ended the war between Britain and the United States, resulting in the Treaty of Paris, which was adopted by the two nations in 1783–84.

France's 1778 entry into the war was not limited to participation in America, however, since international war meant that Britain could no longer afford to concentrate its war effort solely against the United States. France's ally, Spain, declared war on Britain in 1779, expanding the war significantly. With the Netherlands lending support to the United States in violation of treaty, Britain declared war on the nation in 1780. This world war brought fighting to places previously unexpected, such as the Floridas, the Mississippi Valley, the Caribbean, the Bahamas, Nicaragua, Guyana, the English Channel Islands, Minorca, Gibraltar, Senegal, the Gambia, Ghana, and Sri Lanka. Hyder Ali's French-allied Sultanate of Mysor declared war against the British East India Company in 1780, resulting in major fighting throughout southern India. Overwhelmed with enemies the world over, Britain sought to extricate itself and in 1783 agreed to recognize United States independence.

Victory at home and warfare abroad secured independency for the United States, for which the foundations of both were laid at Saratoga.

Colonel Benedict Arnold
by John Ramage, ca. 1781
Private collection; photograph courtesy of Christopher Bryant
This miniature was painted after Arnold betrayed his oath of allegiance to the United States and joined the British Army in the fall of 1780. Made a brigadier-general by the British, Arnold also became colonel (commander) of the American Legion, a corps composed of royalist American volunteers, the uniform of which he wears in this portrait.

Notes

Introduction

1 R. W. Apple Jr., "Best Battle; Benedict Arnold, Hero," *New York Times Magazine*, April 18, 1999, 141. Saratoga's selection was not a result of American history myopia: India was chosen for the "Best Revolution" category.

2 For Wakefield, see Isaac N. Arnold, "Benedict Arnold at Saratoga," *The United Service: A Monthly Review of Military and Naval Affairs* 3 (September 1880): 308; for Woodruff, see William L. Stone, *Life of Joseph Brant-Thayendanegea, including the Indian Wars of the American Revolution* (New York: George Dearborn, 1838), xlix. "Captain" Wakefield's "Recollections of the Campaign of 1777" and Woodruff's published 1827 account exemplify fraudulent source material of this type. Rather than record their service experiences, both veterans created hyperbolized, counterfactual narratives. Conversely, their 1832 pension depositions provide reasonable accountings of their services to the extent of contradicting their narratives. National Archives and Records Administration (NARA), Revolutionary War Pension and Bounty-Land Warrant Application Files, Ebenezer Wakefield (W.18,261) and Samuel Woodruff (W.4,406). Wakefield was a sergeant in Captain Abraham Foster's company, Colonel Samuel Bullard's battalion, Middlesex County, Massachusetts, militia; Woodruff was a private in Captain Asa Bray's company, Brigadier General Oliver Wolcott's battalion, Connecticut militia.

Inevitability

1 Horatio Gates to Benedict Arnold, July 13, 1776, New-York Historical Society, Horatio Gates Papers, microfilm edition, 2:1253.

2 Howe was "General and Commander in Chief of all His Majesty's Forces, within the Colonies, laying on the Atlantic Ocean, from Nova Scotia to West Florida inclusive."

3 Washington was "General and Commander-in-Chief, of the army of the United Colonies, and of all the forces now raised, or to be raised, by them, and of all others who shall voluntarily offer their service, and join the said Army for the Defence of American liberty, and for repelling every hostile invasion thereof."

4   Carleton was "Captain General and Governor in Chief of the Province of Quebec and Territories depending thereon &c &c General and commander in chief of His Majesty's Forces in said Province and the Frontiers thereof." Importantly, Howe and Carleton commanded territories independent of each other.

5   Charles Douglas to John Starke, July 7, 1776, in *Naval Documents of the American Revolution*, vol. 5, ed. William James Morgan (Washington, DC: USGPO, 1970), 957–59. The overland transportation process avoided the river's rapids located between the two towns. H.M. Schooners *Maria* and *Carleton* were disassembled and brought overland, while the largest vessel, H.M. Ship *Inflexible*, was disassembled at Québec and brought to St. Johns for reassembly. Douglas, captain of H.M. Ship *Isis*, was the senior naval officer in the St. Lawrence River. Lieutenant Starke was commander of H.M. Schooner *Maria*. Royal Navy captains ranked as colonels in the British Army; Royal Navy lieutenants ranked as captains.

6   *Naval Documents*, vol. 5, 961. The council of war met on July 7, 1776.

7   Thomas Hartley to Benedict Arnold, July 10, 1776, in *Naval Documents*, vol. 5, 1,009–10. Hartley was lieutenant colonel of the 6th Pennsylvania Battalion.

8   In May 1776 Wynkoop was appointed by Schuyler to the "Command of all the Vessels on Lake Champlain" and he assumed the title of commodore. In August, Wynkoop challenged Arnold's appointed authority over the fleet, from which he was removed.

9   Hazen was colonel of the Battalion of Forces originally embodied as the 2nd Canadian Regiment.

10 Brown was lieutenant colonel of Colonel Samuel Elmore's Connecticut Regiment.

11 Benedict Arnold to Horatio Gates, September 2, 1776, in *Naval Documents of the American Revolution*, vol. 6, ed. William James Morgan (Washington, DC: USGPO, 1972), 654.

12 Horatio Gates to Benedict Arnold, August 7, 1776, in *Naval Documents*, vol. 6, 95–96.

13 Benedict Arnold to Horatio Gates, September 28, 1776, in *Naval Documents*, vol. 6, 1,032–33.

14 John Enys, *The American Journals of Lt John Enys*, ed. Elizabeth Cometti (Syracuse, NY: Syracuse University Press, 1976), 19. Enys was the ensign of Captain James Bassett's company, 29th Regiment of Foot.

15 Isaiah Canfield to Anne Canfield, October 26, 1776, National Archives and Records Administration (NARA), Revolutionary War Pension and Bounty-Land Warrant Application Files, Isaiah Canfield (W.16,883). Canfield was a private in Captain Christopher Ely's company, 10th Continental Regiment. He served aboard the row galley *Trumbull*.

16 Enys, *American Journals*, 19–20.

17 Isaiah Canfield to Anne Canfield, October 26, 1776.

18 Pringle, master and commander of the British armed transport *Lord Howe*, acted as captain of the Lake Champlain fleet, which he commanded from H.M. Schooner *Maria*. Royal Navy master and commanders ranked as majors in the British Army.

19 Arnold's Valcour Island fleet consisted of the sloop *Enterprize*; schooners *Royal Savage* and *Revenge*; row galleys *Congress, Lee, Trumbull,* and *Washington*; and gondolas *Boston, Connecticut, Jersey, New Haven, New York, Philadelphia, Providence,* and *Spitfire*. Only the *Enterprize, Revenge, Trumbull,* and *New York* escaped.

20 James Murray Hadden, *Hadden's Journal and Orderly Books: A Journal Kept in Canada and upon Burgoyne's Campaign in 1776 and 1777*, ed. Horatio Rogers (Boston: Gregg Press, 1972), 34. Hadden was a second-lieutenant of Captain William Borthwick's company, 3rd Battalion, Royal Regiment of Artillery.

21 Due to the lack of waterborne transports, most of Carleton's Canada Army was forced to remain behind.

22 St. Clair's brigade consisted of the 2nd, 5th, 8th, and 15th Continental Regiments.

23 According to Edmund Burke in 1780, Germain's office was "commonly called or known by the name of third secretary of state or secretary of state for the colonies." See Arthur Herbert Basye, "The Secretary of State for the Colonies, 1768–1782," *American Historical Review* 28, no. 1 (October 1922): 13–23.

24 George Germain to Guy Carleton, March 26, 1777, in *Report on the Manuscripts of Mrs. Stopford-Sackville, of Drayton House, Northamptonshire*, vol. 2 (Hereford, UK: Hereford Times, 1910), 60.

25 Guy Carleton to George Germain, May 20, 1777, in *A History of the Organization, Development and Services of the Military and Naval Forces of Canada From the Peace of Paris in 1763, to the Present Time*, vol. 2, ed. Historical Section of the General Staff (Ottawa: Government Printer, 1919), 215.

Stratagem

1 This comment formed part of the 1778 House of Commons "Debate on Mr. Fox's Motion relative to the Failure of the Expedition from Canada." *The Parliamentary Register; or, History of the Proceedings and Debates of the House of Commons*, vol. 8 (London: John Stockdale, 1802), 166.

2 Lieutenant-General John Burgoyne is sometimes confused with his cousin, Lieutenant-Colonel John Burgoyne, who succeeded to his family's baronetcy in 1780 (and was thereafter Sir John Burgoyne, Bt.).

3 George Germain to Guy Carleton, March 26, 1777, in John Burgoyne, *A State of the Expedition from Canada, as Laid before the House of Commons* (London: J. Almon, 1780), vii.

4 John Burgoyne, "Thoughts for Conducting the War from the Side of Canada," in *State of the Expedition*, vi.

5 George Germain to Guy Carleton, March 26, 1777.

6 Burgoyne, "Thoughts for Conducting the War," vi.

Invasion

1 Sir Francis Clerke, Bt., to Alexander Hume-Campbell, Lord Polwarth, July 5, 1777, in Ronald F. Kingsley, "Letters to Lord Polwarth from Sir Francis-Carr Clerke, Aide-de-Camp to General John Burgoyne," *New York History* 79, no. 4 (October 1998): 419. Clerke was a lieutenant and adjutant in the 3rd Regiment of Foot Guards, and thereby ranked as captain in the army. He served as Burgoyne's junior aide-de-camp in 1776–77.

2 Great Britain, The National Archives (TNA), WO27/30, General Review of the 21st Regiment of Foot (Royal North British Fusiliers), June 8, 1774. WO27/35 General Reviews of the 9th (July 17, 1775), 20th (June 7, 1775), and 24th (May 15, 1775) Regiments of Foot.

3 TNA, WO27/35, General Review of the 53rd Regiment of Foot, May 15, 1775.

4 TNA, WO27/35, General Review of the 62nd Regiment of Foot, May 25, 1775. Friedrich Christian Cleve, *Journal of the Brunswick Troops in North America under the Orders of Major-General von Riedesel*, trans. "in England," HZ 156, Hessian Documents of the American Revolution, 1776–1783, Morristown National Historical Park, Lidgerwood Collection, Fiche 180–93. Cleve was a lieutenant and the junior aide-de-camp to General Riedesel.

5 The Canada Army's British grenadier and light infantry battalions included the respective flank companies drawn from the 9th, 20th, 21st (Royal North British Fusiliers), 24th, 29th, 31st, 34th, 47th, 53rd, and 62nd Regiments of Foot. Only the Canada Army's 8th (The King's) Regiment did not provide its flank companies. While combining like flank companies into larger battalions increased the army's tactical flexibility, it also reduced each parent regiment's fighting strength by one fifth, i.e., from ten companies to eight.

6 General Orders, September 6, 1776, in James Murray Hadden, *Hadden's Journal and Orderly Books: A Journal Kept in Canada and upon Burgoyne's Campaign in 1776 and 1777*, ed. Horatio Rogers (Boston: Gregg Press, 1972), 474–75. Fraser, a battalion company captain in the 34th Regiment of Foot, commanded the company. One private from each battalion company of the 9th, 20th, 21st (Royal North British Fusiliers), 47th, 53rd, and 62nd Regiments of Foot, as well as one corporal and one sergeant from each of those battalions, were drafted to serve in this company. The company's subaltern officers were drawn from the British Light Infantry Battalion.

7 Ellis Walker's company was in the 3rd Battalion, Royal Regiment of Artillery. Simon Fraser was lieutenant-colonel of the 24th Regiment of Foot and held the local rank of brigadier-general.

8 John Burgoyne, "Thoughts for Conducting the War from the Side of Canada," in *A State of the Expedition, as Laid before the House of Commons* (London: J. Almon, 1780), iv. The Royal Highland Emigrants, later established as the 84th Regiment of Foot, was considered by Burgoyne too dangerous to deploy since it had "among them considerable numbers of Recruits from the Rebel Prisoners, and to judge of their future behaviour by that of last Summer, great numbers of them may be expected to desert." Only the 29th Regiment

remained unscathed in its review, and was left behind simply because it was "not at present brigaded."

9   TNA, WO27/35, General Review of the 34th Regiment of Foot, July 17, 1775.

10   Orders were for each British infantry regiment (excepting the 24th) to each leave 50 men (300 total) behind in Canada. Additionally, the army's German contingent left 650 men behind. Guy Carleton to George Germain, May 22, 1777, in *A History of the Organization, Development and Services of the Military and Naval Forces of Canada From the Peace of Paris in 1763, to the Present Time*, vol. 2, ed. Historical Section of the General Staff (Ottawa: Government Printer, 1919), 217.

11   George III was simultaneously king of Great Britain, Ireland, and according to the dictates of English tradition, France. He was also the Kurfürst (elector) of Kurfürstentum (Electorate) Braunschweig-Lüneburg, commonly known as "Hanover."

12   John Burgoyne, "Memorandums and observations relative to the Service in Canada, Submitted to Lord George Germain," in *The Parliamentary Register; or, History of the Proceedings and Debates of the House of Commons*, vol. 7 (London: John Stockdale, 1802), 195.

13   For more information regarding the innovative Congreve-pattern light three-pounder and its associated "grasshopper" compatible carriage, see Eric Schnitzer, "A Study in Metamorphosis," in *New Perspectives on "The Last Argument of Kings"* (Ticonderoga, NY: Ticonderoga Press, 2018).

14   These seventy men, all matrosses, were volunteers drafted from the Royal Irish Regiment of Artillery, all of whom were incorporated into the Royal Regiment of Artillery upon embarkation from Cork, Ireland, in April 1777. Although they retained the clothing of their former corps, these men were issued Royal Regiment of Artillery arms and accoutrements. Shepherded to Canada by Captain Thomas Jones, 4th Battalion, Royal Regiment of Artillery, these draftees were distributed to all Royal Artillery companies in the Canada Army, save a cadre of men who served in Jones's artillery detachment.

15   These recruits were commanded by Lieutenant George Anson Nutt of the 33rd Regiment of Foot. While most were intended for that regiment, other recruits were destined for the 15th, 27th (Inniskilling), 35th, 45th, and 54th Regiments of Foot. These men acted as marines for the Lake Champlain fleet during the initial phase of the campaign.

16   Although Riedesel was a baron, he was not the "Baron von Riedesel," nor was his surname "von Riedesel." However, the regiment that bore his name was titled the "Regiment von Riedesel."

17   Because of their traditional predilection for French linguistics over German, most British chroniclers referred to this entire battalion as "Brunswick chasseurs." Common use of the French word *chasseurs* (hunters) has long confused military historians into thinking that the entire battalion was composed of *jäger* (hunters) and thereby armed with rifles.

18   One exception to the well-drilled status of the Braunschweig units was the Infanterie Regiment Prinz Friedrich. Reviewed by General Riedesel in August 1776, he afterward informed its commander that he was "convinced that as long as the regiment has existed,

it has never drilled so badly as on the day I saw it." Friedrich Riedesel to Christian Julius Prätorius, August 27, 1776, HZ 930.

19   The treaty further stipulated that "if the service requires them to be mounted, his majesty engages to do it at his own expense." *Parliamentary Register*, vol. 3, 34.

20   Friedrich Riedesel to Friedrich Baum, August 27, 1776, HZ 928.

21   Wilhelm I was also the eldest son of Frederick II, Landgraf (Landgrave) of Landgrafschaft (Landgraviate) Hessen-Cassel.

22   This regiment was the only one in Burgoyne's army that retained its grenadier company. Being of Hessen origin, it did not form part of the four-company Braunschweig Grenadier-battaillon Breymann.

23   John Burgoyne to Edward Harvey, July 11, 1777, in Burgoyne, *State of the Expedition*, xxxiv. Lieutenant-General Edward Harvey, whose nephew Stephen was a subaltern officer in Burgoyne's army, was adjutant-general of the forces.

24   John Burgoyne to George Germain, May 14, 1777, in Burgoyne, *State of the Expedition*, x.

25   John Burgoyne to George Germain, May 14, 1777.

26   John Burgoyne to Guy Carleton, May 26, 1777, in *History of the Organization*, vol. 2, 218.

27   Guy Carleton to John Burgoyne, May 29, 1777, in *History of the Organization*, vol. 2, 219.

28   Drafting of men for the Canadien companies and the corvée service was performed "upon promise of [their] being allowed to return to their families, by the first of November being the time they expected the Winter to set in . . . unless any of them shall chuse to remain . . . of their own free will and Inclination." Guy Carleton to John Burgoyne, June 13, 1777, in *History of the Organization*, vol. 2, 221.

29   John Burgoyne, *Orderly Book of Lieut. Gen. John Burgoyne, from his Entry into the State of New York until his Surrender at Saratoga, 16th Oct., 1777*, ed. E. B. O'Callaghan, MD (Albany, NY: Joel Munsell, 1860), 17.

Resistance

1   Alexander Scammell to Abigail Bishop, June 8, 1777, in *Collections of the New Hampshire Historical Society*, vol. 9, ed. Isaac W. Hammond, A.M. (Concord, NH: Ira C. Evans, 1889), 197. Scammell was colonel of the 3rd New Hampshire Regiment.

2   Carl Wintersmidt (Charles Wintersmith), *Plan of Ticonderoga and Mount Independence, including Mount Hope, and shewing the Rebel Works & Batteries, as they were when His Majesty's Troops took Possession of them on 6th July 1777*, John Carter Brown Library, JCB Map Collection, 31267. Wintersmidt was an assistant engineer in the Army from Canada, and third lieutenant of Captain August von Hambach's grenadier company, Braunschweig Grenadierbattaillon Breymann.

3   Wintersmidt, *Plan of Ticonderoga*.

4   Arthur St. Clair to Philip Schuyler, June 28, 1777, in *Proceedings of a General Court Martial, held at White Plains, in the State of New-York, by Order of His Excellency General Washington, Commander in Chief of the Army of the United States of America, for the Trial of Major General St. Clair, August 25, 1778* (Philadelphia: Hall and Sellers, 1778), 38.

5   Unlike other Continental regiments in the Northern Army at the time, Long's was formed in summer 1776 and authorized to serve for a single year only.

6   Throughout this text, the numerical designations of Massachusetts Continental regiments are given in parentheses. The numbers associated with the regiments were not settled by the State of Massachusetts (which regulated the matter) until 1779. The numbers given in parentheses are the numbers settled upon in that year. In 1777–79 most of the Massachusetts regiments used different numbers, and some even claimed the same numbers as others, resulting in a confused, unregulated system. In order to avoid confusion, Massachusetts regiments were never identified by number above the regimental level until the 1779 settlement.

7   Richard Varick to Philip Schuyler, June 17, 1777, New York Public Library, Archives and Manuscripts, Philip Schuyler Papers, Letters Received, b. 11, f. 31. Lieutenant Colonel Richard Varick was the Northern Department's deputy muster master general.

8   In 1764 "his Majesty in Council" determined that the Connecticut River formed the "Bounds between New York and New Hampshire" and declared that the long-disputed territory known as the "New Hampshire Grants" belonged to New York. Increasing tensions between those living in the territory and New York's provincial officials flared simultaneously with the revolution's rise in America, and in January 1777 the Grants declared independence. While Vermont remained unrecognized by all extra-government bodies until after the war, it was a self-governed independent republic, and adopted its constitution that July. With New York's claim and governance over the Grants all but eliminated in 1777, Vermont's de facto existence, like that of the United State of America, became reality.

9   Richard Varick to Philip Schuyler, June 17, 1777.

10   Whitcomb was captain-commandant of both his and Aldrich's companies, which were primarily recruited in New Hampshire. Lee's Independent Company of Rangers was raised in Vermont.

11   This number excludes those in the unarmed artificer companies, which was an additional 180 officers and men. Many present with their regiments were sick "on account of the measles . . . but not proper objects for the general hospital," which had less than a hundred patients. *Proceedings of a General Court Martial . . . of Major General St. Clair*, 17.

12   The military designations of "regiment" and "battalion" were often used interchangeably in the American War for Independence, but there were technical differences. Most British, American, and German regiments serving in the war were composed of single battalions, and the words were thereby often used interchangeably, particularly in the Continental Army (for example, the 2nd New Hampshire Regiment was often called the 2nd New

Hampshire Battalion). Some regiments were double, triple, or even quadruple in size and were composed of two, three, or four battalions respectively (for example, the Royal Regiment of Artillery was a single, supersized regiment consisting of four battalions). Further, provisional multi-company corps were designated "battalions," not "regiments," because these units did not operate on permanent footings (such as the Braunschweig Grenadierbattaillon Breymann). Although state militia regiments were permanent, when their officers and soldiers were called to serve, they were usually drawn from across multiple regiments and placed into a single, cohesive, provisional battalion.

13 Wells's and Leonard's militia battalions were from Hampshire County, Massachusetts. The receipt that signified the termination of service for both battalions was signed by their respective lieutenant colonels at Mount Independence on July 5. *Proceedings of a General Court Martial . . . of Major General St. Clair*, 31.

14 These French arms were part of a plethora of military weapons, fabrics, camp equipage and tools, cannons, and ordnance stores delivered aboard the *Amphitrite* at Portsmouth, New Hampshire, on April 20, 1777. Included were 219 chests (30 arms per chest) of surplus French military *fusils* (muskets). Despite this major windfall, close inspection found that many of the muskets were "bad in the Locks." Further, there were "many complaints of the breaking of the main Springs the Cocks and in particular the breaking of the pin or Screw that fixes the Cock to the plate. Some of those purchased by this State [Massachusetts] are scandalously bad Colo. Crafts informs me that of 33, which he proved, 16 burst." William Heath to George Washington, June 30, 1777, in *The Papers of George Washington*, vol. 10, ed. Frank E. Grizzard Jr. (Charlottesville: University Press of Virginia, 1983), 153. Major General William Heath was commander of the Continental Army's Eastern Department.

15 *Proceedings of a General Court Martial . . . of Major General St. Clair*, 25.

16 For example, in spring of 1777 the 430 officers and men in Francis's Regiment had only 56 muskets for the entire regiment (of which 14 had no bayonets). Other Massachusetts regiments were in a similar state. "Return of the 7. Regiments . . . and the Arms and Accoutrements deld [delivered] them," Massachusetts Historical Society (MHS), William Heath Papers, vol. 6.

17 Richard Varick to Philip Schuyler, June 17, 1777.

18 For example, in spring of 1777 the 440 officers and men in Marshall's Regiment had only 197 cartridge boxes and two bayonet belts. Other Massachusetts regiments were in a similar state. Arthur St. Clair to John Hancock, June 25, 1777, in *Proceedings of a General Court Martial . . . of Major General St. Clair*, 8. Hancock was president of the Second Continental Congress. "Return of the 7. Regiments," MHS, William Heath Papers, vol. 6.

19 Richard Varick to Philip Schuyler, June 17, 1777.

20 Philip Schuyler to the commanding officers of corps at Ticonderoga and Mount Independence, June 22, 1777. National Archives and Records Administration (NARA), Papers of the Continental Congress, Letters from Philip Schuyler, vol. 2, 183–87. This letter was sent

in response to a June 21 petition filed by most of the garrisons' regimental commanders, which also included complaints about the lack of blankets, drums, fifes, colours, and other matters related to regimental finances and issues of commissioned rank. Schuyler was effectively a middle man on these matters and deferred these concerns to the Congress and commissary authorities.

21 Henry Sewell to his parents, June 10, 1777, in *The Historical Magazine, and Notes and Queries, concerning the Antiquities, History, and Biography of America*, vol. 2 (Morrisania, NY: Henry B. Dawson, 1867), 7. Sewell was first lieutenant of Captain James Donnell's company, Colonel Samuel Brewer's (12th) Massachusetts Regiment.

22 Thomas Marshall to William Heath, May 19, 1777, MHS, William Heath Papers, vol. 4, Mss. 256.

23 Thomas Marshall to William Heath, June 3, 1777, MHS, Samuel P. Savage Papers, vol. 11, Mss. 163.

24 *Proceedings of a General Court Martial . . . of Major General St. Clair*, 25.

25 Richard Varick to Philip Schuyler, June 17, 1777.

26 Philip Schuyler to John Trumbull, July 27, 1777. Seeing "negroes" in the ranks of his Northern Army constituted a pervasive theme of Schuyler's correspondence in summer 1777. While writing to William Heath, Schuyler wisely asked if it was "consistent with the sons of Freedom to Trust their all to be defended by slaves?" The poignancy of the question is offset by the fact that a majority of African American men serving in the Northern Army were freemen, not enslaved. Philip Schuyler to William Heath, July 28, 1777, in *Letterbook of Philip John Schuyler*, mssHM 649, Huntington Library, Art Collections, and Botanical Gardens.

Catastrophe

1 Patrick Cogan to John Stark, July 17, 1777, in *Documents and Records relating to the State of New-Hampshire during the period of the American Revolution, from 1776–1783*, vol. 8, ed. Daniel Bouton, D.D. (Concord, NH: Edward A. Jenks, 1874), 640. Cogan was quartermaster of the 1st New Hampshire Regiment.

2 MacKay was a half-pay lieutenant in the 60th (Royal American) Regiment of Foot.

3 The party's commanding officer, Nathan Taylor, was wounded. Taylor was a lieutenant in Captain Whitcomb's Independent Company of Rangers.

4 Lt. Col. George F. Stanley, ed., *For Want of a Horse* (Sackville, NB: Tribune Press, 1961), 103. While unattributed, contextual information reveals the journalist was an officer in the light infantry company of the 47th Regiment of Foot, probably Lieutenant Arthur French.

5 Julius Wasmus, *An Eyewitness Account of the American Revolution and New England Life*, trans. Helga Doblin (Westport, CT: Greenwood Press, 1990), 57. Wasmus was the squadron

surgeon (surgeon's mate) of Major-General Friedrich Riedesel's squadron, Braunschweig Dragoon Regiment Prinz Ludwig.

6   The blockhouse was commanded by First Lieutenant John Hewitt of Captain Samuel King's company, Colonel Thomas Marshall's (10th) Massachusetts Regiment.

7   *Proceedings of a General Court Martial, held at White Plains, in the State of New-York, by Order of His Excellency General Washington, Commander in Chief of the Army of the United States of America, for the Trial of Major General St. Clair, August 25, 1778* (Philadelphia: Hall and Sellers, 1778), 36.

8   Moses Greenleaf, "'Breakfast on Chocolate': The Diary of Moses Greenleaf, 1777," ed. Donald H. Wickman, *Bulletin of the Fort Ticonderoga Museum* 15, no. 6 (1997): 496. Greenleaf was a captain in Colonel Ebenezer Francis's (11th) Massachusetts Regiment.

9   The American officer killed was Thomas Wheeler, second lieutenant of Captain Gideon Brownson's company, Colonel Seth Warner's Regiment. The British officer wounded was Lieutenant Richard Houghton, 53rd Regiment of Foot, who served as a subaltern in Fraser's company of British Rangers. Houghton was also the British officer of the Québec Indian Department assigned to the Seven Nations of Canada Caughnawaga people.

10   *Proceedings of a General Court Martial . . . of Major General St. Clair*, 8–9.

11   The militia commanders also informed St. Clair that they were dispatched to search for the enemy's Otter Creek party only, and did not intend to add to St. Clair's garrison. The militia were composed of Colonel Benjamin Bellows's New Hampshire, Colonels Peter Olcott's and Moses Robinson's Vermont, and Lieutenant Colonel Samuel Williams's Hampshire County, Massachusetts, militia battalions. *Proceedings of a General Court Martial . . . of Major General St. Clair*, 18.

12   This party was commanded by Captain James Henry Craig, light infantry company, 47th Regiment of Foot, who was the Army from Canada's deputy judge advocate.

13   Simon Fraser to John Robinson, July 13, 1777, in "Gen. Fraser's Account of Burgoyne's Campaign on Lake Champlain and the Battle of Hubbardton," *Proceedings of the Vermont Historical Society*, October 18 and November 2, 1898, 144. Traditionally, Major-General William Phillips, Burgoyne's second in command, is said to have exclaimed, "Where a goat can go, a man can go; and where a man can go, he can haul a cannon." This quote is a late nineteenth-century contrivance, manipulated from a similar (and perhaps apocryphal) quote from Napoleon concerning traversing the Alps. Alternately, this spurious quote is sometimes attributed to Twiss. Lieutenant and Comptroller William Twiss, a sub-engineer of the Corps of Engineers, was chief engineer of the Army from Canada. The Corps of Engineers was not embodied as a "Royal" corps until 1787.

14   Notably, the British never mounted their medium twelve-pounders in time to force the Americans to evacuate Ticonderoga. The mere sighting of redcoats on Mount Defiance and the expectation of their intentions was enough to do it. *Proceedings of a General Court Martial . . . of Major General St. Clair*, 11–12. Fraser estimated that the "two 12 Prs would

have been there [on the top of Mount Defiance] on the evening of the 6th instant," over twelve hours after the Americans evacuated the region. "Gen. Fraser's Account," 144.

15 Colonel Francis's task force called for 160 from General Poor's Brigade, 150 from General Paterson's Brigade, and "6 captains, 12 subalterns, and non commissioned in proportion" (*Proceedings of a General Court Martial . . . of Major General St. Clair*, 26). During their withdrawal, Francis was joined by an additional 150 troops which formed the piquet in another quarter of the peninsula, thus increasing the strength of his rear guard to about 480 officers and soldiers.

16 The German Division's second brigade was transferred to the New York side of the lake on the evening of July 3. Conversely, Fraser's Rangers were transferred to the Vermont side. *The Specht Journal*, trans. Helga Doblin (Westport, CT: Greenwood Press, 1995), 52. Johann Friedrich Specht was colonel of the regiment that bore his name and brigadier-general of the First German Brigade. The journal is attributed to Second-Lieutenant Anton Adolph Du Roi of Major Carl Friedrich von Ehrenkrook's company, Braunschweig Infanterie Regiment Specht.

17 *Proceedings of a General Court Martial . . . of Major General St. Clair*, 22.

18 These were the same two battalions that were recently discharged and marching home simultaneous to the evacuation. *Proceedings of a General Court Martial . . . of Major General St. Clair*, 27.

19 *Proceedings of a General Court Martial . . . of Major General St. Clair*, 29.

20 *Proceedings of a General Court Martial . . . of Major General St. Clair*, 28.

21 The 9th Regiment's colours were requested out of convenience, since the battalion encamped closest to the Advanced Corps. Fraser was in need of borrowing colours because British flank company battalions had no colours and the 24th Regiment of Foot, as part of the Advanced Corps, left its colours in Canada.

22 The oft-repeated story of four "dead drunk" Americans who remained behind to destroy the bridge with artillery fire first appeared in Thomas Anbury's *Travels through the Interior Parts of America*, vol. 1 (London: William Lane, 1789), 324. However, this is not corroborated by any other source, including Fraser's detailed 1777 letter or St. Clair's 1778 court-martial. In that trial, Colonel Baldwin deposed that he was one of the last to leave the Mount, "just as the enemy came into the works on the hill and fired upon us." As Baldwin and another officer rode off, they soon encountered "four soldiers partly drunk," and while Baldwin tried to force them along, the soldiers were left behind and captured. Anbury, whose narrative is largely a subsummation of other sources, was probably inspired by these four drunk Americans when he wrote his fiction years later. In July 1777 Thomas Anbury was a volunteer in Captain Charles Stanhope, Viscount Petersham's grenadier company, 29th Regiment of Foot.

23 "Gen. Fraser's Account," 144.

24 "Gen. Fraser's Account," 144.

25 "Gen. Fraser's Account," 145.

26 "Gen. Fraser's Account," 145.

27 Ebenezer Fletcher, *Narrative of the Captivity & Sufferings of Ebenezer Fletcher* (New Ipswich, NH: S. Wilder, 1827), 12. Fletcher was the fifer of Captain James Carr's company, 2nd New Hampshire Regiment.

28 George Reid to John Neysmith, July 22, 1777, in Michael Barbieri, "Ti's Evacuation and the Battle of Hubbardton," *Journal of the American Revolution*, July 24, 2014, https://all-thingsliberty.com/2014/07/tis-evacuation-and-the-battle-of-hubbardton. Reid, who was lieutenant colonel of the 1st New Hampshire Regiment, was also second in command of Francis's rearguard task force.

29 "Gen. Fraser's Account," 145.

30 "Gen. Fraser's Account," 146; "The Battles of Saratoga from an 'Enemy' Perspective,'" trans. Helga Doblin, *Tamkang Journal of American Studies* 3, no. 3 (Spring 1987): 8. The unknown journalist was a member of the Infanterie Regiment von Riedesel.

31 "The Burgoyne Expedition—April 1776 to October 13th, 1777—Diary of Joshua Pell, Jr.," *Bulletin of the Fort Ticonderoga Museum*, July 1929, 9. Despite being identified by the editor as a captain of a "New York Regiment of Loyalists," contextual analysis identifies the unknown author as a battalion company officer in the 24th Regiment of Foot. John McNamara Hayes to Charles Mellish, July 13, 1777, University of Nottingham, Hallward Library, MeC 29/17/1-2. Hayes was the senior surgeon of the Army from Canada's General Hospital.

32 Unfortunately for the men of the 24th Regiment of Foot, their cartridge pouches with shoulder belts, issued in 1770–71, were described as "Very good" in 1775. While additional sets of accoutrements were procured for the 1775 augmentation, the colonel did not purchase a new set for the full battalion (full sets were generally replaced once every eight years). As a result, their cartridge pouch capacities would have been typical of those issued in 1770, i.e., with limited carrying capacities, typically twenty-one to twenty-eight rounds. With neither cartridge boxes nor knapsacks (within which some spare ammunition could be stored), the men had limited ammunition on hand. The National Archives (TNA), WO 27/35, General Review of the 24th Regiment of Foot, May 15, 1775.

33 "Gen. Fraser's Account," 146.

34 *Proceedings of a General Court Martial . . . of Major General St. Clair*, 28.

35 *Proceedings of a General Court Martial . . . of Major General St. Clair*, 29.

36 The jäger company was commanded by Captain Maximillian Schottelius; the combined Braunschweig grenadier (about thirty) and light infantry (about fifty) attack was commanded by Carl von Geyso, a captain in the Leichtes Infanterie Battaillon von Bärner.

37 Friedrich Christian Cleve, Journal of the Brunswick Troops in North America under the Orders of Major-General von Riedesel, trans. "in England," HZ 236, Hessian Documents

of the American Revolution, 1776–1783, Morristown National Historical Park, Lidgerwood Collection, Fiche 180–93.

38 John McNamara Hayes to Charles Mellish, July 13, 1777,

39 Cleve, Journal of the Brunswick Troops, HZ 237. This was the remainder of Breymann's Reserve Corps and the Braunschweig Infanterie Regiment von Riedesel, numbering about 1,200 troops.

Flight

1   Duane Hamilton Hurd, ed., "The Gray Family," in *History of Merrimack and Belknap Counties New Hampshire*, pt. 2 (Philadelphia: J. W. Lewis, 1885), 912.

2   Philipp Theobald, "Journal of the Hessen-Hanau Erbprinz Infantry Regiment—June to August 1777," trans. Henry J. Retzer, *Journal of the Johannes Schwalm Historical Association* 7, no. 1 (2001): 42. Theobald was *Feldprediger* (chaplain) to the Regiment Erb Prinz.

3   Julius Wasmus, *An Eyewitness Account of the American Revolution and New England Life*, trans. Helga Doblin (Westport, CT: Greenwood Press, 1990), 59.

4   John Burgoyne to George Germain, July 11, 1777, in John Burgoyne, *A State of the Expedition from Canada, as Laid before the House of Commons* (London: J. Almon, 1780), xvii.

5   The British officer killed was Molesworth Cleland, a second-lieutenant of Captain John Carter's company, 1st Battalion, Royal Regiment of Artillery.

6   The anonymous journalist was an officer serving in a battalion company of the 47th Regiment of Foot. Although the journal is inscribed as being "Richard Pope's Book," no man of that name served in the army. *Journal of an officer of the 47th Regiment of Foot*, mssHM 66, fol. 26v, Huntington Library, Art Collections, and Botanical Gardens.

7   John Burgoyne to George Germain, July 11, 1777, in Burgoyne, *State of the Expedition*, xviii.

8   Roger Lamb, *An Original and Authentic Journal of Occurrences during the Late American War, from its commencement to the year 1783* (Dublin: Wilkinson & Courtney, 1809), 141.

9   Hurd, "The Gray Family," 912.

10 John Burgoyne to George Germain, July 11, 1777, in Burgoyne, *State of the Expedition*, xix.

11   "Other ranks" was the collective term for British infantry corporals and privates. By regulation, other ranks were armed with muskets, while officers and sergeants carried polearms. During the Northern Campaign, all British infantry ranks carried firelocks, officers included.

12   Unfortunately for the men of the 9th Regiment of Foot, their cartridge pouches with shoulder belts, issued in 1770, were still returned as "Good" in 1775. While additional sets of accoutrements were procured for the 1775 augmentation, the colonel did not purchase a replacement set for the full battalion (full sets were generally replaced once every eight years). As a result, their cartridge pouch capacities would have been typical of those issued in 1770, i.e., with limited carrying capacities, typically twenty-one to twenty-eight rounds. With neither cartridge boxes nor knapsacks (within which some spare ammunition could be stored), the men had limited ammunition on hand. The National Archives (TNA), WO 27/35, General Review of the 9th Regiment of Foot, July 17, 1775.

13   Hurd, "The Gray Family," 912.

14   The first wave of reinforcements (sixty) was commanded by Captain Nathaniel Hutchins, 1st New Hampshire Regiment.

15   Van Rensselaer was lieutenant colonel of the 6th Regiment (4th Rensselaerwyck Battalion), Albany County, New York, militia.

16   Lamb, *Original and Authentic Journal*, 142. Lamb was corporal of Major Gordon Forbes's company, 9th Regiment of Foot.

17   Hurd, "The Gray Family," 912.

18   Lamb, *Original and Authentic Journal*, 142.

19   Men of the 9th Regiment of Foot were armed with Pattern 1769 Short Land muskets (Irish) of .75 caliber. Most of the Continental Army soldiers in the battle were armed with French muskets of .69 caliber. Militia musket calibers varied considerably, but most would have ranged in the .50s and .60s. With this difference in caliber, British bullets were too wide to fit down the Americans' musket barrels.

20   Hurd, "The Gray Family," 912.

21   Traditionally, historians have taken Lamb's fabricated claim that Money constituted this reinforcement solo, and that he alone gave the Indian whoop, thereby tricking Americans into thinking that a massive Indian reinforcement was at hand. John Money was a captain in the 9th Regiment of Foot and the Army from Canada's deputy quartermaster general. Claude-Nicolas-Guillaume, the Chevalier de Lorimier, was an official of the Québec Indian Department for the Seven Nations of Canada Caughnawaga people.

22   Hill's second in command, Major Gordon Forbes, admitted that the Americans "certainly would have forced us" had not the Indians arrived in time to save the British. Burgoyne, *State of the Expedition*, 61.

23   Lamb, *Original and Authentic Journal*, 143.

24 John Burgoyne to George Germain, July 11, 1777, in Burgoyne, *State of the Expedition,* xix.

25 *Journal of an officer of the 47th Regiment of Foot,* mssHM 66, fol. 31v.

Fallout

1   Alexander Scammell to James Gray, August 6, 1777, in *The Historical Magazine, and Notes and Queries, concerning the Antiquities, History, and Biography of America,* vol. 8 (Morrisania, NY: Henry B. Dawson, 1870), 142.

2   Henry Dearborn, *Revolutionary War Journals of Henry Dearborn 1775–1783,* ed. Lloyd A. Brown and Howard H. Peckham (Freeport, NY: Books for Libraries Press, 1969), 99. Dearborn was major of the 3rd New Hampshire Regiment.

3   Patrick Cogan to John Stark, July 17, 1777, in *Documents and Records relating to the State of New-Hampshire during the period of the American Revolution, from 1776–1783,* vol. 8, ed. Daniel Bouton, D.D. (Concord, NH: Edward A. Jenks, 1874), 640. Cogan was quartermaster of the 1st New Hampshire Regiment.

4   Letter from persons in the Army belonging to New Ipswich to Ipswich's Committee of Safety, August 11, 1777, in *Documents and Records relating to the State of New-Hampshire,* 667.

5   John Buss to his parents, August 11, 1777, in *The John Buss Letters,* ed. Ed Nash (Leominster, MA: Nashaway Valley Publications, 1996), 11. Buss was a corporal in Captain William Warner's company, Colonel Thomas Marshall's (10th) Massachusetts Regiment.

6   Letter from persons in the Army, belonging to New Ipswich to Ipswich's Committee of Safety, August 11, 1777, in *Documents and Records,* 667.

7   Benedict Arnold to George Washington, July 27, 1777, in *The Papers of George Washington,* vol. 10, ed. Frank E. Grizzard Jr. (Charlottesville: University Press of Virginia, 1983), 434.

8   Patrick Cogan to John Stark, July 17, 1777, in *Documents and Records,* 641. "Caleb" was Caleb Stark, adjutant of the 1st New Hampshire Regiment and son of John Stark.

9   James MacClure to Elizabeth MacClure, July 24, 1777, National Archives and Records Administration (NARA), Revolutionary War Pension and Bounty-Land Warrant Application Files, James MacClure (W.17,475). MacClure was brigade major to Brigadier General John Paterson's Brigade.

10 Letter from persons in the Army, belonging to New Ipswich to Ipswich's Committee of Safety, August 11, 1777, in *Documents and Records*, 667.

11 Patrick Cogan to John Stark, July 17, 1777, in *Documents and Records*, 641.

12 Duane Hamilton Hurd, ed., "The Gray Family," in *History of Merrimack and Belknap Counties New Hampshire*, pt. 2 (Philadelphia: J. W. Lewis & Co., 1885), 912.

13 Jeduthan Baldwin, *The Revolutionary Journal of Col. Jeduthan Baldwin 1775–1778*, ed. Thomas Williams Baldwin (Bangor, ME: De Burians, 1906), 110. Baldwin was colonel and chief engineer of the Northern Department.

14 Philip Schuyler to George Washington, July 14, 1777, in *Letterbook of Philip John Schuyler*, mssHM 649, Huntington Library, Art Collections, and Botanical Gardens.

15 William Weeks to his brother, August 6, 1777, in Hiram Bingham Jr., *Five Straws Gathered from Revolutionary Fields* (Cambridge, MA: Hiram Bingham, Jr., 1901), 12. Weeks was paymaster of the 3rd New Hampshire Regiment.

16 Baldwin, *Revolutionary Journal*, 110.

17 Yates was major of the 1st New York Regiment.

18 Philip Schuyler to Christopher Yates, June 28, 1777, in *Proceedings of a General Court Martial, held at Major General Lincoln's Quarters, near Quaker-Hill, in the State of New-York, by Order of His Excellency General Washington, Commander in Chief of the Army of the United States of America, for the Trial of Major General Schuyler, October 1, 1778* (Philadelphia: Hall and Sellers, 1778), 37.

19 This did not constitute an illegal requisition of rum from the sutlers; Schuyler further stated that the rum would "be left in their own possession."

20 Philip Schuyer to Christopher Yates, July 8 and 9, 1777, in *Proceedings of a General Court Martial . . . of Major General Schuyler*, 45.

21 Baldwin, *Revolutionary Journal*, 110.

22 Colonel John Brown was commander of a battalion of Berkshire County, Massachusetts, militia.

23 Philip Schuyler to Thomas Nixon, July 12, 1777, in *Letterbook of Philip John Schuyler*, mssHM 649. Traditionally, oversight of this destructive operation has been credited to Colonel Tadeusz Kosciuszko, second in command of the Northern Department's Corps of Engineers. Instead, Kosciuszko was overseeing construction of field fortifications for the new camp at Moses Creek, located five miles south of Fort Edward.

24 The remainder of the 1st New York Regiment was transferred south to assist in securing the Mohawk River Valley; with Fort George evacuated, the remainder would soon follow. Half of Bailey's Regiment had been stationed at Fort George, while the other half garrisoned Fort Edward.

25 George Washington to John Hancock, July 10, 1777, in Jared Sparks, *The Writing of George Washington*, vol. 4 (Boston: Russell, et al., 1834), 487.

26 Having been informed by Arnold in person regarding his plan to resign, the timing of Washington's request to have Arnold sent north was neither coincidental nor uncalculated.

27 Philip Schuyler to Jonathan Trumbull Sr., July 21, 1777, in *Letterbook of Philip John Schuyler*, mssHM 649.

28 Philip Schuyler to George Washington, July 21, 1777, in *Letterbook of Philip John Schuyler*, mssHM 649.

Repercussions

1 Daniel Gwynee to his father, August 26, 1777, Pembrokeshire Record Office, Haverfordwest, Wales, D/CT/271. Gwynee was the ensign of Lieutenant-Colonel John Hill's company, 9th Regiment of Foot. Newly commissioned, Gwynee joined the Army from Canada on July 20, thereby missing the Battle of Fort Anne.

2 A retired captain in the 10th Regiment of Foot, Skene headed the Army from Canada's Commission of Supplies and the Commission to Administer the Oath of Allegiance. He was lieutenant-governor commandant of Crown Point and Ticonderoga.

3 The aforementioned provisions were all cattle (in excess of one) that Riedesel ordered Vermont inhabitants to bring into his camp for slaughter, allowing his Germans to enjoy "fresh meat . . . instead of the salted meat." *Hesse-Hanau Order Books, A Diary, and Rosters*, trans. Bruce E. Burgoyne (Bowie, MD: Heritage Books, 2003), 162.

4 The oft-told story that Burgoyne chose this route because he was convinced, or duped, by Philip Skene, who wanted the creek cleared and the road improved for his personal benefit, is baseless.

5 John Burgoyne to George Germain, July 11, 1777, in John Burgoyne, *A State of the Expedition from Canada, as Laid before the House of Commons* (London: J. Almon, 1780), xix.

6 William Digby, *The British Invasion from the North*, ed. James Phinney Baxter, A.M. (Albany, NY: Joel Munsell's Sons, 1887), 233. Digby was a lieutenant in Captain John Wight's grenadier company, 53rd Regiment of Foot.

7 Georg Päusch, *Georg Pausch's Journal and Reports of the Campaign in America*, trans. Bruce E. Burgoyne (Bowie, MD: Heritage Books, 2003), 66. Päusch was captain of the Army from Canada's Hessen-Hanau Artillery Company.

8 This general order was posted on July 12. John Burgoyne, *Orderly Book of Lieut. Gen. John Burgoyne, from his Entry into the State of New York until his Surrender at Saratoga, 16th Oct., 1777*, ed. E. B. O'Callaghan, MD (Albany, NY: Joel Munsell, 1860), 38.

9 Päusch, *Georg Pausch's Journal*, 66.

10 Carl August Sartorius, "Journal of the Hessen-Hanau Erbprinz Infantry Regiment Kept by 2nd Lieutenant Carl August Sartorius," trans. Henry J. Retzer, *Journal of the Johannes Schwalm Historical Association* 6, no. 3 (1999): 35. Second-Lieutenant Carl Sartorious was quartermaster of the Erb Prinz Regiment.

11   Burgoyne, *State of the Expedition*, xiii. Burgoyne's conferences with his Indian allies at the Bouquet River on June 21 and Skenesborough on July 19 stipulated that bloodshed was "positively forbid" outside of combat, that "Aged men, women, children, and prisoners, must be held sacred from the knife or hatchet, even in the time of actual conflict," and that they would "receive compensation" for prisoners. The Indians were permitted to "take the scalps of the dead" they killed, but never "from the wounded, or even dying."

12   Daniel Lane, "Captain Lane's Journal," Maine Historical Society, Special Collections, Coll. 499. The scout's commander, Daniel Lane, was a captain in Colonel Ichabod Alden's (7th) Massachusetts Regiment.

13   National Archives and Records Administration (NARA), Revolutionary War Pension and Bounty-Land Warrant Application Files, Cornelius Laman (S.13,702). Laman was a private in Captain Jeremiah Hickok's company, Colonel John Ashley's battalion of Berkshire County, Massachusetts, militia.

14   NARA, Revolutionary War Pension Files, Isaac Blackmer (S.5,285). Blackmer was a private in Captain Samuel Warner's company, Colonel John Ashley's battalion of Berkshire County, Massachusetts, militia.

15   "Diary of Captain Benjamin Warren on Battlefield of Saratoga," ed. David E. Alexander, *Journal of American History* 3 (1909): 203. Jedidiah Thayer was captain of a carpenter company in Colonel Jeduthan Baldwin's Corps of Artificers.

16   "Diary of Captain Benjamin Warren," 204. Warren was captain in Colonel Ichabod Alden's (7th) Massachusetts Regiment.

17   NARA, Revolutionary War Pension Files, Isaac Blackmer (S.5,285). The "Indian blanket" was most likely a stroud matchcoat, a type of woolen blanket commonly worn as a wrap by Indians.

18   John Buss to his parents, August 11, 1777, in *The John Buss Letters*, ed. Ed Nash (Leominster, MA: Nashaway Valley Publications, 1996), 11. Sawyer was the first lieutenant of Captain Zebedee Redding's company, Colonel Gamaliel Bradford's (14th) Massachusetts Regiment. Rogers was a sergeant of Captain Job Whipple's company, Colonel Rufus Putnam's (5th) Massachusetts Regiment.

19   "Diary of Captain Benjamin Warren," 204.

20   NARA, Revolutionary War Pension Files, Samuel Standish (S.28,899). Standish was a private in Captain Arron Rowley's company, Colonel John Brown's battalion of Berkshire County, Massachusetts, militia.

21   Tobias Van Veghten was the first lieutenant of Captain Andrew Finck's company, 1st New York Regiment.

22   The officer was David Jones, who was the lieutenant in Captain Edward Jessup's company, the King's Loyal Americans. Jones was originally appointed captain in the 13th Regiment (Saratoga District), Albany County, New York, militia, in 1775. Jane McCrea's brother, John McCrea, was the regiment's colonel.

23   NARA, Revolutionary War Pension Files, Samuel Standish (S.28,899).

24 With only certain facts available and no confirmed eyewitness accounts, centuries of purposeful anti-Indian propagandists, and, in reaction, pro-Indian apologists, substantially different narratives of McCrea's death have manifested over time. Even the date she was killed—July 26—is incorrectly given as the 27th in most histories. McCrea was tomahawked, scalped, and shot. Because Indians often stripped men and women alike, including Van Veghten, removal of McCrea's clothing did not constitute a sexual assault, and there's no evidence that such ever took place. The oft-repeated story that her fiancé asked or otherwise paid Indians to secure McCrea from Fort Edward's environs and escort her to the safety of the British camp is preposterous and without founding. Equally ridiculous is the story that the fort's relatively few defenders somehow mounted a counterattack against the Indians and accidentally shot McCrea. Likewise, the story of fort defenders shooting at the Indians from the safety of the fort walls and accidentally hitting McCrea is equally impossible, considering she was killed at a distance of no less than a half mile away. The Indian who killed her was not a Huron or Wyandot—named "Le Loup" or "Panther" or otherwise. McCrea was not wearing her wedding dress when taken, and stories regarding the luxuriousness, color, or length of her hair were the contrivances of obsessive nineteenth-century authors.

25 NARA, Revolutionary War Pension Files, Samuel Standish (S.28,899).

26 NARA, Revolutionary War Pension Files, Luther Shaw (S.22,509). Shaw was a private in Captain Asa Stower's company, Colonel John Brown's battalion of Berkshire County, Massachusetts militia.

27 "Diary of Rev. Enos Hitchcock, D.D., a Chaplain in the Revolutionary Army," ed. William B. Weeden, in *Publications of the Rhode Island Historical Society*, vol. 7 (Providence, 1899): 122. Hitchcock was the Congregationalist chaplain of Brigadier General John Paterson's Brigade. According to William Scudder, Van Veghten was stripped, scalped, and "stabbed . . . in several places." The Indians also "fastened a tomahawk in his breast, sharpened a stick and erected him on his feet, by bracing the sharp part of the stick under his chin." William Scudder, *The Journal of William Scudder, an Officer in the Late New-York Line* (New York: Garland Publishing, 1977), 13. Scudder was the second lieutenant of Captain Robert McKeen's company, 1st New York Regiment.

28 John David Broome, *Life, Ministry, and Journals of Hezekiah Smith 1737–1805* (Springfield, MO: Particular Baptist Press, 2004), 449. Smith was the Baptist chaplain of Brigadier General John Nixon's Brigade. Unlike the British or Germanic militaries, by this time in the war, Continental Army chaplains operated on a brigade level, not a regimental one.

29 Philip Schuyler to George Washington, July 28, 1777, in *Letterbook of Philip John Schuyler*, mssHM 649, Huntington Library, Art Collections, and Botanical Gardens.

30 Stories that Jane McCrea's death became a touchstone for militia volunteerism ("If Burgoyne's Indians will kill a young tory woman, what will they do to us!") have their genesis in nineteenth- and twentieth-century Romantic literature, epitomized by Kenneth Robert's historical fiction *Rabble in Arms: A Chronicle of Arundel and the Burgoyne Invasion*

(New York: Doubleday, Doran, 1933). Militia turnout, or the lack thereof, had no connection to McCrea's fate.

31 "Lord Francis Napier's Journal of the Burgoyne Campaign," ed. S. Sydney Bradford, *Maryland Historical Magazine*, December 1962, 306. Francis Napier, Baron Napier, was a lieutenant in Captain William Cotton's light infantry company, 31st Regiment of Foot.

32 "Diary of Rev. Enos Hitchcock," 123–24. The victims were discovered on July 27 or 28. Because the massacre occurred outside of each army's primary sphere of operation, little is known of the event or its victims, and no formal investigation is known to have taken place. Few people doubted that Burgoyne's Indian allies committed the atrocity. Burgoyne denied any knowledge of the event.

33 Among the wounded was Major Matthew Clarkson, Arnold's senior aide-de-camp.

34 The fort was captured by Lieutenant-Colonel John Anstruther, who, with twenty- six gunboats, led a detachment of the 62nd Regiment of Foot; a detachment from the 3rd Battalion, Royal Regiment of Artillery; and Captain David Monin's company of Canadiens.

35 The Continental portion of Hull's command was drawn from Colonels Bailey's (2nd), Jackson's (8th), and Wesson's (9th) Massachusetts Regiments. Hull was major of Colonel Michael Jackson's (8th) Massachusetts Regiment.

36 NARA, Revolutionary War Pension Files, Simeon Alexander (S.28,966). Alexander was a private in Captain Peter Proctor's company, Lieutenant Colonel Samuel Williams's Hampshire County, Massachusetts, militia battalion.

37 James Freeman Clarke, *Revolutionary Services and Civil Life of General William Hull; prepared from his Manuscripts, by his Daughter, Mrs. Maria Campbell* (New York: D. Appleton, 1848), 79.

38 The mortally wounded officer was Hugh Gray, first lieutenant of Captain Philip Thomas's company.

39 "Diary of Captain Benjamin Warren," 206

40 Hiram Bingham Jr., *Five Straws Gathered from Revolutionary Fields* (Cambridge, MA: Hiram Bingham, Jr., 1901), 15.

Diversion

1 "The Hessen-Hanau Jägers, the Siege of Fort Stanwix and the Battle of Oriskany: The Diary of First Lieutenant Philipp Jakob Hildebrandt," trans. Henry J. Retzer and Thomas M. Barker, *The Hessians: Journal of the Johannes Schwalm Historical Association* 15 (2012): 37. Hildebrandt was the de facto commander of the vacant company, Hessen-Hanau Jäger Battalion von Creutzbourg.

2   St. Leger promoted himself to the rank of brigadier-general in his own general orders dated July 10, 1777. Unlike the "local" promotions held by Burgoyne's brigadier generals, the validity of which was bound to a particular geography, St. Leger could only "act" as brigadier general during the course of the expedition that he commanded. *Orderly Book of Sir John Johnson, during the Oriskany Campaign, 1776–1777*, ed. William L. Stone (Albany, NY: Joel Munsell's Sons, 1882), 66.

3   This detachment was composed of officers and soldiers from the 1st and 3rd Battalions (their parent companies served with Burgoyne) and draftees from the Royal Irish Regiment of Artillery. Although the British Board of Ordnance Establishment of 1764 set the diameter of Coehorn mortars at $4\,\frac{13}{25}$ inches (4.52 inches), those brought with Burgoyne and St. Leger were older and cast according to the slightly larger diameter of $4\frac{3}{5}$ inches (4.6 inches).

4   Sayenqueraghta and Gayentwahga were both from the Seneca Nation, the former from the Turtle Clan and the latter from the Wolf Clan.

5   "The Hessen-Hanau Jägers," 36.

6   "The Hessen-Hanau Jägers," 37.

7   The forty officers and men were detached from Captain Robert Walker's company, which was stationed in Major General Israel Putnam's Highlands Department.

8   This was Captain James Gregg, who survived, and Corporal Samuel Madison, who was killed. Both were in the 3rd New York Regiment.

9   The party was commanded by John Spooner, who was ensign of Captain Thomas DeWitt's company, 3rd New York Regiment. Larry Lowenthal, ed., *Days of Siege: A Journal of the Siege of Fort Stanwix in 1777* (Fort Washington, PA: Eastern National, 2005), 16. The original, unattributed journal came into the possession of William Colbreath, and authorship has traditionally been attributed to him (despite the fact that the journalist referred to Colbreath in the third person). Colbreath was the ensign of Captain Leonard Bleeker's company, 3rd New York Regiment.

10 Lowenthal, *Days of Siege*, 19.

11 Lowenthal, *Days of Siege*, 26.

12 George Clinton to Nicholas Herkimer, August 2, 1777, in *Public Papers of George Clinton, First Governor of New York, 1777–1795, 1801–1804*, vol. 2 (Albany, NY: Wynkoop Hallenbeck Crawford, 1900), 164–65.

13 Philip Schuyler to Nicholas Herkimer, July 18, 1777, in *Letterbook of Philip John Schuyler*, mssHM 649, Huntington Library, Art Collections, and Botanical Gardens.

14 Lowenthal, *Days of Siege*, 29.

15 National Archives and Records Administration (NARA), Revolutionary War Pension and Bounty-Land Warrant Application Files, Henry Walrath (S.28,937). Walrath was a private in Captain John Hess's company, Colonel Jacob Klock's battalion, Tryon County, New York, militia.

16 Sir John Johnson, Bt., was lieutenant-colonel commandant of the King's Royal Regiment of New York.

17 John Butler to Guy Carleton, August 15, 1777, in *The Parliamentary Register; or, History of the Proceedings and Debates of the House of Commons*, vol. 8 (London: J. Almon, 1778), 227. Major John Butler was deputy superintendent of the Six Nations Indian Department.

18 NARA, Revolutionary War Pension Files, Henry Walrath (S.28,937).

19 Despite the fact that these jäger were armed with rifles, most of the pieces proved faulty when inspected at the expedition's conclusion. When the company was rejoined with its parent battalion at Fort Oswego, the commander, Lieutenant-Colonel Carl von Creutzbourg, reported on September 6:

> The brigadier and all other Englishmen have highly praised the vacant company for their valor during the last attack at Fort Stanwix, but openly they complain about their poor marksmanship. This led me to investigate the cause of the above, and I found that the rifles, which were distributed among this company during their hurried departure, were not worth a shot of powder. Therefore, I ordered all noncommissioned officers who were equipped with new rifles to exchange theirs with the old ones of the vacant company. This will give the latter 66 new and the rest old, though fair, rifles.
>
> Carl von Creutzbourg, *Reports of the Hanau Jäger Corps*, trans. John C. Zuleger, Q37, Hessian Documents of the American Revolution, 1776–1783, Morristown National Historical Park, Lidgerwood Collection, Fiche 284–90.

20 John Butler to Guy Carleton, August 15, 1777, in *Parliamentary Register*, vol. 8, 227.

21 The first reference of this having happened was recorded in the nineteenth century. The theory that these troops turned their jackets inside out is unlikely, particularly since the effect would have looked bizarrely suspicious, even at a distance. Additionally, the dense, hour-long summertime deluge would have made the inversion of their rain-soaked jackets insufferable, if not impossible. However, as the KRRNY light infantry company was conspicuously engaged earlier in the action wearing the regiment's uniform green jackets trimmed in red, an officer may have "changed the dress of the detachment of Johnson's Greens, that they appeared like American troops." If so, it was most likely by the wholesale removal of their waterlogged jackets. Their round hats would have appeared similar to those worn by many Continental soldiers. Benson Lossing, *The Pictorial Field-Book of the Revolution*, vol. 1 (New York: Harper and Brothers, 1851), 247.

22 Marinus Willett, August 11, 1777, in William M. Willett, *A Narrative of the Military Actions of Colonel Marinus Willett, taken chiefly from his own manuscript* (New York: G. & C. & H. Carvill, 1831), 132.

23 Lowenthal, *Days of Siege*, 31.

24 "Col. Marinus Willett's Gallant Sortie," in *Public Papers of George Clinton*, 212–13.

25 The amputation of Herkimer's leg was performed on August 16 by Robert Johnson, senior surgeon of the Northern Department's General Hospital. Herkimer died that evening. Despite populist stories to the contrary, Johnson was neither inexperienced nor incompetent.

26 Peter Deygart to Philip Schuyler, May [August] 6, 1777, in *Public Papers of George Clinton*, 191–92. Deygart was a captain in the 1st Regiment (Canajoharie District), Tryon County, New York, militia.

27 Lowenthal, *Days of Siege*, 33;

28 William L. Stone, *Life of Joseph Brant-Thayendanegea: Including the Border Wars of the American Revolution*, vol. 1 (New York: Alexander V. Blake, 1838), 252–53.

29 The officer accompanying Willett was Levi Stockwell, who was first lieutenant of Captain James Gregg's company, 3rd New York Regiment.

30 The British soon realized that their mortars "had only the power of teizing" the fort's walls, by which James Glenie proposed and executed a plan to have the artillery's potency increased by converting the small mortars into howitzers. However, the usefulness of these "moritzers" was offset by "the distance, their chambers being too small to hold a sufficiency of powder." St. Leger to Carleton, August 27, 1777, in *Parliamentary Register*, vol. 8, 231–32. Glenie was a second-lieutenant in the Royal Regiment of Artillery and St. Leger's acting assistant engineer.

31 "The Hessen-Hanau Jägers," 39.

32 "The Hessen-Hanau Jägers," 39.

33 Lowenthal, *Days of Siege*, 39.

34 "The Hessen-Hanau Jägers," 39.

35 Butler was a captain in the Six Nations Indian Department.

36 Barry St. Leger to John Burgoyne, August 27, 1777, in John Burgoyne, *A State of the Expedition from Canada, as Laid before the House of Commons* (London: J. Almon, 1780), lxvii.

Overconfidence

1 Julius Wasmus, *An Eyewitness Account of the American Revolution and New England Life*, trans. Helga Doblin (Westport, CT: Greenwood Press, 1990), 73.

2 John M'Alpine, *Genuine Narratives and Concise Memoirs of some of the most Interesting Exploits and Singular Adventures of J. M'Alpine, A Native Highlander, from the time of his Emigration from Scotland to America, 1773* (Greenock, Scotland: W. M'Alpine, 1780), 27. M'Alpine was an assistant commissary of horse for the Army from Canada.

3   Duer was a representative to the Continental Congress. The area of his home was sometimes referred to as Fort Miller, which was a small, dilapidated French and Indian War post that lay on the west side of the Hudson River across from Duer's house. Directly south were the river's Great Falls, which consisted of a high rift succeeded by a low rift, both of which obstructed navigation and required portaging in order to pass.

4   John Burgoyne to Friedrich Baum, August 9, 1777, in John Burgoyne, *A State of the Expedition from Canada, as Laid before the House of Commons* (London: J. Almon, 1780), xxxiv.

5   These small guns consisted of small pattern bronze barrels and carriages invented by William Congreve. Made at Woolwich, England, in 1776, the carriages were compatible with specially designed shafts, allowing the whole to be pulled by one horse, or by men, without need of a limber. Thus arranged, the ensemble was given the moniker "grasshopper."

6   Wasmus, *Eyewitness Account*, 68.

7   Wasmus, *Eyewitness Account*, 68–69.

8   Importantly, this August 11 entry in the Braunschweig headquarters *Tagebuch* (journal) is the only record of the reason why Burgoyne changed Baum's destination at the last minute. Burgoyne's later intimations—that Bennington was Baum's original destination, and that the town was in part selected based upon Riedesel's recommendation—are fraudulent. While Riedesel did recommend an operation in Vermont, one in which the dragoon regiment could be mounted, the expedition's original destination to the Connecticut River (based upon Riedesel's suggestion) was altered by Burgoyne without consultation with the German general. When Riedesel, who was at Fort George on August 11, returned to Fort Edward, "General Burgoyne told him of this change in the plan as regards Lieutenant Colonel Baum's expedition. The latter [Riedesel] was much astonished, and pointed out the risk incurred by going in the new direction to General Burgoyne, and that it was quite contrary to the first intention." Friedrich Christian Cleve, *Journal of the Brunswick Troops in North America under the Orders of Major-General von Riedesel*, trans. "in England," HZ 265, Hessian Documents of the American Revolution, 1776–1783, Morristown National Historical Park, Lidgerwood Collection, Fiche 180–93. See also Burgoyne, *State of the Expedition*, 12–13.

9   Friedrich Baum to John Burgoyne, August 13, 1777, in Burgoyne, *State of the Expedition*, xxxviii.

10 Friedrich Baum to John Burgoyne, August 14, 1777, in Burgoyne, *State of the Expedition*, xxxxix.

11 Friedrich Baum to John Burgoyne, August 14, 1777.

12 Ira Allen to the New Hampshire Council of Safety, July 15, 1777, in *Documents and Records relating to the State of New-Hampshire during the period of the American Revolution, from 1776–1783*, vol. 8, ed. Daniel Bouton, D.D. (Concord, NH: Edward A. Jenks, 1874), 632. Allen was secretary to Vermont's Council of Safety.

13 *Documents and Records*, 634.

14 "John Wallace's Journal of the Battle of Bennington, August 16, 1777," ed. Michael P. Gabriel, *Walloomsack Review* 22 (Autumn, 2018): 10.

15 "John Wallace's Journal," 10. William Gregg was lieutenant colonel of Colonel Moses Nichols's New Hampshire militia battalion.

16 Wasmus, *Eyewitness Account*, 70.

17 This Braunschweig detachment, consisting of twenty-five grenadiers and nearly forty musketeers drawn primarily from the Regiments von Riedesel and Specht, was commanded by Second-Lieutenant Johann Burghoff.

18 Wasmus, *Eyewitness Account*, 70.

19 Desmaretz Durnford was a sub-engineer in the British Corps of Engineers. Following didactic Germanic military policy, Baum's German soldiers did not build their own fortifications.

20 Claude-Nicolas-Guillaume de Lorimier, *At War with the Americans: The Journal of Claude-Nicolas-Guillaume de Lorimier*, trans. Peter Aichinger (Victoria, BC: Press Porcépic, 1981), 66.

21 Samuel Herrick was lieutenant colonel commandant of a battalion of Vermont Rangers. Moses Nichols was colonel of a battalion of New Hampshire militia.

22 Thomas Stickney and David Hobart were colonels of New Hampshire militia battalions.

23 While people did sometimes chew on lead bullets (musket balls) to stave off pain or thirst, the traditional story of surgery patients being given such an object—an obvious choking hazard—is apocryphal. Michael P. Gabriel, *The Battle of Bennington, Soldiers & Civilians* (Charleston, SC: History Press, 2012), 61. This account was relayed by Thomas Mellen, who was a private in Captain Peter Clark's company, Colonel Thomas Stickney's battalion, New Hampshire militia.

24 Gabriel, *Battle of Bennington*, 51–53. This account was relayed by Jesse Field, who was a private in Captain Elijah Dewey's company, Colonel Moses Robinson's battalion, Vermont militia.

25 Wasmus, *Eyewitness Account*, 71.

26 Joseph Rudd to his father, August 20, 1777, in Gabriel, *Battle of Bennington*, 93. Rudd was a lieutenant in Captain Elijah Dewey's company, Colonel Moses Robinson's battalion, Vermont militia.

27 National Archives and Records Administration (NARA), Revolutionary War Pension and Bounty-Land Warrant Application Files, David Holbrook (S.23,709). Holbrook was a private in Captain Enos Parker's company, Colonel Benjamin Simonds's battalion of Berkshire County, Massachusetts militia.

28 While the dragoons only carried ten rounds on their person, ammunition boxes containing additional cartridges may have been positioned on the hilltop. However, the majority of their hundred-round complements were stored on the ammunition carts located in the baggage park and were therefore inaccessible. Wasmus's claim that the German defenders expended one hundred rounds each is impossible, and is probably based upon

his knowledge that general orders called for each soldier to be issued with one hundred cartridges and the fact that the dragoons expended their ammunition during the fight.

29   Gabriel, *Battle of Bennington,* 54. This deposition, given by Amos Searles in favor of Rudd's widow's pension application, added that "Mr. Rudd said he always regretted Herrick's killing the Hessian for he meant to have him brought in as a prisoner. The sword Mr. Rudd took from the Hessian I have seen. I have also heard Mr. Herrick and others relate repeatedly the same story." NARA, Revolutionary War Pension Files, Joseph Rudd (W.17,582).

30   Wasmus, *Eyewitness Account,* 72.

31   Gabriel, *Battle of Bennington,* 55. This account was relayed by John Orr, who was a lieutenant in Captain Samuel McConnell's company, Colonel Thomas Stickney's battalion, New Hampshire militia.

32   NARA, Revolutionary War Pension Files, Benjamin Bean (S.22,115). Bean was a private in Captain Chase Taylor's company, Colonel Thomas Stickney's battalion, New Hampshire militia.

33   Gabriel, *Battle of Bennington,* 55.

34   Gabriel, *Battle of Bennington,* 55.

35   Ellen M. Raynor and Emma L. Petitclerc, *History of the Town of Cheshire, Berkshire County, Mass.* (Holyoke, MA: Clark W. Bryan, 1885), 50. Stafford, who was wounded in the attack, commanded a body of forty Berkshire County, Massachusetts militia volunteers.

36   Lorimier, *At War with the Americans,* 65.

37   Cleve, *Journal of the Brunswick Troops,* HZ 270.

38   NARA, Revolutionary War Pension Files, Gilbert Bradley (R.21,698).

39   *The Specht Journal,* trans. Helga Doblin (Westport, CT: Greenwood Press, 1995), 67.

40   "Account of an Affair which happened near Walloon-Creek, 16th August, 1777," by Heinrich Breymann, n.d., in *The Parliamentary Register; or, History of the Proceedings and Debates of the House of Commons,* vol. 7 (London: J. Almon, 1778), 238.

41   The instance of the overturned ammunition cart has been conflated with a fabricated story of an exploding ammunition cart, an incident that supposedly occurred during the battle. The story, relayed in "Account of the Battle of Bennington, by Glich, a German Officer who was in the Engagement, under Col. Baum," is a work of fiction, copied word for word from George Robert Gleig's *The Chelsea Pensioners,* vol. 2 (London: Henry Colburn, 1829), 94–124.

42   "Account of an Affair," in *Parliamentary Register,* vol. 7, 238.

43   In his official report, Breymann claimed he was unaware of the battle with Baum when he set off from St. Croix. However, Colin Campbell, who served with the Québec Indian Department, testified that he encountered Breymann about a mile before the Advanced Corps reached the St. Croix bridge and "informed him, in as good French as I was master of, that Colonel Baum, was attacked, mentioning the hour, and the minute," and that Breymann acted upon this information. Colin Campbell to Philip Skene, September 8, 1778, New York

State Library, American Revolutionary War, 1775–1783, Manuscripts and Special Collections, 4959. Campbell was a captain in the 1st Battalion, Royal Highland Emigrants, serving with the Québec Indian Department.

44 "Account of an Affair," in *Parliamentary Register*, vol. 7, 238.

45 Lorimier, *At War with the Americans*, 66.

46 "A Brunswick Grenadier with Burgoyne: The Journal of Johann Bense, 1776–1783," trans. Helga Doblin, *New York History* 66, no. 4 (October 1985): 431. Bense was a soldier in the Braunschweig Grenadierbattaillon Breymann.

47 Gabriel, *Battle of Bennington*, 60. This account was relayed by Jesse Field.

48 NARA, Revolutionary War Pension Files, Daniel Gale (W.16,264). The wound incapacitated him for life. Gale was a private in Captain Taylor Chases's company, Colonel Thomas Stickney's battalion, New Hampshire militia.

49 Gabriel, *Battle of Bennington*, 61. This account was relayed by Thomas Mellen.

50 Limbered guns were incapable of being fired or "whirled around"; certainly, Holbrook meant to say that the unlimbered gun's trail was used to turn the gun around. Portfires were flare-like ignition implements used to discharge loaded artillery pieces. NARA, Revolutionary War Pension Files, David Holbrook (S.23,709).

51 Considering that Baum's expedition had few survivors who returned to Burgoyne's army, a number of its principal officers effected surprising escapes for themselves, including Philip Skene, John Campbell (wounded), the Chevalier de Lorimier (wounded), John Peters (wounded), and Alexander Fraser. Notably, no German officer from Baum's command was able to escape.

Routed

1 Thomas Spencer to the officers of Fort Schuyler and the committee on Mohawk River, so on to Genl. Schuyler, July 29, 1777, in *Journals of the Provincial Congress, Provincial Convention, Committee of Safety and Council of Safety of the State of New-York*, vol. 1 (Albany, NY: Thurlow Weed, 1842), 1,026. An Oneida, Spencer was a blacksmith for the Oneida Nation, so employed by the United States government's Commissioners for Indian Affairs in the Northern Department. He was killed in the Battle of Oriskany.

2 Traditionally, these Continentals have been erroneously identified as belonging to one of the Rhode Island regiments. Instead, they were from Captain Abraham Childs's company, Colonel James Wesson's (9th) Massachusetts Regiment. The Albany County militia contingent was drawn from the 2nd Regiment (Schenectady District).

3 Peter Vroman was colonel of the 15th Regiment (Schoharie and Duanesburgh Districts), Albany County, New York militia.

4 John Harper was colonel of the nascent 5th Regiment of Tryon County, New York militia.

5   Peter Vroman to the President of the [New York] Council of Safety, August 20, 1777, in
    Public Papers of George Clinton, First Governor of New York, 1777–1795, 1801–1804, vol. 2
    (Albany, NY: Wynkoop Hallenbeck Crawford, 1900), 239.

6   John Harper to the President of the [New York] Council of Safety, August 20, 1777, in
    Public Papers of George Clinton, 238.

7   Tradition holds that one of the troop's officers, a lieutenant named David Wirt, died in the
    battle. However, no such man by that name served as an officer or in any position in the
    regiment.

8   Peter Vroman to the President of the [New York] Council of Safety, August 20, 1777, in
    Public Papers of George Clinton, 239.

9   This consisted of Colonels John Bailey's (2nd), Michael Jackson's (8th), and James Wes-
    son's (9th) Massachusetts Regiments, all of which had detachments serving at Fort Schuy-
    ler. While en route, the expedition was joined by Colonel James Livingston's Battalion of
    Forces; a detachment of the 1st New York Regiment, Tryon County militia; and Oneida
    and Tuscarora Nation warriors.

10 Philip Schuyler to Benedict Arnold, August 13, 1777, in *Letterbook of Philip John Schuyler*,
    mssHM 649, Huntington Library, Art Collections, and Botanical Gardens.

11 Benedict Arnold to Horatio Gates, August 21, 1777, New-York Historical Society, Horatio
    Gates Papers, microfilm edition, 5:139.

12 Brooks was lieutenant colonel of Colonel Michael Jackson's (8th) Massachusetts Regiment
    and commanded the regiment throughout 1777 while Jackson was perpetually in absentia.
    Schuyler was a private in Major James Gray's company, the King's Royal Regiment of New
    York.

13 James Thatcher, *A Military Journal during the American Revolutionary War, from 1775 to
    1783* (Boston: Richardson and Lord, 1823), 107. Thatcher was a hospital mate in the
    Northern Department's General Hospital.

14 Larry Lowenthal, ed., *Days of Siege: A Journal of the Siege of Fort Stanwix in 1777* (Fort
    Washington, PA: Eastern National, 2005), 49.

15 "The Hessen-Hanau Jägers, the Siege of Fort Stanwix and the Battle of Oriskany: The
    Diary of First Lieutenant Philipp Jakob Hildebrandt," trans. Henry J. Retzer and Thomas
    M. Barker, *The Hessians: Journal of the Johannes Schwalm Historical Association* 15 (2012):
    44.

16 Barry St. Leger to John Burgoyne, August 27, 1777, in John Burgoyne, *A State of the Expe-
    dition from Canada, as Laid before the House of Commons* (London: J. Almon, 1780), xlvi.

17 Traditional stories outrageously hyperbolize this anecdote, claiming that Hanjost was
    "mentally retarded" and that Indians ostensibly had more respect for someone with a dis-
    ability. These stories further claim that Hanjost's bullet-riddled coat was intended to dupe
    the Indians into thinking that he was magically impervious and, when asked how many
    men Arnold had, that he only gestured to the foliage. This wordless message inferred that
    Arnold's Americans were as numerous as the leaves on the trees, and thereby provided

the Indians with an answer they were capable of understanding. There is no evidence that Hanjost was disabled, or that St. Leger's Indians were tricked by gestures made to tree leaves (the latter story originated from a disassociated 1832 pension claim). As for shooting the coat, the shots were only intended to suggest that he survived near misses during a supposed flight from Revolutionary captivity; there are plenty of references to gunshots tearing through clothing, but missing the wearer, in the American War for Independence.

18   "The Hessen-Hanau Jägers," 41–41.

19   This news was delivered to Burgoyne at Duer's house by Thayendanegea (Joseph Brant) himself. St. Leger's official report of his expedition's failure was delivered to Burgoyne on September 3 by the former's acting deputy quartermaster general, James Lundin. Lundin was the lieutenant of Captain Duncan Campbell's company, 2nd Battalion, Royal Highland Emigrants.

20   Barry St. Leger to Guy Carleton, August 27, 1777, in *The Parliamentary Register; or, History of the Proceedings and Debates of the House of Commons*, vol. 8 (London: J. Almon, 1778), 228.

21   Daniel Claus to William Knox, October 16, 1777, in *Orderly Book of Sir John Johnson, during the Oriskany Campaign, 1776–1777*, ed. William L. Stone (Albany, NY: Joel Munsell's Sons, 1882), 70–71n. Shockingly, St. Leger arrived at this conclusion in early July, weeks before the expedition arrived at Fort Schuyler, based upon intelligence garnered from Spooner and his men. Lieutenant-Colonel Claus was "superintendent of the Indian Department" for St. Leger's expedition. Knox was undersecretary of state for the colonies.

22   Benedict Arnold to Horatio Gates, August 23, 1777, in *Public Papers of George Clinton*, 255.

23   William Scudder, *The Journal of William Scudder, an Officer in the Late New-York Line* (New York: Garland Publishing, 1977), 18–19.

24   John Adams to Abigail Adams, August 19, 1777, in *Letters of John Adams, addressed to his wife*, vol. 1, ed. Charles Francis Adams (Boston: Charles C. Little and James Brown, 1841), 245–46.

25   *Journals of the Continental Congress, 1774–1789*, vol. 9, ed. Worthington Chauncey Ford (Washington, DC: USGPO, 1907), 771–72. This magnificent ca. 1785 French-made sword and scabbard (17.87.3a,b), and Ralph Earl's equally sublime ca. 1791 portrait of Willett (17.87.1), are on display at the Metropolitan Museum of Art, New York.

Galvanized

1   Robert Troup to John Jay, September 14, 1777, in *The Correspondence and Public Papers of John Jay*, vol. 1, ed. Henry Phelps Johnston (New York: G. P. Putnam's Sons, 1890), 166.

Major Troup was senior aide-de-camp to Gates; Jay was chief justice of New York's Supreme Court of Judicature.

2 George Washington to Benjamin Lincoln, July 24, 1777, in *The Writing of George Washington from the Original Manuscript Sources, 1745–1799*, vol. 8, ed. John C. Fitzpatrick (Washington, DC: USGPO, 1933), 463. During Lincoln's absence, his division, which was an element of Washington's army, fell to the command of Brigadier General Anthony Wayne.

3 *Journals of the Continental Congress, 1774–1789*, vol. 8, ed. Worthington Chauncey Ford (Washington, DC: USGPO, 1907), 585.

4 St. Clair left the Northern Army on August 12. The only brigadier general to leave the Northern Army, Matthias Alexis Roche de Fermoy, was dismissed for entirely different reasons. Complaints from his battalion commanders that they "could not understand his language nor he theirs" resulted in Schuyler reassigning de Fermoy's regiments to other brigades. De Fermoy's subsequent assignment to command at Albany was cut short when Schuyler granted his request for leave in early August. Schuyler to Washington, August 4, 1777, in *Letterbook of Philip John Schuyler*, mssHM 649, Huntington Library, Art Collections, and Botanical Gardens.

5 John David Broome, *Life, Ministry, and Journals of Hezekiah Smith 1737–1805* (Springfield, MO: Particular Baptist Press, 2004), 451.

6 Henry Dearborn, *Revolutionary War Journals of Henry Dearborn 1775–1783*, ed. Lloyd A. Brown and Howard H. Peckham (Freeport, NY: Books for Libraries Press, 1969), 102.

7 John Buss to his parents, August 27, 1777, in *The John Buss Letters*, ed. Ed Nash (Leominster, MA: Nashaway Valley Publications, 1996), 13.

8 Brigadier General John Glover's Brigade, sent from the Highlands Department, joined the Northern Army at Saratoga on July 31.

9 "Diary of Rev. Enos Hitchcock, D.D., a Chaplain in the Revolutionary Army," in *Publications of the Rhode Island Historical Society*, vol. 7, ed. William B. Weeden (Providence, 1899), 127.

10 Lincoln was at Bennington one week before the Battle of Bennington in order to coordinate militia there, but Schuyler ordered him to return to the Northern Army upon hearing that Burgoyne gained Saratoga. When intelligence of Baum's expedition was received, Schuyler instructed Lincoln to return to Bennington, where he arrived after the battle.

11 William Smith, *Historical Memoirs from 12 July 1776 to 25 July 1778 of William Smith, Historian of the Province of New York; Member of the Governor's Council, and Last Chief Justice of That Province Under the Crown; Chief Justice of Quebec* (New York: Colburn and Tegg, 1958), 221.

12 Washington's June 1, 1777, general order called for the battalion of riflemen under Morgan's command to be formed of "none but such as are known to be perfectly skilled in the use of these guns [rifles], and who are known to be active and orderly in their behavior." George Washington, *The Writings of George Washington from the Original Manuscript Sources, 1745–1799*, vol. 8, ed. John Clement Fitzpatrick (Washington, DC: USGPO,

1933), 156. Officers and soldiers of Morgan's Rifle Battalion were primarily drafted from the 5th, 6th, 7th, 8th, 9th, and 11th Virginia Regiments; the 1st, 5th, 8th, and 12th Pennsylvania Regiments; and the 1st New Jersey Regiment.

13 John Glover to James Warren, August 6, 1777, in William P. Upham, *Memoir of General John Glover of Marblehead* (Salem, MA: Charles W. Swasey, 1863), 27.

14 Philip Schuyler to George Washington, August 13, 1777, in *Letterbook of Philip John Schuyler*, mssHM 649.

15 Archives and Records Administration (NARA), Revolutionary War Pension and Bounty-Land Warrant Application Files, John Foster (S.13,047). Foster served as a trooper in Captain David McClure's troop, Major Elijah Hyde's battalion of Connecticut Light Horse. The unit had no particular association with Arnold beyond the fact that it was from his home state of Connecticut.

16 Robert Troup to John Jay, September 14, 1777, in *Correspondence and Public Papers of John Jay*, 165.

17 Robert Troup to John Jay, September 14, 1777.

18 Smith, *Historical Memoirs*, 222.

19 Robert Troup to John Jay, September 14, 1777, in *Correspondence and Public Papers of John Jay*, 166–67.

20 Richard Varick to Horatio Gates, September 10, 1777, New-York Historical Society, Horatio Gates Papers, microfilm edition, 5:557. Nixon's Brigade consisted of Colonels Thomas Greaton's (3rd), Rufus Putnam's (5th), Thomas Nixon's (6th), and Ichabod Alden's (7th) Massachusetts Continental Regiments. They were inspected on September 2.

21 Richard Varick to Horatio Gates, September 10, 1777, Horatio Gates Papers, 5:557. Paterson's Brigade consisted of Colonels Thomas Marshall's (10th), Late Ebenezer Francis's (11th), Samuel Brewer's (12th), and Gamaliel Bradford's (14th) Massachusetts Continental Regiments. They were inspected on September 4.

22 Glover's Brigade consisted of Colonels Joseph Vose's (1st), William Shepard's (4th), Edward Wigglesworth's (13th), and Timothy Bigelow's (15th) Massachusetts Continental Regiments. In addition, the brigade included Colonel Abraham Wemple and Lieutenant Colonel Henry R. Livingston's Albany County, New York militia battalions and Colonel Morris Graham's combined Dutchess and Ulster County, New York militia battalion. They were inspected on September 1. Richard Varick to Horatio Gates, September 10, 1777, Horatio Gates Papers, 5:557.

23 Poor's Brigade consisted of Colonels Joseph Cilley's 1st, Nathan Hale's 2nd, and Alexander Scammell's 3rd New Hampshire Continental Regiments; Colonels Philip Van Cortlandt's 2nd and Henry Beekman Livingston's 4th New York Continental Regiments; and Colonels Thaddeus Cook's and Jonathan Latimer's Connecticut militia battalions. They (sans the militia) were inspected on September 5. Richard Varick to Horatio Gates, September 10, 1777, Horatio Gates Papers, 5:557.

24 Richard Varick to Horatio Gates, September 10, 1777, Horatio Gates Papers, 5:557. Learned's Brigade consisted of Colonels John Bailey's (2nd), Michael Jackson's (8th), and James Wesson's (9th) Massachusetts Continental Regiments, and Colonel James Livingston's Battalion of Forces (which is today commonly referred to as the 1st Canadian Regiment). They were inspected on September 7.

25 Although originally including men from the 2nd and 4th New York Regiments, they were returned to their regiments for reasons unknown. See *A Return of the Killed, Wounded, Missing, Absent without Leave, and Not Joined, of the Corps of Light Infantry. Commanded by Major Henry Derborne October 2d 1777,* Horatio Gates Papers, 18:999.

26 These Indians, from Stockbridge, Massachusetts, included Stockbridge, Wappinger, and Munsee war captains and warriors.

27 By September 20 Stevens's artillery corps consisted of one brass nine-pounder, one brass six-pounder, three iron six-pounders, ten of the aforementioned French four-pounders, five iron four-pounders, and two iron three-pounders.

Stymied

1 Sir Francis Clerke to Alexander Hume-Campbell, Lord Polwarth, September 10, 1777, in Ronald F. Kingsley, "Letters to Lord Polwarth from Sir Francis-Carr Clerke, Aide-de-Camp to General John Burgoyne," *New York History* 79, no. 4 (October 1998): 421.

2 Their settlement was located at the confluence of Schoharie Creek and the Mohawk River. After the Oneida settlement at Oriska was destroyed, Oneida and militia allies retaliated by attacking the Mohawk settlement at Fort Hunter. Forewarned of this, the Fort Hunter Mohawks evacuated; most sought refuge with Burgoyne.

3 The Riedesels' daughters were Augusta, Caroline, and Frederica. Also joining the army were Lady Harriet Acland (married to the major of the 20th Regiment of Foot), Honour Harnage (married to the major of the 62nd Regiment of Foot), Anne Reynell (married to a lieutenant in the 62nd Regiment of Foot) and sons Samuel and Thomas, Mrs. Fitzgerald (married to the adjutant of the 62nd Regiment of Foot), and Mrs. Higgins (married to an assistant commissary) and her "family." They were attended by retinues of various servant-class assistants. It is the latter women whom Burgoyne, according to the Baroness, took as his mistress (Higgins's husband was present with the army). If true, the singular reference has nevertheless exploded into ludicrous fiction by many authors writing about the campaign. Frederica Riedesel, Freifrau zu (Baroness of) Eisenbach, *Baroness von Riedesel and the American Revolution,* trans. Marvin L. Brown Jr. (Chapel Hill: University of North Carolina Press, 1965), 55–56. See *The Acland Journal: Lady Harriet Acland and the American War,* ed. Jennifer D. Thorp (Winchester, UK: Hampshire County Council, 1993), for the journal written by Lady Acland and other members of the Acland entourage.

4   La Corne de Saint-Luc to John Burgoyne, October 23, 1778, "A Letter from the Chev. St Luc de la Corne, Colonel of the Indians, to Gen. Burgoyne," *The Scots Magazine* 40 (April 1778): 715.

5   "The Battles of Saratoga from an 'Enemy' Perspective,'" trans. Helga Doblin, *Tamkang Journal of American Studies* 3, no. 3 (Spring 1987): 16.

6   Traditionally, narratives of the Northern Campaign of 1777 must include reference to Burgoyne's supposed thirty "wagonloads" of personal belongings, secured in order to support his lavish, supposed "Gentleman Johnny" lifestyle. The only source for this—general orders dated August 19—specifically states that the carts (not wagons) were not secured at Burgoyne's request, and that "he would on no account suffer his private conveniency to interfere with the public Transports of Provisions." Further, if the rumors were proven true, Burgoyne would "mark the strongest resentment at this very indecent disobedience of General Orders." Whether these thirty carts loaded with Burgoyne's baggage (without his consent), or the baggage of other officers, existed or not is unconfirmed. Either way, any such carts would have been reappropriated for transporting provisions. James Murray Hadden, *Hadden's Journal and Orderly Books: A Journal Kept in Canada and upon Burgoyne's Campaign in 1776 and 1777*, ed. Horatio Rogers (Boston: Gregg Press, 1972), 314–15.

7   Freeman and his son, Thomas, were private soldiers in Lieutenant-Colonel Commandant Ebenezer Jessup's company. Freeman's farm—the centerpiece site for the forthcoming battle—was located in Albany County's expansive Saratoga District. As with most others living in the area, Freeman leased his property. Located within Great Lot 16, the land was owned by Philip Schuyler.

8   *Orderly Book Burgoyne's Campaign of 1777 Ticonderoga to Saratoga 47th Regiment of British Foot*, ed. Frank C. Deering (Saco, ME: privately printed, 1932), 33.

9   Horatio Gates to John Hancock, September 22, 1777, New-York Historical Society, Horatio Gates Papers, microfilm edition, 5:718.

10 This picket was composed of officers and soldiers drafted from Hamilton's Brigade's British infantry regiments. Forbes was major of the 9th Regiment of Foot.

11 Samuel Armstrong, "From Saratoga to Valley Forge: The Diary of Lt. Samuel Armstrong," ed. Joseph Lee Boyle, *Pennsylvania Magazine of History and Biography* 121, no. 3 (July 1997): 245. Armstrong was ensign of Captain John Burnam's company, Colonel Michael Jackson's (8th) Massachusetts Regiment. Armstrong was his regiment's appointment to serve in Dearborn's light infantry corps.

12 Commanded by Captain Thomas Jones (4th Battalion, Royal Regiment of Artillery), the pair of guns attached to the Fusiliers were commanded by Second-Lieutenant George Reid and manned by men recently drafted from the Royal Irish Regiment of Artillery. The pair of guns with the 62nd Regiment were under the command of Second-Lieutenant James Murray Hadden, whose personnel were drawn from Captain William Borthwick's company, 3rd Battalion, Royal Regiment of Artillery.

13   Despite the ridiculous stereotype of British soldiers fighting while wearing knapsacks and other weighty encumbrances, British Army regulations called for British soldiers to remove these impediments and pile them behind their company formations before entering battle. Thomas Simes, *The Regulator: or, Instructions to form the Officer, and complete the Soldier, upon fixed Principles* (London: William Richardson, 1780), 164.

14   The traditional story of British regiments using plodding, tightly packed, rigid formations throughout the war is a pervasive myth inculcated by popular media.

15   Frederic Kidder, *History of the First New Hampshire Regiment in the War of the Revolution* (Albany, NY: Joel Munsell, 1868), 34. The journalist, Thomas Blake, was the ensign of Captain John House's company, 1st New Hampshire Regiment.

16   Henry Dearborn, *Revolutionary War Journals of Henry Dearborn 1775–1783*, ed. Lloyd A. Brown and Howard H. Peckham (Freeport, NY: Books for Libraries Press, 1969), 106.

17   National Archives and Records Administration (NARA), Revolutionary War Pension and Bounty-Land Warrant Application Files, Philo Woodruff (S.15,720). Woodruff was a sergeant of Captain Tarball Whitney's company, Colonel Thaddeus Cook's battalion, Connecticut militia.

18   Horatio Gates to John Hancock, September 22, 1777, Horatio Gates Papers, 5:718.

19   John Money, *A Letter to the Right Honorable William Windham, on the Partial Re-Organization of the British Army* (London: T. Egerton and Carpenter, 1799), 16–17. Money was a captain in the 9th Regiment of Foot and the deputy quartermaster general of Burgoyne's army.

20   Alexander Scammell to Jonathan Chadbourne, September 26, 1777, Schoff Revolutionary War Collection, William C. Clements Library, University of Michigan.

21   Although Burgoyne sent orders for these cannons to be brought up from the valley early in the action (at 2:00 p.m.), Royal Artillery personnel made a circuitous route, retraced their steps back to Swords's house, and followed the road taken by Hamilton in order to arrive at Freeman's farm safely. The four guns brought were medium twelve-pounders or a pair of light twenty-four-pounders and medium twelve-pounders. Friedrich Christian Cleve, Journal of the Brunswick Troops in North America under the Orders of Major-General von Riedesel, trans. "in England," HZ 302–4, Hessian Documents of the American Revolution, 1776–1783, Morristown National Historical Park, Lidgerwood Collection, Fiche 180–93. Royal Regiment of Artillery ordnance inventories included round shot (for cannons), case shot (for cannons, howitzers, and mortars), and shells (for howitzers and mortars), but neither grape nor tin-case (canister). National Archives and Records Administration (NARA), Numbered Record Books Concerning Military Operations and Service, Pay and Settlement of Accounts, and Supplies in the War Department Collection of Revolutionary War Records, vol. 129, roll 39.

22   Unattributed letter, September 20, 1777, Saratoga National Historical Park historian files. Authorship of this letter is attributed to a divisional or brigade staff officer.

23   Hadden, *Hadden's Journal and Orderly Books,* 166.

24   Alexander Scammell to Jonathan Chadbourne, September 26, 1777.

25   "The Burgoyne Expedition—April 1776 to October 13th, 1777—Diary of Joshua Pell, Jr.," *Bulletin of the Fort Ticonderoga Museum*, July 1929, 11.

26   Don N. Hagist, *British Soldiers, American War* (Yardley, PA: Westholme Publishing, 2012), 63. William Crawford, whose autobiography, "A Narrative of the Life and Character of William Crawford," was published in 1823, was, in 1777, a private in Lieutenant-General the Honorable George Lane Parker's company, 20th Regiment of Foot.

27   "Diary of Joshua Pell, Jr.," 11.

28   "Diary of Joshua Pell, Jr.," 11.

29   Philip Van Cortlandt, *The Revolutionary War Memoir and Selected Correspondence of Philip Van Cortlandt*, ed. Jacob Judd (Tarrytown, NY: Sleepy Hollow Restorations, 1976), 47–48.

30   William Gordon, D.D., *The History of the Rise, Progress, and Establishment of the Independence of the United States of America: including an Account of the Late War; and the Thirteen Colonies, from their Origin to that Period*, vol. 2 (London: printed for the author, 1788), 551. Most of Gordon's war narrative was compiled from published primary sources and the accounts of officers with whom he corresponded.

31   Gordon, *History of the Rise*, 550. While not specifically stated, these grenadiers could have been Braunschweig (and thereby identified by their metallic-fronted caps) or British (identified by their felt caps bearing pewter grenade ornaments).

32   William Digby, *The British Invasion from the North*, ed. James Phinney Baxter, A.M. (Albany, NY: Joel Munsell's Sons, 1887), 273–74.

33   James Selkirk, *A New and Complete History of the American Revolution in Three Parts*, pt. 1 (unpublished typescript, 1970), n.p. Selkirk was a sergeant in Captain Timothy Hughes's company, Colonel James Livingston's Battalion of Forces.

34   John Wells to James Milligan, October 4, 1777, in Stanislaus Vincent Henkels, *An Extraordinary Collection of Washington's Letters, Washington Relics, Revolutionary Documents, and The Rarest Works on American History also Scarce American Portraits, Maps and Views* (Philadelphia: Thomas Burch's Sons, 1891), 21. Wells was a Northern Department commissioner for settling army accounts. Milligan was the Continental Army's commissioner for settling army accounts.

35   Cleve, Journal of the Brunswick Troops, HZ 304–HZ 305.

36   Cleve, Journal of the Brunswick Troops, HZ 305–HZ 306.

37   This divisional order, which reiterated that "if the enemy is on a plain, we must take pains to close in on him and, without firing, fall on the enemy with lowered bayonets," was dated August 26. *Orderly Book of the Braunschweig Corps in North America*, trans. Virginia Rinaldy, 56–57, Hessian Documents of the American Revolution, 1776–1783, Morristown National Historical Park, Lidgerwood Collection, Fiche 214–27.

38   Georg Päusch, *Journal of Captain Pausch, Chief of the Hanau Artillery during the Burgoyne Campaign*, trans. William L. Stone (Albany, NY: Joel Munsell's Sons, 1886), 76.

39   Cleve, Journal of the Brunswick Troops, HZ 307–HZ 308.

40   Päusch, *Journal of Captain Pausch*, 76.

41 Captured officers were Captain Peter Drummond (McAlpin's American Volunteers) and two ensigns of the 62nd Regiment of Foot: Louis Joseph, Chevalier D'anterroches, and Levinge Cosby Phillips.

42 John Burgoyne, *Orderly Book of Lieut. Gen. John Burgoyne from his Entry into the State of New York until his Surrender at Saratoga, 16th Oct., 1777*, ed. E. B. O'Callaghan, MD (Albany, NY: Joel Munsell, 1860), 116.

43 Burgoyne, *Orderly Book of Lieut. Gen. John Burgoyne*, 116. The royalists, who would be entitled to a discharge from their new British regiments on December 25, were drawn from Ebenezer Jessup's King's Loyal Americans, John Peters's Queen's Loyal Rangers, Daniel McAlpin's American Volunteers, and Samuel MacKay's Loyal Volunteers. At twenty men each, the recipient battalions were the 9th, 20th, 21st (Royal North British Fusiliers), 24th, 47th, and 62nd Regiments of Foot.

44 Captured officers were Captains Van Swearingen (Rifle Battalion) and Jason Wait (1st New Hampshire Regiment) and First Lieutenant John Moore (1st New Hampshire Regiment). Moore belonged to Captain Ebenezer Frye's company.

45 Lieutenant Colonel Winborn Adams (2nd New Hampshire Regiment) was killed and Lieutenant Colonel Andrew Colburn (3rd New Hampshire Regiment) was mortally wounded (he died the following day).

46 *Orderly book of Capt Thaddeus Cook of Wallingford Connecticut*, American Antiquarian Society, Manuscript Collection, Orderly Books Collection, 1758–1813, octavo volume 12. Despite the erroneous nineteenth-century title written on the orderly book's cover, Cook was a colonel.

Interregnum

1 Henry Beekman Livingston to Robert R. Livingston, October 4, 1777, in George Dangerfield, *Chancellor Robert R. Livingston of New York 1746–1813* (New York: Harcourt Brace, 1960), 102.

2 This message was written at night on September 11 and sent to Burgoyne on September 12. Henry Clinton to Edward Harvey, October 13, 1777, in George Thomas, Earl of Albemarle, *Memoirs of the Marquis of Rockingham and his Contemporaries*, vol. 2 (London: Richard Bentley, 1852), 335.

3 Henry Clinton to Edward Harvey, October 13, 1777.

4 Benjamin Lincoln to the Massachusetts Council, August 25, 1777, in *Correspondence of the American Revolution; being Letters of Eminent Men to George Washington, from the time of taking his Command of the Army to the end of his Presidency*, vol. 2, ed. Jared Sparks (Boston: Little, Brown, 1853), 520.

5 Benjamin Lincoln to John Brown, September 12, 1777, in *Correspondence of the American Revolution*, 525.

6 Benjamin Lincoln to Samuel Johnson, September 13, 1777, in "Brown's Attack of September, 1777," *Bulletin of the Fort Ticonderoga Museum* 11 (July 1964): 213. Johnson was colonel of a battalion of Essex County, Massachusetts militia.

7 Benjamin Ruggles Woodbridge was colonel of a battalion of Hampshire County, Massachusetts militia.

8 "The Journal of Ralph Cross of Newburyport, who Commanded the Essex Regiment, at the Surrender of Burgoyne, in 1777," *Historical Magazine, and Notes and Queries, Concerning the Antiquities, History and Biography of America* 7, ed. Henry B. Dawson (January, 1870): 9. Cross was the lieutenant colonel of Colonel Samuel Johnson's battalion of Essex County, Massachusetts militia.

9 *The American Revolution, Garrison Life in French Canada and New York: Journal of an Officer in the Prinz Friedrich Regiment, 1776–1783*, trans. Helga Doblin (Westport, CT: Greenwood Press, 1993), 78. Authorship of the journal is attributed to Ensign Julius von Hille, Captain Carl von Tunderfeldt's company, Braunschweig Infanterie Regiment Prinz Friedrich.

10 "Journal of Ralph Cross," 9.

11 Brown's force included Whitcomb's Company of Rangers, a detachment from the Green Mountain Boys, Herrick's Vermont Rangers, and various Massachusetts militia battalions, including his own.

12 Thomas Hughes, *A Journal by Thos. Hughes*, ed. E. A. Benians (Cambridge, England: Cambridge University Press, 1947), 12.

13 All Royal Naval officers and men operating on Lakes Champlain and George or with Burgoyne on the Hudson River were drawn from H.M. Ships *Apollo, Blonde, Garland, Isis*, and *Proteus*; the Brig *Canceaux*; and the Sloops *Porpoise* and *Viper*.

14 Hughes, *Journal by Thos. Hughes*, 13. Lord was the lieutenant of Major Alexander, Earl Balcarres's company, 53rd Regiment of Foot. Thomas Hughes was the ensign of Captain William Hughes's company, 53rd Regiment of Foot.

15 Powell was lieutenant-colonel of the 53rd Regiment of Foot and held the local rank of brigadier-general in America only.

16 Taylor was a captain in the 21st Regiment of Foot (Royal North British Fusiliers), on detached service from his regiment.

17 Henry Watson Powell to John Brown, September 18, 1777, in Katharine Kyes Leab and Daniel J. Leab, eds., *American Book Prices Current, 1977*, vol. 83 (New York: Bancroft-Parkman, 1978), 1,027.

18 Brown also burned or destroyed a number of gunboats, bateaux, outbuildings, carts, and military stores and dispersed numerous horses and cattle.

19 Aubrey was a captain in the 47th Regiment of Foot. Diamond Island's garrison consisted of most of two companies of the 47th Regiment of Foot, small detachments of British officers and men from other regiments, and a ninety-man guard of Braunschweig infantry under

the command of Ensign Johann Gödeke. Gödeke was the ensign of Major Balthasar von Lucke's company, Braunschweig Infanterie Regiment von Rhetz. Although Fort George lay in ruins, a forty-man detachment garrisoned the site under the command of Lieutenant Gerard Irvine. Irvine was the lieutenant of Captain Thomas Gamble's company, 47th Regiment of Foot.

20 National Archives and Records Administration (NARA), Revolutionary War Pension and Bounty-Land Warrant Application Files, Elkanah Sprague (S.11,445). Sprague was a private in Captain Seth Hodges's company, Colonel Joseph Marsh's battalion, Vermont militia.

21 Jeduthan Baldwin, *The Revolutionary Journal of Col. Jeduthan Baldwin 1775–1778*, ed. Thomas Williams Baldwin (Bangor, ME: De Burians, 1906), 121.

22 Only Brown's battalion of Berkshire County, Massachusetts militia, which was formed under the auspices of a twenty-day alarm, was discharged.

23 Ezra Badlam to unknown correspondent, September 28, 1777, "Letter of Ezra Badlam," in *The New England Historical & Genealogical Register*, vol. 2 (Boston: Samuel G. Drake, 1848), 48. Badlam was the major of Colonel James Wesson's (9th) Massachusetts Regiment.

24 William Smith, *Historical Memoirs from 12 July 1776 to 25 July 1778 of William Smith, Historian of the Province of New York; Member of the Governor's Council, and Last Chief Justice of That Province Under the Crown; Chief Justice of Quebec* (New York: Colburn and Tegg, 1958), 221.

25 Jonathan Trumbull Jr. to Jonathan Trumbull Sr., October 6, 1777, in "The Trumbull Papers," *Collections of the Massachusetts Historical Society* (Boston, 1902), 153. Jonathan Trumbull Jr. was the Northern Department's deputy paymaster general. Son of Connecticut governor Jonathan Trumbull Sr., he should not be confused with his younger brother and artist, John Trumbull.

26 Philip Schuyler to George Washington, August 1, 1777, in *Letterbook of Philip John Schuyler*, mssHM 649, Huntington Library, Art Collections, and Botanical Gardens.

27 Journals of the Continental Congress, *1774–1789*, vol. 8, ed. Worthington Chauncey Ford (Washington, DC: USGPO, 1907), 624. Yea votes were Nathaniel Folsom (New Hampshire), Henry Marchant (Rhode Island), Eliphalet Dyer (Connecticut), James Duane (New York), Daniel Roberdeau (Pennsylvania), and George Walton (Georgia). Nay votes were John Adams, Samuel Adams, Elbridge Gerry, and James Lovell (Massachusetts); Philip Livingston and William Duer (New York); Jonathan Sergeant and Jonathan Elmer (New Jersey); Robert Morris, James Wilson, and George Clymer (Pennsylvania); Nicholas Van Dyke (Delaware); Samuel Chase and William Smith (Maryland); and Thomas Burke and Cornelius Harnett (North Carolina).

28 Livingston, the son of New Jersey's governor, was Arnold's junior aide-de-camp and should not be confused with Colonel Henry Beekman Livingston, commander of the 4th New York Regiment.

29 Horatio Gates to John Hancock, September 22, 1777, New-York Historical Society, Horatio Gates Papers, microfilm edition, 5:717.

30 Benedict Arnold to Horatio Gates September 22, 1777, Horatio Gates Papers, 5:726.

31 Horatio Gates to John Hancock, September 23, 1777, Horatio Gates Papers, 5:742.

32 Benedict Arnold to Horatio Gates September 23, 1777, Horatio Gates Papers, 5:744.

33 Horatio Gates to Benedict Arnold, September 23, 1777, Horatio Gates Papers, 5:739.

34 Traditionally, historians have manipulated the meaning of this order to show that Arnold was relieved of his command or otherwise supplanted. This was never the case.

35 James Wilkinson to Arthur St. Clair, September 21, 1777, in William Henry Smith, *The St. Clair Papers: The Life and Public Services of Arthur St. Clair*, vol. 1 (Cincinnati: Robert Clarke, 1882), 443.

Enterprise

1 Israel Putnam to George Clinton, October 8, 1777, in *Public Papers of George Clinton, First Governor of New York, 1777–1795, 1801–1804*, vol. 2 (Albany, NY: Wynkoop Hallenbeck Crawford, 1900), 385.

2 Like Carleton, Howe, and Burgoyne, Clinton held the army rank of major-general with a commission date of May 25, 1772. Also like Burgoyne, Clinton's local rank of lieutenant-general—valid "in America only"—was dated September 1, 1775. All four were among those elevated to the army rank of lieutenant-general on August 29, 1777.

3 William Howe to George Germain, April 2, 1777, in *Report on the Manuscripts of Mrs. Stopford-Sackville, of Drayton House, Northamptonshire*, vol. 2 (Hereford, UK: Hereford Times, 1910), 63–64.

4 William Howe to Guy Carleton, April 5, 1777, in *Report on the Manuscripts of Mrs. Stopford-Sackville*, 65–66.

5 This statement was made on March 19, 1778, as part of the "Debate on Mr. Fox's Motion relative to the Failure of the Expedition from Canada." *The Parliamentary History of England, from the Earliest Period to the year 1803*, vol. 19 (London: T. C. Hansard, 1814), 956.

6 William Howe to George Germain, August 30, 1777, in *Report on the Manuscripts of Mrs. Stopford-Sackville*, 74–75. The inordinate three-month delay between the date that Germain wrote Howe of the king's approval (May 18) and the date when Howe received the letter (August 16) has given rise to outrageous stories of missing or undelivered orders for the British general to ascend the Hudson and assist Burgoyne. Not only was there never an order for Howe to ascend the Hudson and capture Albany, but the delayed letter in question only gave formal approval of the sea-bound approach to Philadelphia, something that Howe had already embarked upon.

7   William Howe to Henry Clinton, July 30, 1777, in *The Parliamentary Register; or, History of the Proceedings and Debates of the House of Commons*, vol. 11 (London: John Stockdale, 1802), 339.

8   The Detached Corps consisted of the light infantry and grenadier companies of the 7th (Royal Fusiliers) and 26th Regiments of Foot, as well as the grenadier company of the Ansbach Infanterie Regiment von Eÿb. Like Braunschweig, Hessen-Hanau, and other German states, Markgrafschaft Brandenburg-Ansbach und Bayreuth supplied German subsidiary troops for the British war effort.

9   Philemon Dickinson to George Clinton, October 12, 1777, in *Public Papers of George Clinton*, 420. Dickinson's observation of "Regiments of Greens" was in reference to royalist American uniform coat color.

10 Hotham's flotilla included H.M. Ship *Preston*; Frigates *Mercury* and *Tartar*; Brig *Diligent*; Galleys *Crane, Dependence,* and *Spitfire*; Sloop Tender *Hotham*; and over fifty flat boats, bateaux, and other small vessels.

11 The general geographic region of the department roughly consisted of New York State south of Kingston, inclusive.

12 This assembly, commanded by Captain John Hodge, included the frigates *Montgomery* and *Congress*, sloop *Camden*, and galleys *Lady Washington* and *Shark*.

13 These were Colonels William Allison's and Jesse Woodhull's Orange County and Colonel Jonathan Hasbrouck's and Lieutenant Colonel James McClaughry's Ulster County, New York militia battalions.

14 The officer, who delivered the message on October 5, was Captain Colin Campbell. Historians have oft mistaken this officer for Alexander Campbell, captain of the light infantry company, 62nd Regiment of Foot.

15 "Conversation with Captain Campbell sent by General Burgoyne to me [General Clinton]," in *The Parliamentary Register; or, History of the Proceedings and Debates of the House of Commons*, vol. 8 (London: J. Almon, 1778), 246.

16 *Parliamentary Register*, vol. 8, 246–47.

17 "Diary of Johann Christoph Doehlemann, Grenadier Company, Ansbach Regiment, March 1777 to September 1778," trans. Henry J. Retzer, *The Hessians: Journal of the Johannes Schwalm Historical Association* 11 (2008): 13. Döhlemann was a corporal in Captain Ludwig von Erckert's grenadier company, Ansbach Infanterie Regiment von Eÿb.

18 "Diary of Johann Christoph Doehlemann," 13–14.

19 "Copy of a Journal of an officer of the 31st Regiment, serving in the Expedition up the North River, October 9th, 1777," in G. D. Scull, ed., *The Evelyns in America: Compiled from Family Papers and other Sources, 1608–1805* (Oxford: Parker, 1881), 347. The officers killed were Major Francis Bushil Sill, 63rd Regiment of Foot, who commanded his battalion on the expedition, and Captain Francis Stuart, grenadier company, 26th Regiment of Foot, who commanded the Detached Corps.

20 "Diary of Johann Christoph Doehlemann," 14. Fort Clinton's commander—Brigadier General James Clinton, who was Brigadier General and Governor George Clinton's brother—was bayoneted but escaped.

21 Mungo Campbell was lieutenant-colonel of the 52nd Regiment of Foot.

22 George Clinton to George Washington, October 9, 1777, in *Public Papers of George Clinton*, 393. William Smith Livingston was lieutenant colonel of Colonel Samuel Webb's Additional Continental Regiment, serving on detached duty.

23 George Clinton to George Washington, October 9, 1777, in *Public Papers of George Clinton*, 393–94.

24 National Archives and Records Administration (NARA), Revolutionary War Pension and Bounty-Land Warrant Application Files, Joel Bower (S.29,020). Bower was a private in a detachment of carpenter artificers under the direction of Thomas Machin. Machin was captain lieutenant of Captain Theodore Bliss's company, Colonel John Lamb's (2nd) Continental Artillery Regiment, and acting engineer of the Highlands defenses.

25 Also killed was Major Alexander Grant, commander of the royalist New York Volunteers.

26 Among the principal officers of the garrisons captured were Colonel William Allison (Orange County, New York militia), Lieutenant Colonel William Smith Livingston (Colonel Samuel Webb's Additional Continental Regiment), Lieutenant Colonel James McClaughry (Ulster County, New York militia), and the 5th New York Regiment's lieutenant colonel and major, Jacobus Bruyn and Samuel Logan.

27 Only the galley *Lady Washington* was saved.

28 New York had two governors serving simultaneously for most of the war: New York State's Revolutionary governor, Brigadier General George Clinton, and the Province of New York's royal governor, Major-General William Tryon.

29 Library of Congress, George Washington Papers, Series 4, General Correspondence: Henry Clinton to John Burgoyne, October 8, 1777. This message was concealed "in a small silver ball of an oval form, about the size of a fusee bullet, and shut with a screw in the middle." Its carrier, Daniel Taylor (a sergeant in the King's American Regiment), was caught by the redcoated soldiers of Webb's Additional Continental Regiment on October 9. Taylor swallowed the ball, "but a strong Dose of Tarter emittic brought it forth." He swallowed it again, only to give it up once more after being threatened with death. His secret revealed, Taylor hoped to save himself from the hangman's noose by claiming to be a lieutenant in the 9th Regiment of Foot. The ruse didn't work, and he was hanged on October 18. *Public Papers of George Clinton*, 398–404, 412–14, 443.

30 The officer who delivered the message on October 9 was Captain-Lieutenant Thomas Scott, 24th Regiment of Foot, who departed from Burgoyne's camp on September 27. For Scott's memorial in which he described this journey, see "Captain Scott's Journal," in Edward Barrington De Fonblanque, *Political and Military Episodes in the Latter half of the Eighteenth Century* (London: MacMillan, 1876), 287–90.

31 Henry Clinton to Edward Harvey, October 13, 1777, in George Thomas, Earl of Albemarle, *Memoirs of the Marquis of Rockingham and his Contemporaries*, vol. 2 (London: Richard Bentley, 1852), 337.

32 The Advanced Squadron, commanded by Captain Sir James Wallace, consisted of H.M. Brig
Diligent, Sloop *Hotham*, and the Galleys *Crane*, *Dependence*, and *Spitfire*. Flatboats transported
Vaughan's troops, consisting of the 7th (Royal Fusiliers), 26th, and 63rd Regiments of Foot,
and one company of the 71st Regiment of Foot. The *Hotham* was left behind at Pollepel
Island near New Windsor in order to prevent the Americans from obstructing the river
behind the northbound flotilla.

Ascendancy

1 *The Specht Journal,* trans. Helga Doblin (Westport, CT: Greenwood Press, 1995), 90.
Authorship of the Specht journal, the official record of the First German Brigade, commanded by Brigadier Specht, is attributed to Du Roi.

2 This divisional order was dated October 2, 1777. *Orderly Book of the Braunschweig Corps
in North America,* trans Virginia Rinaldy, Hessian Documents of the American Revolution, 1776–1783, Morristown National Historical Park, Lidgerwood Collection, Fiche
214–27.

3 The claim that the flour cakes (also known as ash or fire cakes) were as "relishing with
the best Bread" was indoctrination codified by Burgoyne in general orders dated June
24. John Burgoyne, *Orderly Book of Lieut. Gen. John Burgoyne, from his Entry into the State
of New York until his Surrender at Saratoga, 16th Oct., 1777,* ed. E. B. O'Callaghan, MD
(Albany, NY: Joel Munsell, 1860), 7.

4 *The Specht Journal,* 97.

5 *The Specht Journal,* 89.

6 Friedrich Christian Cleve, Journal of the Brunswick Troops in North America under
the Orders of Major-General von Riedesel, trans. "in England," HZ 332-3, Hessian Documents of the American Revolution, 1776–1783, Morristown National Historical Park,
Lidgerwood Collection, Fiche 180–93. While the intention of Burgoyne's reconnaissance-in-force has long confounded historians, the only contemporary record of the
secret meeting between Burgoyne, Philips, Riedesel, and Fraser makes its purpose clear.
The probing force was never intended to, nor was it equipped to, attack the American
lines, nor was it capable of taking high ground west of the Summit in order to blaze away
with artillery in the hope of forcing the Americans to escape.

7 While the translation to "White House" appears obvious, consistent capitalization of the
place-name, as well as variant German grammatics and spellings, confound meaning. No
known British source describes the structure.

8   "Colonel Brooks and Captain Bancroft," in *Proceedings of the Massachusetts Historical Society* 3 (February 1855): 275. Brooks added that the "opinion General Arnold expressed in this discussion was probably the cause why Gates was afraid to trust him to go out when the firing was first heard, lest he should bring on an engagement in the open field, and contrary to his own opinion of its expediency." Historians have traditionally claimed that Brooks's date must have been in error, and that this dinner—an afternoon meal—somehow occurred on the morning of September 19. This arbitrary determination was made solely to fulfill the requirements of the long-standing story, wholly contrived by James Wilkinson, that Arnold had been relieved of command.

9   Henry Dearborn to James Wilkinson, December 20, 1815, in Henry Dearborn, "A Narrative of the Saratoga Campaign," *Bulletin of the Fort Ticonderoga Museum* 1 (January 1929): 7.

10 Nathaniel Bacheller to Susanna Bacheller, October 9, 1777, Saratoga National Historical Park historian files.

11 Nathaniel Bacheller to Susanna Bacheller, October 9, 1777. It's notable that most Americans, including Arnold, believed that the British forces were trying to claim the heights west of Bemus Heights. Not being privy to Burgoyne's operational plans, Americans (and everyone except Burgoyne and his three top generals) were of course ignorant of his intentions. Despite this, traditional interpretations of the purpose of Burgoyne's October 7 reconnaissance rely on Americans' misperceptions. Bacheller was adjutant of Colonel Abraham Drake's battalion, New Hampshire militia.

12 Oliver Walcott to Jonathan Trumbull Sr., October 10, 1777, in "The Trumbull Papers," in *Collections of the Massachusetts Historical Society* (Boston, 1902), 160. Walcott was brigadier general and commander of a volunteer Connecticut militia battalion, signer of the Declaration of Independence, and representative to the Continental Congress.

13 Samuel Armstrong, "From Saratoga to Valley Forge: The Diary of Lt. Samuel Armstrong," ed. Joseph Lee Boyle, *Pennsylvania Magazine of History and Biography* 121, no. 3 (July 1997): 248.

14 Henry Dearborn to James Wilkinson, December 20, 1815, in Dearborn, "Narrative of the Saratoga Campaign," 7.

15 John Burgoyne, *A State of the Expedition from Canada, as Laid before the House of Commons* (London: J. Almon, 1780), 43.

16 Georg Päusch, *Journal of Captain Pausch, Chief of the Hanau Artillery during the Burgoyne Campaign*, trans. William L. Stone (Albany, NY: Joel Munsell's Sons, 1886), 167–68.

17 Päusch, *Journal of Captain Pausch*, 169.

18 Henry Dearborn to James Wilkinson, December 20, 1815, in Dearborn, "Narrative of the Saratoga Campaign," 7.

19 Päusch, *Journal of Captain Pausch*, 168.

20 Burgoyne, *State of the Expedition from Canada*, 53.

21 Burgoyne, *State of the Expedition from Canada*, 172.

22 Henry Dearborn to James Wilkinson, December 20, 1815, in Dearborn, "Narrative of the Saratoga Campaign," 8. Since the nineteenth century, historians have ascribed the shot that mortally wounded Fraser as having come from the rifle of Timothy Murphy, William Critchlow, Thomas Scott, or a supposed "elderly man, with a long hunting gun." These unsupported claims are illustrative of the fact that no contemporary reference exists that testified to the shot having come from any known individual. Deducing who shot one of the few British officers conspicuously riding on horseback in an open field within range of rifles and muskets alike is impossible. Nonsensical nineteenth-century dialogue-laced anecdotes to the contrary, the earliest legitimate hint of who may have shot Fraser was recorded by a British officer, Samuel Graham. Graham, who was captured when Cornwallis surrendered at Yorktown in October 1781, recalled having dinner with Daniel Morgan at Winchester, Virginia, in early December of that year. The timing of this meeting is codified in context with a letter written to Graham from Morgan dated Saratoga, Virginia, November 28, 1781. While dining, Morgan recalled that during the Battle of Bemus Heights, he singled out a mounted British officer—"a devilish brave fellow"—for death. Accordingly, Morgan relayed the story: "says I to one of my best shots . . . you get up into that there tree, and single out him on the white horse. Dang it, 'twas no sooner said than done. . . . I jist tuck my eyes off him for a moment, and when I turned them to the place where he had been—pooh, he was gone!" Graham admitted that he assumed Fraser was the officer, but it could have been another (such as Sir Francis Clerke). If mentioned in the conversation, the marksman's name went unrecorded. Samuel Graham, "Traditions of the American War of Independence," in *The United Service Journal and Naval and Military Magazine*, pt. 3 (London: Henry Colburn, 1834), 312–13. Graham was captain-lieutenant of the 76th Regiment of Foot.

23 This was Captain Ellis Walker's company, 3rd Battalion, Royal Regiment of Artillery, which manned the fort's two light six-pounders, four light three-pounder "grasshoppers," and two royal howitzers.

24 Philip Van Cortlandt, *The Revolutionary War Memoir and Selected Correspondence of Philip Van Cortlandt*, ed. Jacob Judd (Tarrytown, NY: Sleepy Hollow Restorations, 1976), 48.

25 MacKay was captain-commandant of this independent corps, a position to which Burgoyne appointed him after the death of its original commander, Franz Pfister, who was mortally wounded in the Battle of Bennington.

26 Henry Dearborn to James Wilkinson, December 20, 1815, in Dearborn, "Narrative of the Saratoga Campaign," 8. Joseph Morris was major of the 1st New Jersey Regiment and major of Colonel Morgan's Battalion of Riflemen.

27 Armstrong, "From Saratoga to Valley Forge," 248

28 Friedrich Julius von Papet, *Canada during the American Revolutionary War: Lieutenant Friedrich Julius von Papet's Journal of the Sea Voyage to North America and the Campaign Conducted There, 15 May 1776 to 10 October 1783*, trans. Bruce E. Burgoyne (Bowie, MD:

Heritage Books, 1998), 78. Von Papet was first-lieutenant of Captain Conrad Anton Alers's company, Braunschweig Infanterie Regiment von Rhetz.

29 Ernst von Speth was the lieutenant-colonel of the Braunschweig Infanterie Regiment von Riedesel. Captured alongside him, from the same regiment, were Ensigns Friedrich Denecke and Raimund Häberlein. Notably, the officers and soldiers sent to retake the camp not only had not been part of its garrison, but had probably never been to it, even in daylight. Their royalist guide was probably who he claimed to be; MacKay's company formed part of Breymann's camp, and many of its soldiers, men from Albany County's Hoosick District, were German-speaking. The fact that he led von Speth to where he wanted to go was no ruse.

30 In addition to the aforementioned von Speth, these were Burgoyne's junior aide-de-camp (Captain Sir Francis Clerke, Bt., who was also mortally wounded), the British artillery commander (Captain and Major Griffith Williams, 1st Battalion, Royal Regiment of Artillery), deputy quartermaster general (Captain John Money), and the British Grenadier Battalion commander (Major John Acland, who was also wounded).

Endgame

1 Richard Varick to Philip Schuyler, October 12, 1777, New York Public Library, Archives and Manuscripts, Philip Schuyler Papers, Letters Received, b. 11 f. 86.

2 Benjamin Lincoln to William Heath, March 19, 1799, in Jared Sparks, *Lives of Daniel Boone and Benjamin Lincoln* (Boston: Charles Little and James Brown, 1847), 260–63.

3 Frederica Riedesel, Freifrau zu (Baroness of) Eisenbach, *Baroness von Riedesel and the American Revolution*, trans. Marvin L. Brown Jr. (Chapel Hill: University of North Carolina Press, 1965), 53.

4 John Burgoyne, *A State of the Expedition from Canada, as Laid before the House of Commons* (London: J. Almon, 1780), 170.

5 *The Specht Journal*, trans. Helga Doblin (Westport, CT: Greenwood Press, 1995), 93.

6 The surgeon left behind to oversee the hospital was John McNamara Hayes.

7 *Orderly Book of Colonel Timothy Bigelow's (15th Massachusetts) Regiment, August 12 to November 4, 1777*, American Antiquarian Society, Manuscript Collection, Orderly Books Collection, 1758–1813, octavo volume 11.

8 Only some Massachusetts militia regiments from Brigadier General Jonathan Warner's brigade remained behind in camp at Bemus Heights.

9 Frederic Kidder, *History of the First New Hampshire Regiment in the War of the Revolution* (Albany, NY: Joel Munsell, 1868), 37.

10 Oliver Walcott to Jonathan Trumbull, Sr., October 10, 1777, in "The Trumbull Papers," *Collections of the Massachusetts Historical Society* (Boston, 1902), 163.

11   Samuel MacKay, *The Narrative of Captain Samuel MacKay, Commandant of a Provincial Regiment in North-America* (Kingston, Jamaica: Douglas & Aikman, 1778), 11.

12   Henry Dearborn, *Revolutionary War Journals of Henry Dearborn 1775–1783*, ed. Lloyd A. Brown and Howard H. Peckham (Freeport, NY: Books for Libraries Press, 1969), 110–11. Killed in this attack was First Lieutenant John Buchannan of Captain Thomas Posey's company, Colonel Morgan's Rifle Battalion. Buchannan was drafted from Captain Charles Flemming's company, 7th Virginia Regiment.

13   Library of Congress, George Washington Papers, Series 4, General Correspondence: Rufus Putnam to Horatio Gates, October 26, 1778. Captured was Lieutenant William Pendred Naylor, 62nd Regiment of Foot, and Hospital Mate Robert Kerr. Goodale was a captain in Colonel Rufus Putnam's (5th) Massachusetts Regiment.

14   *The Specht Journal*, 97.

15   Riedesel, *Baroness von Riedesel*, 58.

16   Elizabeth Fisher, *Memoirs of Mrs. Elizabeth Fisher of the City of New-York* (New York: printed for the author, 1810), 18–19. Her "biscuit" is a reference to British Army–issue biscuit, also known as ship's bread, the predecessor of hardtack. Fisher and her infant son were refugees from Hebron, New York. Her husband, Donald Fisher, was a royalist serving with Burgoyne's army.

17   Don N. Hagist, *British Soldiers, American War* (Yardley, PA: Westholme Publishing, 2012), 208. Fox's undated postwar memoir, "The Narrative of George Fox," was recorded by his nephew. In 1777 Fox was a private in Lieutenant-General Sir Guy Carleton's company, 47th Regiment of Foot.

18   *The Specht Journal*, 96.

19   *The Specht Journal*, 97–98.

20   New-York Historical Society, Horatio Gates Papers, microfilm edition, 5:1076.

21   *Lieutenant-general Burgoyne's Proposals*, Horatio Gates Papers, 5:110–12.

22   *The Specht Journal*, 98.

23   *The Specht Journal*, 98.

24   Whipple was also a signatory of the Declaration of Independence. Kingston and Major Isaac Peirce, Gates's secretary and a supernumerary aide-de-camp, worked as secretaries for the negotiators. Gates never saw fit to include his army's deputy judge advocate, George Smith, in the proceedings. Smith was the second lieutenant of Captain Samuel Sacket's company, 4th New York Regiment.

25   James Wilkinson, *Memoirs of My Own Times*, vol. 1 (Philadelphia: Abraham Small, 1816), 310–11.

26   Bettys was a volunteer in Captain-Commandant Daniel McAlpin's corps of American Volunteers.

27   Friedrich Christian Cleve, Journal of the Brunswick Troops in North America under the Orders of Major-General von Riedesel, trans. "in England," HZ 354, Hessian Documents of the American Revolution, 1776–1783, Morristown National Historical Park, Lidgerwood Collection, Fiche 180–93.

28   Ironically, Americans usually called the village Kingston, while the British usually referred to it as Esopus. In 1777 Kingston was located in Ulster County's Esopus District.

29   John Vaughan to Henry Clinton, October 17, 1777, in *Naval Documents of the American Revolution*, vol. 10, ed. Michael J. Crawford (Washington, DC: USGPO, 1970), 192.

30   The one home purposefully spared was owned by royalist Jacobus Lefferts.

31   The officer was Lieutenant James Clark of H.M. Galley *Dependence*.

32   Sir Henry Clinton, *The American Rebellion: Sir Henry Clinton's Narrative of his Campaigns, 1775–1782, with an Appendix of Original Documents*, ed. William B. Willcox (New Haven, CT: Yale Historical Publications, 1954), 80.

33   All told, Vaughan's expedition netted 14 cannons, 150 stands of arms, 12 barrels of flints, and 6 sloops "loaded with Provisions of all Kinds &ca: &ca: &ca:." Counted among the supplies successfully destroyed were 1,150 stands of arms, 44 barrels of gunpowder, 80 small vessels, and a shocking 400 houses, barns, mills, and other outbuildings. *Naval Documents*, vol. 10, 301.

34   Traditionally, historians ascribed Vaughan's withdrawal as fallout from Howe's call for reinforcements. While Vaughan's expedition was recalled, he received the order to do so while already en route to the Highlands.

35   Cleve, Journal of the Brunswick Troops, HZ 355.

36   Horatio Gates Papers, 5:1153.

37   Horatio Gates Papers, 5:1174.

38   Cleve, Journal of the Brunswick Troops, HZ 356.

Surrender

1   Dudley Coleman to Moses Little, October 28, 1777, in *Reminiscences of a Nonagenarian*, ed. Sarah Anna Emery (Newburyport, MA: William H. Huse, 1879), 152. Coleman was lieutenant colonel of Colonel Edward Wigglesworth's (13th) Massachusetts Regiment.

2   An exception were the nine-round-capacity cartridge boxes issued to light infantry companies; because they were purchased by regimental colonels for their men, they were, like pouches, also private property.

3   These consisted of five pairs of British colours and four sets of five German colours (for a total of thirty). Because colours were seen as an encumbrance incompatible with the tactical doctrine of the Advanced Corps, the 24th Regiment's colours remained in Canada. Each Braunschweig and Hessen-Hanau infantry regiment had five colours—one for each musketeer company.

4   Friedrich Christian Cleve, Journal of the Brunswick Troops in North America under the Orders of Major-General von Riedesel, trans. "in England," HZ 360, Hessian Documents

of the American Revolution, 1776–1783, Morristown National Historical Park, Lidger-wood Collection, Fiche 180–93.

5   Frederica Riedesel, Freifrau zu (Baroness of) Eisenbach, *Baroness von Riedesel and the American Revolution*, trans. Marvin L. Brown Jr. (Chapel Hill: University of North Carolina Press, 1965), 72.

6   John Burgoyne, *A State of the Expedition from Canada, as Laid before the House of Commons* (London: J. Almon, 1780), 85. This was from the testimony of Lieutenant-Colonel Robert Kingston. Traditional stories of "Burgoyne's gold" being buried before the surrender are, of course, baseless. Other stories—even contemporary reports—of the hefty treasury somehow being whisked away at night by trusty royalists are also apocryphal and contrary to facts.

7   *Articles of Capitulation Between Lieutenant-General Burgoyne and Major General Gates*, New-York Historical Society, Horatio Gates Papers, microfilm edition, 5:1160.

8   John Peters to Thomas Townshend, Viscount Sydney, September 6, 1785, New York State Library, Manuscripts and Special Collections, John Peters Loyalist Claim Papers, CL 3576. Because his Queen's Loyal Rangers was not recruited to completion, Peters ranked as lieutenant-colonel commandant.

9   "Memorial of Captain Hugh Munro, Montreal January 10, 1778," Library and Archives of Canada (LAC), Haldimand Papers, Add. MSS 21827, 120–21. Hugh Munro was captain of a company of royalist bateauxmen in Captain-Commandant Daniel McAlpin's American Volunteers.

10 Elisha James to Sara James, October 19, 1777, The James Library & Center for the Arts, Special Collections. James was a private artificer in Captain Ezra Eaton's Company of Blacksmiths, Colonel Jeduthan Baldwin's Corps of Engineers and Artificers.

11 John David Broome, *Life, Ministry, and Journals of Hezekiah Smith 1737–1805* (Springfield, MO: Particular Baptist Press, 2004), 453–54. Unfortunately, contrived nineteenth-century stories of this exchange have dominated traditional histories. This account of the words spoken between the two generals, recorded only hours after their meeting, constitutes the only contemporary report of it. Smith's journal entry also acknowledged that the quotes may have been "Words to that Effect," noting the unlikelihood of recording an unscripted conversation with perfect exactitude even hours afterward.

12 Howard Kendall Sanderson, ed., *Lynn in the Revolution*, pt. 1 (Boston: W. B. Clarke, 1909), 165–66. Hallowell was a private in Captain Nathan Goodale's company, Colonel Rufus Putnam's (5th) Massachusetts Regiment.

13 "America: Civilities to Prisoners," *The Scots Magazine* 39 (December 1777): 664–65. The account was relayed by an anonymous British officer who was in attendance.

14 The fantastic claim that there were upward of 2,000 women followers with Burgoyne's army was no more than a specious contemporary accusation made by a Member of Parliament in 1779. Instead, victualing returns proved that there were instead "very very few" women (nearly 300 women and as many children by the campaign's end). Burgoyne called the accusation "preposterous, as well as false" and "maliciously intended," claiming the women were neither a detriment to his army's progress nor taxing upon his provisions. See Burgoyne, *State of the Expedition*, 88–89, 127.

15 Burgoyne was a member of Parliament for Preston Borough; Major-General William Phillips was a member of Parliament for Boroughbridge Borough; and Captain Charles Stanhope, Viscount Petersham, was a member of Parliament for Westminster City. A fourth representative, Major John Dyke Acland, captured on October 7, was a member of Parliament for Callington Borough.

16 *The Specht Journal*, trans. Helga Doblin (Westport, CT: Greenwood Press, 1995), 101–2.

17 Elisha James to Sarah James, October 19, 1777.

18 M. M. Quaife, "A Boy Soldier Under Washington: The Memoir of Daniel Granger," *Mississippi Valley Historical Review* 16 (March 1930): 547. Granger was a drummer in Captain John Adams's company, Colonel Samuel Johnson's battalion (Major Benjamin Gage's detachment), Essex County, Massachusetts militia.

19 Hannah Winthrop to Mercy Otis Warren, November 11, 1777, Massachusetts Historical Society (MHS), Mercy Otis Warren papers, Ms. N-17.

20 National Archives and Records Administration (NARA), Revolutionary War Pension and Bounty-Land Warrant Application Files, Isaac Quackenboss (S.11,275). Quackenboss was a private soldier in Captain Jacob Lansing's company, Colonel Abraham Wemple's battalion of Albany County (Schenectady District), New York militia.

21 Samuel Harris Jr., *The Journal of Samuel Harris Jr. of Boston. Written while in the Army in 1777*, Harvard University, Houghton Library, MS Sparks 25, 139b-140a. Harris was a private in Captain Ebenezer Lathrop's company, Colonel Jonathan Latimer's battalion, Connecticut militia.

22 At the height of his British Army career, Gates was the major of the 45th Regiment of Foot, which commission he sold in 1769. References to the idea that Gates and Burgoyne had previously served together or even met before October 17, 1777, are baseless.

23 "Conversation between Major-General Gates and Lieutenant-Colonel Kingston," in *The Parliamentary Register; or, History of the Proceedings and Debates of the House of Commons*, vol. 11 (London: J. Almon, 1779), 213.

24 Glover's, Paterson's, Poor's, and the Massachusetts Regiments of Learned's Brigades were transferred to Washington's army. Nixon's brigade remained in the Northern Department.

25 Articles of Capitulation, Horatio Gates Papers, 5:1160.

26 This, despite the fact that Gates admitted to the president of Congress that "The Mentioning of the Accoutriments was forgotten in the Convention." Horatio Gates to Henry Laurens, December 3, 1777, Horatio Gates Papers, 6:573. Laurens succeeded to the presidency of the

Continental Congress on November 1, 1777. During its investigation, Congress determined that the British garrison at St. Johns, Canada, surrendered its arms and accoutrements to American forces in 1775, despite the fact that the *Articles of Capitulation* only stipulated that the surrendering soldiers should "ground their Arms." This inexact precedent provided Congress with its reasoning for demanding the same of Burgoyne. See *Articles of Capitulation Proposed by Major Charles Preston for His Majesty's Forts at St. John's, in the Province of Canada* [with Brigadier General Richard Montgomery's answers], November 2, 1775, in Peter Force, *American Archives: Fourth Series. Containing a Documentary History of the English Colonies in North America*, vol. 3 (Washington, DC: M. St. Clair Clarke and Peter Force, 1840), 1,394.

27 Horatio Gates to Henry Laurens, December 3, 1777, Horatio Gates Papers, 6:573.

28 *Journals of the Continental Congress, 1774–1789*, vol. 9, ed. Worthington Chauncey Ford (Washington, DC: USGPO, 1907), 1,064. Beyond the missing colours and "cartridge boxes," the congressional resolution also cited two additional reasons why the Convention was suspended. First, Burgoyne's "refusal to give descriptive lists of the non-commissioned officers and privates, belonging to his army." Second, that a:

> charge made by Lieutenant General Burgoyne in his letter to Major General Gates, of the 14 November, of a breach of public faith on the part of these States is not warranted by the just construction any article of the Convention of Saratoga; That it betrays a disposition of availing himself of such declaration in order to disengage himself and the army under him of the obligations they are under to these United States, and that the security which these States have hitherto had in his personal honor is hereby destroyed.

Legacy

1 Franklin, Deane, and Lee to the Congressional Committee of Foreign Affairs, December 18, 1777, in Francis Wharton, ed., *The Revolutionary Diplomatic Correspondence of the United States*, vol. 2 (Washington, DC: GPO, 1889), 452. Franklin, Deane, and Lee were ministers plenipotentiary in France.

2 "Last Journals of Horace Walpole," December 2, 1777, in Horace Walpole, *Journal of the Reign of King George the Third, from the year 1771 to 1783*, vol. 2, ed. Dr. Doran (London: Richard Bentley, 1859), 170.

3 This statement was made on March 19, 1778, as part of the "Debate on Mr. Fox's Motion relative to the Failure of the Expedition from Canada." *The Parliamentary History of England, from the Earliest Period to the year 1803*, vol. 19 (London: T. C. Hansard, 1814), 953. Fox was a member of Parliament for Malmesbury Borough.

4   This statement was made on March 19, 1778, as part of the "Debate on Mr. Fox's Motion." *The Parliamentary History of England*, 954. William Jolliffe was a member of Parliament for Petersfield Borough.

5   Austin, secretary to the Massachusetts Board of War, left Boston aboard the brigantine *Perch* on October 31 and arrived at Nantes, France, on November 30. Jones, a captain in the Continental Navy, left Portsmouth, New Hampshire, in command of the U.S. Sloop *Ranger* on November 1, which arrived at Nantes on December 2. At Passey, Austin was first to inform Franklin of Burgoyne's surrender on December 4.

6   John Langdon to Franklin, Deane, and Lee, October 29, 1777, in *The Papers of Benjamin Franklin*, vol. 25, ed. William B. Willcox (New Haven, CT: Yale University Press, 1986), 120–21. Langdon served as captain of a small independent company of New Hampshire volunteers.